The Anthropology of Love and Anger

The Anthropology of Love and Anger provides remarkable evidence that anthropology is a thriving subject. In this highly original discussion the editors have brought together papers that question the very foundations of Western sociological thought.

In their examination of the 'social structure', or rather 'sociality', (the former expression being inapplicable in this context) of indigenous peoples from across the South American continent, the contributors have come to realise that Western thought does not possess the vocabulary to define the very fundamentals of indigenous thought and practice. The rigid dualities of public and private, political and domestic, individual and collective, even male and female, on which Western anthropology was founded cannot be so neatly applied to peoples whose 'sociality' is based upon an 'aesthetics of living' that follows altogether different criteria.

For indigenous peoples success is measured by the extent to which conviviality (all that is peaceful, harmonious and sociable) has been attained. Yet it is not just a conviviality or 'sociality' which relies on love and 'the good'; instead it is one that recognises a continuous interplay between the constructive and destructive emotions and reasonings. It is a sociability that depends on the negotiation of the negative features of communal living, anger, jealousy, hate and greed, toward the end of promoting ones that are positive.

With its cogent Introduction and case studies from across Latin America, ranging from the (so-called) fierce Yanomami of Venezuela and Brazil to the Enxet of Paraguay, and with discussions on such topics as the embodiment of sociality, the efficacy of laughter, the role of language, and anger as a marker of love and even homesickness, *The Anthropology of Love and Anger* is a seminal, fascinating work which should be read by all students and academics in the post-colonial world.

Joanna Overing is Professor and Chairperson of the Department of Social Anthropology, University of St Andrews and Director of the Centre for Indigenous American Studies at St Andrews. **Alan Passes** is a novelist, film writer and anthropologist.

The Anthropology of Love and Anger

The aesthetics of conviviality in Native Amazonia

Edited by Joanna Overing and
Alan Passes

London and New York

First published 2000 by Routledge
11 New Fetter Lane, London EC4P 4EE

Simultaneously published in the USA and Canada
by Routledge
29 West 35th Street, New York, NY 10001

Routledge is an imprint of the Taylor & Francis Group

© 2000 Joanna Overing and Alan Passes

Typeset in Baskerville by BC Typesetting, Bristol
Printed and bound in Great Britain by
Biddles Ltd, Guildford and King's Lynn

British Library Cataloguing in Publication Data
A catalogue record for this book is available from the British Library

Library of Congress Cataloging in Publication Data
The anthropology of love and anger: the aesthetics of conviviality in
    Native Amazonia [edited by] Joanna Overing and Alan Passes.
    Includes bibliographical references and index.
    1. Indians of South America – Amazon River Region – Social life
    and customs.   2. Social interaction – Amazon River Region.
    3. Community life – Amazon River Region.   I. Overing, Joanna.
    II. Passes, Alan, 1943–

    F2519.1.A6 A58 2000
    306′.09811–dc21   00-032835

ISBN 0–415–22418–7 (pbk)
ISBN 0–415–22417–9 (hbk)

Contents

List of contributors

Catherine Alès is attached to the Centre National de la Recherche Scientifique, Paris, and is Visiting Research Associate of the Centre for Indigenous American Studies and Exchange, within the Department of Social Anthropology, University of St Andrews.

Luisa Elvira Belaunde teaches Social Anthropology at Durham University.

Juan Alvaro Echeverri teaches Social Anthropology at the Universidad Nacional de Colombia (Amazonas), and is currently a researcher on Programa COAMA – Fundación Gaia Amazonas (Colomia).

Marco Antonio Gonçalves is a Lecturer in Social Anthropology at the Universidade Federal do Rio de Janeiro.

Peter Gow teaches Social Anthropology at the London School of Economics and Political Science.

Mark Jamieson is a Lecturer in Social Anthropology at the University of Manchester, where he has been awarded a Simon Fellowship.

Stephen W. Kidd is a Lecturer in Social Anthropology at the University of Edinburgh.

Elsje Maria Lagrou is a Lecturer in Social Anthropology at the Universidade Federal do Rio de Janeiro.

Carlos David Londoño-Sulkin is currently at the University of St Andrews, where he is in the final stages of writing his doctoral thesis.

Peter Mason is a freelance writer and translator, and consultant on art and anthropology to the Fundación América, Santiago de Chile.

Joanna Overing is Professor and Chair of Social Anthropology at the University of St Andrews.

Alan Passes is a novelist, screenwriter and anthropologist, affiliated to the Centre for Indigenous American Studies and Exchange (University of St Andrews).

Peter Rivière is Professor of Social Anthropology at the University of Oxford and a Fellow of Linacre College.

Dan Rosengren is a Lecturer in Social Anthropology at Gothenburg University, Sweden.

Fernando Santos-Granero is a staff scientist at the Smithsonian Tropical Research Institute in Panama.

Preface

This book is a collection of papers on Native American, and especially Amazonian, practices, notions and feelings relating to everyday communal life and, in particular, some of the different ways of constructing, experiencing and embodying it – ways to which, for reasons explained in the Introduction, we have given the overall, and hopefully thought-provoking and fruitful, name of Love. It owes its inception to a conference on the 'aesthetics of emotions', funded by the British Academy and held in May 1998 at the Centre for Indigenous American Studies and Exchange, in the department of anthropology at the University of St Andrews, Scotland.

The aim, as initially proposed by Joanna Overing who set up the conference, was to explore the relation of aesthetics to virtues and affective life within a variety of Amazonian cultures, and in the process to foster the beginning of a conversation that takes us beyond the sociological framework that we inherited from our training. The topic constitutes a relatively new field of study in Amazonia. It is nevertheless becoming clear, it seems to us, that a focus upon conviviality and 'aesthetics of community' sheds considerable light upon indigenous social, economic and political life, especially as the ethnographic gaze converges increasingly on the ethical, the aesthetic, emotion talk, and styles of relating and speaking. The informal and egalitarian sociality of many Amazonian groups tends to offend anthropological susceptibilities on a number of fronts. How do we understand peoples who appear to disdain the 'sociological' and, instead, stress a high degree of emotional comfort in their daily life, and the quality of its interpersonal relations – an affective emphasis which is given expression intellectually and practically by the political one that prioritises the realisation of conviviality through the productive capacities inherent in those relations? Amazonian people – which here includes those like the Nicaraguan Miskitu, the subject of Jamieson's chapter, who are Amazonian in the wider sense of possessing a similar type of lifestyle – often gauge the success of sociality according to its degree of intimacy and informality, and to the extent to which conviviality has been attained. Consequently a person's place within a social network of relations is judged by what they do and how they act, rather than in terms of prescribed roles and statuses.

We wish to pay more attention to the indigenous 'sense of community', in Vico's sense of the collective good which has both a political and a moral meaning, as well as an aesthetics of action. For, as we will discuss, there is an aesthetics to Amazonian ways of acting, and styles of everyday relating that are morally – and therefore aesthetically – not only proper but beautiful and pleasing. In respect of Amazonian peoples, we can correctly speak of the 'culinary arts', the art of feeding, of speaking, of working, and that of nurturing.

While casting light, as mentioned, upon indigenous conviviality, particularly in the areas listed above (the ethical, the aesthetic, emotion talk, styles of relating and speaking), to date almost all research on the Amazonian 'aesthetics of community' has dealt with those peoples who stress harmony in everyday life. It is obviously the case that among the Native peoples of the Americas there are many 'styles of relating'; we therefore require not only more work on Amerindian aesthetics and associated virtue-centred ethics, but also on those 'styles of relating' which reputedly value more belligerent or aggressive expression, and we are consequently pleased to include among our chapters Catherine Alès's study of the Yanomami, who, for all their reputation as fierce and warlike, are shown here also to esteem friendship, concord and compassion no less than other, more pacific peoples. Thus, if a more general understanding of Amerindian conviviality is to be gained, further comparative and problem-centred studies are necessary.

A short word about 'conviviality'

Today, no less than in the earliest years of our contact with them, Amazonian peoples continue commonly to be portrayed by observers, and in the European imagination, either as fierce and bellicose, and living lives filled with control, cruelty and fear (e.g. Chagnon's Yanomamö[1]), or on the contrary as peaceful, gentle and affable (e.g. Huxley's Kaapor or Goldman's Cubeo[2]). Thus, in archetypal terms, a stark and seemingly changeless dichotomy: Hobbesian brutes and demons versus Rousseauesque paragons. The Introduction, as well as some of the chapters (notably those by Mason and Santos-Granero), deals with this disagreement in perspective and stance which is a critical part of the background debate against which the present work, like the conference which initiated it, first arose. It also establishes concerns, considerations and motives connected with our choosing to focus on, and to seek to dissipate some of the more simplistic or plainly wrong-headed fancies, whether for or against, relating to the second kind of representation – or actuality: the Native American as sociable, amicable, peace-loving, etc.; as existing in short, and essentially, in a state of what we have already designated as *conviviality*. Since this term, together with its derivatives, appears extensively, not to say emblematically, throughout the book, either as a gloss or, at other times, to denote something more specific, it would be appropriate here to look more closely both at the word and the concept, as a way of providing some kind of a take on the type of lifestyle or, perhaps more precisely, of social life, referred to by them in respect of the peoples we study and write about.

We will start by saying what, from our point of view and for our purposes, conviviality is not. First, our use of the word, which broadly defines an Amazonian mode of sociality, eschews, yet also at another level transcends, the particular English sense of simply having a good (and, it is implicit, slightly inebriated) time in the company of others: i.e. a jovial, festive, companionable state, occasion or atmosphere. Even less does 'our' conviviality match the common and yet narrower French meaning attaching to the word *convive*, namely, guest, (fellow) diner; although *convivialité* signifying, as an extension of bonhomie and joviality, amicable social relations and interaction, does approach our own use. As will be seen in a number of the chapters, these sociable, congenial and even commensal aspects are not absent from Amerindian conviviality; but while important constituents of it, they are not the entire thing itself. The idea inherent in, and also literally conveying the original Latin root meaning of, the Spanish words *convivir*, to live together/to share the same life, and *convivencia*, a joint/shared life, is much more in the area of what we ourselves *basically* intend. But of what, though, does this Native American communal living, this conviviality, actually consist?

In the end, of course, this can only be a matter of interpretation, our own and that of the peoples concerned. This said, one possibly more pertinent and helpful notion of the *wider* sense(s) operating in our version of the term is to be found in Ivan Illich's *Tools for Conviviality* (1973). Here a view of 'conviviality' premised on an Ancient Greek (and Thomist) understanding of friendship and playfulness in personal relations is borrowed in order to describe, and support a thesis about, the manufacture and control of the social environment through the creative and communal, yet free and individually autonomous, agency of its members. Thus, on one hand, the psychological, moral and practical state of collective being implied by such amity and productive social play, and on the other hand, egalitarianism, co-operation, non-coercion, and freedom of personal thought and action. Now were we to add to these further complementary, and equally vital, features which may be encountered in the Native context, then we would begin to get a fuller, albeit necessarily still approximate, grasp of Amazonian conviviality, at least as perceived by us. These features would include peacefulness, high morale and high affectivity, a metaphysics of human and non-human interconnectedness, a stress on kinship, good gifting–sharing, work relations and dialogue, a propensity for the informal and performative as against the formal and institutional, and an intense ethical and aesthetic valuing of sociable sociality.

It is this particular guise of conviviality, in all its complexity, which we maintain is characteristic of so many Amazonian socialities, and not only in terms of an ideal way of living. As the chapters below variously aim to show, it also manifests itself in a concrete and quotidian sociopolitical sense, with sociability (interlocution, friendliness, mutuality and joyfulness) and sociality being considered as one, and something to be constructed daily by, and in, each and every community co-resident and co-producer.

However, Amazonian social life is not just a matter of peace and harmony. Danger, violence and disharmony also exist, whether actually or potentially, and need to be dealt with. Consequently, in contrast to the foregoing picture, a number of contributors will be looking at more negative, community-threatening situations (e.g. fighting, illness, death), and antisocial affective states (e.g. anger, jealousy, 'fierceness', loneliness); and also at the ways in which practices and strategies entailing the avoidance of negative emotions may be said to be as integral to the creation and maintenance of conviviality as the positive ones.

The Anthropology of Love and Anger, whose contributors range widely in terms of approach and style no less than in those of nationality, background and professional experience, does not, however, adopt a unitary position on the subject – which is as it should be. For, as the reader will see, it is also our aim to promote and welcome a free and creative multiplicity of perspectives, understandings and interpretations of the topic, linked not by a uniform vision or ideology but, rather, by shared concerns and a belief in an anthropology of engagement.

Joanna Overing and Alan Passes (February 2000)

Notes

1 Chagnon (1968).
2 Huxley (1963); Goldman (1979).

References

Chagnon, N.A. (1968) *Yanomamö. The Fierce People*, New York: Holt, Rinehart & Winston.
Goldman, I. (1979 [1963]) *The Cubeo*, Urbana: University of Illinois Press.
Huxley, F. (1963 [1956]) *Affable Savages*, London: Rupert Hart-Davis.
Illich, I. (1973) *Tools for Conviviality*, London: Calder & Boyars.
0

Introduction

Conviviality and the opening up of Amazonian anthropology

Joanna Overing and Alan Passes

For many of us who work among the indigenous peoples of Amazonia, the recent critiques of the grand narratives of modernist thought as formulated within the human sciences, and through which anthropology as a discipline was conceived and hatched, have come as both a relief and a liberating breath of fresh air. Most importantly, we are now allowed, even within the confines of academia, to shed the bonds of all those master tropes of Western sociological theory that have militated against a Western understanding, much less appreciation, of Amazonian social philosophies and associated everyday practice. Our academic forebears, in objectifying major categories of Western social thought, especially such notions as society, culture, community and the individual, also incorporated modern Western distinctions of judgement and worth into the very analytic constructs through which they then gazed at, assessed and recorded all other types of socialities. As a result the nature of indigenous sociality in Amazonia has always been resistant, rebellious even, to most anthropological categorisation (see Overing Kaplan 1977; Seeger *et al.* 1979; Rivière 1984).

Although somewhat of an exaggeration, the anthropological space of Amazonia became filled with either a litany of negations and lack ('they have no lineages, no corporate groups, no land-holding groups, no authority structure, no political and social structure')[1] or structuralist templates of the cognitive domains of myth and kinship through which anonymous rationalities belonging to no one – or anyone – were unfolded (cf. de Certeau 1988). In both instances, the sentient, living, experiencing, speaking indigenous person was irrelevant, and the contents of an indigenous sociality remained elusive. The interactive, intersubjective social self has, as Michel de Certeau notes (ibid., p. xi), been concealed by the type of formal rationality dominant in the academic culture of the modernist West. Thus, the very interesting question still remains: what paths *do* we follow to understand the social life of Amazonian peoples who seem so adamant in their rejection of the 'sociological' (as defined by Western theory), and who desire above all else a high degree of emotional comfort in daily life, a stress substantiated by the political and moral one that sets as first priority the achievement of conviviality in the productive relations of community life?

Whenever indigenous sensibilities, values and reasonings *have* been success-fully grasped by the ethnographer, they almost always turn out to be judge-ments thoroughly loathsome to the sensibilities of Western sociological thought. In the contributions to this volume we do find considerable consen-sus on this 'contrariness' in Amerindian attitudes and points of view. On the following points most of us are in accord: (1) there is the idea widespread in Amazonia that the self who belongs to a collective is an independent self, and that the very creation of the collective is dependent upon such autonomous selves who have the cognitive/affective skills for congenial, social interaction; (2) at the same time, the moral gaze is other-directed, where the autonomous I is ever implicated within and joined with an intersubjectivity (see Gow, this volume, and, on the embodiment of self and community, particularly see the contributions of Jamieson, Kidd, Lagrou, Londoño-Sulkin, Overing); (3) Amazonian peoples, who notably value their ability to be social, have as well an antipathy to rules and regulations, hierarchical structures and coercive constraints (Overing 1993a, 1993b; cf. Clastres 1977); (4) in other words, they tend to be short on anything Western theory might deem as 'societal structure', or even 'social structure' or formal jural groupings; (5) Amazonian peoples do not tend to talk about roles and statuses as might relate to a particular type of hierarchical corporate structure;[2] (6) what they *do* talk about at great length is how to live well, happily, in community with others; (7) they talk about how to go about creating 'good/beautiful' people who can live a tranquil, sociable life together, and the difficulties of achieving this task; (8) they talk much about how to avoid dangerous anger, and how to love appropriately and to be 'compassionate'; (9) *their* emphasis is upon achieving a comfortable affective life with those with whom they live, work, eat and raise children, and not upon the building of societal structures. The anthropological point is this: it clearly makes an enormous difference to the results of an anthropological study – on all kinds of grounds, but certainly in its success in grasping key aspects of Amazonian sociality and experience – when *from start to finish* attention is focused upon indigenous voices and points of view, rather than upon grand structures of mind, culture or society, unconscious or otherwise.[3]

The anthropology of love and anger: the debates

The title of this volume has been chosen to capture the perspectives of Amazonian peoples with regard to the more noticeable tenets of their 'socio-logically wayward' sociality. Much of the technical language of anthro-pology, with its interest centred upon the jural domain, is for the most part irrelevant to Amazonian social concerns, and thus unenlightening of them. It is nevertheless the case that each of the Amazonian peoples that feature in this volume has its own strikingly rich lexicon through which its members are able to speak of, and reflect upon, what are, for them, the salient features of their own sociality. The distinctive feature of Amazonian social talk is that it pertains to a language of affect and intimacy that *conjoins thinking and the sensual life*, where the concern is with the attributes of the everyday moral agent in ordinary interpersonal pursuits. In other words, their 'emotion talk' is also 'social talk' in that they consider the management of their affective life *vis-à-vis other people* to be constitutive of moral thought and practical reason. It is a language that speaks axiologically of the social benefits of the practice of the everyday virtues of love, care, compassion, generosity and the spirit of sharing (see most contributions to this volume). It dwells equally upon the antisocial inclinations of anger, hate, greed and jealousy that are disruptive to the human social state.[4] Thus love and anger, as Alès, this volume, notes of the Yanomami, are in many respects but two sides of the same sociopolitical coin: love cannot be understood without the backdrop of the spectre of anger. For Amazonian people, love and anger are the very strong markers that tell respectively of the success or failure of social process.

Insofar as we insist in this volume upon the absolute importance of linking an engagement with indigenous moral thought and practice to the anthropological task of beginning to understand the sociality of Amazonian peoples, our discussions can be seen as contentious. This is because many of them are directed toward overcoming a prejudice inherent in Western political, legal, social and moral theory which separates the dominant 'domain of the public' (the cool and rational space of societal relationships which are ruled through contract and law) from the contingent 'domain of the domestic' (the hot and affective space of personal family relationships centred around the everyday care and responsibility of children). Both anthropology and moral philosophy inherited this point of view, and the problems of unravelling its distorting effects upon our translations of other peoples' reasoning about the world of the social are immense. As but one example, there is a strong assumption in anthropology that 'domestic relationships' do not pertain to the social, while in moral philosophy a prevalent view of 'the domestic' is that it is, moreover, irrelevant to the realm of the moral (e.g. Rawls 1971; Kohlberg 1981, 1982; Habermas 1990). Sahlins, in his assessment of the 'domestic mode of production' of 'tribal' folk, argues that its social defect is that it only serves intimate and therefore ultimately selfish familial satisfactions, and not those of the wider whole (Sahlins 1972: 86, 97–8). The intimate relationships which Sahlins thereby declares asocial are those that are centred on the caring and raising of children (see Rapport and Overing 2000b). For him, only the public domain, within which the chief operates through means of political coercion, merits the label of 'social' (Sahlins, op. cit., p. 134). In this narrative of society, to be social is to engage in hierarchical relationships that are enacted coercively.

The debates in the last couple of decades, especially those initiated by feminist theorists across the disciplines within the human sciences, centre upon the neglect of the personal everyday within misogynist, universalistic moral theory (cf. Gilligan 1982; Benhabib 1992; Baier 1995).[5] In anthropology, Strathern observes (1988: 94–5) about such Western ideas of social order, that the larger whole, the controlling, collective force of society, is said to coincide with the public domain of men, while the subordinated, individuating, familial domain of the asocial (and amoral) domestic is relegated to women – and their biologically based activities. She argues that such a gendered distinction between public and private concerns is not necessarily helpful for the understanding of indigenous socialities, for among indigenous peoples of Melanesia, the goals of 'the domestic' and 'the collective' merge to such an extent that most of the men's endeavours are 'directed toward the same production of domestic kinship, growth and fertility' as concern the women (Strathern, op. cit., p. 318). The same observation can be made of the indigenous peoples of Amazonia (see Overing 1999; and Alès, Belaunde, Echeverri, Lagrou, Londoño-Sulkin, Overing, this volume).

An interdisciplinary, and similar, sharp debate is in progress over the respective value of a 'rights-centred' and a 'virtue-centred' moral system. It is a discussion pertinent to anthropology in that Amazonian peoples adhere to a 'virtue-centred ethics' that is primarily centred upon the quality of 'the good life' which is engendered through the artful[6] practices and skills of those who personally and intimately interact in everyday life. There is an aesthetics to Amazonian morality, which also centres upon intent and desire (see Echeverri, this volume). In contrast, the dominant trend in contemporary moral philosophy, since Kant's recasting of it, has been to purify ethics of all aesthetics and desire (see Gadamer 1979: 35–9) and to narrow the definition of the moral domain so as to centre moral reason upon abstract issues of justice, and the rights and obligations adhering to it within the context of the impersonal relations of the *public* domain. As Annette Baier has argued (op. cit., pp. 4–5, 13–14, 116), the overly coercive models of morality (and society) that are depicted in rights-centred theory are attached to such notions as the rule, and its obedience, and the justification of coercion when rules are broken. Thus the moral concentration is upon obligations, and not the virtues (see Benhabib, op. cit.). Much of modernist social theory, including that of anthropology, is derived from the same rationalist, formalist and juridical model of a 'rights-centred' view of society.

Standing against the universalism, formalism and rationalism of the 'rights-centred' theorists, the advocates of a virtue-centred ethics, many of whom are feminists,[7] oppose the immorality of moral theory that removes from its discussion the everyday, interactive relationships that might lead to the creation of a high quality of personal relations among those within the same life-world, such as, for instance, those concerned with the care, trust and responsibility for the raising of children. Such feminist critique has played its crucial part in decentring the construct of society as it sits within modernist social theory. In rethinking the grand narratives of Western social thought, one salient aim, as Benhabib (op. cit., pp. 5–10) so aptly phrases it, has been to shift the conceptualisation of 'the moral point of view' so as to include the 'evaluative questions of the good life', and thus the intimate relationships of care within Western discussions of the moral – and therefore the social.

However, the problem of gendering domains needs to be further considered. Outside of anthropology, the feminist debate has largely been pursued from a Western standpoint, where the concern for care and trust is assumed to be principally a matter of gender, of interest to females but not males.[8] The genders are thought to have different moral outlooks, that is, while contemporary men tend to phrase morality in terms of obligation, contract and justice (a reflection of their own concern with personal autonomy and independence), women are more 'domestic' in view, being most concerned with a virtue-centred morality relevant to the bringing up of children, and engendering of love, care, trust and cooperation. However, from a cross-cultural point of view, anthropology can argue, as has Strathern (op. cit.) for Melanesia, and Overing for Amazonia (1999; see Alès, this volume), that an antagonism about matters of morality that distinguishes public and domestic concerns is not always typical of gender relations. As many of the contributions to this volume make clear, the values of care, trust and cooperation are equally relevant to judgements of actions of men and women (see Gow 1989, 1991; McCallum 1989; Belaunde 1992). Likewise, the right to personal autonomy in Amazonia is more often than not an ungendered value. Anthropology has not been especially perspicacious in its insights into indigenous sorts of moral systems, and the main reason for this is that a dominant strand in Western moral theory, from which anthropology is not exempt, does exclude 'domesticity', certainly as it might relate to a vision of personal autonomy. It is, however, with the everyday relations of the ordinary moral agent, male or female, that Amazonian sociality is usually about.

There is also an argument going on presently within Amazonian debate, which when stripped of all the rhetoric, is precisely over the relevance of these Western grand narratives of society to any satisfactory understanding of indigenous Amazonian social life. What *is* this domain of 'the social'? As noted, most of our contributors wish to centre the discussion upon indigenous notions of sociality, which means that the Western separation of the 'public' and the 'private', the formal versus the informal (see Alès, this volume), the domestic versus the collective – with all their layers of signification which are local to the Western imagery of society – is clearly obstructive to this task. The notion that we then ignore the wider intercommunity, intertribal and cosmic relationships, and overlook, as well, the effects of conflict and violence, the negative passions of anger, hate and distrust, along with the widespread

Amazonian understanding of the link of affinity with predation, is patently wrong.[9] Rather, the case is that many of us (in this volume) see most of these wider relationships, and the cultural elaboration upon them, as indeed belonging to the Native Amazonian narratives of sociality, that is, insofar as these are exactly those elements of lived experience that most Amazonian peoples construe as asocial, even *non-human*, and certainly amoral. As such, they serve as negative examples of just what sociality should not be. As Alès, in this volume, argues, intercommunity relationships among the Yanomami (whose vision of a distinction between the formal and the informal is not that of Western theory) are considered sociable *only* insofar as they are enacted in accordance with the expectations of their code of caring, loving friendship – the intimate state of social engagement that is paradigmatic for all close, personal, trusting relationships.

In other words, and in like manner to the Yanomami, all those attributes and relationships we dub as 'domestic', most Amazonian peoples identify with the realm of the social. To exclude what we see as 'domestic' in discussing the sociality of Amazonian peoples would be equivalent to restricting the discussion to such topics as their engagement with the great Carib trade and cannibal raids (of earlier centuries), or to the present-day warrior/shamanic dealings with the spirit world and the cannibal gods, and their sorcery or warfare against human enemies. Such a sociological reduction would be nothing less than a strong form of modern exoticism. It would be equally reductive, of course, to restrict the discussion of sociality to the internal world of 'domesticity'.

Thus, it is also correct to note that we agree that Amazonian sociality cannot be understood without the backdrop of the wider cosmic and inter-community and intertribal relationships. The forces for conflict, violence, danger, cannibalism, warfare and predation do penetrate to the heart of the Amazonian social, as most of the contributions to this volume make clear. This in fact is the paradox facing many Amazonian people in their daily construction of the sociable, fertile conditions for sociality: it is not an unusual cosmogonic vision that all forces for life, fertility, creativity *within* this world of the social have their origin in the dangerous, violent, potentially cannibalistic, exterior domains beyond the social (cf. Overing Kaplan 1981; Overing 1985a; Echeverri and Londoño-Sulkin, this volume). Nonetheless, these forces in and of themselves are not conducive to sociality, but destructive of it, and they cannot be generative of human social life until transformed through human will, intent and skill. As Echeverri's discussion of the poetics of the salt ritual among the Uitoto comprehensively unfolds, the lived social existence of human beings can only be achieved through the suffering and hardship of enduring a multiplicity of difficult, treacherous paths that eventually enable a person to *transform* the violent, angry, ugly, capricious forces of the universe into constructive, beautiful knowledge and capacities. These, in their changed state, and in contrast to their former sterile, destructive constitution, then become *generative* of sociality and the type of affective–fertile existence of which human beings, and human beings alone, are capable (see Belaunde, Gow, Londoño-Sulkin, Santos-Granero, this volume; McCallum 1994; Overing 1999). However, because the source of the conditions for the peaceful, fertile social life that humans can achieve is also born in violence, the latter's presence is ever potential, lurking at the heart of the social to disrupt the sociality so preciously wrenched from the universe (Belaunde, this volume). This is one explanation for the immense value that Amazonian peoples set on the *tranquillity* of their social life, and upon the quality of its affective state of being. It is why they place so much attention upon the positive dispositions conducive to amiable peace, and are deeply wary of those threatening to it, such as anger and greed.

From the indigenous point of view, it would be impossible for their hard-won sociality to be 'encompassed', as Viveiros de Castro suggests (1992), by the wider forces of affinal, cannibalistic violence – and still remain 'social'. As Rivière observes (this volume), the *raison d'être* of peaceful social relation-ships of community life is their very exclusion from its kinship space (except, as noted, as forces tamed, mastered and *transformed*: the affine remade into kin). This human *sociable* world is often understood as distinct from all other agential worlds of the cosmos. The link of sociality with outside forces is hardly straightforward, and the (indigenous) sociological thrust is cate-gorially to separate the two: agents of the exterior are viewed as *incapable* of sociality until transformations prove otherwise. Thus, although there is truth to the idea that Amazonian sociality appears to follow an *inclusivist* view of alterity, it is always an alterity *transformed*. There is no homology therefore between the way people enact their *sociable* relations with each other and the way they treat other kinds of beings in the universe (see Gow on the Piro, this volume). This would be impossible since ontologically no other beings are capable, in and of themselves, of sociality. The sociable sociality cannot be encompassed because non-human beings are not governed by the other-regarding virtues, which as Gow stresses in his chapter, *do* make up everyday social reality. For Piro people, kinspeople create together an intersubjective multiplicity, which is an impossible task for other beings of the universe.

An anthropology of the everyday

Our quest is to begin the process of creating an 'anthropology of the every-day' through which to explore, with greater insight, the 'contrary' ways of Amazonian sociality where the moral virtues and the aesthetics of inter-personal relations, and not structure, are the overriding concern. This focus upon the everyday is not banal or insignificant, for its aim is to capture the indigenous stress, which is of course the point of the exercise. Time and again the Amerindian emphasis (with regard to the world of the social) is upon the artful skills for living together in convivial *intimacy* (see most contributions to this volume), and upon the teaching of such competence to their children and young people (see especially Belaunde, Echeverri, Kidd, Lagrou, Londoño-Sulkin, this volume).

For the anthropologist to engage with Amazonian views of sociality, a good many boundaries of Western social thought must as a matter of course be disrupted, as for instance is particularly the case with respect to some of the major dualisms of Enlightenment thought: the contrast between civil society and the domestic, society and the individual, reason and emotions, mind and body, subject and object, art and work. In Brady's words (1991: 8–9), everyday reality is a 'polyphonic, symbolically layered environment' which has elusiveness as a permanent, inbuilt characteristic (cf. de Certeau, op. cit., p. xi). This is the lived world about which Amerindian people most reflect and intellectually elaborate upon through the poetics of their social theory (see especially Echeverri, this volume). There is no uniform closure to it, be it institutional or performative. It is a world at one with poetics and aesthetics, which contrasts with our modern Western sensibilities where the work of the poet and artist must be kept separate from (what is viewed as) the tedium of workaday, everyday life (see most of the contributions to this volume and, before, Overing 1989, 1996, 1999; Witherspoon 1977; Witherspoon and Peterson 1995).

The aim, then, is an ethnography of 'the ordinary' and the local, a grassroots ethnography. To reach the goal of an ethnographic everyday, we are here paying attention to the relation of aesthetics to virtues and affective life in Native American (and mainly Amazonian) cultures, and to the ways in which such a relation itself becomes constitutive of indigenous social ethics, and 'everyday' sociality, conviviality and practice. While the various contributions explore, and seek to describe and explain, the topic each in their different manner and from a different angle, their common focus (with one exception) is upon indigenous understandings of community (their ways of thinking and speaking about it), the sociocultural practices linked with such interpreting and the emotional states attendant on them.

To attain such connections, different domains and current concerns of anthropology are here being brought together, namely, the emotions, cognition, aesthetics and poetics, dialogics, phenomenology and social organisation. To this list must be added the topic of morality, the stepchild of anthropology, and upon which there is a dearth of studies. There is the logical convergence of social with cultural anthropology, and the dialogue is fruitful in this volume between some of the normally isolated parts of our studies, such as ethnolinguistics (see Gow, Jamieson, Kidd, Passes, Rivière), ethnohistory (see Santos-Granero) and ethnopsychology (see most chapters; also see Schwartz *et al*. 1992), as well as with symbolic, economic and sociopolitical anthropologies. In order, then, to move more closely to what we consider to be the daunting task of understanding Amerindian lifeways, with their subtleties and richness, their coherencies, fluidities and contradictions, we wish to contribute to the process, already engaged in by others,[10] of widening and extending the anthropological endeavour beyond the self-imposed borders of the sociological.

The overall stance of our book is integrative, incorporative, synthetic. *It must be*, in light of the fact that the academic sociological notion of 'society' excludes much of what Amazonian people most value in life, and also experience and do – an observation which probably holds, albeit in relative degrees, for most other people in the world. The list that is taboo for 'society' and 'societal relations' is endless: there is the life of experience, of laughing and crying, of loving and hating, of caring and feeding; there is the talking, chatting and telling, the singing and playing, the laughter in work, the tact and aesthetics of interpersonal dealings (and their infringement and breakdown) – all those elements that contribute to the creation or destruction of 'the beautiful good life', the intimate, informal relationships of the everyday, which are the primary concern of most Amazonian peoples, and which seem to take up most of their time and energy. The received wisdom of sociological theory places all of this richness of living and everyday life, along with its aesthetics and poetics, outside society's boundaries, and into the (subsidiary, subordinate) domain of the domestic, and thus beyond the pale of the sociological. We must dislodge the rigid boundaries of the scientific endeavour that turn into mere leftovers and footnotes the lifeways of living, experiencing people (see de Certeau, op. cit., p. 6). The modernist notion of 'society' is beyond morality; it is always beyond sentient, phenomenal, creative human beings, for whom styles of relating and moral codes of decorum, followed or infracted, are of paramount ongoing concern. In Amazonia, this is precisely, however, what life *is*, or at least what a *human social life* is. Not a single one of the structures of modernist sociological theory will in itself further our understanding of it. As Roy Wagner has proclaimed (1991), in his article 'Poetics and the recentering of anthropology', we must overcome the effects of a sociological scientism which has 'nickeled and dimed' (i.e. devalued and debased) *human* realities to death.

To do so, we must also overcome our tendency to denigrate the everyday. We, as professional anthropologists, are inclined to view the matters of the everyday as tedious and irrelevant, and are therefore disposed to seeing its practices and expressions as but mere epiphenomena of grander and more 'interesting' schemes. Or, as already noted above, we impose a wall between 'the public' and 'the private', where only the former is considered to be worthy of attentive analysis. There is as well the allure of the exotic, which bewitches us. We long to see the remarkable, while we regard the world of the everyday as *un*remarkable and boring (see Gow, this volume). Certainly, from the viewpoint of many anthropologists, shamans interacting with cannibal gods, warriors lopping off the heads of enemies and hunters shooting wild peccary with blowguns and curare are much more exciting prospects than people preparing communal meals or training and caring for children. As a result, the anthropologist has become better trained in capturing the exotic display of alien minds and actions than in expressing the significance of the 'normal' skills of everyday behaviour. Because we perceive as trivial many matters of daily life, we end up actually refusing to see them. As Jacob Meløe says for philosophy (Meløe 1988: 95), a lot of anthropology is about 'not seeing and not knowing that we are not seeing'. In this volume, we wish to talk about the ways in which indigenous peoples of the Amazon can be powerful philosophically in their reflections about matters of everyday concern. It is only by paying close attention to the details of this everyday life that we can begin to understand the relation between their strong valuation of everyday skills and their egalitarian practices, between personal autonomy and sociality, and their linking of the metaphysical and the beautiful with the accomplishment of everyday sociality.

The conscious everyday

The thread common to most of the recent writings within anthropology that have been involved in unravelling the splits of modernist social theory, particularly subject and object, is a dedication to the creation of an 'anthropology of consciousness', where the conviction is to 'decolonialise' the human subjects of our studies. The 'anthropology of consciousness', which rebels against the grand narratives upon which modernist epistemologies rest, is an important element of an 'anthropology of the everyday'. As Rapport and Overing note (2000a), it is no longer acceptable to claim a consciousness for ourselves which we deny to others. As encouragement for anthropologists to descend from their intellectual high ground, they should recall the oft repeated proclamation of a certain Amazonian people to their resident ethnographer (Oldham 1996), along the lines of: 'In our experience, it seems that we are much more profound as anthropologists than those who label themselves as such!'[11] Truth or not, the indigenous peoples have good reason to fight for their own intellectual integrity.

Our arrogant Eurocentrism, and its systematic denial to others of an intelligence (pro)claimed for self, has imperialist roots, as Mason reminds us in his discussion (this volume) on the violence of the Western gaze as trained on the indigenous other by sixteenth-century observers during the initial contact following the invasions of the New World. From the European perspective, Amazonian people were ugly (with tails and no necks) and therefore cannibals; they ate dreadful food: an indication of their inability to distinguish correctly between the edible and inedible; they were naked, and thus did not know the difference between nudity and dress, or private and public. In brief, the Natives lacked the intelligence to discriminate properly – they had no faith, king or law (see Clastres, op. cit., p. 156) – *ergo* they lacked knowledge, reason and order. Mason's point is that the colonialist eye that perceived, interpreted instantaneously. Through but a glance, the

Amerindian was classed as either on the side of bestiality or belonging to a Golden Age that was close to nature, both conditions being obverse to the state of the civilised European: Noble Savage or Pagan Cannibal, yet essentially, as Sally Price puts it (1989: 37), one and the same person described by a Westerner in 'two frames of mind'. By contrast, the Europeans were adult: they possessed reason, technological advancement, the knowledge of letters and money; *they*, unlike the Natives, had monarchs, manners, garments and a true religion (see Pagden 1982; Todorov 1987; Hulme 1986; Mason 1990; Corbey and Leerssen 1991; Palencia-Roth 1996).

The apparent transparency of these perceived 'primitive symptoms' of lack, each of which conveyed and compounded the same message of primitiveness, was in fact, Mason argues, an opacity, 'tautologously' revealing nothing that was not already 'known' – or assumed. Such European images of New World peoples had prime force in the sixteenth century as valued tools of denigration, exclusion, conquest and the colonialist endeavour (Arnold 1996; Hulme, op. cit.; Mason, op. cit.; Pagden, op. cit.). What is troublesome is that they held sway until but very recently in Western social theory, where the gaze is still sufficiently violent to create Natives who are ignorant children without the intelligence, or even interest, to engage in conscious reasoning. As Mason observes, the supposed 'communication' between sixteenth-century Europeans and Natives – and by inference between twentieth-century anthropologists and indigenous Amazonian people – has been in effect a European monologue, where no convivial, conversing relations could possibly be established.

There has been a very long history to Europe's creation of its imaginary worlds of Amazonia and its accompanying discourse on lack, and on the cannibal, pathological other. Furthermore, it has been anthropology, the science of alterity *par excellence*, that has provided the objectified, simplified imagery and the 'technical' language through which all those peoples who were conquered and colonised by the Western state could be digestibly incorporated into, and depreciated by, a supremacist European mental framework.

Since dialogue is our interest, one of the tasks of this volume is to engage with indigenous social philosophies, and thus with indigenous metaphysics. To do so means to *listen* well to what the people have to *say*, and to recognise the face-value worth of their words (an embarrassing intent to have to make overt, when the hopeful expectation is that it would be taken for granted). The decent academic and political goal of the anthropologist should be at the very least the reappropriation of language by its speakers, without which no conversation with the other (as interlocutor) can begin (see de Certeau, op. cit. p. xiii). From Amerindian perspectives, their own capabilities for achieving sociality also have their history: they can be, for instance, the outcome of specific cosmogonic happenings, often brutal and whimsical in their pre-social stages (see Echeverri, Gonçalves, Londoño-Sulkin, Overing, Rosengren, Santos-Granero, this volume). Because of this past, and the violence of remnants of it in the present, sociality today is never a given, or a gift: it must be daily and precariously achieved through the careful actions of reasoning, practising human beings. If intellectual *decolonisation* is *our* aim, we cannot with justice reduce this Amazonian sociality – as has been our habit in the past when communication was more of a monologue for Western consumption only – to structures of kinship and affinity, or to such equally reductive principles as exchange, reciprocity and hierarchy. In order to understand an indigenous metaphysics of sociality, we must take another road, for when it comes to explanations, theirs is a logic that is expansive, not reductive (see Echeverri, this volume).

To decolonise Amazonian ethnography, we must familiarise ourselves with indigenous poetics, and their aesthetics of living a human sort of life (see most chapters, this volume). There are all those beautiful ornamentations of self, beautified artefacts – and beautiful behaviours. We may well ask, why such stress among Amazonian peoples upon the beauty of the everyday? And, how do we, as anthropologists, go about studying it? How do we 'verify' the design on a canoe paddle, the artistry in a feathered head-dress, and the beauty of words, or of a posture? Wagner suggests (op. cit., p. 40) that what we must become are poets of 'the here and now', of the everyday, accepting of its surprise as we shed the cool, aseptic scepticism of the scientist *vis-à-vis* what is 'out there' (cf. de Certeau, op. cit., p. xiii).[12] Certainly, to clarify the Amerindian stress upon the *need for beauty* in the everyday, we must understand the verses of their chanting and the poetics of their everyday speech, their artful use of copulas, affixes, noun classes and possessives, and understand their humour and irony, and their crafty, complex wordplay (see Alès, Echeverri, Jamieson, Kidd, Overing, Passes, this volume), all expressive of their strong sense of the follies of existence, its myriad of interconnections within an animated universe, its ambiguities and dangers and its possibilities for beauty. As the reader will see, Amazonian sociality is achieved at great effort against a cosmic background of danger and folly (see Belaunde, Echeverri, Gow, Londoño-Sulkin, Overing, Rivière, Rosengren, Santos-Granero, this volume).

It does make a difference for us to pay full attention to indigenous thinking about being in the world which is substantial, coherent – and often different from our own.[13] In engaging in an 'anthropology of consciousness and the everyday', we hope to undo some of the outrage that has been committed in the past to the philosophies, knowledges and experiences of other people, all in the name of one paradigm or the other forthcoming from high modernism (see especially Lagrou, this volume, on representational theories of meaning). We would like our endeavour to be seen instead to fit comfortably within the domain of comparative aesthetics, moral philosophy and social psychology (cf. Witherspoon and Peterson 1995: 78). Our difference from the other is not to be 'construed as vacancy, awaiting the inscription of its blankness by those who wield the power to confer meaning' (Mason, this volume). We want to converse with Amazonian peoples, and not hover over them, as Brady has nicely phrased it, 'in analytic neutral' (op. cit., p. 11).

The Western monologue on society and collectivity

We find, however, that when it comes to discussing, describing, expressing the daily collective life of Amazonian peoples words fail us; we falter over the clumsy technical vocabulary of our discipline: the rules and regulations of social life, the hierarchical structures of society, the jural rules of social structure, the distinction between the individual and society – all those sociological means through which we are directed to understand another people's collectivity. It has become normal in modernist thinking about the social to view collectivity as a heavily repressive mechanism, with the force of coercive power on its side.

Raymond Williams tells us (1983: 293) that 'society' as an abstract notion was not used until the eighteenth century, at which time the term began to take on its modernist, general sense of denoting particular 'social orders', an idea that grew out of the debates upon the state's hierarchical and hegemonic institutions of control as might be associated with the new (bourgeois) political order. This Western, abstract sense of 'society' (e)merged, then, with the notion of 'civil society' and the development of contract theories of the state. There is a local *history* to the development of the modern usage of the word 'society' that led to the *impersonal and coercive* sense of the term as used in modernist social theory.[14]

If, however, we define the collectivity in terms of institutions of hierarchy and coercion, it is clearly the case that many Amazonian peoples do not have much of it, nor do they want it (e.g. Clastres op. cit.; Overing 1993b). Yet surely something is faulty with our definition, for the indigenous peoples of Amazonia are undoubtedly social beings, and they also happen to have their own strong views about proper human sociality, where the stress is often upon its intimacy, its informality, its egalitarian ways of doing things.

Amazonian people deeply value not only their personal autonomy, but (almost) equally their ability *to be social* (especially on this interplay see Alès, Rivière and Rosengren, this volume; and Goldman 1963; Thomas 1982; Rivière 1984; Overing 1989, 1993a, 1999). On this point, it is perhaps enlightening to note that the so-called bellicose Yanomami appear to be attached to 'more' collectivity than the more 'peaceful' peoples in the volume, such as the Trio, Piaroa and Matsigenka. According to Rosengren (this volume), among the Matsigenka the group exists only at the moment of its constitution, whereas Alès observes that for the Yanomami their beloved personal autonomy is encompassed by a principle of collective solidarity. Whichever the case, the ethnographer's problem has been that our modernist notion of the social, or 'collectivity', is no more suitable for the purposes of translating most of the social practices and perspectives of indigenous Amazonia than are all the other master terms that have fallen recently into anthropological disrepute, such as 'society', 'culture', 'community' and 'the individual'.

To understand the difference between Western theory and the Amazonian vision and practice, the distinction must be made between collectivity as might be expressed through social-structural imperatives (through roles, statuses and juridical rules) and the collective *as an* attachment to (or among) the people who follow specific cultural and social ways of being. Many indigenous peoples of Amazonia are strongly, adamantly, fond of their own cultural and social ways of *doing* things, and of the people with whom they share them, but not of heavy imperatives of social structure or collectivity (cf. Overing 1999). Again, we need to find the paths into *their* sociality, and the one that we suggest to be followed pays closer attention to the ways and wherefores of Amazonian peoples' attachment to people: what for them are the conditions for human sociability?

Why conviviality?

Of interest to us in this volume, in the exploration of paths to Amazonian sociality, is the earlier usage in the West of the term 'society' to convey a sense of '*personal* belonging', or the face-to-face relationships of a community. Before the eighteenth century the term denoted sociability, companionship, fellowship, or a mode of living (Williams, op. cit., pp. 291–2). It is this earlier meaning that many anthropologists are now saying is closer to an acceptable view. Today, though, in order to sidestep the objectifications and valuations of the modernist use of the term 'society', the yet more acceptable preference is 'sociality' (cf. Strathern, op. cit.; Ingold 1994; Fardon 1992), the idea being, first of all, that the social requires individual agency (acting, reflecting, moral agents) and thus the two are constitutive of one another.

However, the term most contributors to this book have chosen as especially appropriate to translate Amazonian sociality or collectivity is 'conviviality', a term that can overlap in many respects with the earlier understanding of 'society' as amiable, intimate sets of relationships which carry, as well, a notion of peace and equality.[15] Conviviality seems best to fit the Amazonian stress upon the *affective* side of sociality. In the modernist, abstract use of the word 'society', there is no place for affect. We can almost say that affect is inappropriate to modern conceptions of society, and certainly to the *notion* of its state or character, a rational, impersonal, serious matter, to be sure. Whereas, on the contrary, Amazonian sociality could not be understood without paying attention to it, in that affect, and especially the establishment of a state of *convivial affect*, is what it is all about. The social, interactive, inter-subjective side of Amazonian collectivity is there from the start, so much so that if relationships are not convivial, then there is no sociality (see Belaunde, Gow, Kidd and others, this volume).

We must be quite clear, however, as was stressed in the Preface, that we are *not* using the term 'conviviality' in the usual English sense, that is, of having a festive, hearty, jovial, and usually inebriated, good time in the company of others. It is because of this English meaning that Rivière (this volume) remains adverse to it being used to characterise Amazonian sociality, which is only sometimes festive, intense and inebriated. One matter to consider is the fact that the *styles of relating* do vary considerably in Amazonia, where one people's normal jovial and raucous *daily* interactions, as for instance with the Pa'ikwené (Passes, this volume) and the Yanomami (Alès, this volume), would from an outside observer's perception be similar to the festive-only style of behaviour of the relatively less overtly intense Piaroa and Piro, or the soft-spoken Trio (see respectively Overing, Gow, Rivière, this volume). It is very interesting that the quiet-loving Trio lexically distinguish two states of sociality, the euphoric once-in-a-while festive and the daily calm, tranquil style of the everyday, where noise is kept at a very low level. While styles of sociability (and for that matter, tranquillity) may very well vary, the dangers of the inebriations of the festival and their tendency to disrupt the values of normal interaction are probably recognised by most of the indigenous peoples of Amazonia (e.g. see Kidd and Rosengren, this volume).

As noted in the preface, some of the other European languages come closer to the intent of our use of 'conviviality' in this volume, and we find, for instance, that the English obsolete meaning of 'society' is semantically similar to the Spanish word *convivir*. Such an idea of a sociable, jovial, shared life also underlies the stress of Erasmus (1941: 28, 35) on the importance of folly to the ongoing success of personal relations, and the work that is enacted through them. It, moreover, approaches Hume's notion of the contagious serenity and cheerfulness that relates to those social capacities that contribute to the quality of life (see Baier, op. cit., p. 59). Anthropology has for the most part neglected the role that humour and laughter play in human social relations (cf. Hobart 1995; Overing 1985a, and this volume).[16] The art of folly and laughter has been firmly demoted as one of those irrational practices, belonging to the emotive side of life *and thus* to the realm of the experiential, the illogical, the childish. It is judged to be irrelevant and marginal to societal concerns (cf. Sherzer 1990: 93). In contrast, most Amazonian people recognise, as Boon (1984) and Hobart (op. cit.) have also made clear for the Balinese, the significant part that folly plays in the attainment of a comfortable, *knowledgeable*, and therefore successful, sociality. For these people humour is constitutive of the social. Sherzer (op. cit., p. 87) has said the following of one Lowland Amerindian people, the Kuna:

> Humor is a salient and central feature of the Kuna world. In fact the intersection of speech play, verbal art, and humor penetrates every

aspect of Kuna social, cultural, and especially verbal life . . . [Speech] play involves both harmony and tension and is both verbal and social . . . Verbally artistic language for the Kuna, in ritual and everyday speech, involves an actualization of various potentials of speech play . . . [Among the Kuna] laughter is omnipresent.

It is also in large part through their humour that Amerindians not only express their reflections upon, and elucidations of, their social world, but construct it. As Sherzer comments for the Kuna, their humorous discourse 'is a *concrete actualization and recreation of*, reflection and exaggeration of, as well as commentary on what happens in real Kuna life' (Sherzer, op. cit., p. 93, our emphasis). Passes, in this volume, stresses the value of convivial speech for the Pa'ikwené as a force that is morally, affectively and socially productive in its own right. And, as Overing remarks about the Piaroa, there is a fecundity to laughter and good, strong words. Among the Pa'ikwené and the Piaroa, an aesthetics of work carries with it an aesthetics of speech. To understand the convivial sociality of Lowland Native Americans, and the social philosophies that underpin it, we must shed our own prejudices with regard to the banality of laughter – and reject any assumptions we might have with regard to the irrelevance of verbal expression, and its manner, in daily life.

Among the Piaroa, the ludic has a powerful part to play within their practices of everyday sociality, where a bantering, slapstick, and even bawdy humour is constitutive of such daily social activities as gardening, gathering, food preparation and shamanic narrations (Overing, this volume). Various of the other contributions also dwell upon the social, joyful, dialogical quality of daily work, both as ideal and in practice (see Alès, Belaunde, Echeverri, Lagrou, Passes, and by implication others). The congenial, convivial relations of work are essential to a sociality that allows for very little coercive force, and no discord, with respect to the matter of work. We can, with reason, and from an indigenous point of view, speak of the work of conviviality, and its tools (cf. Illich 1990; and Alès, Overing, Passes, this volume). For instance, contributors dwell upon the role of friendship within the same context of practical workaday life (see Alès, Gonçalves and Santos-Granero), and of the qualities of care and compassion (see Alès, Gow, Jamieson, Kidd, Lagrou and Londoño-Sulkin), and of the generous, sharing spirit that is generative of a convivial mutuality (see Alès, Gonçalves, Gow, Jamieson, Kidd, Lagrou, Rivière, Rosengren and Santos-Granero).

As most of the contributions to this volume indicate, the idea of a convivial sociality in the non-English sense described earlier captures, better than most of our notions of social relatedness, the enormous valorisation which the indigenous peoples of Amazonia place upon good humour, affective comfort and a sociable mutuality in their everyday, intimate relations and practices of community living. The fact that many Amazonian peoples equate sociality with the convivial personal is not trivial to our anthropological task. *Their* quest for a convivial sociality is the product of a powerful and highly egalitarian ethics and social philosophy, where humour, generosity and goodwill provide its sustenance; whereas *our* anthropological tools of the trade have been created to unfold the grave structures of hierarchy and formal order.

The affective conditions for Amazonian sociality

The art of social living: the good life and its moral sentiments

The most obvious thread joining the peoples discussed in this volume is their united vision of 'the good life' being the achievement of a high level of affective contentment (as Rivière, this volume, phrases this value for the Trio) among those who interact in daily intimacy. The social itself is defined as a *personal, intimate, harmonious* space of interaction, and judgement of it is ever geared toward the success of its affective life, and the comfort of it. As we will see, what is prized most is the attainment of a companionable and congenial mutuality that is engendering of a tranquil everyday existence through which, as Belaunde says for the Airo-Pai, 'good beautiful' people can be created, or, as Kidd explains of the Enxet, through which children can be raised to have 'good/beautiful *wáxoks*' (their affective/cognitive capabilities that are seated in their stomachs) with the artful skills for community life.

Happiness – which of course, in the sense of psychic comfort, is desired by the individual – has as well its potent social end, for a fertile community is a sign in Amazonia of its high morale. As Lagrou's contribution recounts, the Cashinahua insist that a *happy* village is one where many babies are born. In other words, as Overing has suggested elsewhere (1999), indigenous sociality in Amazonia is more about the issues of fecundity than those of status, role and property. The emphasis is upon creativity, for the individual's skills for a convivial life have their beautiful generative and productive power (see Overing 1989 and this volume; also Belaunde, Echeverri, Lagrou, Londoño-Sulkin, Passes, this volume).

There is an aesthetics to the indigenous emphasis upon happiness and love. For instance, from the perspective of the Enxet (Kidd, this volume), the healthy, happy community is one where its members have the embodied skills to interact appropriately through the practice of love in a good and beautiful way, while the Piro (Gow, this volume) tell of the importance of the process of good/beautiful love, thought and memory to the creation of kinsmen, and for the health that allows them to live well. And the 'fierce' Yanomami (yes, they are included here, for they too yearn for the tranquil, peaceful life) speak of how consequential it is for each individual to retain a beautiful, quiet vital soul, without which the intense, loving relationships necessary for successful community life would be impossible (Alès, this volume). Among the Yanomami, according to Alès, the entire community feels responsible for helping the one who suffers to regain his or her 'beautiful soul', and thereby health, propriety and happiness. The social attention to the aesthetics of love, and to the related virtues of sharing and generosity, has moral persuasion, for the emphasis is upon their other-regarding quality, and the (loving) necessity of preventing those with whom you live from suffering (see Alès, Belaunde, Gow, Lagrou, Overing, this volume). As already noted, we find that the language of loving compassion is especially marked, for many of the peoples described in this volume, as a moral virtue (see Alès, Gow, Jamieson, Kidd, Rosengren). In short, the convivial sociality so longed for and sought after by these peoples as a mode of communal living prioritises the language of intimacy (see Jamieson, this volume) and such other-regarding social virtues and emotional conditions as love, sociability, cooperativeness, peacefulness, affability, amity, generosity and compassion.

The idea whereby community is linked with an aesthetics of social existence is not alien to Western philosophy; indeed it was once general to Western thought as an inheritance from the Roman notion of *sensus communis*. In Vico's rendering of the concept (cf. Gadamer, op. cit., pp. 19–24), the notion of the 'sense of community' is the sense of 'the right and the general good' that is acquired through living in community and which is related to its specific goals and organisation (Gadamer, op. cit., p. 22). It has both political and moral meaning, and embraces an aesthetics, and also metaphysics, of practice. This image of an aesthetics of community coincides with the indigenous American view, but is now foreign to our modern Western one of both collectivity and aesthetics, wherein the two cannot be joined. This disjuncture stems from Kant's refashioning of moral philosophy in such a manner as, on the one hand, to separate aesthetics from the domain of knowledge (theoretical and practical) and, on the other hand, to remove the activity of aesthetic judgement in the area of law and morality from philosophical attention (cf. Gadamer, op. cit., pp. 35–9). The Enlightenment's revised view of aesthetics as yet one more autonomous realm, alongside religion, science, economics and politics, became our inheritance in the social sciences. We are now faced with recognising the implications of the insistent entanglement of the everyday with aesthetic judgement and activity in Amazonian peoples' visions and narratives of the social. As Overing has earlier argued (1989), it is only by acknowledging aesthetics in the broader sense of its meaning, where beauty in daily practice is understood as an expression of moral and political value, that anthropologists can begin to perceive the characteristics and affective conditions of everyday social life in Amazonia, and indigenous reasonings about them (see Echeverri, Jamieson, Kidd, Lagrou, this volume). For instance, there is an aesthetics to the practice of the culinary arts (see Echeverri, Lagrou, Passes, this volume; Overing 1989). In addition, the consistent emphasis upon the social value of intimacy and informality in Amazonia (the so-called 'looseness of structure' of Amazonian social life) not only has its political, productive intent, but a moral/aesthetic one as well. To understand this point requires us to comprehend the social sense of Amazonian people, that is, their 'sense of community'.

The embodied community and its aesthetics

This rich language of affect and intimacy that is linked to Amazonian sociality is not to be mistaken for evidence of a prioritising of emotions over reason. For sure, the path of Lévy-Bruhl (1966), who provides a caricature of the affective–mystical, and therefore 'prelogical', nature of 'primitive mentality', ill equips us, for we find on the contrary that Amazonian peoples deeply value their cognitive capabilities (see Overing 1985a; Belaunde 1992; and most contributions to this volume). It is a matter of utmost importance that it is not the case that the affective conditions of community life in Amazonia are 'just a matter of emotion', and as such 'felt, not thought'. Rather they are integrally linked to knowledge and moral value, and *therefore* to a type of sociality that continually demands reflection upon the moral virtues and their practice (see most contributions). However, it is also the case, from the evidence of Amerindian discourse, that they consider not only that *both* cognitive and affective capacities are embodied, but also that, for them, the capability to live a moral, social existence *requires* that there be no split between thoughts and feelings, mind and body. The Amazonian vision of the social and its practice serves as an excellent antidote to Western grand narratives, for in it there can be no such absolute positioning of the emotions on the side of 'nature', with thinking and the intellect on the side of 'culture' and 'society'. The idea that there is an aesthetics involved in belonging to a community of relations that conjoins body, thought and affect is widespread in Amazonia, and is given attention in most of the contributions to this volume.

An extensive anthropological literature has recently been produced on the cultural construction of emotions. Such writings should be read as a counteraction to a prevailing Western notion that emotions and feelings are private to the individual, and pertain to the body alone. Building on Mauss's concept of socially acquired 'body techniques' (Mauss 1979), anthropologists such as Heelas (1986), Lutz (1988),[17] Myers (1979), Rosaldo (1984) and many others have firmly established the idea of a socialised and situated body. Such writers have gone a considerable way toward overcoming the biological universalism that has long crippled and restricted anthropology's capacity to study such an important aspect of the sociality of human beings. Because affective life has so often been defined as outside the range of the human sciences by virtue of the 'corporeality' of emotions (for one famous example, see Lévi-Strauss 1981), we still know little about its place in the creation of everyday social life. This has been a true gap in our understanding.

Thanks to the recent work in the anthropology of emotions, they and the body are now recognised to be no less social and cultural than physical – a point of great relevance to Amazonia where we find 'body creation' rituals (see Echeverri, Lagrou, Londoño-Sulkin, this volume) and the idea of the embodiment and/or the mutuality of sociality (see most contributions, this volume, and especially Gow, Jamieson and Londoño-Sulkin on the notion of the embodied intersubjectivity of community). The 'emotional', though, should no more be seen solely in terms of social constructiveness than of biologic universalism, and there are some extremes of which we must beware. In stressing the cultural, intellectual aspect of emotions, some of the scholars writing within the anthropology of emotions have, at the same time, denied the 'feeling' side of affective life (cf. Leavitt 1996). Thus, instead of the emotions being considered in terms of the interesting marriage of intellect and feeling, the problem of our tendency to split the two persists. As Leavitt points out (ibid.), an emotion is something both cognitive and internally 'felt', but not one more than the other. Amazonian peoples appear to share this view. As our examples illustrate, 'Amazonian' emotions as feeling–thoughts are social, cultural experiences learned and expressed in the body in the daily process of personal interactions.

Anger, grief and jealousy: the other side of the coin

Many contributors to this volume have explored not only those virtues that Amazonian peoples find conducive to community life, but also the character-istics viewed as the most destructive of its creation and maintenance. What is more, Amazonian discourse on their affective life seems to elaborate as much upon these negative dispositions, those prejudicial to the achievement of community tranquillity, as on the ones that are constitutive of its well-being. It appears that there are two affective inclinations that Amazonian peoples almost unanimously dwell upon as the most injurious to the tranquillity and health of their cherished social state, namely, anger and suffering, which for some are strongly interrelated (on the make-up of anger/suffering see Alès on the Yanomami and Rivière on the Trio, this volume).

Anger, always conceived of as an interactive, relational state, is understood as a sign of violence and aggression against others. For the Airo-Pai, anger is envisioned as a 'monster' within the affected person that causes him or her to see kinspeople as prey or enemy: the angered person loses all sense of moral action, and is no longer in a human state of being (Belaunde, this volume). For most of the peoples discussed in the volume, the display of anger is the worst offence to community well-being (see Belaunde, Gonçalves, Jamieson, Kidd, Londoño-Sulkin, Overing, Rivière, Rosengren). The amoral state of anger tends to be seen as the final stage of any number of other affective states (envy, jealousy, grief, arrogance, loneliness, 'kinsickness'), not all of which are treated negatively in themselves, e.g. grief and loneliness (see Alès,

Gow, Lagrou, Rivière, this volume). The positive virtue of compassion is often cited as the means for preventing the grief of a kinsperson from transforming into the more dangerous state of anger. By directing compassion to the kinspeople who are suffering, the latter are thereby drawn back to a state in which they can once again interact with others through, as Gow says for the Piro, 'beautiful, loving thoughts'. The one who suffers is in a lonely, asocial state, where s/he withdraws into the self and is no longer able to participate convivially with others, and thus loses the primary capability for a human type of sociality. It is through the intensification of their own sociability that his or her kinspeople recreate a space and memory for him or her to once again engage within a human collectivity (Gow, this volume). The Yanomami solution is somewhat different, though the intent is the same: to enable someone who grieves to regain the affective state of health, sociality and happiness, it is incumbent on their kinspeople to provide them solace by acting out the suffering person's anger on their behalf through physical attacks on enemies, i.e. those responsible for the grief. It is only through revenge that the pain of the beloved grieving one can be assuaged (Alès, this volume). The Piaroa act similarly, but only through sorcery against enemies who are personally unknown (Overing 1986).

For the most part, however, these are peoples who loathe physical violence and the display of anger. They also have very few collective means for handling psychologically, or otherwise, actual acts of conflictive violence within the context of community life (especially see Belaunde, Rivière, Rosengren, Santos-Granero, this volume). The emphasis, instead, is upon the personal mastery of the life of affect in both its positive and negative manifestations. Children and young people are carefully trained to contain their own asocial inclinations, such as anger, avarice, self-centredness, and to master the positive virtues that make the convivial social state possible (especially see Alès, Belaunde, Echeverri, Kidd, Lagrou, Londoño-Sulkin, Rosengren). This is why we can say that it only through the personal autonomy of individuals, that is, the skills for social living that each individual acquires and masters – for friendship and compassion just as much as those necessary for the culinary arts – that Amazonian sociality can be built.

In many respects, the two sets of attitudes, the constructive and the destructive, are mutually implicated. If there is love and compassion to everyday practice that are engendering of its beauty, there is its danger as well: the possibility of practice gone wrong, and of becoming an ugly, destructive manifestation of anger and hate. The contributors have tended to concentrate upon two factors in their explanations of this interplay between the forces of amity and discord within Amazonian communities. First, there is the cosmological element, and secondly the level of intensity through which the personal relations of community are played out. Both are problematic.

Most Amazonian peoples understand the cosmos as a violent, dangerous space. The capricious and asocial forces of their animated universes can make the day-by-day maintenance of sociable and healthy interpersonal relationships of human beings exceedingly difficult. The paradox is that such disruptive cosmic forces are at the same time, as noted earlier, the original source for all life within the human community, and its health. A theme common to many of the peoples of this volume is that the onus for handling such disruptive forces is upon the individual. In other words, the transformation of dangerous, destructive elements of the cosmos into good and beautiful forces that allow for the health and fertility of the community is seen as the identical process as the transformation of the disruptive elements of self into good, beautiful ones that are conducive to human fecundity (see Belaunde, Echeverri, Kidd, Londoño-Sulkin).

While anger might in origin be a diabolical monster from outside, it remains a monstrous force within only if not sufficiently transformed by the active will and work of the individual. This is one obvious reason for the Amazonian rhetoric upon the importance of personal vigilance against one's own anger. As Belaunde argues in this volume, for the Airo-Pai the force of anger, although cosmological, is an *internal* matter, for dangerous, disruptive anger is always forthcoming from within, through a kinsperson who has not taken the responsibility for converting the cosmological forces within the self into the fertile, healthy, *human* forces for social living. And Londoño-Sulkin tells us that among the Muinane the process of curing the 'diseases of anger and jealousy' is through the act of work itself, e.g. the hunting of game, the building of a house. Through the creative effort of human work, the cosmological forces for affective disorders become transformed into the proper dispositions for health and the raising of children.

On a more existential note, Gow observes in his chapter that for the Piro, as for many other Amazonian peoples, one important means for keeping the antagonistic cosmic forces at bay is through maintaining a collective state of tranquillity. This is precisely why the peaceful, quiet life is so valued. Thus, what appears to us Westerners as a 'flatness of the everyday' is not only fully intentional, but also, for not a few of these peoples, the highest achievement of the collective state of existence. As Gow says, 'it is won from a cosmos that is governed by other kinds of reason, and which invades Piro people's lives with dramatic events of emotional extremity'. Thus 'living well' becomes the 'key value of an aesthetic of social life in which mastery lies with making sure that nothing ever happens', at least of a noisy emotional sort (contrast the Yanomami or Pa'ikwené). The alternative to 'doing nothing' (to be translated as an invitation for sociable visiting in Piro etiquette) is to suffer even more than is necessary the whims of the unfriendly universe. Volatile emotions are a sign of the presence within of an untamed malicious cosmos.

The second stress focuses upon the intensity or fragility of the affective life expected within the convivial sociality, and the dangers, either structural or psychological, involved when ill will erupts. Santos-Granero, the first among us to write (1991) on the concept of love as a significant principle of

Amazonian people's understanding of the social state, argues (this volume) that the frailty of Amazonian sociality where handling conflict is concerned resides in the sheer intensity through which conviviality (along with its strong feelings of love, friendliness, trust and generosity) is lived. Any fracture in those intimate affective relations will, he concludes, generate the equally intense emotions of anger, hate, shame and guilt, all dispositions militating against the continuation of conviviality. To illustrate his point, Santos-Granero describes the collapse of two modern Yanesha communities as the result of discord and political rivalry between consanguineally related leaders, the conflictive emotions engendered in the wider population, and the apparent lack of means to resolve the friction and thus maintain conviviality.

There are various ways, however, through which Amazonian peoples *can* handle what Rosengren refers to in this volume as 'the delicacy of community life'. The Yanesha communities described by Santos-Granero were large nucleated, modern, state-endorsed ones, *comunidades nativas*, involved in the process of economic, social and religious change, and it is thus not surprising or atypical that they should follow such cycles of development and decline. Previously, when the settlement pattern was more dispersed, individuals were better able to regulate the intensity of their convivial relations (Santos-Granero, this volume). Settlement dispersion, and the relative distancing it provides, is a strategy common to many Amazonian peoples for maintaining their deeply valued harmonious quality of life (see Rivière and Rosengren, this volume). There is at the same time the ease with which individuals or families can move between settlements when affective discomfort begins to be felt, a typically Guianese solution (cf. Rivière 1969, 1984; Overing Kaplan 1975; Thomas, op. cit.). Some peoples, like the Tsimanes of Bolivia, avoid conflict by making the continual travel between settlements of kins-people an integral aspect of their way of life (Ellis 1997). Such flexibility of movement must certainly be understood as intrinsic to the accomplishment of convivial sociality and the playing out of the positive virtues it requires. An attachment to an exceedingly low-key expression of affective life, as is found among the Matsigenka, Piro and Trio (see respectively Rosengren, Gow and Rivière, this volume), is yet another such strategy for enabling its success. The Yanomami, on the other hand, prefer a stronger collectivity as the solution most protective of their passionate sociality, where there is not always such an easy balance between their more overt expression of intense love and equally intense hate.

In the end, we cannot generalise for Amazonia about social-structural imperatives, because other matters, those linked to the 'feeling–thoughts' considered necessary to the actualisation of the dream of the convivial sociality, are of equal import – and also connected to them in surprising ways. Such a conception centres upon a notion of an embodied unity of kinspeople, while the specification of the category of kinsperson who might be viewed as problematic varies. As Gonçalves illustrates with the Paresi and Santos-Granero

with the Yanesha (both in this volume), it is the expectations for extreme
affective intensity between consanguines that can make these relationships
the most vulnerable and potentially violent of all. We also see, with both the
Airo-Pai and the Yanomami, that violence too has its source within the community of close relationships. In the former case, the love for a kinsperson
can transform into enmity, while among the latter it is the deep love for close
kin that leads to violence without (Belaunde and Alès respectively, this
volume). In all of these cases, the 'structural' unease comes from the kin relationship *within*, and not from the affinal relationship without. Even when the
guilt for collective discomfort lies with the affinal relationship the case is not
so clear; for, as for example with the Piaroa (Overing Kaplan 1975), the
source of social discord is the affine within, and not without, that is, with the
affine transformed into a consanguine. Ultimately, the dangers to the convivial sociality prove to be the very forces through which it is created, and
these are as much the affective as the structural conditions of its existence. As
the peoples of Amazonia recognise, these matters of affect require constant
work, vigilance, and even suffering to maintain.

Notes

1 Cf. Rivière (1984: 4, 87).
2 This is not say that Amazonian peoples do not envision categorial ways of
   behaving, but such behaviour is ever contextualised to take into account situation,
   personal choice, the affective state of relationships and judgements about them
   (e.g. Overing Kaplan 1975; Thomas 1982; Kidd, this volume).
3 This is of course not to say that Amazonian peoples are not capable of creating
   extensive external networks of relationships that, from their point of view, have
   their order – as with those between long-distance trade partners.
4 Amazonian emotion terms are clearly not just about emotions, as we might
   narrowly define them. Cf. Lutz (1988: 119) on the Ifaluk (Micronesian) word
   fago, which is usually translated as 'love', but not 'love' as 'White Americans'
   might interpret it, i.e., in terms of sex and romance. Rather, what the Ifaluk
   mean by 'love' is to be more broadly read, as is the case in Amazonia, to imply
   caring, responsibility and compassion, all states of being that are not just 'felt',
   but very much require the intellect.
5 There is a growing philosophical counterculture to contemporary coercive models
   of morality that includes both men and women, e.g. see Michael Stocker (1976a,
   1976b); Alasdair MacIntyre (1980); Lawrence Blum (1980); Susan Wolf (1982);
   Michael Slote (1983); Alison Jaggar (1983); Claudia Card (1994, 1995).
6 'Artful' is used in its old sense of 'being characterised by art, beauty', and not in
   the modern meaning of 'using deceit or cunning'.
7 Especially see Gilligan (1982); Benhabib (1992); Baier (1995).
8 For example, see Baier (1995: 323), and also Gilligan (1982).
9 The current debate was initiated by Viveiros de Castro (1996) in his classification
   of three theoretical tendencies that, in his mind, typified contemporary
   Amazonian studies (see Gonçalves, Rivière and Santos-Granero, this volume,
   who discuss this debate). These were the 'political economy of control' (cf.
   Rivière's discussion, this volume), the 'symbolic economy of alterity' (to which

Viveiros de Castro subscribes), and the 'moral economy of intimacy' (to which many of the contributors of this volume supposedly belong). The latter group has been accused of dwelling only upon the domain of the 'domestic' and the local, and of excluding the wider domain of (more important) sociological interest. We argue that we do not exclude the 'wider' network of relationships, cosmic and otherwise. Indeed, as this volume describes, they are crucial to understanding any Amazonian vision of sociality. To argue further, however, would be to engage in the grand narratives of society upon which the first listed approaches are embedded. We, after working toward the *de*centring of the construct of society as envisioned within grand narrative texts, would be led to argue once again within modernist theory, which holds to a world-view that is incommensurable with the indigenous one. Translation we must do, but not translation through the grand narratives of Western social theory. For a start on such translation see, for example, Overing (1985c, 1987, 1988, 1989, 1990, 1993a, 1993b, 1999); McCallum (1989); Gow (1989, 1991); Belaunde (1992); Santos-Granero (1991); Ellis (1997); Lagrou (1998); Passes (1998); Kidd (1999); Storrie (1999); Pauli (2000).

10 Obvious examples are the 'radical empiricism' of Jackson (1989), the anthropological poetics of Brady (1991), the anthropology of experience of Turner and Bruner (1986), the critique of the Western dualism of mind and body by Myers (1979) and Rosaldo (1984), the critique of modernist anthropology by Fabian (1983, 1998), Bruner (1984) and Wagner (1991), the joining of literature and anthropology by Rapport (1994), the bringing together of thought and action by Ingold (1994) and the deconstruction of 'society' by Strathern (1988).

11 The indigenous peoples are 'one-upping' Wittgenstein's quip of 'when we do philosophy we are like savages, primitive people, who hear the expressions of civilized men, put a false interpretation on them, and then draw the queerest conclusions from it' (Wittgenstein 1976: §194, 79). The indigenous rendering would be: 'when you do anthropology you are like savages, primitive people, who hear the expressions of civilised people, put a false interpretation on them, and then draw the queerest conclusions from it'.

12 Also see Augé (1997: 8), who argues that, on the contrary, anthropology 'has always dealt with the here and now'.

13 Contrast this view with that of Descola, who when speaking on the 'animic systems' of Amazonia says: '[E]xcept in the western scientific tradition, representations of non-humans are not usually based on a *coherent and systematic corpus of ideas*'. Rather, 'Anthropologists reconstruct these *mainly non-verbal models of practice* from bits and pieces, from all sorts of apparently trifling acts and disconnected statements which they [the anthropologists] weave together so as to produce meaningful patterns' (Descola 1996: 86, our emphases). In other words, the Native's representations are expressed, he says (ibid.), contextually, in 'daily actions . . . in lived-in knowledge and body techniques, in practical choices and hasty rituals, in all those little things that "go without saying" (Bloch 1992)'. In this view the anthropological chore is to decontextualise all this unconscious 'habitus'-embodied knowledge in order to create a meaningful, rational and textual order, which the native him- or herself would not be capable of verbalising – or, it seems, understanding. We, on the other hand, in this volume, are insisting on privileging both context and the indigenous practitioners of the art of speaking. In this contrasting view, poetic ways of 'making do' have their own coherencies, fully realised by the speakers (cf. de Certeau 1988: xv, 56–8). It is this more poetic coherency which it is in fact our task to understand. It cannot, however, be the same coherency seen and created by the practitioner of formal analysis.

Any coherency consciously recognised by the indigenous speaker would not only be seen as (sociologically) 'untrue' by such a specialist of Western formalist arts, but, even more to the point, impossible!

14 Particularly suspect for contemporary sensibilities in anthropology is the abstract notion of society, forthcoming from Durkheimian theory, as the weighty collectivity that imposes, opposes and constrains all those extra-social individuals who compose it, and in so doing transcends the individual and his or her conscious life of thought and action (e.g. see the discussions of Strathern 1988; Fardon 1992; Ingold 1994; Rapport 1997).

15 Cf. *The Compact Edition of the Oxford English Dictionary* (1971, p. 2902).

16 It is not only anthropology that has ignored the significance of humour in human social relations, for this has been the trend in all the human sciences, which, as Hobart comments (1995), suffer a severe case of *gravitas*. See Bremmer and Roodenburg (1997) on analyses of just why this might be the case.

17 Also see Lutz and White (1986); Lutz and Abu-Lughod (1990); cf. Overing (1985c).

References

Arnold, A.J. (ed.) (1996) *Monsters, Tricksters, and Sacred Cows: Animal Tales and American Identities*, Charlottesville: University of Virginia Press.

Augé, M. (1997 [1992]) *Introduction to an Anthropology of Supermodernity*, trans. J. Howe, London: Verso.

Baier, A. (1995) *Moral Prejudices: Essays on Ethics*. Cambridge, Mass.: Harvard University Press.

Belaunde, L.E. (1992) 'Gender, commensality and community among the Airo-Pai of West Amazonia (Secoya, Western-Tukanoan speaking)', unpublished Ph.D dissertation, University of London.

Benhabib, S. (1992) *Situating the Self: Gender, Community and Postmodernism in Contemporary Ethics*, Cambridge: Polity Press.

Bloch, M. (1992) 'What goes without saying: the conceptualization of Zamaniry society', in A. Kuper (ed.) *Conceptualizing Society*, London and New York: Routledge.

Blum, L. (1980) *Friendship, Altruism, and Morality*, London: Routledge & Kegan Paul.

Boon, J. (1984) 'Folly, Bali, and anthropology, or satire across cultures', in E. Bruner (ed.) *Text, Play, and Story: The Construction and Reconstruction of Self and Society*, Prospect Heights, Ill.: Waveland Press.

Brady, I. (1991) 'Harmony and argument: bringing forth the artful science', in I. Brady (ed.) *Anthropological Poetics*, Savage, Md.: Rowman & Littlefield.

Bremmer, J. and Roodenburg, H. (eds) (1997) *A Cultural History of Humour*, Cambridge: Polity Press.

Bruner, E. (1984) 'Introduction: the opening up of anthropology', in E. Bruner (ed.) *Text, Play, and Story: The Construction and Reconstruction of Self and Society*, Prospect Heights, Ill.: Waveland Press.

Card, C. (1994) *Choices and Values*, New York: Columbia University Press.

—— (1995) *Character and Moral Luck*, Philadelphia: Temple University Press.

Clastres, P. (1977) *Society against the State: The Leader as Servant and the Humane Uses of Power among the Indians of the Americas*, Oxford: Basil Blackwell.

Compact Edition of the Oxford English Dictionary (1971) Glasgow and New York: Oxford University Press.

Corbey, R. and Leerssen, J. (eds) (1991) *Alterity, Identity, Image: Selves and Others in Society and Scholarship*, Amsterdam and Atlanta, Ga.: Rodopi.

de Certeau, M. (1988) *The Practice of Everyday Life*, Berkeley: University of California Press.

Descola, P. (1996) 'Constructing nature: symbolic ecology and social practice', in P. Descola and G. Pálsson (eds) *Nature and Society: Anthropological Perspectives*, London: Routledge.

Ellis, R. (1997) 'A taste for movement: an exploration of the social ethics of the Tsimanes of Lowland Bolivia', unpublished Ph.D dissertation, University of St Andrews.

Erasmus, D. (1941 [1511]) *The Praise of Folly*, trans. H.H. Hudson, Princeton, NJ: Princeton University Press.

Fabian, J. (1983) *Time and the Other: How Anthropology Makes its Object*, New York: Columbia University Press.

—— (1998) *Moments of Freedom: Anthropology and Popular Culture*, Charlottesville and London: University of Virginia Press.

Fardon, R. (1992) 'Postmodern anthropology? Or, an anthropology of post-modernity?', in J. Doherty, E. Graham and M. Malek (eds) *Postmodernism and the Social Sciences*, London: Macmillan.

Gadamer, H.-G. (1979) *Truth and Method*, London: Sheed & Ward.

Gilligan, C. (1982) *In a Different Voice: Psychological Theory and Women's Development*, Cambridge, Mass.: Harvard University Press.

Goldman, I. (1963) *The Cubeo*, Urbana: University of Illinois Press.

Gow, P. (1989) 'The perverse child: desire in a Native Amazonian subsistence economy', *Man* (n.s.) 24: 299–314.

—— (1991) *Of Mixed Blood: Kinship and History in Peruvian Amazonia*, Oxford: Clarendon.

Habermas, J. (1990) 'Discourse ethics: notes on a program of philosophical justifica-tion', in *Moral Consciousness and Communicative Action*, pp. 43ff, Cambridge, Mass.: MIT.

Heelas, P. (1986) 'Emotion talk across cultures', in R. Harré (ed.) *The Social Construc-tion of Emotions*, Oxford: Basil Blackwell.

Hobart, M. (1995) 'As I lay laughing: encountering global knowledge in Bali', in R. Fardon (ed.) *Counterworks: Managing the Diversity of Knowledge*, London: Routledge.

Hulme, P. (1986) *Colonial Encounters: Europe and the Native Caribbean 1492–1979*, London: Methuen.

Illich, I. (1990 [1973]) *Tools for Conviviality*, London: Marion Boyars.

Ingold, T. (1994) 'Introduction to social life', in T. Ingold (ed.) *Companion Encyclopedia of Anthropology*, London and New York: Routledge.

Jackson, M. (1989) *Paths toward a Clearing: Radical Empiricism and Ethnographic Inquiry*, Bloomington: Indiana University Press.

Jaggar, A. (1983) *Feminist Politics and Human Nature*, London: Rowman & Allenheld.

Kidd, S. (1999) 'Love and hate among the people without things: the social and economic relations among the Enxet of Paraguay', unpublished Ph.D dissertation, University of St Andrews.

Kohlberg, L. (1981) 'Justice as reversibility: the claim to moral adequacy of a highest stage of moral judgment', in *Essays on Moral Development*, San Francisco: Harper & Row.

—— (1982) 'A reply to Owen Flanagan and some comments on the Puka–Goodpaster exchange', *Ethics* 92: 316.

Lagrou, E, (1998) 'Cashinahua Cosmovision: a perspectival approach to identity and alterity, unpublished Ph.D dissertation, University of St Andrews.

Leavitt, J. (1996) 'Meaning and feeling in the anthropology of emotions', *American Ethnologist* 23(3): 514–39.

Lévi-Strauss, C. (1981) 'Finale', in C. Lévi-Strauss, *The Naked Man*, New York: Harper & Row.

Lévy-Bruhl, L. (1966 [1910]) *How Natives Think*, New York: Washington Square Press.

Lutz, C.A. (1988) *Unnatural Emotions: Everyday Sentiments on a Micronesian Atoll and their Challenge to Western Theory*, Chicago: University of Chicago Press.

Lutz, C.A. and Abu-Lughod, L. (eds) (1990) *Language and the Politics of Emotion*, Cambridge: Cambridge University Press.

Lutz, C.A. and White, G. (1986) 'The anthropology of emotion', *The Annual Review in Anthropology* 15: 406–36.

McCallum, C. (1989) 'Power, gender and social organisation among the Cashinahua of Brazil', unpublished Ph.D dissertation, University of London.

—— (1994) 'Ritual and the origin of sexuality in the Alto Xingu', in P. Harvey and P. Gow (eds) *Sex and Violence: Issues in Representation and Experience*, London: Routledge.

MacIntyre, A. (1980) *After Virtue*, Notre Dame, Ind.: Notre Dame University Press.

Mason, P. (1990) *Deconstructing America: Representations of the Other*, London: Routledge.

Mauss, M. (1979 [1935]) 'Body techniques', in *Sociology and Psychology*, pp. 95–123, London: Routledge & Kegan Paul.

Meløe, J. (1988) 'Some remarks on agent perception', in L. Hertzberg and J. Pietarinen (eds) *Perspectives on Human Conduct*, Leiden: E.T. Brill.

Myers, F. (1979) 'Emotions and the self: a theory of personhood and political order among Pintupi Aborigines', *Ethos* 7: 343–70.

Oldham, P. (1996) 'The impacts of development and indigenous responses among the Piaroa of the Venezuelan Amazon', unpublished Ph.D dissertation, University of London.

Overing, J. (1985a) 'There is no end of evil: the guilty innocents and their fallible god', in D. Parkin (ed) *The Anthropology of Evil*, Oxford: Basil Blackwell.

—— (1985b) 'Introduction', in J. Overing (ed.) *Reason and Morality*, London: Tavistock.

—— (1985c) 'Today I shall call him "Mummy"', in J. Overing (ed.) *Reason and Morality*, London: Tavistock.

—— (1986) 'Images of cannibalism, violence and domination in a "non-violent" society', in D. Riches (ed.) *The Anthropology of Violence*, London: Basil Blackwell.

—— (1987) 'Translation as a creative process: the power of the name', in L. Holy (ed.) *Comparative Anthropology*, pp. 70–87, Oxford: Basil Blackwell.

—— (1988) 'Styles of manhood: an Amazonian contrast in tranquillity and violence', in S. Howell and R. Willis (eds) *Societies at Peace*, pp. 79–99, London: Tavistock.

—— (1989) 'The aesthetics of production: the sense of community among the Cubeo and Piaroa', *Dialectical Anthropology* 14: 159–75.

—— (1990) 'The shaman as a maker of worlds: Nelson Goodman in the Amazon', *Man* (n.s.) 25: 601–19.

—— (1993a) 'The anarchy and collectivism of the "primitive other": Marx and Sahlins in the Amazon', in C. Hann (ed.) S*ocialism: Ideals, Ideologies, and Local Practice*, London: Routledge.

—— (1993b) 'Death and the loss of civilized predation among the Piaroa of the Orinoco Basin', *L'Homme* 126–8, 33(1): 191–211.

—— (1996) 'Aesthetics is a cross-cultural category: against the motion', in T. Ingold (ed.) *Key Debates in Anthropological Theory,* London: Routledge.

—— (1999) 'Elogio do Cotidiano: a Confiança e Arte da Vida Social em uma Comunidade Amazônica' (In praise of the everyday: trust and the art of social living in an Amazonian community), *Mana* 5(1): 81–108.

Overing Kaplan, J. (1975) *The Piaroa, a People of the Orinoco Basin*, Oxford: Clarendon.

—— (1977) 'Introduction', in J. Overing Kaplan, org., 'Social Time and Social Space in Lowland South American Societies', in *Actes du XIIIe Congrès International des Américanistes, 1976*, Paris: CNRS and Fondation Singer-Polignac.

—— (1981) 'Review article: "Amazonian anthropology"', in *Journal of Latin American Studies*, 13(1), May.

Pagden, A. (1982) *The Fall of Natural Man: The American Indian and the Origins of Comparative Ethnology*, Cambridge: Cambridge University Press.

Palencia-Roth, M. (1996) 'Enemies of God: monsters and the theology of conquest', in A.J. Arnold (ed.) *Monsters, Tricksters, and Sacred Cows: Animal Tales and American Identities*, Charlottesville: University of Virginia Press.

Passes, A. (1998) 'The hearer, the hunter, and the agouti head: aspects of intercommunication and conviviality among the Pa'ikwené (Palikur) of French Guiana', unpublished Ph.D dissertation, University of St Andrews.

Pauli, G. (2000) 'The creation of real food and real people: gender complementarity among the Menkü of Central Brazil', unpublished Ph.D dissertation, University of St Andrews.

Price, S. (1989) *Primitive Art in Civilized Places*, Chicago: University of Chicago Press.

Rapport, N. (1994) *The Prose and the Passion: Anthropology, Literature and the Writing of E.M. Forster*, Manchester: Manchester University Press.

—— (1997) *Transcendent Individual: Towards a Literary and Liberal Anthropology*, London: Routledge.

Rapport, N. and Overing, J. (2000a) 'Consciousness', in N. Rapport and J. Overing, *Key Concepts in Social Anthropology*, London: Routledge.

—— (2000b) 'Society', in N. Rapport and J. Overing, *Key Concepts in Social Anthropology*, London: Routledge.

Rawls, J. (1971) *A Theory of Justice*, 2nd edition, Cambridge, Mass.: Harvard University Press.

Rivière, P. (1969) *Marriage among the Trio*, Oxford: Clarendon.

—— (1984) *Individual and Society in Guiana: A Comparative Study of Amerindian Social Organization*, Cambridge: Cambridge University Press.

Rosaldo, M. (1984) 'Toward an anthropology of self and feeling', in R. Shweder and R. LeVine (eds) *Culture Theory: Essays on Mind, Self and Emotion*', Cambridge: Cambridge University Press.

Sahlins, M. (1972) *Stone Age Economics*, London: Tavistock.

Santos-Granero, F. (1991) *The Power of Love: The Moral Use of Knowledge amongst the Amuesha of Central Peru*, London: Athlone Press.

Schwartz, T., White, G. and Lutz, C.A. (1992) *New Directions in Psychological Anthropology*, Cambridge: Cambridge University Press.

Seeger, A., da Matta, R. and Viveiros de Castro, E. (eds) (1979) 'A construçao da pesoa nas sociedades indígenas Brasileira' (The construction of personhood among indigenous societies of Brazil) *Boletim do Museu Nacional* 32: 2–19.

Sherzer, J. (1990) 'On play, joking, humor, and tricking among the Kuna: the agouti story', in E. Basso (ed.) *Native South American Cultures through their Discourse*, pp. 85–114, Bloomington: Indiana University Folklore Institute.

Slote, M. (1983) *Goods and Virtues*, Oxford: Clarendon Press.

Stocker, M. (1976a) 'The schizophrenia of modern ethical theories', *Journal of Philosophy* 73: 453–66.

—— (1976b) 'Agent and other: against ethical universalism', *Australasian Journal of Philosophy* 54: 206–20.

Storrie, R. (1999) 'Being human: personhood, cosmology and subsistence for the Hoti of Venezuelan Guiana', unpublished Ph.D dissertation, University of Manchester.

Strathern, M. (1988) *The Gender of the Gift: Problems with Women and Problems with Society in Melanesia*, Berkeley: University of California Press.

Thomas, D. (1982) *Order without Government: The Society of the Pemon Indians of Venezuela*, Urbana: University of Illinois Press.

Todorov, T. (1987) *The Conquest of America*, trans. R. Howard, New York: Harper & Row.

Turner, V. and Bruner, E. (eds) (1986) *The Anthropology of Experience*, Urbana: University of Illinois Press.

Viveiros de Castro, E. (1992) *From the Enemy's Point of View: Humanity and Divinity in an Amazonian Society*, Chicago: University of Chicago Press.

—— (1996) 'Images of nature and society in Amazonian ethnology', *Annual Review of Anthropology* 25: 179–200.

Wagner, R. (1991) 'Poetics and the recentering of anthropology', in I. Brady (ed.) *Anthropological Poetics*, Savage, Md.: Rowman & Littlefield.

Williams, R. (1983) 'Society', in R. Williams, *Keywords*, London: Fontana.

Witherspoon, G. (1977) *Language and Art in the Navajo Universe*, Ann Arbor: University of Michigan Press.

Witherspoon, G. and Peterson, G. (1995) *Dynamic Symmetry and Holistic Asymmetry: In Navajo and Western Art and Cosmology*, New York: Peter Lang.

Wittgenstein, L. (1976) *Philosophical Investigations*, Oxford: Basil Blackwell.

Wolf, S. (1982) 'Moral saints', *Journal of Philosophy* 79: 419–39.

Conviviality as a creative process

The aesthetics of the passions and embodiments of community

Part I

Conviviality as a creative process

The aesthetics of the passions and embodiments of conviviality

Chapter 1

The first love of a young man

Salt and sexual education among the Uitoto Indians of Lowland Colombia

Juan Alvaro Echeverri

Men must eat many a peck of salt together before the claims of friendship
are fulfilled
(*Dialogus de Amicitia: Laelius*, XIX, 67, in Latham 1982: 57)

The Uitoto and other neighbouring groups from the Colombo-Peruvian
Amazon used not to consume mineral salt – sodium salt, NaCl. They have
learned to eat it since the middle of the twentieth century following their
incorporation into market relations through the rubber industry and, latterly,
Catholic Mission education and permanent contact with non-Indians.
Formerly, they extracted salts from plants, mainly palms, and they continue
doing so today. To obtain these vegetable salts, the plant matter (buds,
flowers, bark) is burned, water is filtered through the ashes to leach out the
minerals, and the resulting brine is boiled down until the salts are desiccated.
These vegetable salts are potassium salts very rich in microelements. Indians
use them mostly as an alkaline mixture for tobacco paste (*yera*),[1] as well as
for healing and some limited culinary consumption.

Vegetable salts have been extracted by many peoples throughout the
world, e.g. the Azande of Central Africa (Prinz 1993: 344–5) and the Anga-
speaking groups of Papua New Guinea, mainly the Baruya, for whom salt
serves as a kind of money (Godelier 1969; Lemmonier 1984). In the American
continent there have been numerous reports since the earliest times of
European occupation of the use of vegetable salts.[2] Most are just anecdotal,
but they seem to point to its widespread utilisation, which is not a mere substi-
tute for sodium or mineral salt (many of these groups having easy access to
natural sources), and which in most cases seems to be closely associated with
ritual purposes. The production and consumption of vegetable salts no
longer exist among many of the groups that formerly used them. In Northwest
Amazonia they are still to be found mainly among the Eastern Tukano-
speaking, Uitoto-speaking, Bora Miraña-speaking and Andoque-speaking
groups, who occupy a continuous area on the borders of the Colombian,
Peruvian and Brazilian Amazon, where they continue to be actively produced

and circulated, mostly for everyday and ritual consumption of tobacco, ritual exchange, initiation rites and healing.

Ethnographic reports of these groups refer but summarily to the production, consumption and circulation of vegetable salts, let alone to the meanings associated with them in indigenous thought.[3] Much attention has been paid to other ritual substances, such as tobacco, coca, hallucinogenic plants and medicinal plants, but *salt* seems to have gone unnoticed. For the Vaupés region, at least two anthropologists have, in passing, hinted at the potential meaning of the substance. Reichel-Dolmatoff writes that according to the Tukano, 'the main energy in the cosmos is generated by the sun and is called *bogá*, a fundamental vital force of an essentially spermatic character' (1996: 32). And he adds in a note: 'The root of *bogá* (*bo, bu, po, pu, mo, mu*) can be found in a number of words that refer, literally or metaphorically, to a conceptual field that has to do with procreation, insemination and impregnation' (ibid., p. 190). Among the words he lists as derived from that radical (manioc starch, phallus, to inseminate, cultivated field, etc.), he cites '*~moá/* salt, metaphorically sperm' (ibid.). The spermatic character of salt among the Vaupés Indians is confirmed by Christine Hugh-Jones in her reference to the process of the preparation of meat among the Eastern Tukano-speaking Barasana, in which she states that 'salt and pepper added during the boiling could be made comparable to semen and blood. Not only are their colours white and red appropriate for semen and blood, but also the Barasana terms for them relate them to the sexual roles in conception. Salt is *moa*, "activating substance" (*moa-*, to move, to work)' (1979: 195).

This seminal sense of salt, only intimated at by these authors, is shared by the Uitoto and other neighbouring groups. This has become clear to me after a number of years of research on the meaning of vegetable salts for the Uitoto, with the elder Enókakuiodo. Our inquiry arose from a common interest in understanding the interplay of desire in human relations, which can evolve into love, hate, miscommunication, or life. This has led to a compilation of oral narratives about salt, which are the subject matter of this chapter. I have done research and collaborative work with the Indian groups of the Caquetá-Putumayo region in the Colombian Amazon, in the context of their growing political awareness, the legal recognition of lands, and their re-creation of collective identities in the aftermath of their violent insertion into market relations which has taken place since the first decades of the twentieth century. I became involved in institutional work to support 'grassroots initiatives', concerning indigenous research on territory, alternative market products, indigenous education, indigenous political organisations and legal advice. After a number of years I, and others who worked with me, grew increasingly disappointed with the results of such well-intentioned attempts: delays, failures, mutual misunderstandings, problems with financial resources were constant and recurring. My concern with these issues of 'intercultural communication' was shared by Enókakuiodo, who, as a sort of privileged outsider (he was not involved in any project), used to employ sexual jokes to comment on the everyday trials and tribulations of relations between institutions and Indians (cf. Overing on the potency of bawdy humour, this volume). Enókakuiodo would refer to communities as 'women who are jealous', to a project as a process of seduction and to the barrenness of such polygamous marriages.

In particular I remember one very potent image which he constructed to express his understanding of the relationships between non-Indians and Indians, in that context and in general. He likened the situation to that of a woman showing her vagina to a man: non-Indians showed the Indians 'that woman's vagina', that is, money, alcohol, merchandise, technology, and, in a perfectly symbolic and literal sense, '*their* salt'. Formerly, when baptised, Indians were given a taste of (chloride) salt, which, for many elders today, was their first-ever experience of mineral salt.[4] 'As they gave it once, now they have to keep giving it to us', is something I have heard from several older Indians. This baptismal salt is a metonym of 'white people's stuff' and carries a sexual sense of sharing body fluids: semen, milk. It creates bonds and desire.[5] So, 'we had a glimpse of that woman's vagina, and we want more', Enókakuiodo asserts: 'we don't know where to stop'. That is why institutions, so to speak, feel so uncomfortable and disappointed in their dealings with Indians, as the latter lose their heads when handling money and alcohol, and normal relations get strained or broken.

But, conversely, Indians have also shown non-Indians their own 'vagina', that is, their ritual substances, their sorcery, their knowledge about the forest and nature, and their shamanic power and skills. Because we glimpsed that vagina without preparation, we then want more: we want to taste, we want to touch. We do not know how to deal with the Indians' 'salt'. Indians consequently feel that non-Indians do not relate to them on fair terms, and that they want to inquire into matters that are very private and esoteric, while seemingly failing to understand the most obvious.

For Enókakuiodo, the whole matter is thus a question of sexual education: of how to regulate desire, how to know the limits. This sexual education may help to turn barren relations into productive ones, allowing for mutual nurturing and feeding; it may open up what he calls 'a playground', where such exchanges are regulated and maintained. Thus, 'salt' became our research subject. We began a long work, carrying out a full empirical investigation of the vegetable salts utilised by the Uitoto, extracting, processing and analysing a total of sixty types from different vegetable species. In the process we recorded in the Uitoto language, then transcribed and translated many hours of Enókauiodo's explanation about the meaning of salt, addressed to one of his sons. He stressed the subject's importance by stating repeatedly that this work was actually a way of bequeathing a 'heritage' to his children and grandchildren. At the same time, according to him, our project was a sort of 'laboratory' in which to probe and test the regulation and management of such a sexually charged 'playground': space of meeting, space of attraction, space of exchange, feeding space, breathing space, space of creation – surrounded by dangers, illness, fatigue, distrust, anger; space of processing and transformation.

Enókakuiodo's initial aim was to reach a better understanding of the relations between persons and groups, modelled on those between husband and wife or, rather, between ritual allies, contending parties who keep growing in their ceremonial careers by exchanging work, songs, knowledge – and modelled also on the exchange of coca or of tobacco in the ritual place of coca, and on the rules for *mambe*-ing[6] coca (cf. Londoño-Sulkin, this volume), for men sitting together in dialogue, 'cool' and 'sweet'. His perspective then became an open-ended consideration of the processes of insemination, fecundation, conception, birth and development of life: the constitution of a 'ground': i.e. consciousness, society, the world – the ongoing agonistic process of battling, suffering, transforming, processing.

Thus, from these two contrasting portrayals of the circulation of 'salt' – salt as semen that impregnates a ground and salt as circulation of substances in a 'playground' – I have chosen a sort of intermediate image to start with: a young man in love, at the end of this process of formation and full of salt for exchange.

A young man's basket

Let us focus our attention on a young Uitoto man beginning to weave a basket. Crouching in front of a bunch of vines, he tries to figure out how to start, where to place the first knot, which fibre to insert next, so as to give form to the entangled ensemble. His body shifts this way and that, his face bends toward the floor, he keeps attempting to start. 'This is the first moving around', says the discourse on salt, 'this is the first looking around; this is, truly, the first tasting'. And it continues:

> For this reason a young man
>> does not
>> at once pick up *rafue*.
> Out of weariness, out of suffering
>> he understands *rafue*, he picks up *rafue*.
> But then, when he becomes dextrous, he shows it in work,
>> he teaches [it]
>> to another,
>> he shows it:
>> 'Here, this is my work,
>> I have baskets, I have firewood.'

This is the origin
   of the first love
   of a young man.
Formerly, the Father Buinaima
   settled
   this
   strength,
   this
   woman's desire.

This is woman, this is the wooing basket.
Who can turn his face away
   from that basket?
Who can say 'I can'? No one can say that.
   In that basket,
   many former generations lost their faces,
   many spirits lost their faces.
There is nowhere else to go,
   there is no other track,
   there is no other path.
The path we tread is the only one.
It is the path of our birth,
   it is the path through which we came forth.

Thus we are observing the moment of trying to start, to give form, to bring order to the tangled set of vines. What is referred to may in effect be a material basket, or an attempt to instil life in a woman's womb, or the work of the Creator to give form to the world. Similarly, one could also understand that what is being described are the efforts to make sense of a situation, to open up a path of knowledge – 'knowledge', a first attempt to translate the Uitoto word *rafue*.

In ordinary language, *rafue* means 'news, matter, affair'. In the above excerpt, it signifies knowledge, but it is a knowledge that has to be made to act upon the world and produce tangible results: baskets, firewood, the first love of a young man. *Rafue* refers neither to words nor things, but to the activity through which words are turned into things, the movement from the named to the tangible through time. The two roots that compose the term *rafue* (*raa*, 'a thing', and *ifue*, 'something spoken') synthesise this movement. Most crucially, for Enókakuiodo, his discourse on salt is also *rafue*. Rather than an explanation of a system of meanings, it is a process of instruction, whose result is the realisation of a vital reappropriation by the listener–apprentice. It is meant to bring about the latter's own interpretation based on lived experiences: 'Out of weariness, out of suffering/he understands *rafue*, he picks up *rafue*.'

Rather than on a system of thinking, my focus here is on the process of instruction that lays out a discourse that produces multiple images each of which may be interpreted in several ways. The discourse extends like a net that defies any attempt to structure a coherent narrative out of it. I feel like that young man set before many strands (images, concepts), trying to weave them into a basket. Another listener, one of Enókakuiodo's sons, say, may be able to construct it as a discourse on the process of formation of life inside a woman's womb, given his own worries concerning his wife's fertility. The key to the matter is the vital experience that the listener can bring into his/ her reflection upon the *rafue* of salt: human reproduction, good intercultural communication, understanding of a system and so forth.

That reflective capacity of *rafue* is obtained through a 'poetic' use of language: 'poetic' understood as linguistic artefacts that slide along paradigms of meaning. 'Basket', for instance, can be taken as referring to the womb, a person, knowledge, power, ceremonial career. These poetic artefacts transform into others – 'basket' is also a path, the birth path. The images flow and subside in the *rafue* of salt along the drama of creation, of battling, suffering, succeeding, never arriving at an ultimate conclusion. I try to represent this poetic imagery and flow through a transcription of the discourse in versified form, as shown in the excerpts quoted.

A full demonstration of this mode of narration requires a rendition of longer sections. Here, however, I will focus on two guiding principles or notions that allow a view of this process of transmission of knowledge through poetic artefacts: the notions of 'ground' and of *rafue* itself. My first approach to the two notions is the image of a young man weaving a basket, articulated by vital experience: sexual impulse – *jiruifue*, which I translate as 'love'. 'Ground' is the object of that sexual impulse, in this case named as a basket, which can be understood as woman, food plot, etc. The exercise of that impulse upon that ground is the path of *rafue*.

This ground–*rafue* system of construction of knowledge contains a statement about proper social behaviour, implicit in the control of that sexual impulse through what is the ultimate goal of *rafue*: to ensure good human life, expressed in knowledge, wisdom, human fertility, regeneration, love, speaking and food. This is most clearly depicted in the following excerpt of the *rafue* of salt in respect of the basket of humanity:

> This is the basket of *mambe*-ing coca,
>   this is the basket of knowledge,
>   this is the basket of endurance,
>   this basket
>   is the basket of advising,
>   basket of wisdom;
>   this basket
>   is the basket of holding the phallus,

basket of humanisation;
this basket
is the basket of love,
basket
of the Word;
this is the basket of our life.

The *rafue* on *rafue* and the 'ground': the path of life

The image of a young man beginning to weave a basket is but one transformation of the master story of the creation of the world. The Creation is indeed a myth, but in the *rafue* of salt it is never narrated as a separate story. Myths derive their power from always being susceptible to multiple interpretations, transformations, displacements, lack of closure. One would prefer to 'understand' the narration of a myth in some kind of chronological order – what comes first, what follows next, which character is different from which other character, who is the son, wife or brother-in-law of whom and so forth. Fixing the myth destroys its power. The *rafue* of salt is full of mythic references that are never fully revealed, never transparent. The myths are always half-concealed, their apparent narrative structure perpetually being modified. Once told, they are promptly devalued as 'just stories'. I will try to 'detain' for a moment the story of creation, inasmuch as it contributes to our argument, before it is shortly consigned again to oblivion.

It is said that, in the beginning, Father Buinaima, the Creator, is everything in himself. He has no 'ground'. His first creative accomplishment is to burn himself; with his ashes he fertilises 'the ground'. He mixes, he combines, he impregnates, he fertilises so as to give form to this 'ground'. He then 'processes' it – and out of such processing, the path of humanity is configured. The following excerpt narrates what I just described:

Now then, formerly,
  Father Buinaima
  burns himself in that place,
    like rock-of-salt, like plant-of-salt,
  to impregnate this ground-whole,
  for the new generation of life
  not to be in confusion.
Because [the pollution of the ground] stands in the way,
  Father Buinaima processes it,
  he processes
  this ground-whole,
  this earth,
  the whole earth-of-birth.

> It is said that at that moment,
> – now, then, there –
> the Word comes forth.

Each verse of this excerpt has one of several words which I variously translate as: 'in that place', 'this ground-whole', 'earth', 'the whole earth-of-birth' and 'there', all of them ending with the morpheme *-ni: bigini, nagini, biini, nani, binikoni*. These are not common words but specialised ones employed only in ritual discourse. I initially thought this set of nouns referred to 'the earth', but my Indian friends promptly stated this was inaccurate, because what was meant by the terms was not yet the earth and not necessarily the earth. They may refer to the earth, to a human body, or to *rafue*. Enókakuiodo himself advised that the closest translation would be 'sex'. I opted for 'ground', the translation–interpretation used here. This first act of creation may then be understood as the constitution of space and corporeality. But this 'ground' is not an object apart from the Father. The great feat of the Creator is to be able to create his own corporeality. He accomplishes this by burning himself.

From now on, as we will see below, the activity of Father Buinaima will be a constant burning. It is tempting to view the 'ground' as the female counterpart of the Father, a sort of Mother Earth. However, it is precisely this burning, this fire, which will be conceived of as the Mother.

By burning himself, the Father impregnates (*iinote*) the 'ground' and makes it stable; he fertilises it. The same word *iinote* is used to describe the action of mixing tobacco paste with vegetable salt, or the mixing of clay with vegetable substances to make it stable. Through impregnation, the ground becomes firm, stable. The *rafue* of salt employs other verbs referring to culinary operations to represent that ground-stabilising activity of the Creator: to mix meat with cassava (the proper way to eat), to season food with peppers. After this the Father has to process the 'ground'.

'To process' (*finode*) literally means 'to make, to build, to prepare', but here it has the particular meaning of 'making good (edible, usable, harmless)': 'Because [the pollution of the ground] stands in the way' he has to process it. This preparation starts the great process of separation, which inaugurates the cycle of events of mythic times, in which the Creator separates the good from the evils of the world and transforms the latter into animals, rocks, lakes – the entire natural world, antagonistic to the world of true humanity. In this manner he obtains the perfect substance of humanity. This process is comparable to the separation of the starch from the pulp of the manioc. The starch is going to be humanity, the pulp the rest of nature. What is obtained from this process is a name, a power for humanity, symbolised in several ways, as salt rock, enlightenment, power, emblem. The processing leads to a hardening of the ground, and to the quintessential human capability and goal: the reproduction of human life.

It is said that at that moment 'the Word comes forth'. What I translate as 'Word' is the term *rafue* (cf. Passes on the value and power of the word, this volume). This is the very beginning. The creative process differentiates the world and, at the same time, creates speech – advice, counsel for humanity. It is both a food and the knowledge for humans to act in the world. It is 'the path of the Creator', what the human race, 'the future generation to come', has to enact in order to have a good life.

The *rafue* of salt goes on for hours narrating the ceaseless suffering of Father Buinaima and his opening of the path through burning and 'processing': the Father falls ill, endures suffering, discovers, burns, processes. When *rafue* is born, Father Buinaima is a single being; everything is in him, both evil and good. He is full. Then he falls ill, ill with the most fundamental of illnesses: he is full of salt, he is full of semen; he loses his breath, he is exhausted, he is in agony. He tries to find the source of his condition. After struggling with illness, he pulls out the mucus from his nose and throws it away. He then observes what he has thrown out and is relieved. That mucus, that salty thing that was making the Father ill, is now a world. He burns it, tastes its salt, and says: 'So, this is what was making me ill, but now, it is nothing, now it is food; thus will it be for future generations'.

After this, Father Buinaima again and again falls ill with all kinds of illnesses and problems: he feels paralysed, then he is pricked by thorns; thereafter he suffers all sorts of mental diseases or delusions: he believes he is already grown up, he is attracted to women who want to devour him, he feels very hot, he is lazy, he wishes to rush things and so on. The process continues in a similar fashion as before: he endures a problem, discovers its cause, throws away its manifestation, burns it, and then tastes a purified product which he leaves as a power and a counsel for the coming human generations. He cleans up the path of humanity, he tightens up the basket of humanity, he fills up this basket with words and food. Each illness he throws out becomes a tree, an animal, or some other natural element which bears in its name the memory of the Father's particular suffering, each representing a type of vegetable salt.

This process of creation is replicated by the actual technical process of making vegetable salt: burning down the vegetable matter, filtering the ashes to separate the minerals and boiling down the brine to dry the salts. These salts contain only the mineral elements of the living plant. Each salt has its own name and is like a trace and a memory of the events of the creation. But this is 'just material . . . a mere tree . . . a substance', Enókakuiodo would constantly repeat to me. This salt process replicates what goes on within the self; it resembles alchemy, in that what is intended with the process of transformation of matter is the transformation of the operator him- or herself.

The creation process does not end there. The travails of Father Buinaima and his defeat of so many illnesses is just the first cycle, the products of which were buried under this earth. It happened in 'another planet', as

Enókakuiodo likes to say. We have not yet arrived at this world, this layer of earth, this generation. All the beings which the Father threw out later rebel against him; it becomes the task of the Son of the Father, called Añiraɨma, to burn all those evils yet again and arrange this world in proper order. In that ancient world all those powers were rampant; they were put to sleep so that nowadays a fertile soil is established for the new generation of humanity to live.

Enókakuiodo constantly reiterates concerning this: 'Don't be misled; perhaps you believe we are talking about things that happened long ago or far away. Actually, we are talking about our own bodies.' Inasmuch as the vegetable salts obtained are 'just material, just a substance', the story of Creation is 'just a story'. The vital experience of the listener is the 'ground' where he/she constitutes a *rafue* through the process of enduring, burning, processing and condensing the salt – experience, voice, memory, food.

The sexual education of the Mother

It is this transmuting power of fire which accomplishes the great feats of creation, clears the path of humanity and consolidates the 'ground'. The Father is not so much the agent of creation as the patient of the actions of fire, which the discourse on salt most beautifully names as the Mother:

> This fire is the true Mother,
>   this heart,
>   this flame,
>   fire of abundance,
>   fire of humanisation.
> By this fire I sleep,
>   this fire feeds me.
> Whatever comes to this fire
>   never returns.
> This fire is processing fire.
>
> It is not I,
>   it is not I who knows,
>   it is the Mother who processes,
>   it is the Mother who devours,
>   it is the Mother who knows how to devour.
>   I do not know,
>   I suck from her breast,
>   I only know how to suck from her breast.
> On the Mother's lap, on this ground,
>   I lie down.

A transforming, purifying power, Mother-Fire turns everything into ashes, then into pure mineral salt. That is the food a human creature was fed in that other planet, the mother's womb. Then, on this earth, one has to transform plants and animals through 'processing' (fire) to keep oneself fed. That 'salt' – the purified substance resulting from processing with fire (tobacco, coca, food . . .) – will keep accumulating in the human body and will constitute the source of its capacity for action.

The image of human capacities and abilities that surfaces throughout the discourse on salt is that of a person who is alert. It is described through several verbs which mean 'to be trained and dextrous' (*fibide*), 'to be aware, to be in tune' (*fidide*), 'to hit, to find, to discover' (*baite*), 'to be agile, quick' (*iyúirede*), 'to listen' (*kakade*), 'to know' (*onode*), 'to see' (*kiode*) and, finally, 'to be full of words, to speak' (*uáirede*). These abilities derive from the successful 'hardening' of salt in the body, until it forms a kind of a rock, a power, which is called *riado*, 'power rock', or *fiókie*, 'charisma'. It is said that in former times powerful sorcerers who had sufficiently 'hardened' their rocks could actually pull them out from their foreheads and display them to other sorcerers. These were, it is said, little shiny rocks; some were green, others yellow, yet others red.

But those were sorcerers; the power rock of a 'true' man is his offspring, his food plot, his accomplishments. When you work, you sweat; your sweat (salt) impregnates the soil; as Enókakuiodo explains, it is like taking a woman, or slashing a patch of forest to open a food plot. Once you take that woman or make that wound in the forest, you have to persevere; that is the path of the Creator, that is the birth path. You will keep impregnating that ground so as to make it produce tangible results: offspring, food. Such activity is *rafue*. On that path of *rafue* many problems will arise: anger, laziness, impatience, pain, disorientation, confusion and so forth, just as happened to Father Buinaima in the story of Creation. Father Buinaima already opened that path, he already processed it and advised humanity of what he had suffered. The Mother, Fire, is constantly burning these states and turning them into salt; this is the substance of her breast. That is why the discourse on salt says: 'I do not know, I suck from her breast, I only know how to suck from her breast'. Conversely, if you do not follow the path of the Creator, you will be devoured by the Mother.

Sorcerers displaying their power rocks is a negative example for Enókakuiodo. It may appear as a great accomplishment for an individual. But for a 'true' man, his accomplishment is to overcome this illusion of individuality, by displacement and enlargement. I shall explain: for a young man his 'ground' is his body, he has to displace his 'salt' (sweat, semen) into the soil, through work, or into a woman, through marriage. His power rock is now a woman's power, a woman's desire, which enlarges the path of *rafue*. An individual does not accomplish the path of *rafue*; his power is now a woman's, it is generation, it is reproduction. It is said that in dance rituals women danced with a parrot perched on their shoulders (actually, 'parrot' is the meaning of the name Enókakuiodo). These parrots represented their power, their emblem, their power rock, their children.

The first love of a young man is a most dangerous moment, the constitution of an individuality that soon has to be discarded, displaced, enlarged. Like the myths of Creation, the power of a man is a momentary illusion which cannot be sustained. The ground is constantly displaced and constantly being consumed by fire. What is constructed soon returns to ashes to keep nourishing that moving ground.

That is why, perhaps, the discourse on salt is also constantly mocking its own coherence, its own closure. Always displaced, constantly appearing and perishing, what remains is a mineral, salt, milk from the breast of the Mother. I recover here a little taste of the saline residue.

Acknowledgements

Research for this article was funded by the COAMA Program for the Consolidation of the Colombian Amazon of Fundación Gaia (Colombia), the Instituto Colombiano de Cultura COLCUTURA of the Colombian Government and the Earth Love Fund (UK). The ideas in this chapter are the result of an ongoing process of work and research with the elder Enókakuiodo (Oscar Román) and his son Simón Román. I am indebted to Carlos Londoño-Sulkin and Alan Passes for their generous editorial support in the preparation of the final manuscript, and to Joanna Overing for her encouragement and ideas.

Notes

1 The use of tobacco paste for licking is very restricted in Native South America. It is found only in the region of Lake Maracaibo (by the now extinct Timote-Cuica), in the Caquetá-Putumayo region (by the Uitoto and neighbouring tribes: Nonuya, Ocaina, Muinane, Miraña, Bora and Andoque), in the region of the Sierra Nevada de Santa Marta, Colombia (by the Kogi, Ijka and Sanka) and in some isolated regions of the Peruvian Montaña (by the Piro and Campa [?]) (Wilbert 1987: 40–2).

2 See Patiño (1992: 34–7), who cites reports of the use of vegetable salt by ten Amerindian groups from the fifteenth century through the eighteenth; also Farriss (1984: 24, for the Maya of Yucatan); Humboldt (1981: 261–2, for the Casiquiare-Orinoco); Domínguez et al. (1996: 138, for the Carib-speaking Carijona).

3 Reports about the production and use of vegetable salts are found in Schultes and Raffauf 1990; Garzón and Makuritofe 1992; Galeano 1991; La Rotta n.d.; López 1989. All these are works by botanists or ethnobotanists, and mainly concerned with reporting the species employed for the elaboration of salts.

4 Vatican Council II modified the Catholic baptism rite by eliminating, among other things, the administration of salt to the baptised.

5 It is interesting that for the Semites 'salt' possessed a very similar sense: 'Those who eat the same food are considered to have the same blood. The meal taken in

common, symbolised by salt, either confirms the blood relationship or established it' (Latham 1982: 53).
6 '*Mambe*-ing' coca means to ingest coca by putting *mambe* (the powder obtained by toasting, pounding and straining coca leaves together with the ashes of leaves from the *Cecropia* tree) inside the cheeks, where it is slowly absorbed through the mouth and digestive tissues. As this action does not correspond to 'eating coca' or 'chewing coca', I introduce this new verb, borrowed from Spanish.

References

Domínguez, C.A., Gómez, A.J. and Barona, G. (eds) (1996) *Geografía física y política de la Confederación Granadina. Estado del Cauca, Territorio del Caquetá. Obra dirigida por el General Agustín Codazzi*, Bogotá: Coama–Unión Europea, Fondo Fen-Colombia, Instituto Geográfico Agustín Codazzi.

Farriss, N.M. (1984) *Maya Society under Colonial Rule: The Collective Enterprise of Survival*, Princeton, NJ: Princeton University Press.

Galeano, G. (1991) *Las palmas de la región de Araracuara*, Estudios en la Amazonía colombiana, vol. 1, Bogotá: Tropenbos-Colombia.

Garzón, C. and Makuritofe, V. (1992) *La noche, las plantas y sus dueños: Aproximación al conocimiento botánico en una cultura amazónica*. Bogotá: Corporación de Araracuara.

Godelier, M. (1969) 'La "monnaie de sel" des Baruya de Nouvelle Guinée', *L'Homme* 9(2): 5–35.

Hugh-Jones, C. (1979) *From the Milk River: Spatial and Temporal Processes in Northwest Amazonia*, Cambridge: Cambridge University Press.

Humboldt, A. de (1981) *Del Orinoco al Amazonas*, Barcelona: Labor.

La Rotta, C. (n.d.) *Especies utilizadas por la comunidad miraña: Estudio etnobotánico*, Bogotá: World Wildlife Fund, Fen-Colombia.

Latham, J.E. (1982) *The Religious Symbolism of Salt*, Théologie Historique, vol. 64, Paris: Éditions Beauchesne.

Lemmonier, P. (1984) 'La production de sel végétal chez les Anga (Papouasie-Nouvelle-Guinée)', *Journal d'Agriculture Tropicale et de Botanique Apliquée* 31(1–2): 71–126.

López, M.C. (1989) 'La palabra y la planta: Una aproximación a la botánica uitoto', Tesis de grado, Departamento de Antropología, Universidad Nacional (Colombia).

Patiño, V.M. (1992) *Historia de la cultura material en la América equinoccial*, Vol. 5: Tecnología, Santafé de Bogotá: Instituto Caro y Cuervo.

Prinz, A. (1993) 'Ash salt, cassava and goitre: change in the diet and the development of endemic goitre among the Anzande in Central Africa', in C.M. Hladik, A. Hladik, O.F. Linares, H. Pagezy, A. Semple and M. Hadley (eds) *Tropical Forests, People and Food: Biocultural Interactions and Applications to Development*, pp. 339–48, Paris: Unesco-Paris and The Parthenon Publishing Group.

Reichel-Dolmatoff, G. (1996) *The Forest Within: The World-View of the Tukano Amazonian Indians*, London: Themis Books.

Schultes, R.E. and Raffauf, R.F. (1990) *The Healing Forest: Medicinal and Toxic Plants of the Northwest Amazonia*, Historical, Ethno- and Economic Botany Series, vol. 2, Portland, OR.: Dioscorides Press.

Wilbert, J. (1987) *Tobacco and Shamanism in South America: Psychoactive Plants of the World*, New Haven, Conn. and London: Yale University Press.

Chapter 2

Helpless – the affective preconditions of Piro social life

Peter Gow

This chapter explores the dynamics of a particular experiential state, which I here term 'helplessness', among the Piro people of Peruvian Amazonia, to shed light on the specific Piro conception of the human condition, and of the place of humanity in the cosmos. It draws on and extends a larger body of work concerned to develop a phenomenological account of the lived world of these people (Gow 1989, 1990, 1991, 1993, 1994, 1995a, 1995b, 1997, in press). My analysis in this chapter directly addresses the issues raised by Overing in her work on the aesthetics of community (Overing 1989, 1999), and by Taylor's critique (Taylor 1996) of the very distinctive analytical style that Overing has created: now that we are able to talk of love and of hate in the context of ethnographies of indigenous Amazonian peoples, what other emotional states can we talk about?

Here I want to discuss an aspect of indigenous Amazonian lived worlds which has received surprisingly little attention to date: experiences of grief, suffering, compassion and consolation. Our naive everyday phenomenology would be shocked to discover that indigenous Amazonian people had no experience of these phenomena, and the fieldwork experiences of those who have worked in the region doubtless present much material on which to elaborate accounts of them, but there is very little literature on these states.[1] So, here I want to look at experiences of grief, suffering, compassion and consolation in the Piro lived world, and at the purchase a consideration of these experiences gives in ethnographic description and analysis.

The Piro people are an indigenous Amazonian people with existing communities in four areas of Western Amazonia: on the Bajo Urubamba, Cushabatay and Manú rivers in Peru and on the Iaco river in Brazil.[2] I know best the people living along the Bajo Urubamba river, which has the largest Piro population, and my account here refers exclusively to them. They live in villages ranging in size from about fifty to three hundred people, and to over a thousand people in the special case of the mission of El Rosario de Sepahua, and depend for their living on shifting agriculture, fishing, hunting and commercial work in lumbering and other activities. They speak a Maipuran (Arawakan) language. All Piro people are involved in dense relations with non-Piro people such as, on the Bajo Urubamba river, the Campa-Asháninca, Matsiguenga and *mestizos*. A far fuller account may be found in the book, *Of Mixed Blood* (Gow 1991).

To be helpless and to be seen to be helpless

The Piro terms I address here are *wamonuwata*, 'to do/to be *wamonu-*' and *getwamonuta*, 'to see *wamonu-*'. The term *wamonuwata*, can be translated as 'to grieve, to be sad, to suffer, to be cute, to be cuddly'. This experiential state elicits, in others, *getwamonuta*, 'to see the grief, sadness, suffering, cuteness, cuddliness of another'. The diverse range of states designated by *wamonuwata* have, at least to this English-speaker, little in common. I argue here that what these people, cute babies and grieving adults and older children, have in common, for Piro people, is their aloneness, their singularity as humans, and that the best translation of the term *wamonuwata* is 'to be helpless', in the idiomatic sense that this term shares with the Spanish *desamparado*. Similarly, I translate *getwamonuta* as 'to compassionate', in the idiomatic sense that this term shares with *compasionar*. I hasten to add that these are my translations: Piro people, when speaking the local Ucayali dialect of Spanish, habitually use *estar triste*, 'to be sad', for *wamonuwata*, and *dar pena*, 'to feel sorry for', for *getwamonuta*.

Clearly, these English and Spanish translations of mine carry a theological loading likely to be absent or different in the Piro case. Indeed I argue that the interplay between the states of 'being helpless' and 'compassionating' are the affective preconditions of Piro humanity and its intrinsic sociability, and not, as in Judaeo-Christian cosmology, preconditions of humanity in the regard of an extra-human divinity.

Little babies *wamonuwata*, 'are helpless', and elicit in others *getwamonuta*, 'compassion'. Why? Because they are alone. They are humans who lack kinspeople. When a Piro baby is born, the first question asked about it is, 'Is it human (*yineru*)?'. This question addresses the bodily form of the baby: is it a human, or a fish, or a tortoise or 'an animal nobody had ever seen'. The bodily form of the baby is an intrinsic identity form, which is uninfluenced by parental behaviour. Only those babies born with human form have potential to be 'kinspeople': others are expelled out of social space into the realm of otherness, the river or forest. A human baby is divided from its placenta, and only the placenta is expelled from social space. Such a baby has the potential to be a 'kinsperson', but it is not a kinsperson to anyone yet. To become a 'kinsperson', it must be fed 'real food', and respond with kin terms (cf. Belaunde, Kidd, Lagrou, Londoño-Sulkin, Overing, this volume).

Mourning adults *wamonuwata*, 'are helpless', and elicit in others *getwamonuta*, 'compassion'. Why? Because they are alone. They are humans who lack kinspeople. Here the missing kinsperson is a specific known dead person. A once-living kinsperson has died, and left the surviving kinsperson as one who is 'alone'. Piro people do not mourn collectively, or in small defined groups of mourners. They mourn alone, because each person has lost part of themselves. This is because kin relationships are, as has been pointed out on numerous occasions by Rivière, Overing and Viveiros de Castro among others, radically 'ego-centric' in Amazonian systems such as the Piro one: each link in the chain that establishes a person as a kinsperson is focused on the 'ego', rather than on broad classes or groups. Just as Piro people do not identify themselves with other kinspeople in defining their own specific kin relations, they do not identify themselves with other kinspeople when those kin relations are unmade in the ontogenetic processes of death (cf. Alès, Belaunde, Jamieson, Lagrou, this volume).

On hearing one of my earlier accounts of Piro experiences of mourning, a Melanesianist ethnographer of psychoanalytic bent described them as 'extreme narcissists', and questioned the veracity and plausibility of my account. While I strenuously defended my material and analysis, the Melanesianist was making an important point. For Melanesianists, and presumably for Melanesian people themselves, social life is predicated on the anti-narcissus of exchange, and ethnography after ethnography demonstrates how, in that region, it is exchange that overcomes the self-regard of other people (cf. Wagner 1967; Munn 1986; Strathern 1988). There, gift exchange transforms egocentric emotions into sociocentric actions. Among Piro people, and more widely in Amazonia, where elaborated gift-form exchanges are absent, the person stands revealed fully as a person, and hence does indeed resemble one of the manifold psychic disorders treated by psychoanalysts.

The Melanesianist was right: it is indeed true that the grief of mourning plunges Piro people into a condition we might recognise as 'melancholy', at least in terms of the devastating honesty with which they habitually talk of it. But if we think about the notion of narcissism, and the myth of Narcissus, we gain a new insight into the Piro lived world. Unlike Narcissus, who fell in love with his own reflection, Piro people are in love with their multiple other selves. That is, Piro people are not 'extreme narcissists' because it is not their solitary reflections they love, but their multiplicity. Let me explain why.

I borrow the term 'multiple other selves' from Joanna Overing's elucidation of the Piaroa lived world.[3] It provides an excellent fit with two aspects of the Piro lived world. First, there is the predication of 'humanity' and 'kinspeople' as intrinsically multiple. Second, there is the predication of one's own selfhood, one's own definition of one's humanity, as lying with other people, in 'the eye of the beholder': this is the Piro formulation of self in *nshinikanchi*, 'mind, love, memory, thought'. I take each in turn.

For Piro people, 'humanity' is intrinsically multiple. In Piro, the words *yine*, 'humans, people, Piro people', and *yineru/yinero*, 'male/female human', have an unusual characteristic. *Yine* is technically a plural of the noun root *yi-* + *-ne*, 'pluraliser', but this noun root cannot take a singular form, for no word **yi* exists in Piro.[4] Thus the singular forms of humans (by gender, *yineru* and *yinero*) are the singularisations of what is intrinsically plural. This formulation is very unusual in Piro, and is only shared with the names of the *neru*, 'endogamous groups', the units Piro people say their ancestors were divided into, and which exist today as surnames (cf. Gow 1991). All other 'ethnic' labels in Piro, such as *kajitu*, 'white man', *gashanigka*, 'Campa person', *chayiko*, 'Conibo person', etc., exist as singular forms that must be pluralised to attain multiplicity.[5] The same is true of all other entities. Therefore, 'humanity' is multiple, and uniquely so.

Further, unlike the modern Western core idioms of kinship, which stress profound and originary ties between formally separate entities (such that, for example, two individuals can be consanguines), the Piro core idiom of kinship stresses the multiplication of identical entities. The Piro term *nomolene*, 'my kinspeople', has the root *mole-*, which means 'to be related to as a kinsperson', 'to heap up a bunch of like things' and 'ten'. It therefore refers to the grouping together of elements which are separately alike into a multiplicity of identical elements: 'kinspeople', 'things', 'numbers' (i.e. the digits of two hands). A kinsperson, *nomole*, 'my kinsperson', does not therefore refer to a special relationship between ego and alter, but to ego and alter's common membership in a set with multiple members. Within this set, any given person is related in specific mode to any given other (as 'son', 'father', 'brother' and so on), just as each element of a 'heap of like things' or the constituent integers of 'ten' stand in specific relations to each other. I stress that the metaphors I am using here are drawn from mathematics, not anthropological kinship theory.[6]

Nomolene and *yine* are two manners by which Piro people designate, in normal circumstances, the collectivity I here term 'Piro people'. In most circumstances, the two terms are interchangeable and coterminous: 'my kinspeople' are 'humans' and vice versa. There are, however, key moments when they become separated, such as in birth ritual, the making of affinity, in shamanry, etc. For example, in birth ritual, the umbilical cord must be cut by someone who is not a kinsperson to the parents. But since all Piro people are kinspeople to each other, the father must often redefine a 'distant kinsperson' as not *nomole*, 'my relative': the cord-cutter becomes thus a 'human' who is not a 'kinsperson'.[7] Similarly, when people say of a normally nonhuman entity, such as a kind of deer or palm tree, that '*Yinerni*', 'It is human', there is no implication of kinship here, for this statement signals the speaker's entry into a specifically shamanic discourse where, as I discuss further below, different rules apply.

Getwanonuta, 'to compassionate', is grounded in this sense of the intrinsic multiplicity of 'humans' and 'kinspeople' when these coincide. When Piro people see the 'helplessness/aloneness' of another, their own sense of their humanity as intrinsically multiple leads them to intensify their regard for that other person (cf. Alès, Jamieson, Kidd, Lagrou, Londoño-Sulkin, Rivière, this volume). The person who is 'helpless' is one of other Piro people's multiple selves and so must elicit their compassion. They solicit the regard of the one who *wamonuwata*, 'is helpless', and so insist on their own mutual co-presence.

From the start, from the moment that the people assembled at the birth have decided that it is human, the neonate is the object of other people's compassion. Usually, this compassion is expressed by the baby's parents, but it is not uncommon for another adult to do so. One woman told me, of her ninth child,

> When she was born, she was so small! Just tiny! I looked at her and said, 'This one will not be able to live.' My father said, 'Oh, my daughter, how can this one survive? She's far too small!' But my oldest daughter said, 'I feel sorry for her, she is beautiful. Let's see if we can make her live.' So my daughter breastfed her, I had no milk then. My daughter fed her until my milk came. It is because of her older sister that my little daughter is alive now.

In another case, a married couple insisted that a newborn baby be given to them, on the basis that they had only one child, the mother had already had fourteen, and she had no husband. Their argument received general support in the village, but the mother refused, saying, 'No, I want to keep him. He is a beautiful little boy, I feel sorry for him.' Little Samuel stayed with his mother, and village opinion shifted to an amused tolerance of his mother's eccentricity.

Older babies are subjected to a ceaseless stream of attention, as they are called to across the village, joked with, and picked up and played with. A visiting baby, sitting on its mother's hip, will often be greeted before its mother, and when in the care of perhaps bored older siblings, will be easily relinquished into the solicitous arms of others. At the very least, a baby will be turned towards anyone soliciting its attention, and any fear on its part will call forth a warm but mildly disapproving cry of 'Waaaaa!', followed by laughter. This attitude towards babies is the elicitation of the baby's 'mind', in the sense of its regard for others. The stereotypic response to a friendly reaction from the baby is '*Ralukno!*' or '*Talukno!*', 'He/she loves me!'

Getwamonuta, 'to compassionate', leads the person to *giglenshinikanuta* the one who *wamonuwata*, 'is helpless'. *Giglenshinikanuta* means 'to mind well, to remember well, to love well, to console': it is a combination of *gigle-*, 'beautiful, good', and *nshinikanu-*, 'memory, love, thought, thinking about'. Therefore, the 'helplessness' of a singularised human leads the other 'to see suffering, to compassionate' and then 'to mind/think/love well, to console' the other. This consolation is not a special act, as it might be in Western cultures, but an intensification of the general sociability that characterises

Piro village life. Insofar as relations between villagers are by definition kin relations, and insofar as all kin relations originate in an adult's compassion for and consolation of a helpless baby, Piro village life is a sustained and generalised form of compassion and consolation. Its everyday form is the mutual recognition of fellow villagers' hunger and the consequent distribution of game. Here, hunger is the everyday equivalent of the more extreme state of 'helplessness': it is that little bit of suffering that all Piro people may experience any day (cf. Gow 1989, 1991).

The term *nshinikanchi* can be translated as 'memory, love, thought, thinking'. But it cannot be simply so translated, for it is not construed as a bodily interior state after the manner of these English words. *Nshinikanchi* is immediately perceptible in another person, such that Piro people do not need to speculate whether an alter 'remembers, loves, thinks about' them. This is because, as noted above, the supreme manifestation of *nshinikanchi* is co-residence. That is, two people manifest their *nshinikanchi* to each other by living together in the same village, and by sharing game with each other. Likewise, two people manifest their lack of *nshinikanchi* to each other by living apart in different villages, and by never sharing game with each other. Piro people who live apart are still kinspeople to each other, but they are very bad kinspeople to each other, as Piro people are always quick to point out (cf. Gow 1991 for how such relations are negotiated).

As might be imagined, this faculty of *nshinikanchi* is entirely relational, and indeed ego-centred. Those with whom one lives and to whom one is closely related have more *nshinikanchi* than others. This has the interesting effect that Piro people experience themselves as their own paragons of virtue in this regard. Indeed, Piro people consider themselves, as a whole, to be *kshinikanpotu*, 'with lots of *nshinikanchi*', and they array all other beings below them. Thus, they consider the neighbouring Campa people to have less *nshinikanchi*, while white people and animals are *mshinikatu*, 'thoughtless, forgetful, without *nshinikanchi*' (although pets, missionaries and anthropologists can, with time and careful handling, develop a certain degree of *nshinikanchi*).

However, although *nshinikanchi* is radically ego-centred, it is also radically alter-centred too. This is because it is only really possible to be *kshinikanu* with other people who are also *kshinikanu*. As I have discussed at length elsewhere, *nshinikanchi* develops in a child through the care it receives from others, and is manifest in its spontaneous use of kin terms to address those others. Similarly, *nshinikanchi* is maintained and manifest in the willingness to co-reside with other kinspeople, such that it is necessarily a feature of human multiplicity.

Because kinship ties, in the sense I use this term here, are modes of intersubjectivity, the *nshinikanchi* is fully intersubjective. Indeed, the *nshinikanchi* can be thought of as the intersubjective 'organ' of kinship. The *nshinikanchi* is both the organ of sociality/kinship and the surface of a person, or rather, that surface as it is constituted in the mutual visual experience of related persons.

I must stress that *nshinikanchi* is the bodily exterior of the person, but not the skin, *mtachri*. It is, rather, the availability of the other person to ego's everyday perceptual experience. A salient contrast here is with the bodily interior, which is the locus of the key transformational processes that generate *nshinikanchi*. The bodily interior is not available to casual inspection by others, and it can only enter the realm of the intersubjective when it is reported on by ego, when it is viewed in hallucinatory state by shamans, or when it is finally revealed long after death as the *gipnachri*, 'bone demon' (cf. below). *Nshinikanchi*, by contrast, is what you see, because in everyday village life, what you see is what you get.[8] As my *comadre* Sara perceptively put it, referring to two foreign women, 'Fulana is a nice woman, every time you see her she is smiling. Mengaña is maybe not so nice. She only smiles when she sees you looking at her. Perhaps she is angry.' For good reason, and precisely to avoid such judgements, Piro people strive for and admire a placid easy-goingness in daily life.

There is another possible translation of *nshinikanchi*, 'respect'. Piro people are, and seek to be, 'respectful' of each other (cf. Kidd, Rivière, this volume). This is a generalised social value, but it is manifested in its particularities. That is, the nature of 'respect' depends entirely on the nature of the relationship between the two people involved, whether they stand to each other as father and son, brother and sister, mother-in-law and son-in-law, and so on. When Piro people say they are *kshinikanpotu*, 'very respectful', they refer to their careful mutual attention to the multiplicity of their kin relations. When they say that white people are *mshinikatu*, 'disrespectful', they refer to the shockingly disrespectful manner in which white people treat each other and everyone else. As they say, 'Go to the white man's house and see if he will feed you! That's where you will learn how to suffer!' White people either do not notice other people's hunger, or they do notice it and do not care.

Piro social life is the ongoing realisation of their multiplicity in a ceaseless round of attention towards others as kinspeople. This multiplicity leads to the supreme Piro value of *gwashata*, 'to live well'. Literally the term means 'to reside and do nothing else': it refers to the day-to-day tranquillity of village life, where no grievances, sadness or dissatisfaction leads a person to seek to move elsewhere. It is based on the orchestration of life-courses of different people of different ages and sexes, in the production of villages where life is good, and tranquil. 'Living well' is what we would have to define as kinship for Piro people.

Alone

My account here of *nshinikanchi* helps to explain the dynamics of 'helplessness', 'compassion' and 'consolation'. To 'be helpless' means to lie outside of the generalised mutual attention of 'living well'; to 'compassionate' means to see another who is in such a condition; and to 'console' is to intensify attention toward the one who is helpless to bring them back into 'living well'. But if these are the dynamics of 'helplessness', 'compassion' and 'consolation' in Piro social life, what are the interior dynamics of 'helplessness'? What does it mean, for Piro people, to be alone?

If Piro people experience their condition as social humans as a manifestation of *nshinikanchi*, 'mind, memory, love, thought', then their experience of a non-social condition lies with the *samenchi*.[9] I have translated this term previously as 'soul', following Piro people's own translation of the term into Ucayali Spanish as *alma*, but without wishing to imply any specific religious content to the term. Now I would prefer to translate it as 'self', in the sense of the radical experience of personal uniqueness. As I have been discussing, for Piro people, the self, this radical experience of personal uniqueness, is not the basis of social life, for that is based on *nshinikanchi*, 'mind, memory, love, thought', a faculty generated by others. It is, however, at the basis of much cosmological action in the Piro lived world, and in particular, of the experience of 'helplessness'.

The most common everyday experience of *samenchi* for Piro people is in dreaming (*gipnawata*). The self who experiences and acts in dreams is the *samenchi*. During sleep, a person's *samenchi* wanders around, experiencing things. What it sees is the future, but in a metaphorical sense. Piro people know a set of standard metaphors for translating dream experiences into predictions of the future, although not all dreams are easy to analyse. Dream-analysis is a collective act: people tell their dreams to others, and ask for interpretations. However, during dreaming, and in the later remembering of the dream for collective analysis, Piro people experience themselves as intimately unique. As one man put it, 'At night, it seems as if we wander around, doing all sorts of ridiculous things. It's not true! We're just there, lying in bed!' This raises an important point, for all perceptual experience of the *samenchi* is, from the point of view of the everyday waking state, delusional.[10] The self sees the future in dreams, it is true, but it experiences the real future as a set of bizarre and improbable events, i.e. in delusional form, rather than as it will be. For example, a young man anxiously recounts that he has dreamt that his entire body was covered in caterpillars with poisonous spines, saying, 'It was revolting, and I was very frightened!' Making no comment on his expressed emotions, which were delusional and hence do not matter, his kinspeople speculate as to whether this means he will live a long time (the caterpillar's spines are grey like the hair of very old people) or whether all his children will be daughters (girls have long hair like the caterpillar). Opinions are expressed, but no consensus is sought. The young man calms down.

The *samenchi*, experienced in a dream state, has an origin and a future. Consideration of this trajectory of the *samenchi* will help to explain the nature of 'helplessness' as an experiential state. Piro people are born with *samenchi*, that is, with intimate personal uniqueness. Indeed, until the child develops *nshinikanchi* ('mind, memory, love, thought'), all experience is of the *samenchi* (the 'self'). This accounts for the strange actions of infants: the infant's *samenchi* wanders after its parents when they go to the river or the forest, and hence falls easy prey to demons disguised as its parents, who lure it away. This is the illness known as 'soul loss' (cf. Lagrou, this volume). Similarly, infants make augury: for example, if an infant arches its back and raises its tongue onto the roof of its mouth, it is an augury of death, for this behaviour means, 'it sees its own coffin'. Like the dreaming adult, the infant sees the future, and communicates this future involuntarily as augury.[11] As the infant grows and develops *nshinikanchi*, the *samenchi* does not cease to perceive, but shifts locus. In a formulation that would surely please Lacanians, it is the development of language which shifts the *samenchi* out of its central place and into the world of dreams.

It is this full existence in the delusional world of *samenchi* experience which renders the infant *wamonuwata*, 'helpless' in the eyes of others. By eliciting its attention towards themselves, older Piro people lead the infant to generate *nshinikanchi*, and hence to attend to its kinspeople in the here and now, rather than to the future. Here, the dynamics of compassion render the infant as 'human' in the full sense described above, the combined 'human' and 'kins-person'.

The relationship between *nshinikanchi* and *samenchi* is manifested most powerfully at death. At a person's death, the *samenchi* separates from the body. The latter rots down in the grave to the skeleton, which eventually reanimates and leaves the earth to prowl about as the very dangerous 'bone demon', in a process that necessarily takes quite a long time. By contrast, *samenchi* retains its agency immediately after the death. This is because it retains *nshinikanchi*. It continues to haunt the living, crying in loneliness for them, and evoking in them a lethal nostalgia. However, the *samenchi*, separated from the body, cannot generate the *nshinikanchi* of others, so must depend on its agency in the *nshinikanchi* of those who are already linked to it. It is only those who are already bound to the dead soul through *nshinikanchi* who can be objects of its actions. That is, only those who have known a dead person as a once-living person need fear the attentions of his or her *samenchi*. As each of those who have known a person during life die in turn, his or her soul ceases to act and is totally forgotten. As the SIL (Summer Institute of Linguistics) missionary Matteson put it, the *samenchi* 'lingers by the grave, living on papaya, suffering and crying when soaked by the rain, until it eventually passes out of existence' (1965: 337). This fate of the dead *samenchi* helps to underscore the meaning of *nshinikanchi* as embodied intersubjectivity. It is *nshinikanchi* which holds people together, and leads them to feed each other and to live together. The dead *samenchi* lives in the forest, eating non-human food, and suffers in the rain.

This account of the *samenchi* helps us to understand the peculiar nature of *wamonuwata*, 'being helpless', in the case of the mourning adult. From the point of view of other people, the mourning adult is alone, abandoned by the dead person. But from the point of view of the mourning adult, he or she is not alone, for he or she is subjected to the constant sight of the dead person's *samenchi*, who calls to them, begging them to keep it company. Here it is the *samenchi* who 'is helpless', *wamonuwata*, and the mourning adults who 'are compassionate', *getwamonuta*, towards it. However, as I have discussed elsewhere (Gow 1991), such 'compassion' is delusional and lethal, for it leads to death.

Here, the 'compassion' of other living kinspeople, and their 'good thinking', leads them to intensify their solicitude for the mourning adults, searching them out, keeping them company, and insistently and steadily replacing the presence of the dead *samenchi* in the experience of the mourning adults with the presence of themselves. Eventually, the mourning adult 'forgets' the *samenchi*, which thereby ceases to act. Through other people's *giglenshinikanuta*, 'thinking well, consolation', the *nshinikanchi* of one who *wamonuwata*, 'is helpless', is brought back to the only place where it has meaningful social efficacy, the immediate world of living kinspeople.

Dead or dying

This pattern of consolation explains two features of Piro sociability that genuinely shocked me by their extreme differences from my own notions of humanity. The first is what I here term 'death-throe narratives', detailed accounts given to those who were absent from an event of death of exactly how that person died, and the second are jokes about dead people. The first appalled me with their horrific honesty, while the second appalled me by their callousness.

Returning in 1995 to the village of Santa Clara after an absence of seven years, I was told of the death of my *compadre* Artemio Fasabi during the epidemic of cholera. This news was bad enough, but I was not simply told that he was dead. His close relatives took me aside to tell me in excruciating detail exactly how he had died. These accounts numbed me, for dying is never pleasant, and death by cholera is particularly frightening. I had no idea of how to respond to them. The same happened with other people I had known well and who had died during my long absence, like Artemio's older sister Lucha and his brother-in-law Pablo. Even at the time, it was clear to me that the survivors wanted me to know the terrible details of these deaths, and even seemed to feel that I had some sort of right to know them. But I did not know why.

I have never been able to bring myself to discuss this matter with Piro people, but my sense now is that the death-throe narratives are, in themselves, a mode of 'consolation' directed at those who have returned after a long absence. Because such travellers have not actually witnessed the death, they might be tempted to disbelieve that it had really happened: Piro people do regularly lie about these matters to humorous effect. Were the returnee to imagine that the death-throe narratives were lies, and that the death in question had not in fact occurred, they would be dangerously open to the imprecations of the dead person's soul. It is as if the death-throe narratives are saying, 'Believe us, the real living people, and not that dead person!' Because the *samenchi* of the dead person is still operative in the *nshinikanchi* of the person who has just discovered that the death has occurred, the death-throe narrative forces the listener to accept the reality of the death, and consequently the delusional nature of the wandering *samenchi*. As with all Piro personal experience narratives, it is the wealth of the detail provided that underwrites the credibility of the account. My experience was thus a simple effect of coming from a world where all people are said to 'die peacefully in their sleep'.

The second feature of Piro sociability which I found shocking is their remarkable gallows humour. Piro people will make jokes or comments about dead people which I found to be in extremely poor taste. For example, when I asked about a former resident of Santa Clara village with whom I had spent many happy times, I was told, 'Oh, she died! She went to Pucallpa, and starved to death. She'll be sitting in a hole there now!' The assembled people roared with laughter. It seems to me that the reason such stories are funny is that they demonstrate to Piro people that they have ceased to 'be helpless', that 'compassion' and 'consolation' have worked, and that the remembered dead, now that they are fully dead, are ludicrous. Collective laughter manifests that triumph, and the temporal distance travelled.

I hasten to add that this collective laughter is never fully triumphant, for Piro people will remain capable of sadness when they think about particularly close kinspeople throughout life. But such sadness is highly attenuated, as the person becomes capable of talking (and presumably thinking) of the dead kinspeople without the morose withdrawal that characterises *wamonuwata*. Overcome, the intense loneliness of 'helplessness' becomes a general attitude to the human condition, marked by the facticity of mortality.

I return to the Melanesianist's comment. Piro people probably are extreme narcissists, but of a very interesting kind. They are narcissistically attached to their own identities, but their version of Narcissus's reflection is their 'multiple other selves', their kinspeople. They know this to be true of themselves, for their core social value is *gwashata*, 'to live well, to live quietly': that is, to live in a good village in harmony with all one's close kinspeople. And they know this also to be true through their compassion for the helpless: they know that helplessness, and the compassion it elicits in others, are the affective preconditions of Piro social life.

Consolation ignored

There is, however, an exception: *kagonchi*, shamans. If asked why they underwent the rigorous training and continue to undergo the discomforts of their practice, shamans give one stereotypical response. The shamanic career originates in the unbearable grief, experienced or simply feared, of losing a child to illness. The loss of a child provokes a particularly intense *wamonuwata* in many men, since men tend to live in the villages of their wives, and hence to depend on their children as a means to relate to their co-residents. The death of a child, and the subsequent state of *wamonuwata*, tends therefore to subvert the key value of 'living well' much more radically for a man than for a woman. Women also become shamans, but they do not, to my knowledge, engage in long shamanic apprenticeships. While this was never made explicit to me, I have the impression that women attain their access to shamanry through miscarried foetuses and children who died in infancy. A further condition of female shamanry is marriage to a male shaman, and the subsequent constant contact with the hallucinatory state and other shamanic activities.

Inconsolable over the loss of a beloved child, some men withdraw from social life, remaining inattentive to the solicitude of others. They fall quiet, talking little, 'thinking, loving, remembering' one who is now dead. The souls of young children are by no means as feared as those of adults, but they seem to stimulate an especially intense *wamonuwata*, perhaps due to the sense of the child's total helplessness in its condition of dead *samenchi*. Such men brood on their own inability to protect their children's lives, and fear that their other children will die too.

Contemplating his condition, the grief-stricken man conceives the project of becoming a shaman, and hence acquiring the knowledge and powers to defend his other children and other kinspeople. To do so, however, means forsaking a large part of the pleasures of life, for shamanry means avoiding sex as much as possible, not eating many things, and especially it involves the frequent consumption of hallucinogens. Apprentice shamans do not drink beer with their kinspeople, and avoid their company.

Shamanry involves a progressive increase in contact between the apprentice shaman and powerful beings. Increasingly, the shaman begins to live much of the time in a hallucinatory state of consciousness. There he acquires another 'social life': as the powerful beings begin to 'like' (*galuka*) him, and seek out his company. He becomes, so to speak, a double being, living 'here in the village' and simultaneously 'off there with powerful beings'.

This duplication is more than a metaphor for Piro people. A twin, a person who was born one of two, is an innate shaman.[12] Only one twin can survive, Piro people say. One woman (herself the mother of a twin and grandmother of another) told me, 'One of them just dies. If we struggle to keep both alive, then both of them will die.' The living twin is a shaman from birth, and already in a permanent state of dual consciousness: he or she can not only see the future, but is able to describe it to others.

The shamanry of twins is largely passive, but that of men who have trained as shamans is active. Because they have refused the 'good thinking' of their co-resident kinspeople, and hence refused to be consoled by them, they enter another form of multiplicity, that of the multitudes of powerful beings met in hallucinatory state. In hallucinatory state, these powerful beings reveal themselves to the shaman as *yine*, 'humans', and in turn they treat the shaman as *yineru*, 'a human'. The shaman therefore becomes one of the elements in the multiplicity of given powerful beings/sets of powerful beings. This multiplication of the shaman was vividly expressed to me as follows, by Don Mauricio Fasabi, 'A man who takes drugs no longer sleeps. The things you have learned don't let you sleep. The things you know are walking around and around, they won't let you get to sleep any more.' For non-shamans, insomnia is caused by hunger, and leads to unhealthy broodings on close kinspeople who are far away or dead. Shamans, by contrast, experience the insomnia generated by the multiplication of their being through their acquired knowledge.

The doubling of the shaman makes him a member of otherwise diverse sets of human multiplicity, and sets up the dynamic connectivities that characterise shamanic action. In shamanry, the everyday form of the village full of co-resident kinspeople gives way: to visions of non-humans as 'human', *yine*; to the non-human spaces of the river and forest as the houses and villages of the powerful beings; to the 'here and now' as past, present and future; and to sick kinspeople as the wounded prey animals of powerful beings and other shamans. And, it should be added, in the seldom-voiced but ever-present language of sorcery, visions emerge of 'kinspeople' in other villages as potential prey animals of oneself.

In shamanry, the cosmos is revealed to be governed by the same actions which make up everyday life. But there is one key difference: the cosmos is not governed by the cycling of 'helplessness', 'compassion' and 'consolation' which make up everyday sociability. There is no suggestion in shamanry that shamans are 'compassionated' in their 'helplessness' by the powerful beings, nor that they are helped because the powerful beings seek to 'console' them. How indeed could the powerful beings 'compassionate' the shaman? For the former are immortal, and, knowing nothing of death, do and could not share the initial condition which drives a man to become a shaman.

The justification of shamanry, in relations with other people, is, however, 'compassion': shamans cure because they 'compassionate' their patients. They are, of course, also paid, but their primary motivation is 'compassion', the 'seeing of the helplessness' of others. This was a point all shamans I spoke to stressed, and some went as far as to insist that they prefer not to be paid. This is a tricky issue, for all non-shamans know that shamans lead a double life, and hence cannot necessarily be trusted. After all, it is widely known that sorcery is much easier to learn than curing, and it is by no means certain that shamans tell the truth when they say that they, personally, would never use it. This is why Piro people say, with a slightly resigned tone, 'There have to be shamans, those who know these things'.

The necessity of shamans in the Piro lived world brings us to the issue I raised at the beginning: the Piro conception of the human condition, and of the place of humanity in the cosmos. Piro humanity, as I have said, is intrinsically multiple, and relations between people are governed by *nshinikanchi*, 'mind, love, respect, thought, memory'. *Nshinikanchi* is a temporal phenomenon, developing in the growing child as it responds to others, and surviving the death of the person in the memories of others. The temporality of social life is a product of a key fact of the human condition: mortality. Social life is only possible because people are born and die, for it is generated in the relations people develop as a consequence of those experiences. The newborn baby and the mourning adult are in 'helplessness', other people 'compassionate' and 'console' them, and so make the Piro social world. Surrounding them is a cosmos based on very different principles, ever ready to impinge on their lives, and whose existential implications are constantly glimpsed in dreams, in helplessness and in hallucinations.

A plateau of consolation

When I was living in Santa Clara, the sound of shamans singing the drug songs would make the hairs stand up on my arms. Out of the pitch darkness, and from a cacophony of retching, vomiting and spitting, would come the thin sound of the whistled melody of a drug song. The shaman was now hallucinating very strongly, and he was beginning the process of taming the drug spirit people through the entrancing artistry of his voice. Then the shaman would start to sing the strange words of these songs, coming from languages nobody here speaks. This man was now fully alone, far out there in that separate reality. Using all of his courage and all of his accumulated knowledge, the shaman was now singing powerfully, as he sought to beguile the torrent of imagery cascading over him into yielding up the secret he needed to know in order to cure this sick person. Out of their compassion for him, other people would join in, wordlessly accompanying the shaman's song in an unfamiliar counterpoint, or they would sing their own songs, thereby generating spectacular harmonic convergences which chased each other through the night air. And when I had taken the drug too, this unearthly concert would reveal itself to be an extraordinary opera, played out by multitudes of uncanny creatures on an enormous stage of vast complexity. I would be completely overwhelmed.

Daily life in Santa Clara, by contrast, was often very boring. Nothing much seemed to happen beyond the to-and-fro of people gardening, fishing, visiting, sending food, getting firewood, cooking, bathing, gossiping and so on. It was all perfectly pleasant, but I often longed for something, just anything, to happen. I would grow restless and peevish, irritated by every host's polite response to every visitor's enquiry about their current activities, 'I'm doing nothing'. How very true, I would comment bitterly to myself, and I would wonder at why local people seemed to be content with doing so little when they had the proven capability to do so much. And these feelings were compounded by my sense of their total unworthiness, and that it was I who was at fault, and not they. A constant consolation to me in these moments was the memory of those two chapter titles from Peter Rivière's study of the Trio (1969), 'Life's dull round I' and 'Life's dull round II'. Well then, I thought, so it's not just me.

This sense of the assailing boredom of life in indigenous Amazonian communities is not restricted to Rivière and myself, for it has been noticed by others, even if they are seldom willing to comment on it to a wider public. Cecilia McCallum remarked, on a visit to Santa Clara, 'Gosh, these people keep themselves busy! They're always doing things. Cashinahua people just sit about all day doing nothing!' I was bemused, but later discovered that Cashinahua people are capable of having even less happen in their villages than Piro people. Other Europeans have commented to me on the extreme tedium that they have felt in Campa villages and in Yaminahua villages, so the pattern seems quite general. A whole eternity seems to have passed, but it is still only eleven o'clock in the morning.

This boredom is not really an ethnographic fact about indigenous Amazonian peoples, since in each case the informant is European. This boredom doubtless tells us much about a specific middle-class European aesthetic of social life, in which 'doing nothing' is strongly frowned upon (cf. Passes, this volume). Even if it is one's current state, European convention demands that it be carefully masked, at the very minimum, by the claim to be 'just watching television'. That said, however, ethnographers must proceed in their work by attending to the mismatch between their own prejudices and expectations and those of the people they are studying, so perhaps it is possible to translate this experience of 'boredom' into an ethnographic insight. What does it mean that Piro people openly assert that they are 'doing nothing'?

In part, the statement, 'I'm doing nothing' is an invitation to interact: the hosts are assuring the visitors that there is nothing already happening to distract their full attention from the manifold pleasures of this new activity, 'being visited'. But more than this, we have seen that this is an aesthetic of life that asserts that company is, in and of itself, desirable. People should be 'doing nothing' when visitors come, for nothing is more important than everyday sociability. Of course, visits can be untimely and visitors unwelcome. Piro people like to have a good view from their houses, in order to see visitors early enough to hide any object or activity that they would not want those visitors to see, and it is also common practice to avoid unwelcome visitors by hiding inside the walled-off section of the house. But in general, Piro people spend large amounts of their time sitting openly in their houses, 'doing nothing', and ready for interaction with anyone who approaches. And when they are not doing this, they are often off visiting others in turn.

The key to 'doing nothing' lies in its possible alternatives. In my early months in Santa Clara, I would confuse my own visitors by trying to specify what I was up to when they asked me. I slowly learned that 'I'm reading this book', 'I'm thinking about my family', or 'I'm trying to decide when to go to Lima', were not acceptable Piro responses. Such answers confused and worried them. Some of my responses were presumably simply too bizarre for them to hear, but some lay dangerously close to genuine and alarming Piro responses to the question, 'What are you doing?' Such answers can be: 'I'm lying here sick', 'I am dying', or the sullen silence that leaves the visitor wondering what exactly might be wrong. Such answers cause fear and consternation. The alternative to 'doing nothing', I thus discovered, is 'suffering'.

So, the something that does not happen in these villages is 'helplessness', suffering. The flatness of everyday life turns out to be fully intentional, it is an achievement. It is won from a cosmos that is governed by other kinds of reason, and which invades Piro people's lives with dramatic events of emotional extremity. In the face of such events, Piro people know themselves to be helpless, for they know themselves to be virtually powerless to change the given structure of a cosmos which was not created for their benefit and which is totally indifferent to their fate. Knowing this, Piro people know they must help each other. Piro people know that they have been and will be helpless. They see the helplessness of others, and this compassion leads them to heighten their social regard for them, in specific acts of consolation. In everyday life, when things are going well, this 'thinking beautifully' transforms into the sustained plateau of kindness and companionship that Piro people call 'living well'.

'Living well' is the key value of an aesthetic of social life in which mastery lies with making sure that nothing ever happens for, like every plateau, this one is surrounded on all sides by sharp descents into very different regions. I used to find it boring, and to long for the nights of shamanry, when the exotic show would be performed. In retrospect, I was in blissful ignorance. I knew that the nocturnal operas of the shamans were directed at curing illness, to be sure, but I had not realised then how these spectacles originated within the terrors of suffering, nor how these songs, which could take me to those places of such otherworldly beauty, were a courageous transformation of the singer's former state of silent pain.

Acknowledgements

My fieldwork on the Bajo Urubamba between 1980 and 1999 was funded by the Social Science Research Council, the British Museum, the Nuffield Foundation and the British Academy. This chapter was written, at the invitation of Anne-Christine Taylor for the session on 'Mind, Affect, and the Image of the Self' at the International Congress of Americanists, in Quito in July 1997, and I thank her, Joanna Overing and all of my peers in the British

school of Amazonianists for their perceptive comments and questions, and
Alan Passes for his excellent editing. Comments from Christina Toren,
Heonik Kwon, Edward Schieff[in and Olivia Harris seeded some key ideas,
and a conversation with Claire Jenkins allowed me to think its conclusion. I
owe a very special debt to Aparecida Vilaça, who first helped me to talk
about Piro death-throe narratives.

Notes

1 There are excellent accounts of grief and mourning from Basso on the Kalapalo
   (1985, 1995) and from Taylor on the Achuar (1993, 1996).
2 Isabella Lepri informs me (personal communication) that there is also a Piro
   community in northern Bolivia.
3 See Overing (1996).
4 This is likely to be a relatively recent development in Piro from a proto-Maipuran
   form which was not intrinsically plural. Piro *yine* is cognate with Campa *-shani-*,
   Amuesha *yanesha* and Terena *shane* (see Payne 1991).
5 There are two exceptions: the Panoan-speaking Amahuaca people are *gipetuneru*,
   'Capibara People', while the Machiguenga people are *kiruneru*, 'Peach Palm
   People'. They are thus treated as if they were Piro endogamous groups, and the
   Amahuaca and Machiguenga peoples have long occupied a rather special place
   in Piro regard in more ways than this.
6 See Gow (1997) for discussion of this theme (also Mimica 1992 and Urton 1997).
7 See note 3.
8 Piro people seem much less animated by a concern for other people's ultimately
   unknowable intentions than Melanesian people (Wagner 1967; Munn 1986;
   Strathern 1988).
9 *Samenchi* is the Absolute form of the root *-samenu*. As with the Campa cognate
   samentsi, this Piro Absolute form can strictly speaking only refer to a dead
   '*samenchi*'. Here, I use it quite ungrammatically for both living (attached) and
   dead (detached) souls.
10 The only dreams defined as 'true' by Piro people, those taken as actual experiences
   of lived reality, are those mediated by hallucinogens, particularly *toé/gayapa*.
11 Body parts, like the upper arm, can also make augury quite independent of
   personal will. Many other objects in the world are attributed the same power.
12 This is literally true: the Piro word for 'innate' also means 'twin'.

References

Basso, E. (1985) *A Musical View of the Universe: Kalapalo Myth and Ritual Performances*,
   Philadelphia: University of Pennsylvania Press.
—— (1995) *The Last Cannibals: A South American Oral History*, Austin: University of
   Texas Press.
Gow, P. (1989) 'The perverse child: desire in a Native Amazonian subsistence
   economy', *Man* (n.s.) 24: 299–314.
—— (1990) 'Could Sangama read? The origin of writing among the Piro of Eastern
   Peru', *History and Anthropology* 5: 87–103.
—— (1991) *Of Mixed Blood: Kinship and History in Peruvian Amazonia*, Oxford Studies in
   Social and Cultural Anthropology, Oxford University Press.

—— (1993) 'Gringos and wild Indians: images of history in Western Amazonian cultures', *L'Homme* 126–8, 33(2–4): 331–51.

—— (1994) 'River people: Shamanism and history in Western Amazonia', in C. Humphrey and N. Thomas (eds) *Shamanism, History and the State*, pp. 90–113, Ann Arbor: University of Michigan Press.

—— (1995a) 'Land, people and paper in Western Amazonia', in E. Hirsch and M. O'Hanlon (eds) *The Anthropology of Landscape: Perspectives on Place and Space*, pp. 43–62, Oxford: Clarendon Press.

—— (1995b) 'Cinema da floresta: filme, alucinação e sonho na Amazônia peruana', *Revista de Antropologia*: 37–54.

—— (1997) 'O Parentesco como Conciência Humana: O Caso dos Piro', *Mana* 3(2): 39–65.

—— (in press) *An Amazonian Myth and its History*, Oxford: Oxford University Press.

Matteson, E. (1965) *The Piro (Arawakan) Language*, Berkeley and Los Angeles: University of California Press.

Mimica, J. (1992) *Intimations of Infinity: The Cultural Meanings of the Iqwaye Counting and Number System*, Oxford: Berg.

Munn, N.D. (1986) *The Fame of Gawa: A Symbolic Study of Value Transformation in a Massim (Papua New Guinea) Society*, Cambridge: Cambridge University Press.

Overing, J. (1989) 'The aesthetics of production: the sense of community among the Cubeo and Piaroa', *Dialectical Anthropology* 14: 159–75.

—— (1996) 'Under the sky of the domesticated: in praise of the everyday', Inaugural Lecture for the Professorship and Chair of Social Anthropology, University of St Andrews, 4 December.

—— (1999) 'Elogio do Cotidiano: A cofiança e a arte da vida social em uma comunidade amazonica', *Mana* 5(1): 81–107.

Payne, D.L. (1991) 'A classification of Maipuran (Arawakan) languages based on shared lexical retentions', in D.C. Derbyshire and G.K. Pullum (eds) *Handbook of Amazonian Languages*, Vol. 2, Amsterdam: Mouton de Gruyter.

Rivière, P. (1969) *Marriage among the Trio. A Principle of Social Organization*, Oxford: Clarendon Press.

Strathern, M. (1988) *The Gender of the Gift: Problems with Women and Problems with Society in Melanesia*, Berkeley, Los Angeles and London: University of California Press.

Taylor, A.-C. (1993) 'Remembering to forget: identity, memory and mourning among the Jivaro', *Man* 28: 653–78.

—— (1996) 'The soul's body and its states: an Amazonian perspective on the nature of being human', *Journal of the Royal Anthropological Institute* 2: 201–15.

Urton, G. (1997) *The Social Life of Numbers: A Quechua Ontology of Numbers and Philosophy of Arithmetic*, Austin: University of Texas Press.

Wagner, R. (1967) *The Curse of Souw: Principles of Daribi Clan Definition and Alliance in New Guinea*, Chicago: University of Chicago Press.

Chapter 3

The efficacy of laughter
The ludic side of magic within Amazonian sociality

Joanna Overing

The role of laughter is vital to the everyday life of an Amazonian community. The relish of many Amazonian peoples for humorous and bawdy play has intrigued me for many years.[1] My clearest memories of the Piaroa, an indigenous people of Venezuela who dwell along tributaries of the Orinoco, was of their laughter. A Piaroa was most happy when with close relatives, gathered all together within the bounds of the large communal house. At such times, when the house was filled with people, laughter filled the air, bouncing off the walls of the forest surrounding it. These are a people who are lovers of slapstick, and of witty or outrageous play on words. When I lived with them, their ritual and even nightly chanting were broken by the amusing story, the inevitable laughter. It was in hilarity that I felt I actually understood and was at one with them.

The Piaroa are not alone among Amazonian peoples in their love for the bawdy, the slapstick, the scatological, the absurd and most importantly the good-humoured banter or tease. I have experienced the raucous repartee of the Yanomami, neighbours of the Piaroa. Viveiros de Castro writes (1992: 9) of the exuberance and joyfulness of the Araweté of Central Brazil. He observes that the Araweté are '[f]ond of touch and physical closeness, . . . exaggerated in their demonstrations of affection, lovers of the flesh and of the feast, free with tongues and constant in their laughter, sarcastic and at times delirious'. Laughter and the ludic obviously play a large part in the everyday life of these peoples, so much so that it becomes an important clue to the very distinctiveness of their sociality.

Why then have we paid so little attention to the role of the ludic in Amazonia? Why indeed are there so few works in anthropology that deal at depth with the topic of humour?[2] We only have flashes of insight here and there of its significance. James Boon writes on the love of the Balinese for the burlesque (1984: 168). Mark Hobart, on the same people, says (1995: 66) that he was struck how often Balinese conversation was interspersed with laughter, as too were the healer's séances – and all teaching and learning. Most likely our own lack of scholarly attention to foolery has been because we stress both the gravity of knowledge and the triviality of jest (cf. Hobart, ibid.). This lack of a sense of humour in our work can be a very serious deterrent to understanding, and the most ironic anthropological predicament of all would be for the ethnographer to take as (seriously) literal a people's ironic commentary on the world and their own behaviour (cf. Bruner 1984: 12). I am certain that many analyses of myth suffer this illness of *gravitas*, particularly when examples of the genre are earnestly treated as decontextualised texts, as collectors' tales on the written page.

Every example of myth telling that I witnessed among the Piaroa was a piece of drama, a performance that smacked of ribaldry and parody, interspersed with a heavy dose of irony. Far from being solemn and awesome tales of godly omnipotence and omniscience, these performances created instead an audience delight in godly buffoonery, and a pleasurable understanding of the absurdity of the human predicament. The behaviour of the Piaroa creator gods was decidedly indecorous. Brothers squabbled while vying with each other over which could toss the moon and the sun the highest into the sky: one leapt so hard to push his moon higher that he banged his head, leaving forever his facial imprint, while the other suffered a short-lived death, burning in the fire of the sun; the creator of people grabbed a wandering penis hovering above him to give form to man; the creator of fire and agriculture, cursing, ran round and round in circles, made mad by the potency of his own powers which came from the rust of the sun; a goddess refused to stay with her husband and chose instead to lead a life of ribald promiscuity. She did this as revenge against her creator god brother who had sold her to her husband for only six boxes of matches.

Boon links (op. cit., p. 169) the burlesque of the Balinese to an epistemology of folly, an attitude to the world that the Piaroa clearly share. Something of importance is obviously going on in their myths – intellectually, socially, politically. We may well ask, why *do* Piaroa myths centre upon the risible, the erotic and the obscene? Or better put, why do they underline the scatological and hilarious side of godly behaviour? Why are their strongest obscenities and most colourful dirty words to be found in the sacred language of chants? I shall return later to this topic of the ludic in myth, as well as to the ludic and the social, but for now it is important to note that these are relationships barely touched in the literature – a fact not shedding good light on anthropological perspicacity, or the capacity to grasp humour crossculturally. Thus a word needs to be said on the development of certain Western views of laughter, and their unfortunate effects upon the outlook of the social theorist.

The banality of laughter, or the 'authority is a serious matter' approach

In the preface to their recently published *A Cultural History of Humour*, Bremmer and Roodenburg note (1997a: xi) that it is only recently that historians have come to see humour as an incisive key to cultural codes and sensibilities. They observe that historians have displayed a decided lack of interest in the topic of humour, and thus for the most part the historical and social context of the ludic has not been previously treated. They wish to rectify this lapse by demonstrating how attitudes toward laughter and the risible have often changed through the course of Western history, and that they have done so in line with influences from the church and state, the growth of science and the industrial revolution, and the related social changes forthcoming from such developments. It is noted that the *aesthetics* of laughter in the West have changed over time, along with attitudes toward laughter as a *bodily* practice (Le Goff 1997: 42–6). This is a history that sheds considerable light upon why so little attention has previously been paid to humour, not only by the historians, but by the anthropologists as well.

In much of early modern Europe we find an increase in the policing of the frontiers of jokes and comic domains, which became considerably reduced, as too were the occasions and locales where laughter was allowed (Burke 1997: 72). By the twelfth century the church, always suspicious of laughter, reached a sort of codification of the practice of laughter, by distinguishing admissible from inadmissible (ribald) ways of laughing (Le Goff, op. cit., p. 44). Laughter, in an extraordinary Christian physiology, was understood to have a dangerous relation with the body, as the worst pollution of the mouth. With Calvinism laughter became especially alien to workaday Christian behaviour (Bremmer 1997: 22); it became increasingly understood as a *banal* practice, a sign of idleness and lack of humility indicative of the out-of-control behaviour of the non-Christian – and members of the working classes (Le Goff, op. cit., pp. 43–4). The rules of decorum allowed wit within the domain of 'proper' conversation for ladies and gentlemen, but no longer the burlesque. The court fool made his exit, as too did the lords of misrule, the licensed buffoons of the English countryside (Bremmer and Roodenburg 1997b: 8). Thus in the early modern period the values of sobriety and gravity gained the upper hand (ibid., pp. 6–7), the view being that weighty areas of life, particularly those dealing with the authority of the church and state, were not a joking matter (cf. K. Thomas 1977). At the same time, with the growth of industrial society and the development of the professions, laughter became unseemly to the serious practices of civil society. From an Ivan Illich point of view (1973), the West began – with a vengeance – to undervalue its 'tools for conviviality', as it increasingly overvalued those of productive efficiency.

The human sciences have of course been affected by these trends. The very fact that the social role of the (dangerous) ludic has been so little studied and its importance neglected in anthropology speaks of their effect.[3] The ludic is not expected in other peoples' religious, political and economic life. Or, if there, it is considered banal, *irrelevant* – or inappropriate – to the study.

Frivolity does not belong to the workplace, the pulpit, the political committee and the academic manuscript. It is interesting that the one area of experience where the humorous has been anthropologically well documented is that of 'ritual play', for instance through the superb writings of the anthropologists Bateson (1958) and Turner (e.g. 1982; also see Fernandes 1984). Although Turner (1982), for one, disagrees with this view, it is as if it were only in that *non-everyday* realm of liminal ritual that we can expect, or accept, the whimsical or ludicrous. Laughter is not expected in everyday working relationships of hunting, gathering, gardening. A cogent query is why then is so much laughter *visually* recorded in the ethnographic films of everyday pursuits in Amazonia, on the building of fishing traps, or the telling of myths?[4]

The play of work and collectivity

As already mentioned, ludic play is often used in Amazonia as a powerful tool for social living, and is considered necessary by indigenous people to many aspects of living successfully in village life. Thus, the congenial collectivity is highly valued by many Amazonian peoples, but it is also understood as a form of sociality that can only be attained with difficulty. The convivial collectivity enabling of health and well-being must be created through its '*tools* of conviviality' (cf. Illich op. cit.),[5] which must be ever sharpened and honed by the members of a community (as most of the other chapters in this book also stress). It is for good reason that one of the main duties of good leadership in Amazonia is to create and maintain the high morale of the group (e.g. see Goldman 1963 on the Cubeo; Overing 1989 on the Piaroa). The leader cannot order people about, for this role is not a coercive one: Amazonian people do not obey, but perhaps follow or join in (see Lévi-Strauss 1967; Overing Kaplan 1975, 1993; Clastres 1977; D. Thomas 1982; Rivière 1984). Lévi-Strauss, in an incisive moment of social astuteness when trying to understand *the reason* for an Amazonian chief among such egalitarian peoples, notes of the Nambikwara leader that he 'must be a good singer and dancer, a merrymaker always ready to cheer up the band' (1967: 53). It is my argument that it is precisely through these ludic skills that the leader *enables* collectivity among an otherwise vehemently anarchic people. It is the leader who, in large part through his skills for merriment, for jesting, clowning and dancing, provides the impetus, and even possibility, for these people to fulfil their desire for collective togetherness, or union.

Note that I speak of the leader's *skills* for conviviality. There is an *art* to merriment in Amazonia, which is not the same thing as the art of the performer in our Western culture where performance has its designated, formal stage. In Amazonia the art of performance pertains to an aesthetics of *everyday life*, where humour is often constitutive of the daily *social* activities of gardening, gathering, the preparation of food, the building of a house, a curing ritual. Conviviality is an intrinsic *ethical* value for many Amazonian peoples, and its mastery speaks of high social worth. Thus the leader is expected to be more talented in the *art* of humour than anyone else – and this within a culture that is in general engendering of skills for play and laughter.

Among the Piaroa, one finds high value placed upon creative play in the use of language, with the leader being the great master of metaphor. The 'technical words' of this chant language are constructed through the complex and artistic use of affixes, and it is also through the same principle that everyday metaphors are constructed. In wordplay, children construct colourful metaphors through the clever use of affixes. Through the shrewd use of an infix, a child can jokingly characterise a man as pointed or round, a mountain or a banana, a monkey, snake or pig. The more mature will use elements of the esoteric chant language to make a quip: thus the jest, 'red quakamaya flies high', in answer to the question of 'where are you going?', meaning that the person was going bathing. The reasoning is that red quakamaya is the 'master of fire', which was born in the depths of a sacred lake of origin. 'To swim' and 'to burn oneself' is the same word in Piaroa language. As 'master of fire', the speaker would fly high (out of the depths) in swimming in the terrestrial space of a river. Individuality and creativity play a significant part in Piaroa ordinary language use.

Work and play are not distinct domains of activity in Amazonia. I well remember the slapstick of a Piaroa husband and wife returning to their village after a successful hunting and gathering trip, and the gay laughter with which they were greeted. The wife bounced into the plaza with a basket on her back filled with thirty kilos of their bounty, the fruit and game that they had accumulated from the jungle. In contrast, the husband, a fit man in his prime, studiedly stumbled into view, holding high a huge flat basket that held one sole jungle fruit right in its centre. This jungle foray had provided more pleasures than the joy of discovering ripened fruit and docile prey, and since it is a cultural fact among the Piaroa that men are depleted of energy if they indulge in sex, while women are not, the message of their antics was thoroughly enjoyed by the other residents of the community.

More generally, the Piaroa highly prize convivial friendship in the partners with whom they work side by side in all their daily tasks (cf. Alès, Passes, this volume). Husbands and wives engage in light banter in their shared work. A man, who might spend hours in the day weaving baskets or making a quiver or set of darts, does so in the congenial atmosphere of the communal house, where he can banter with children, or with women preparing food. A lad *chooses* the man he wants to teach him to hunt, so that he can enjoy what might be otherwise tense jungle pursuits. Children choose to go on lengthy collecting trips with a congenial grandmother, who is not their own. On the other hand, a man usually does not share a garden and its work with his brother-in-law, because men do not banter with their brothers-in-law about the earthy matters usual to their humour – repartee about the breaking of wind ('you are blowing out your father-in-law'), or things of sexual interest. The in-law relationship between men is not as comfortable as other relationships, and thus a brother-in-law may well misinterpret what is meant to be light-hearted joking and repartee. Women, however, often tend their gardens with a sister-in-law, whose company they enjoy almost as much as their sisters'. Although the content of daily work is often gender-specific, men and women do carefully coordinate their tasks, and cooperate in many of them – the preparing of game for cooking, the making of tools for vegetable processing.

One of the most telling examples in the ethnography of Amazonia is David Thomas's description of the joking of men and women among the Pemon (a people neighbouring on the Piaroa). Thomas tells how they bantered over who was more important to the productive process, men or women:

> The discussion started out with the brother avowing that meat was really important food, and that it was, after all, the men who brought in the meat. But who, his sister shot back at him, prepares the manioc cakes and *cachiri* [beer] that give the men the strength to go out and hunt? And who, the brother replied in turn, cuts the forest so that the manioc can be planted? and who, the sister and her sister-in-law asked, tends the plots so that the manioc will not be swamped with weeds, and who brings it home and grates, squeezes, and bakes it? . . . Round and round it went, for the space of half an hour or so, till finally the discussion left off in a few joking barbs and the grudging admission on both sides that one thing supported another, *ad infinitum*.
>
> (D. Thomas 1982: 91–2)

It was the humour of the repartee that intrigued Thomas (op. cit., p. 92), and its outcome. No one could be topped. There was always a comeback. There is an edge to much of the humour of the indigenous Guianas, whether among the Piaroa, or their neighbours, the Pemon and the Yanomami.

Certainly for the Piaroa, there are general, but crucial, guidelines to the expression of humour and laughter. A person only works with those with whom one can have an easy bantering relationship. There is therefore the need for *trust* between partners of an activity, and if two people do not emotionally trust each other they will not willingly work together (cf. Alès, this volume). Also, earthy banter is not really appropriate with a parent or parent-in-law, and this is perhaps one reason that young men tend to shun garden work and other labour that demands the company of their elders. Men become fully productive when they have their own children and are of an age themselves to master the adult skills for living, and therefore can be equals with other men in their work. It is then that they can enjoy work by conjoining it with easy play. There is a discipline required of the use of humour, for a person must be careful about the context of humour, and be sensitive to whether banter will bring enjoyment or give offence. There is a code of decorum to their humour, and thus laughter should not be overly disruptive or excessive. The raucous laughter of children may offend the sacred mountains and waterfalls, who might retaliate with illness and other troubles. Conviviality is an ethical value intrinsic to Piaroa sociality, but it also has its dangers.

The power of jokes and the work of myth

The idea that jokes have power is more than likely usual to most peoples, and it is also the case that the potency of joking and laughter may be variously received. Mary Douglas has noted (1973: 14) that, 'in any of a number of social systems the idea of loud vociferous laughter may be unseemly in polite company. But what counts as loud and vociferous may vary greatly', as too, we might add, what is considered 'polite'. Laughter almost always has its limits, although their boundaries may vary greatly. It seems from the literature that the Araweté are much noisier in laughter than the Piaroa – while the Trio are more quiet (cf. Rivière, this volume) and the Yanomami more aggressive (cf. Lizot 1985). Certainly the Piaroa have placed fewer boundaries than we do upon laughter's place. For instance, they see slapstick humour as essential to the success of any shared physical effort. They do not separate work from play because they recognise the *social* side of work (cf. Passes, this volume). Because their stress is upon work as a social matter that serves a social purpose (the feeding and growing of people), working alongside other people must be socially good, and therefore emotionally pleasurable. At the same time the 'high conviviality' of festival time is also valued, when there is a 'no holds barred' approach to sociability, which would be more in keeping with the particular definition of conviviality in English, one that is usually induced through the pleasures of inebriation, as well as good company (cf. the note on 'conviviality' in the Preface to this volume, and the Introduction; also see the chapters by Rivière and Santos-Granero). However, because of its dangers such high conviviality must be short-lived. The Piaroa recognise that the humour so important to the *everyday* process of living requires the use of the intellect and practical judgement; it should not give expression only to laughter which is 'felt' as might happen at moments of collective euphoria (cf. Rivière, this volume).

Although the social benefits of humour for Amazonian people are clear, the importance for them of the play of jokes can be more deeply understood when it is placed within the wider context of cosmology. It is not sufficient merely to say that the Piaroa do not like out-of-control laughter, that it offends their code of decorum. With this we would only have a modicum of understanding. The emphasis they place upon the power of laughter in creating a desirable state of sociability would be trivialised, but what would also be missed would be the significant role of myth in framing the experience of joking and laughter. The imagination and reason that centres their affective life of living in communities would go unnoticed. What the Piaroa treasure, and what the myths in unexpected ways underline, is *the quality* of their affective life (cf. Echeverri, Londoño-Sulkin, Santos-Granero, this volume). As we will see, while the Piaroa logic is that convivial emotions must be felt, they also must be *thought*.

The Piaroa recognise an illness of minor madness called *k'iraeu*, which can become symptomatic in various ways, one being crazy (or unmastered) laughter. Children and young people tend to be prone to this symptom. Another symptom is diarrhoea, which everyone can suffer, but it is especially serious for children, and yet another is sexual promiscuity, or 'monkey urine madness', as it is called, a danger for adults. Thus the illness of *k'iraeu* can manifest itself as excessive laughter, diarrhoea, or promiscuity. For the sake of social tranquillity and personal health the illness must be withdrawn from its victim through shamanic means. It is obvious that each of these illnesses is associated with a particular bodily orifice, and what these diseases have in common is that they all have to do with disorders of the bodily orifices, and their excessive use (or, excessive openness, as Lévi-Strauss (1969: 135–6) would explain). To understand the complexity of the associations between these illnesses of the various bodily orifices we must turn to myth, where the *social* origins of the forms of the madness of *k'iraeu* are also explained.

The hilarity of some of the scenes the myth teller unfolds dramatically is conspicuous when listening to the mythic vignettes, but it is also a humour that is difficult to translate out of the context of their own use of language and the cultural setting. The words of the myth teller, usually a shaman, are much stronger, more interesting and more comic, than any that I will use in this text (but see Overing 1986 for more of the flavour). An apt telling of the myth is always supported by mimicry and pantomime, through gestures of the body, face and hands, all a performance central to the ludic effectiveness of the myth (cf. Driessen 1997). As I have mentioned, ribald humour is an integral aspect of the telling of myths. There is good reason for the incorporation of the scatological and the bawdy, as there also is for the inclusion of the strongest swear words in Piaroa language, words too robust to be used in ordinary lay speech. These words, used in the public speech of the skilled shaman (as for instance for the interesting private parts of the promiscuous female who later became the supreme deity, and the enormous ones of her brothers), play an important part in the potency of their mythic language, but they must be left for the most part to the reader's imagination. It is our decorum that academic writing will not overly use such robust phrases.

I shall begin with the origin of *k'iraeu* as crazy laughter, and turn later to the origin of promiscuity and diarrhoea. The myth teller, a powerful shaman whose Spanish name was Jose Luis, entitled this vignette as here:

Howler Monkey looked for laughter not sleep

The creator gods could not sleep because there was no night, only day.
The sun hadn't gone to the other side of the earth because it was stuck
against a mountain. The creator gods went to the Rock of Black Liquid
(Yuri'do), a mountain and the house of the Grandfather of Sleep. They
went with Howler Monkey (Hichu), who was still a man. This is before
he became transformed into Howler Monkey. They all went to the
Rock of Black Liquid to ask their Grandfather for sleep. He presented
the box of sleep to them, and the creator gods, Buok'a and Wahari, took
it. But Howler Monkey refused the gift, saying that he only wanted
'laughter craziness', *k'iraeu*. 'I came to get *k'iraeu*', he said. So the Grandfather of Sleep told him that he had a little on top of his house. Howler
Monkey tried to climb up the [mountain] house to get it, but the beams
were so slippery that he slid down, flattening out the end of his private
member in the process. His companions, Buok'a and Wahari, *laughed at
him* [a laughter that will prove significant].

Howler Monkey watched them laughing at him, and remarked,
'I should be looking for laughter, and not listening to you!' The Old
Grandfather replied that Monkey had already caught *k'iraeu*, for it had
been in the beam of the house that he slid down. So Monkey told the
creator gods, 'I'll give you "Laughter Craziness" too. Which way do
you want to laugh?', he asked, 'men together over women? or women
together over men?' They did not want either, but wanted instead to be
able to laugh *with* women, not *at* them.

And this was the birth of *k'iraeu* , crazy laughter, as humans suffer it
today. Wahari gave it to the Piaroa. It is when men laugh together over
women, and women laugh together over men.

The story continues:

> The creator gods, Wahari and Buok'a, left for their own home, and on
> the way they came across a tree with a good fruit, *turí*. Wahari *ordered*
> Howler Monkey to climb up the tree to get the fruit for them. Howler
> was a little crazy by this time, with his 'laughter madness'(*k'iraeu*), so
> once up the tree he urinated on Wahari and Buok'a, and yelled, '*here*
> comes the fruit!' Howler then defecated on Wahari. Wahari had been
> standing under the tree, looking up, waiting for the treat of sweet fruit!
> But, being hit in the face by the uneatable, he suggested to his brother,
> Buok'a, 'let's climb the tree ourselves, and find another branch just for
> us, because they [Howler had transformed into a group of monkeys] are
> *laughing* at us!'

The episode ends with Monkey becoming lost, and never returning to the
company of the gods.

Now we may ask, what is significant in this myth on the origins of 'Crazy Laughter' illness? It is obvious that crazy laughter is understood to be disruptive of ordinary social relations, even for such simple tasks as the collecting of fruit. However, in the telling there is also an attribution of blame. Who is at fault in this myth? Is it the crazy Howler Monkey? It is Howler Monkey who asks for and receives the illness of Crazy Laughter, and who then passes it on to the creator gods, but he is not the culprit. Culpability is not where you might expect it, for Howler Monkey is in fact understood to be the victim.[6] Although the myth most certainly serves as a lesson on the proper expression of emotions, it is a tutoring that has its subtlety. Fault lies with the creator gods, for it is they who begin the mayhem through their own thoughtless emotional reactions. And this is a pattern that runs through all Piaroa myth where it is consistently explained that all misfortunes that human beings today must suffer took root in the irresponsible emotional reactions of the creator gods. In this case the primary, instigating misdeed was thoughtless mockery of the worst sort. Notice that Howler Monkey decided to give the illness of *k'iraeu* to the creator gods only after they had *mocked* him by laughing at his painful injury. The consequence of their crass lack of sympathy was retaliation, *which they had asked for*! There is yet more evidence.

Later in the story, note that instead of throwing fruit to the creator gods, Howler Monkey defecates and urinates on them. He is said thereby to mock ('laugh at') them. The bodily orifices are a key to understanding this symbolic play, for Howler Monkey's unsocial laughter is expressed not through the mouth, but ludicrously through the wrong bodily orifices, because he is suffering Crazy Laughter illness. But even so he is not the instigator of this sequence. He was but responding to Wahari's arrogance of 'ordering' him up the fruit tree. In Piaroa etiquette no one has the right to command another to do anything. The major lesson of the myth is that thoughtless mockery and arrogance creates victims who then set into motion a further sequence of socially irresponsible reactions. This is why a man must not tease his brother-in-law who can so easily interpret a joke meant in lightness as one made without good intent.

With the following mythic vignettes, we find again a dance of unsocial emotions and disorderly orifices where the dangers of anger, arrogance and resentment are each given their (laughable) turn. The next episode is about the origin of Monkey Urine Madness, or the illness of sexual promiscuity, which is a second symptom of *k'iraeu*. It involves the relationship between the creator god, Wahari, and his sister, the goddess Cheheru, and tells how she came to suffer the plight of Monkey Urine Madness. The Howler Monkeys reappear. Here they receive their animal form of monkey. The myth is also about the creation of perfume, which is to the Piaroa mind a disruptive love magic. The structure of the myth is similar to the preceding one, in that we find repeated a command being made, and a command being violated (or interpreted as so being).

The Birth of Howler Monkeys and Monkey Urine Madness

The brother and sister creator gods, Wahari and Cheheru, hold a feast at their house. Many foreigners come, beautifully decorated, painted and perfumed. *All* parts of their bodies are perfumed! Wahari, worried about his sister's virtue, commands her to be careful with her drink. He then proceeds to drink to the full with the women visitors, and deep in the house, where there is laughter and where love affairs go on, he spends delightful time with them.

Cheheru also likes their visitors, and she drinks a lot because she likes these men who are so nicely perfumed. She nevertheless remains chaste, following, she thought, the intent of her brother's commands.

Later, furious with her brother for his hypocrisy, Cheheru refuses to speak to him. She thinks bitterly about how the men had spoken so well to her. 'Let's go', they had said, and she had been stupid enough to refuse. Swinging in her hammock, she sings about her desire for the beautiful men; she sings about how she wants 'to make a monkey' [a consequential turn of phrase].

Wahari, in turn, becomes infuriated with Cheheru – she hadn't *listened* to him! So he mocks his sister: 'Why didn't you go off with these men?' He becomes so angry he throws her powers of sorcery to the Mountain of Sorcery, and tosses her there too. There, where she fell, she creates Howler Monkey, giving him his animal form. She becomes the 'Mother of Monkey', and she makes perfume there too. She creates the Craziness Disease of 'Monkey Urine Madness' (*k'iraeu*) – the illness of sexual promiscuity – which comes from the perfume she gave the monkeys. This perfume is in fact the monkeys' own urine that she made for them. The crazy monkeys use their own urine as a love potion.

Cheheru then leads a wandering life, as too does Wahari. She visits one group of foreigners after another, creating their perfume for them, making love, creating more monkeys. She even makes perfume for the white people, the kind that comes in liquid form, in bottles. Wahari announces that the Piaroa who live afterwards would also go crazy if they used perfume: they too would suffer from Monkey Urine Madness. They would go crazy and make love with their brother or sister, with all their friends, and with foreigners.

In this episode, the fault is more clearly stated than in the first. Again the culprit is Wahari. He arrogantly orders Cheheru to behave, while he himself plays as he pleases. He then responds angrily, mockingly and then even aggressively to her justifiable reactions of desire and resentment. The result is Cheheru's promiscuous wandering and the creation of Monkey Urine Madness, but she is nevertheless the victim of this story – just as Howler Monkey was in the previous vignette when he was made angry by Wahari's thoughtless mockery and arrogant command.

In a final episode on the origins of the illness of *k'iraeu*, the origins of the symptom of diarrhoea are told. The setting underscores the association of the onset of *k'iraeu* (in this case as diarrhoea) with the thoughtless expression of feelings, a lack of respect for appropriate conviviality. It is the story of the birth of a boy by the name of Wiritsa and his relationship with his father, the creator god, Wahari. The setting for the story is Wahari's madness after he received his mighty sorcery powers for creation. He arrogantly proclaims his own greatness by announcing that he is now the 'Master of the Rivers and Rapids', the 'Master of the World'. Becoming obsessed with his own importance he turns his back on his own kinsmen, to become a wandering man:

> Back at home, his sister, Cheheru, in retaliation, uses her sorcery to seduce him, her own brother. This is a strange event that he won't remember. Some time later, when Wahari drops by Cheheru's house he is shocked to find a young boy there [Cheheru had miraculously grown their son]. This is Wiritsa, but Wahari doesn't know who he is. The boy becomes curious about Wahari's hunting equipment, and Wahari *orders* him not to touch it, as it is dangerous. The boy *doesn't listen* and handles the blowgun, the bows and arrows; it is with this touch that he receives diarrhoea. Wahari announces to Wiritsa that he would now be the original source for the illness of diarrhoea, he'd be called the 'Father of Diarrhoea'.
>
> The next day the boy follows Wahari on the hunt, calling to him, 'papa, papa!'. Wahari, irritated, tells him he is wrong, to go away and stop pestering him, and never again to call him 'papa', but Wiritsa finally persuades Wahari that he is indeed his father because they look just like each other.
>
> Wahari is shocked and infuriated, and strikes his son through sorcery with such force that he is thrown stunned to a far-away place, and Wahari announces, 'Now you are the Master of Diarrhoea!'. Wahari thinks he has killed his son, and so goes off to the rapids, muttering that now that he has killed his son, he was going to kill fish. But the boy is alive. He creeps up behind Wahari, who is busy fishing, to say, 'hello papa, how are you?' Outraged, Wahari threatens to kill him. His son persuades him not to, suggesting that by killing him Wahari would at the same time be killing himself, as they have now the same hunting powers [from the boy's handling of Wahari's hunting equipment]. Wahari then decides to test the boy's hunting abilities, so he hands his bow and arrow to his son. Wahari *mocks* his son's lack of skill, until the boy shoots Wahari's arrow far up into the sky which in falling strikes a deer, which then becomes ill with diarrhoea. This diarrhoea, that the deer now gives people, is called the 'illness of Wahari's arrow'.

The pattern should by now be clear. Here the myth focuses specifically upon familial relations, and the appalling effects of the denial of kinship (cf. Belaunde, this volume). Wahari becomes so outrageously arrogant that he neglects his own people – so much so that he wanders with foreign women, and then commits incest with his own sister – a ludicrous scene in the telling. His shock upon discovering that he had done so serves him right. But instead of remorse he is foolishly angry with his own son, he mocks him, refuses kinship with him, and even attempts to kill him – all a reflection of his unmastered emotions. His only response to his realisation that he had probably killed his son is to go and kill some fish, a ridiculous response. Wahari's out-of-control emotions are crucial mythic operators, a signal of his lack of sociality and the dire consequences that must follow. His neglect of familial conviviality leads to the birth of the illness of diarrhoea, yet another form of *k'iraeu*. A proper father teaches his son, and finds no need to command.

In all three of the mythic episodes we find that the display of dangerous emotions results in a disturbed sociality, made specific through the onset in a victim of one of the three symptoms of the illness of *k'iraeu*: i.e. excessive laughter, excessive sex or excessive defecation. The demonstration of mockery, anger or arrogance is the most important of all mythic operators, for it gives evidence of an asociality, a contempt and lack of respect, that causes significant others to lose mastery over their own bodily orifices (cf. Belaunde, this volume). Such disturbance in turn interferes with the creation of the good health and daily goodwill between those who live together, where good sociality, physical health and proper sex are all prerequisites to their collective existence (cf. Echeverri and Londoño-Sulkin, this volume). Bad laughter and angry words disturb the high morale that is so necessary to the viability of the relatively egalitarian relations through which Amazonian community life is lived (cf. most of the other contributions to this volume).

This has been about 'bad laughter'. Let us return to 'good laughter', and its relation to the 'magic of words'.

The magic of words and the play of the ludicrous, a return to good laughter

Good laughter is essential to the health of the community. As the first mythic episode indicates, good laughter is when men and women can laugh together, rather than at each other. The Piaroa leader must be a master of laughter, and nowhere is this more evident than in the telling of myths. The absurdities of myth are good theatre. Because of their play on the ludicrous, the words of the myth give pleasure. They also have their force, these words, as good magical words must. The Piaroa recognise the power of words, and this includes the everyday ordinary use of them (cf. Jamieson, Passes, this volume). They label the sounds of village laughter and talking, when heard from afar in the forest, as *huruhuru*. Also, in the telling of myths, the setting is often an approach to a village, which is recognised through the sounds of *huruhuru*, people's voices and laughter. Literally translated this word means 'jaguar's roar'. The same word is used for a sorcerer's might. There is then a wizardry to words. Pleasure in them is not only conducive to good health, but also to the fecundity that allows for the creation of good food and healthy children (cf. Echeverri, this volume). Good, strong words have a positive effect upon the body, just as bad words have ill effect. Good words lead to a laughter that is also intellectually appreciated, while bad words just act (irrationally) upon the senses. The felt and intellectual sides of humour are *equally valued,* but they must go hand in hand to provide wizardry sufficiently powerful to create a healthy community life. The Piaroa would agree with Lévi-Strauss (1971: 678) that the operations of the senses have an intellectual aspect, but only insofar as one is talking about an *appropriate* operation of the senses. It is their understanding that the joining of the senses with thought is a learned response that must be constantly invigilated through personal reflection (cf. Belaunde, Jamieson, Kidd, Lagrou, Londoño-Sulkin, this volume). Piaroa social philosophy is more akin to a social psychology than a code of rules and regulations (cf. most other contributions to this volume). Myth telling among the Piaroa is best understood as an exploration of this social psychology. It is all about the creation of a feeling of well-being among those who live together, and what happens when this fails.

Frazer (1960), in *The Golden Bough*, insists that magical words, being all about the control of natural forces, are therefore false words that have no relationship to reality. You cannot control natural forces with words, he says. I am arguing that the magical words of Piaroa myths have a good deal of efficacy because they have first and foremost to do with *human* forces. They are about the difficulties of creating the relations of trust that are so necessary to the successful carrying out of the everyday conditions of an Amazonian community of relationships. *Human* forces can be productive, conducive to convivial living, but they also can be absurd, ludicrous and destructive.

The generative power of bawdy words

We return to the puzzle of why the sacred myths are filled with bawdy language. To answer this question we must ask what is life about for these Amazonian people? What is most important to them? Life for them is about the events that surround them in daily life. We tend to forget such daily concerns, or do not put them as the highest priorities – those of giving birth, the growing of crops and hunting for food, the preparation of food for those with whom you live. Their priorities also include the suffering of falling ill, and of experiencing death. For Amerindians, all these things are what life is. To live a productive human life is about being fertile, which is to be taken in the more general sense of referring first and foremost to those capabilities of creating relationships with others that are conducive to a healthy environment in which to raise children, which includes the existence of a healthy set of adults (cf. Belaunde, Echeverri, Gow, Londoño-Sulkin, this volume). The primary duties of the leader have to do with this fertility: they must protect and enable the fertility of their people, as they also do for the land and the rivers the people use. Thus the myths the leader tells are about the conditions for human fecundity, which include their dangers as well as their social possibilities (cf. Echeverri, this volume). The myths are in the main concerned with the fecundity that is engendered through conviviality, which only human beings are capable of achieving, and they talk about the dangers of the neglect of such conviviality. The leader, being a specialist on fertility, is also a specialist on conviviality.

The bawdiness of the myths has partly to do with the contrast between dangerous and beneficial fertility. The ribaldry also has to do with the myths being the place for 'technical' talk. This technicality is from the Piaroa view, and it is the 'technical talk' of the powerful shaman. We must, however, contrast our own specialist talk about fertility with theirs. Ours is 'technical', we might think, with all those Latin words that are used to describe the physical aspects of the body and bodily processes. These are 'clean' words, we might argue; they are 'neutral' words, and as such have no emotive connotation. For us, 'neutral' means cleansed of the irrelevant emotional (ribald, fun, dangerous) side of human procreation. The magic of our Latin words is that they are 'scientific' words, and thereby have hard, rational, scientific efficacy. In contrast, the words of the Piaroa specialist are not neutral, and are never meant to be. The shaman's myth is all about emotion – wrong emotions, right emotions, ridiculous emotions. Dangerous emotions, those expressed without the clothing of thought, are ruinous to sociality, and therefore also destructive of human fecundity, while the expression of convivial emotions is conducive to it.

In unfolding the dangerous, the myth teller uses the dangerous, strong, comic words to strike home the message that human beings can act absurdly, outrageously, destructively, that is, without thought. The irresponsible creator gods made this absurdity an inevitable possibility of human conduct, and it is the leader's job to tell just how ludicrous and destructive this is. In this egalitarian culture, arrogance, contempt and anger are placed firmly on the side of the ridiculous, the asocial – and also the infertile, or wrongfully fertile, when bodily parts and orifices become ridiculous, obscene, grotesque, as happened with the creator gods and those with whom they interacted. The shaman's concern is a holistic one. The first desire is for the audience to laugh, a sign itself of the efficacy of the magical words as they play their role in facilitating the health of the people. Also, the technical words about physical aspects of the human body are always shown to be only part of the equation, for these technical smutty words are always signs of emotions that have gone awry. The emotive side, and the extent to which good laughter and the intellect have played their role, are of greater importance than the specific physical parts in the understanding of human fertility. It is for this reason that the technical, efficacious words of the chants are also bawdy.

I conclude by making a plea for the development of a perspicacious anthropology of humour. There are many reasons for anthropologists having taken the 'art of play' away from the everyday. There are our own notions of decorum, and our scholarly emphasis upon a certain sort of intellect (the unconscious operations of analogic thought), and our neglect of embodied thought and practice (cf. Belaunde, Jamieson, Kidd, Lagrou, Londoño-Sulkin, Rivière, this volume); there is our own lack of regard for folly, and our separation of work and play (cf. Passes, this volume); there is our own lack of respect for the volitional, conscious, acting, feeling, eating, mating, birthing, dying, fully experiencing subject (cf. Gow, this volume). There is also our distinction between thinking and living, and our idea that conscious thought pertaining to practice always deceives. For all these reasons, and more, we need to take the advice of our cultural historians and recognise laughter as an important cultural and social matter. There is a climate growing within anthropology to return to Dilthey's formulation of the subject matter of the human sciences, namely, to consider first and foremost *lived* experience, which of course includes thought, but thought charged with volition and emotion, with value-judgements, and specific aesthetics of being in this world (cf. most other contributions to this volume).[7] We need to begin to understand the particular rules of decorum, which vary greatly in time and place, that relate to the propriety of humour and laughter. In short we need to understand the codes of civility relating to the ludic, and the reasons for the tremendous variation between them in allowing for openness in humour's expression.

Notes

1 I have touched on the topic of the ludic in myth among the Piaroa (see Overing 1985, 1986), and discussed briefly the importance of wordplay in their everyday life. An earlier version of the present chapter was given as the Frazer Lecture, in Liverpool, 20 November 1998.

2 See Henk Driessen (1997) for a summary of the handful of works in anthropology on the topic of humour and its role in social relationships. See Mary Douglas (1975) for one of the more interesting discussions in the anthropological literature.

3 *The Compact Edition of the Oxford English Dictionary* (1971: 1579) defines laughter as having 'the emotion (of mirth, amusement, scorn) which is expressed by laughing'. Laughter is 'to manifest the combination of bodily phenomena (spasmodic utterance of inarticulate sounds, facial distortion, shaking of the sides, etc.) which forms the instinctive expression of mirth or of the sense of something ludicrous'. Laughter in this view is a distorted, instinctive bodily state associated with the 'utterance of inarticulate sounds'. The act of laughter is then, as a first definition in the English language, placed on the side of animality, and not sociality.

4 On the importance of 'the everyday' to the understanding of Amazonian sociality, see Overing 1999, and the Introduction to the present work.
5 The Amazonian 'conviviality of the everyday' is very similar in flavour to the conviviality that Illich champions in his plea for fundamental changes in the inter-personal social practices relating to work within modern industrial nations.
6 It was Dell Hymes's insights in *In Vain I Tried to Tell You* (1981) that taught me to look for such subtleties in the sequences of response.
7 See Victor Turner's discussion (1982) of the importance of Dilthey to the anthropo-logical approach. Also see Brunner (1984) for the discussions by a group of anthropologists who have the desire to 'open up' anthropology in these directions. For a set of more recent papers of great relevance on the topic see Brady (1991).

References

Bateson, G. (1958) *Naven*, 2nd edition, Stanford, Calif.: Stanford University Press.
Boon, J. (1984) 'Folly, Bali, and anthropology, or satire across cultures', in E. Bruner (ed.) *Text, Play, and Story: The Construction and Reconstruction of Self and Society*, Prospect Heights, Ill.: Waveland.
Brady, I. (ed.) (1991) *Anthropological Poetics*, Savage, Md.: Rowman & Littlefield.
Bremmer, J. (1997) 'Jokes, jokers, and jokebooks in ancient Greek culture', in J. Bremmer and H. Roodenburg (eds) *A Cultural History of Humour*, Cambridge: Polity Press.
Bremmer, J. and Roodenburg, H. (1997a) Preface, in J. Bremmer and H. Roodenburg (eds) *A Cultural History of Humour*, Cambridge: Polity Press.
—— (1997b) 'Introduction: humour and history', in J. Bremmer and H. Roodenburg (eds) *A Cultural History of Humour*, Cambridge: Polity Press.
Bruner, E. (1984) 'Introduction: the opening up of anthropology', in E. Bruner (ed.) *Text, Play, and Story: The Construction and Reconstruction of Self and Society*, Prospect Heights, Ill.: Waveland Press.
Burke, P. (1997) 'Frontiers of the comic in Early Modern Italy', in J. Bremmer and H. Roodenburg (eds) *A Cultural History of Humour*, Cambridge: Polity Press.
Clastres, P. (1977) *Society against the State*, trans. Robert Hurley, Oxford: Basil Blackwell.
Compact Edition of the Oxford English Dictionary (1971) Glasgow and New York Oxford University Press.
Douglas, M. (1973) *Natural Symbols: Explorations in Cosmology*, Harmondsworth: Penguin.
—— (1975) *Implicit Meanings: Essays in Anthropology*, London and Boston: Routledge & Kegan Paul.
Driessen, H. (1997) 'Humour, laughter and the field: reflections from anthropology', in J. Bremmer and H. Roodenburg (eds) *A Cultural History of Humour*, Cambridge: Polity Press.
Fernandes, J. (1984) 'Convivial attitudes: the ironic play of tropes in an international kayak festival in Northern Spain', in E. Bruner (ed.) *Text, Play, and Story: The Construction and Reconstruction of Self and Society*, Prospect Heights, Ill.: Waveland Press.
Frazer, J. (1960) *The Golden Bough* (Vol. 1, Abridged Edition), New York: Macmillan.
Goldman, I. (1963) *The Cubeo*, Urbana: University of Illinois Press.

Hobart, M. (1995) 'As I lay laughing: encountering global knowledge in Bali', in R. Fardon (ed.) *Counterworks: Managing the Diversity of Knowledge*, London: Routledge.

Hymes, D. (1981) *'In Vain I Tried to Tell You'*, Philadelphia: University of Pennsylvania Press.

Illich, I. (1973) *Tools for Conviviality*, London and New York: Calder & Boyars.

Le Goff, J. (1997) 'Laughter in the Middle Ages', in J. Bremmer and H. Roodenburg (eds) *A Cultural History of Humour*, Cambridge: Polity Press.

Lévi-Strauss, C. (1967) 'The social and psychological aspects of chieftainship in a primitive tribe: the Nambikwara of Northwestern Mato Grosso', in R. Cohen and J. Middleton (eds) *Comparative Political Systems*, Garden City, NY: The Natural History Press.

—— (1969) *The Raw and the Cooked: Introduction to a Science of Mythology*, trans. J. and D. Weightman, New York and Evanston: Harper & Row.

—— (1971) *The Naked Man: Introduction to a Science of Mythology, Volume 4*, trans. J. and D. Weightman, New York and Cambridge: Harper & Row.

Lizot, J. (1985) *Tales of the Yanamami*, Cambridge: Cambridge University Press.

Overing, J. (1985) 'There is no end of evil: the guilty innocents and their fallible god', in D. Parkin (ed.) *The Anthropology of Evil*, Oxford: Basil Blackwell.

—— (1986) 'Men control women? The "Catch 22" in gender analysis', *International Journal of Moral and Social Studies*, 1(2): 135–56.

—— (1989) 'The aesthetics of production: the sense of community among the Cubeo and Piaroa', *Dialectical Anthropology* 14: 159–75.

—— (1999) 'Elogio do cotidiano: a confiança e a arte de vida social em uma comunidade Amazônica' (In praise of the everyday: trust and the art of social living in an Amazonian community), *Mana* 5(1): 81–108.

Overing Kaplan, J. (1975) *The Piaroa, a People of the Orinoco Basin*, Oxford: Clarendon.

Rivière, P. (1984) *Individual and Society in Guiana: A Comparative Study of Amerindian Social Organization*, Cambridge: Cambridge University Press.

Thomas, D. (1982) *Order without Government: The Society of the Pemon Indians of Venezuela*, Urbana: University of Illinois Press.

Thomas, K. (1977) 'The place of laughter in Tudor and Stuart England', *Times Literary Supplement*, 21 January, pp. 77–81.

Turner, V. (1982) *From Ritual to Theatre: the Human Seriousness of Play*, New York: Performing Arts Journal Publications.

Viveiros de Castro, E. (1992) *From the Enemy's Point of View: Humanity and Divinity in an Amazonian Society*, trans. Catherine Howard, Chicago and London: University of Chicago Press.

Chapter 4

Compassion, anger and broken hearts

Ontology and the role of language in the Miskitu lament

Mark Jamieson

> Alas, mother, poor mother! alas, mother, where have you gone?
>   Here are your children crying for you;
> Yesterday we were talking together, but now you are lying there.
> Alas, mother, did you go from among us in anger?
>   Did we not love you?
> Your husband sits outside with his head hung down.
> Here the women are sitting with their heads covered,
>   All for love of you.
>   But you have abandoned us.
> Alas, that I shall never see your face again;
> That I shall never hear your voice again!
>
> (Bell 1989: 91)

The text given above is the English translation of a Miskitu lament from the mid-nineteenth century. In 1992, in Kakabila (the Miskitu village in which I conducted fieldwork), I attended the mortuary rites for a 60-year-old woman and, as her coffin was lowered into a grave dug by her daughters' husbands and other male affines, I heard her eldest daughter Amanda cry out a lament which in many respects was identical. This lament was produced at the exact moment the coffin was being lowered into the grave, a very public moment in which almost the entire village and several visitors were present and focused on this scene. As was customary, a close female relative (in this case Loyola, Amanda's mother's sister's daughter) was on hand; first, to prevent her kinswoman throwing herself into her mother's grave; second, to cover the grieving daughter's head with a shawl (a symbol of illness or vulnerability); and third, to lead her away from the scene of her distress. At this moment a Creole woman from the regional capital Bluefields turned to two fellow Bluefields women and whispered in English, 'she did all the work', implying that the other two surviving daughters should have put on a customary demonstration of grief equivalent to Amanda's. In this chapter I am not concerned with the question of why Amanda's sisters did not cry laments as she had done, or whether it was usual in Miskitu villages for more than one kinswoman to have done so, but rather to interrogate the apparent claim by this Creole woman that such expressions of emotion are 'work' and, as such, culturally constructed before they are felt. The evidence I will consider is both sociocultural and linguistic.[1]

'Living good', compassion and emotions

Kakabila is a small Nicaraguan Miskitu- and English-speaking village with fewer than three hundred people, situated in the Pearl Lagoon basin on Nicaragua's Caribbean coast. Like many other communities in this low-lying region Kakabila is a nucleated village sitting on top of a bank, surrounded on one side by the lagoon's edge and on three sides by dense 'bush' (secondary rainforest) and swamp. All transport to and from the village is therefore waterborne, mostly by 'dory' (dugout canoe with sheet sail) or 'motor' (dugout canoe with in-board motor), and it is extremely diffi-cult to walk to even the closest villages of Raitipura and Brown Bank, neither of which is more than five miles distant. Isolated from other people by geography, it is not surprising to learn that Kakabila people consider them-selves to constitute a bounded community.

Kakabila people have a strong sense of the right way to be with other people, a notion expressed in the English phrase 'living good' (*pain iwaia* in Miskitu), and this is best exemplified by relations with fellow Kakabila people. As I noted above, the geography of the village provides people with a convenient means of imagining inclusiveness.[2] Kakabila, for villagers, is thus a well-defined moral universe and as such is often compared and contrasted (usually favourably) with other moral communities in the region, most of which are similarly defined by geography. This is not to say that Kakabila people consider their relations with people in other villages and communities unimportant, but rather to emphasise that Kakabila as a place is very much thought by villagers to embody a shared understanding of what it means to 'live good', in other words, convivially, with other people.

'Living good' in Kakabila is usually represented as not 'rowing, fighting or cursing' (all manifestations of 'living bad' – *saura iwaia*) with one's neigh-bours. In short it means living frictionlessly with one's neighbours, an ideal to which all village people, at least theoretically, aspire.[3] 'Living good' also means the absence of politics,[4] give and take, negotiation, hustle and com-promise (all of which provide potential threats to harmony), and the presence of an atmosphere in which villagers exercise concern for one another's well-being. Kakabila people like to believe that they are, by and large, successful in 'living good' together in this way and therefore represent Kakabila to themselves and outsiders as a community whose members do live in harmony with one another in contrast to other communities supposedly riven by strife and disharmony. Kakabila people, in other words, 'pull together' with one another, not 'against' each other.

Kakabila prides itself on its harmony and its members' concern for one another. A death, therefore, such as that of Amanda's mother, is a matter of significance for everybody (cf. Alès, Belaunde, Gow, Lagrou, this volume). The tranquillity of the community is threatened as people consider both the possibility of the death being caused by sorcery ('science' or *sika*) and the likelihood of the deceased's 'ghost' (*wlasa*) seeking revenge or provoking mischief among the living. In other words, there are anxieties about the well-being of the village. Furthermore there are concerns for the well-being of the most severely bereaved, especially for those described as *taya* or 'family' and for the spouse (*maia*).[5] These concerns – directed towards one another as fellow villagers, and towards the surviving spouse and *taya* of the deceased – are described with the word *latwan*, a term which captures many of the meanings projected by the English words 'pain', 'love' and 'compassion' (cf. particularly Gow, this volume).

Latwan is, apparently, a rather versatile word, as evidenced by the fact that it can be used to refer to the pain associated with a backache, compassion for an obviously disabled person and the feeling engendered by romantic infatuation. It is, in other words, used to describe physical, mental and emotional states of being. However, *latwan*'s versatility is not so striking when one comes to consider linguistic evidence for the proposition that Kakabila people do not make clear-cut distinctions between mind and body or between physical and mental states. I will for now provide two examples for this (though more are given below). When Kakabila people wish to say that they forget, they use the expression *aya tiwan* meaning 'my liver is lost'. This is because the liver is understood to be the locus of one's memory. Similarly when they wish to say that they get angry, they use the expression *yang kupi baiwisa* meaning 'my heart is breaking'. This is because the heart is understood to be the site of one's composure. Those states usually described in the West as mental and/or emotional states are thus, for Kakabila, located in one's physical being.

Of course, it is possible to find similar examples in English. For example, the English expression 'to break one's heart' means to be deeply saddened. This, however, is generally understood to be a metaphor in no way indicating that English-speakers in the West consider the heart to be the site of one's contentment. Examples like this, however, need not invalidate my understanding of the ontological status of these Kakabila expressions. Up until the emergence and popularisation of psychology in the early part of this century, similar expressions locating states of mind within the physical body were evidently understood by many people (not to mention phrenologists!) in entirely literal terms.[6] I have no problem, therefore, in believing that Kakabila people understand that there might be an intrinsic relation between particular physical organs on the one hand, and particular states of mind on the other, a view supported, I believe, by the evidence presented below.

The states of mind of others are, for Kakabila people, theoretically problematic. When asked to suggest motives and intentions for the actions of others, Kakabila people often say that they cannot possibly know, implying that it would be improper, even foolish, to guess.[7] The hearts (*kupia*) of others are, in the final analysis, closed to them, and even to ask what these might be is considered rude. One never, therefore, asks another what he or she is thinking (*lukaia*) but rather whether that person is in the act of thinking.[8] This gives the hearer the space to answer the question politely without elaborating if he or she feels so inclined. One is, however, entitled to speculate about the feelings of one's kin and, contextually, one's fellow community members (those with whom one 'lives good'), since the well-being of those close to oneself and one's own well-being are inextricably bound together. Because one wishes well for those with whom one 'lives good', it is legitimate to speculate on their experiences of love, compassion, pain, anger, remembering and forgetting. Similarly one's own experiences of love, compassion, pain, remembrance, as well as anger and forgetfulness, are likely to be directed towards these same people: those with whom one 'lives good' or convivially. In summary, Kakabila people's ruminations on states of mind are centred on those closest to them, especially those considered kin.

Emotions, parts of the body and kin are thus, for Kakabila people, co-constituents of a single ontological domain in which the first, emotions and other states of mind, are conceptually situated in the second, that is, various parts of the physical body, while at the same time only those pertaining to the third, one's kin, are deemed truly knowable.[9] Interestingly, this ontological articulation is represented linguistically in a rather peculiar and anthropologically intriguing aspect of Miskitu morphology.

The language of compassion

Like many languages, Miskitu marks possession with affixes selected to distinguish between first, second and third persons. In most instances these are as follows:

1st person -*ki*
2nd person -*kam*
3rd person -*ka*

The first-person -*ki* is affixed to nouns to mean 'mine' and 'our' in the exclusive sense, the second-person -*kam* is employed to mean 'your' in the singular and plural senses, while -*ka* is used to mean 'his', 'her', 'its', 'their' or 'our' in the inclusive sense.[10] This is demonstrated below using the Miskitu word *aras*.

aras (horse)
aras-ki   my, our (excl.) horse
aras-kam   your (sing. or plural) horse
aras-ka   his, her, its, their, our (incl.) horse

Now, the vast majority of nouns are marked for possession using *-ki*, *-kam* and *-ka*. In the CIDCA publication (1985, chapter three) these are referred to as 'Class 1' nouns. There is, however, an important group of nouns which employ other means of marking possession. These are the 'Class 2' nouns (ibid., chapter three). Class 2 nouns are distinctive in that where phonological conditions permit, they mark possession with either the infixes *-i-*, *-m-* and *-ø-* (no infix at all), the suffixes *-i*, *-am* and *-a*, or other forms whose variants are conditioned by the varying phonological environments offered by the Miskitu nouns.[11] Three examples are presented below.

latwan (pain, love, compassion)
la-i-twan   my, our (excl.) pain (love, compassion)
la-m-twan   your (sing. or plural) pain (love, compassion)
la-ø-twan (i.e. *latwan*) his, her, its, their, our (incl.) pain (love, compassion)

napa (tooth)
na-i-pa   my, our (excl.) tooth
na-m-pa   your (sing. or plural) tooth
na-ø-pa (i.e. *napa*)   his, her, its, their, our (incl.) tooth

tubani (sister's son, nephew)
tuban-i   my, our (excl.) sister's son
tuban-am   your (sing. or plural) sister's son
tuban-a   his, her, its, their, our (incl.) sister's son

The attentive reader will notice that these words, *latwan*, *napa* and *tubani* refer to an emotion (or state of mind), a part of the body, and a kinsperson, exactly the three categories (in Western ontologies) which I argue are closely linked in the Miskitu conceptual universe. To quote from *Miskitu bila aisanka: gramática miskita* (CIDCA, op. cit.) (where a good many other examples are given),

> If we concentrate our attention on . . . the list corresponding to Class 2, we can see that all the nouns included are kinship terms or words refer- ring to parts of the body. If we were to complete the list we would see that besides having to also include words referring to sentiments and sensations such as *latwan* (love) and *brinka* (wish), nearly all of the other nouns of the group would be entered into these two categories: parts of the body or kinship terms.
>
>   (ibid., p. 70, my translation from the Spanish)

Taking exceptions into consideration the authors then ask, 'what do kinship terms, words referring to parts of the body and words which describe sensations and sentiments have in common?' (ibid., p. 70, my translation). The answer, they claim, is to be found in a distinction between 'alienable possession' (*posesión alienable*) and 'inalienable possession' (*posesión inalienable*), the latter referring to those entities which cannot be lost, given, exchanged or sold to others (ibid., p. 71). Kin, parts of the body, sensations and sentiments (items in the Class 2 noun class) are all linguistically marked as 'things' which cannot be alienated from oneself, while other kinds of 'thing' (almost all in the Class 1 noun class) are linguistically marked as 'things' which conversely can.

First, a caveat must be considered. French and Spanish, for example, have noun classes which have been described as 'masculine' and 'feminine', but, as many authors on gender (in the linguistic sense) have written, this does not entail that Native speakers of these languages consider items in these classes to be intrinsically male or female (Corbett 1991). There are two answers to this. First, the terms 'masculine' and 'feminine' to describe the noun classes in French and Spanish are terms from studies of language, not popular ontology. Conceivably the distinction between the two classes might be understood in other ways that have yet to be understood properly. Second, and more significantly, the fact that noun classes in some languages are not given significance by their speakers does not mean that the same is true for other languages. In some languages noun class membership is flexible and the phenomenon of reassignment of nouns from one class to another is linguistically productive, thereby highlighting the importance of the classificatory character of each class. Consider, for example, the nineteen or so noun classes found in many of the Bantu languages, where switches of noun from one class to another (not possible in French or Spanish) are frequently used for pragmatic (often humorous) effect (Corbett, ibid., pp. 43–6, 48–9, et passim). Indeed speakers of Miskitu can, phonological conditions permitting, choose between two or more affixes to represent possession on Class 2 nouns, as the possible variants of the following example (all considered well-formed by Native speakers) demonstrate.

lapia (ritual birth friend)
(a) *la-m-pia*   your (sing. or plural) *lapia*   Class 2 infix -*m*-
(b) *lapi-am*   your (sing. or plural) *lapia*   Class 2 suffix -*am*
(c) *lapi-kam*   your (sing. or plural) *lapia*   Class 1 suffix -*kam*

In summary, the word *lapia* can be used with Class 1 or Class 2 affixes. The first two variants (a and b), both Class 2, however, connote greater intimacy between the addressee and his/her *lapia* than the third (c), which is Class 1. This, to my mind, shows that, as with many of the Bantu languages, subtle nuances or shifts in meaning can be produced by shifting nouns from one class to the other through the strategic use of particular affixes. Evidence for this idea also comes from the observation that sometimes people seem deliberately to use Class 2 nouns for effect.[12] One day in Kakabila, for example, I witnessed a small child ask an old woman, Kuka Libias, for something which her mother required. Kuka Libias did not have what this child asked for and, in having to deny him, addressed him indulgently as '*pla-i-sni*' (my youngest child), employing the constituents *plasni* (youngest child) and the Class 2 first-person infix *-i-*. Even though this particular child was not a member of Kuka Libias's 'family', she sought to mollify him with the most inclusive term of address she could think of,[13] and did so employing the Class 2 infix rather than the equally possible, though less intimate, Class 1 alternative, *plasni-ki*.

In characterising Class 1 and Class 2 nouns as grammatically marked for 'alienable possession' and 'inalienable possession' respectively, the authors of *Miskitu bila aisanka* cleverly identify an inalienable quality they consider common to the members of Class 2, leaving the members of Class 1 as a default or residual category. Although the authors of this book, clearly linguists, demonstrate no awareness of the writings of Mauss (1966), Marx (1967), Sahlins (1972), Weiner (1976), Taussig (1980), Gregory (1982) and Carrier (1998), for example, their characterisation of these noun classes as 'alienable' and 'inalienable' does, in the light of insights offered by these and other authors on alienation as an anthropological concept, invite discussion.[14] Particularly interesting in this respect is the observation made by the authors that nouns loaned into Miskitu from other languages, principally English, to refer to concepts properly belonging in Class 2 appear to be grammatically treated unambiguously as Class 1 nouns (CIDCA, op. cit., p. 71). Hypothetically, as commodities increasingly came into the Miskitu world through purchase rather than exchange, a function of the Miskitu's engagement with the periphery of the capitalist system during the last century and a half (Helms 1969, 1971, 1983; Noveck 1988), all terms of foreign origin might have reflected a Miskitu perception of this other world as one characterised by purchase, through being assigned to the 'alienable' Class 1. The 'inalienable' Class 2, with its sense of inclusiveness, was thus reserved for 'true' Miskitu words. For example, the kin term *anti* (aunt or mother's sister) from the English 'auntie' which has now all but replaced *yapti diura*.

In my view, however, an attempt to understand this distinction between the noun classes in purely economic terms is not adequate. Consideration of the complexities of Miskitu economics, both 'traditional' and 'modern', on the basis of gift/commodity and inalienable/alienable distinctions, while potentially useful in considering movements of goods and services between the Miskitu-speaking peoples and their neighbours (Helms 1983), does little to explain why kin, parts of the body, sentiments and sensations should be grouped together in the fashion described above. While considerable credit is due the authors of *Miskitu bila aisanka* for pointing out the congruences found among the concepts represented by the words in Class 2, they did not, I believe, choose the best term ('inalienable') to capture these congruences.

In my view the concepts expressed by words in Class 2 – kinship, sentiments and sensations (about which only those of one's kin are truly knowable), and parts of the body (themselves sites of those sentiments and sensations) – are better understood in terms of niceties of intimacy. So when Kuka Libias chose to address a small boy as '*plaisni*', she was not only addressing him as 'my youngest child', a particularly intimate kind of kin but was also, through her choice of a Class 2 infix for first person possession, summoning up resonances of consubstantiality, sensation and sentiment. This was clearly a motivated act in that she was making an apology which she hoped the child would pass on to his mother when he returned empty-handed. On another occasion she might have ignored him (if he simply walked past) or referred to him affectionately as '*papa*' (father), another, less charged, kin term of endearment for males younger than oneself.[15]

In Kakabila and other Miskitu villages 'living good' with one's neighbours is ideally achieved without 'politics'. Reality, however, determines that, from time to time, neighbours have to be dealt with, and since engagements with neighbours are usually mediated through speech, modulations in the use of language assume considerable importance. Miskitu villages like Kakabila (population less than 300) are small and since neighbours know one another all too well, often living close to each other during the course of their entire lives, engagement is, as Kuka Libias knows, best conducted through a language of intimacy in which neighbours are best treated as kin.

Death and the language of compassion

The body, for Kakabila people, is deeply implicated in the negotiation of intimacy. Body organs – heart (*kupia*), liver (*aya*), tongue (*twisa*) and so on[16] – are sites where sensations and sentiments towards others – pain, compassion, love (*latwan*), sorrow (*sari*) and so on – are experienced and expressed, and the proper workings of both – organs and sensations/sentiments – are in no small measure both mutually dependent and dependent on the capacity for 'living good' (*pain iwaia*) with others. The most serious threat to all of these arrives with a death in the village. Convivial relations with the deceased are extinguished and the *isingni* or life force which animates his or her sensations and sentiments becomes detached from his or her body organs. Literally disembodied, these sentiments residing in the dead person's *isingni* now consti-tute a threat to the integrity of both community and the bodies of the living (cf. Belaunde, Gow, Lagrou, this volume). They now exist in the form of dangerously unpredictable *wlasa* ('ghosts' or 'duppies') and they need to be dispatched through a series of rituals which, among other things, render the community safe again.[17]

News of a death in the village is greeted by loud laments or ritual wailings of the type given at the beginning of this chapter from the deceased person's kinswomen. One of the town bells is rung and villagers quickly arrive at the dead person's house, motivated by both curiosity and concern for the grieving women who, it is believed, will attempt to harm themselves. Messengers, often male affines, are then dispatched immediately to neighbouring villages to inform kin, *compadres* and friends, and once they have arrived, a church service is organised, to be followed by a funeral. Close kin are not expected to attend the church service, lest they be overcome with grief, but they do join the procession of mourners, usually composed of the entire village as well as visitors, as it heads to the cemetery (*raiti*) for the burial. At the grave-side a short lesson is read out by the catechist (in Kakabila a shaman of considerable repute) after which time the coffin, which has been sitting in the deceased's hall up to then, is lowered into a grave previously dug by male affines (typically sons-in-law). At this point at least one female relative, usually the eldest daughter, cries a lament of the kind presented above, and the coffin is lowered into the grave, after which those present disperse.

The following days are given up to a vigil ('set up' or 'nine nights') when mourners periodically visit the deceased's house to sing 'sankey' (mourning songs) and drink coffee and rum. On 'the tenth night which broke the nine', 'sankeys' are sung up until midnight, at which point the mourners 'turn the bed' round, thereby releasing the 'spirit' or *isingni* of the deceased and sing 'Go Spirit Go', a song only ever sung at this particular moment. The *isingni* (life force) of the deceased departs, never, it is hoped, to return and 'molest' the living as a 'ghost' or *wlasa*.[18] More rum and coffee are drunk and as dawn rises the mourners are given breakfast. Normal life resumes as community, bodies, sensations and sentiments are returned to their informal order, except for the very closest relatives, many of whom continue to mourn ritually in a more attenuated fashion for a year.[19]

As I showed earlier, for Miskitu speakers Noun Class 2 constitutes a grammatical categorisation where kinship, community, bodies, emotions, sentiment and sensation are grouped together in an ontological domain. I also noted that Miskitu speakers are, at some level, aware of this and manipulate the boundaries between Class 2 and the residual Class 1 in order to achieve pragmatic effect. Nowhere, to my mind, is this more evident than in the funeral lament which is, as the reader will remember, produced at exactly the moment in which the integrity of this domain, that of 'living good' with one's neighbours, is most threatened. Although the Miskitu language contains nouns which regularly employ few Class 2 affixes, the funeral lament is typically absolutely packed with them, with references to kin, body parts, emotions and also, significantly, language.[20]

I now present the lament given earlier in this chapter both in Miskitu and, for convenience of presentation, once again in English.[21] Class 2 affixes are given in italics.

Alai yapti yapti umpira! alai yapti, ansara waram?
     Sark-*am* atia luhpi-*am* nani ini bangwiba
Nawala yawan wal aisikata, kuna nanara bara prawisma.
Alai yapti tila wina kupi-*am* baiwi auma ki?
     La-*m*-twan apia katna ki?
Latara mai-*am* aimakupi iwiba.
Nahara mairin nani ai wita-*ø* sruki iwi bangwiba,
     Sark-*am* atia sika.
     Ban ba kuna ai lulkisi waram.
Alai maw-*am* kli kaikamna apia ba;
Kli bil-*am* baikra walamna apia ba!

                              (Bell. op. cit., p. 312)

Alas, mother, poor mother! alas, mother, where have you gone?
     Here are your children crying for you;
Yesterday we were talking together, but now you are lying there.
Alas, mother, did you go from among us in anger?
     Did we not love you?
Your husband sits outside with his head hung down.
Here the women are sitting with their heads covered,
     All for love of you.
     But you have abandoned us.
Alas, that I shall never see your face again;
That I shall never hear your voice again!

                              (Bell, op. cit., p. 91)

With respect to the ontological analysis given above, three kin terms *yapti* ['mother'], *luhpia* ['son' or 'daughter'] and *maia* ['spouse']; four parts of the body (*kupia* ['heart'], *wita* ['head'], *mawa* ['face'] and *bila* ['mouth' – used here in *bila baikra* meaning 'mouth breaker' or 'voice']) and four sensations or sentiments, *kupia baiwi* ['getting angry' – literally 'heart breaking'], *sarka* ['sorrow' or 'love' (twice)], *latwan* ['love', 'compassion' or 'pain'], appear with Class 2 morphology for possession. Besides these one sensation expressed in purely verb form (*ini* ['crying']) and one kin term without possessive morphology (*yapti* ['mother']) also feature.

In terms of the pragmatics of this lament, the loading of so many Class 2 affixes into this short piece represents a poetic *tour de force*, the speaker densely packing it with images of separation, the significance of talk, the anger of the deceased's *isingni*, and the sense that the deceased and the bereaved 'lived good' together before being separated.[22] Without detracting from the no doubt very real grief of the woman delivering it, this lament truly represents, at least to me, 'work' in the senses of it (a) doing the very real job of appeasing, and indeed chastising, the deceased's *isingni*,[23] and (b) truly being a work of what Sherzer (1998) calls 'verbal art'.[24]

The lament is the focus of the Miskitu community's reaction to the threats posed by death to community life, bodies and emotions (cf. Alès, Belaunde, Gow, Lagrou, this volume). So, when an older woman dies, it is the duty of the daughter (or daughters) of the deceased to confront the *isingni* or life force which objectifies these threats. The importance of the lament is evident in that it is produced at the graveside when the coffin is lowered into the grave, a very public event witnessed by the entire village as well as visitors. The work of the lament is to project forcefully the sacredness of this moment.[25]

The lament is closer in some ways to an oration than a spontaneous outburst in that it has to conform to a set of poetic preconceptions.[26] It is, therefore, usefully readily susceptible to ethnopoetic analyses of the kind I have tried to employ in this chapter. A complete analysis of the Miskitu lament, of course, would require analysis of other aspects of language, parallelism and prosody in particular, and would be a very much lengthier piece of work.[27] In this chapter I have chosen to focus on its 'work' in providing an aesthetically appropriate emotional mood at the graveside by the ontological assignment of Class 2 possessive affixes to nouns. The selection of Class 2 possessive affixes, in contrast to Class 1 affixes, emphasises community, bodies, sentiment and inclusivity. The aesthetically appropriate mood at the graveside is achieved in part by the bombarding of the audience (mourners and *isingni* alike) with as many of these as possible while their attention is most focused. While noun class selectional possibilities perhaps offer a less constrained range of choices to Miskitu-speakers in other kinds of speech event, it is perhaps the daughter's lament which best foregrounds the significance of the extraordinary Class 2.

Acknowledgements

This chapter is based upon ethnography collected during eighteen months' residence in Nicaragua in 1992–3, fifteen of which were spent in the village of Kakabila in the Pearl Lagoon basin. This work was conducted as a postgraduate student in the Anthropology Department of the London School of Economics, and as an associate researcher with CIDCA (el Centro de Investigaciones y Documentación de la Costa Atlántica). It was recently supplemented by shorter periods of fieldwork also spent in Kakabila in 1997 and 1998. I am most grateful to both institutions for their considerable assistance. This work was also made possible by fieldwork grants from the Wenner Gren Foundation for Anthropological Research and the Emslie Horniman Trust, and I would like to thank the trustees of both for their confidence in my ability to carry out this research. Above all, I would like to thank the people of Kakabila – in particular Mister John and Miss Chavela Schwartz, their daughter and my *comadre* Lorna Schwartz, my *compadre* Mister Palford Theodore, Miss Rachel Schwartz MacPherson, Miss Buelah Theodore, Mister Rafael Bonilla and Mister Mercado Garth – for teaching me the Miskitu language and for making my stays in their village so memorable and pleasurable.

Notes

1 See Urban (1988) for discussion of laments or ritual wailing among the Shokleng, Shavante and Bororo of Brazil, Graham (1987) for the Shavante, and Briggs (1992, 1993) for the Warao of Venezuela. Urban (1988: 392) notes that death is certainly 'the principal situation throughout native South America' in which ritual wailing (or the lament) occurs.

2 With the village so clearly defined in relation to other communities by the facts of geography, villagers do not imagine their moral universe so easily in terms of numerous concentric circles of inclusiveness as the Matsigenka evidently do (Rosengren, this volume).

3 See Goldman (1963) and Overing Kaplan (1975) for useful discussions of this idea among the Cubeo of the Northwest Amazon and the Piaroa of the Guiana region, and Overing (1989) and Rivère (1984) for useful comparative discussions.

4 Interestingly, Kakabila people reserve the English-language word 'politics' to mean precisely these micro-interactions. To say of another in the Kakabila variety of Nicaraguan English, 'I no like hi' politics' does not mean that one disapproves of another's affiliation to, say, the FSLN (Sandinistas) but that one does not like the way they either use and manipulate others or conduct interactions with them.

5 In simple terms, *taya* or 'family' are consanguineal kin. 'Family' members are not defined by household membership. Nor are spouses considered 'family'. See Jamieson (1996, 1998) for more nuanced discussions of kinship in Kakabila.

6 This of course does not mean that since the rise to prominence of popular psychology, we have become more 'rational' about the relationship between 'mind' and 'body', only that we have come to reinvent this relationship in new and anthropologically interesting ways. Metaphors aside, I am not at all convinced that most of us in the West really do make a cut-and-dried Cartesian distinction between mind and body in either day-to-day discourse or thought. The Cartesian distinction between mind and body is, arguably, a product of the culture of the academy rather than the various cultures of the peoples of the West, and a relatively recent one at that. See Leavitt (1996) for the view that the distinction between mind and body has impeded the development of an adequate anthropology of emotions, and Briggs (1992: 348) on this point more specifically in the context of a discussion of laments among the Warao.

7 Though, of course, close friends often do speculate privately on the motives and intentions of others.

8 *Lukaia* often carries an overtone of melancholic contemplation. To ask the question '*lukisma?*' (are you thinking?) suggests that addressee appears to be sad. See Gow, this volume, for a similar idea expressed by the Piro.

9 It is interesting to note that some kin terms are also homonyms for parts of the body. So, for example, *waika* (brother-in-law, same-sex male cross-cousin) also means 'tail', while *klua* (opposite-sex cross-cousin – no longer used) means 'belly button'. The word *taya* (consanguineal kin) also means 'skin'. I am not yet sure of the significance of these observations. Joanna Overing (personal communication) has some similar data for Piaroa. Noun classes similar to the Miskitu Class 2, where special affixes marking possession for kin and parts of the body, can be found in a number of other Central American languages (Suarez 1983: 84–6). I suggest that more research would reveal the same to be true in many South American languages. Joanna Overing (personal communication) informs me that noun classes among the Piaroa might similarly be analysed through the notion of inclusivity.

10 Exclusive 'our' (*-ki*) is used when the hearer(s) is excluded. Inclusive 'our' (*-ka*) is used when the hearer(s) is included.

11 Readers interested in a more linguistically nuanced discussion should consult CIDCA (1985, chapter 3).

12 I can only think of two examples from English where a pronominal noun class is switched to produce effect in a similar way. The first is the feminist hypercorrectional regendering of the supposed masculine possessive 'his' in 'history' in order to produce 'herstory'. Here, of course, as sharp-eyed linguists will notice, it is the supposed pronoun ('his') which is regendered and not the supposed noun ('story'), while in Miskitu, a number of Amerindian languages discussed in Suarez (1983), and most Bantu languages it is inevitably the gender of the noun itself which is reassigned. The second example is the different effects produced by referring to a ship with either the feminine 'her' or the neuter 'it'.

13 The *plasni* (youngest child) is the favourite and most indulged child in many Miskitu households.

14 Neither anthropologists nor economists are cited at all in this book. *Miskitu bila aisanka*, it should be emphasised, is not a work of linguistic anthropology but simply a grammar and exercise workbook written primarily for Spanish-speaking Nicaraguans wishing to acquire some basic Miskitu.

15 '*Papa*' never employs a possessive affix when used as a term of address. When used with a possessive affix referentially (almost always then to refer to a 'real' father), it employs Class 1 suffixes (*papi-ki, papi-kam, papi-ka*). This allocation of *papa* to Class 1 is undoubtedly a function of the fact that *papa* is a borrowing from English and/or Spanish.

16 All Class 2 nouns of course.

17 Following this death of Amanda's mother and before her *isingni* was set free, some people asked me if I was frightened to sleep alone, the implication being that I would make an easy target for her 'ghost'.

18 The *isingni* of the deceased is deemed particularly dangerous up to the moment the 'bed is turned'.

19 Widows and widowers often state, after the death of their spouse, that they will not remarry until a year has elapsed. It is also deemed inappropriate to 'tomb' the deceased (cover the grave with a cement case) until a year has gone by, lest others construe an enthusiasm for 'tombing' the deceased by relatives as evidence of 'a quick death' (a euphemism for murder by poisoning or sorcery).

20 According to Urban (1988), Bororo laments also contain many possessive pronouns, though he give no transcriptions of the kind provided in this chapter. Briggs (1992: 343), considering Warao laments, also notes that 'many phrases or refrains begin or end with a kin term preceded by a genetive prefix'. Graham (1987) also notes that morphology is employed in significant ways in Shavante laments but unfortunately provides no examples.

21 I have taken the liberty of reproducing this text in modern Miskitu orthography. Bell's rather idiosyncratic spelling of Miskitu words makes the original very hard to read. Otherwise it is unchanged.

22 'In short, [Warao] textual phrases are so packed with semantic content that they often seem to be bursting at their poetic seams' (Briggs 1992: 343–4). 'Nearly every line', he notes, 'contains a kin term that indexes the relationship between the performer and the person she is mourning' (ibid., p. 346).

23 In contrast to Miskitu women who chastise the deceased, Warao women produce laments which chastise the living (Briggs 1992, 1993).

24 Gell (1998, especially chapter 1) contains an absorbing discussion of the problems in using the term 'art' for cultures without the particular category 'art', though

there is nothing in Sherzer's account that might be substantively problematised by Gell's analysis. Bell's lament, possibly not a real lament but the essence of several he heard, and the one I heard given by Amanda are both 'retentions' and 'protentions' of a 'style' (to use Gell's terms) which has evidently changed little in the last 150 years at least. As Bauman and Briggs (1990: 77) note, '[a]n authoritative text, by definition, is one that is maximally protected from compromising transforming'.

25 Urban (1998) makes this point particularly strongly. In his view (p. 386) 'ritual wailing contains with it the secret of social order, how culture comes to exercise control over affective process'. In the view of Bauman and Briggs (1990: 73), '[p]erformance puts the act of speaking on display – objectifies it, lifts it to a degree from its interactional setting and opens it to scrutiny by an audience'. It is these aspects of the work of Amanda's lament to which the Creole woman mentioned at the beginning of this chapter was referring. Urban (1988: 398) adds that '[d]espite the fact that actors in some sense "know" what they are doing, they must not let on that they know'. It is this work of producing an appropriate aesthetics (Overing 1989) that the Miskitu consider important.

26 Particular phrases are clearly chosen for the most part on the spur of the moment. So, for example, Amanda, addressing the fact that her mother had died from cerebral malaria, cried out 'Mother! Why didn't you put up your mosquito net?' These improvisations, however, are clearly selected to enhance, rather than subvert, the lament's form. See Briggs (1992: 341) for similar constraints and spaces for improvisation in Warao laments.

27 See Urban (1988), Graham (1987) and Briggs (1992, 1993) for this kind of analysis.

References

Bauman, R. and Briggs, C.L. (1990) 'Poetics and performance as critical perspectives on language and social life', *Annual Review of Anthropology* 19: 59–88.

Bell, C.N. (1989 [1899]) *Tangweera: Life and Adventures among Gentle Savages*, Austin: University of Texas Press.

Briggs, C.L. (1992) 'Since I am a woman I will chastise my relatives: gender, reported speech, and the (re)production of social relations in Warao ritual wailing', *American Ethnologist* 19: 337–61.

—— (1993) 'Personal sentiments and polyphonic voices in Warao women's ritual wailing: music and poetics in a critical and collective discourse', *American Anthropologist* 94(4): 929–57.

Carrier, J. (1998) 'Property and social relations in Melanesian anthropology', in C.M. Hann (ed.) *Property Relations: Renewing the Anthropological Tradition*, Cambridge: Cambridge University Press.

CIDCA (1985) *Miskitu bila aisanka: gramática miskita*, Managua: Serie Lingüística Colección Autónoma, CIDCA.

Corbett, G. (1991) *Gender*, Cambridge: Cambridge University Press, Cambridge Textbooks in Linguistics.

Gell, A. (1998) *Art and Agency: An Anthropological Theory*, Oxford: Clarendon Press.

Goldman, I. (1963) *The Cubeo: Indians of the Northwest Amazon*, Urbana: University of Illinois Press.

Graham, L. (1987) 'Three modes of Shavante vocal expression: wailing, collective singing, and political oratory', in Joel Sherzer and Greg Urban (eds) *Native South American Discourse*, Berlin: Mouton de Gruyter.

Gregory, C.A. (1982) *Gifts and Commodities*, London and New York: Academic Press.

Helms, M.W. (1969) 'The purchase society: adaptation to economic frontiers', *Anthropological Quarterly* 42: 325–42.

—— (1971) *Asang: Adaptations to Culture Contact in a Miskito Community*, Gainesville: University of Florida Press.

—— (1983) 'Miskito slaving and culture contact: ethnicity and opportunity in an expanding population', *Journal of Anthropological Research* 39: 179–97.

Jamieson, M. (1996) 'Kinship and gender as political processes among the Miskitu of Eastern Nicaragua', unpublished Ph.D dissertation, London School of Economics.

—— (1998) 'Linguistic innovation and relationship terminology in the Pearl Lagoon basin of Nicaragua', *Journal of the Royal Anthropological Institute* 4: 713–30.

Leavitt, J. (1996) 'Meaning and feeling in the anthropology of emotions', *American Ethnologist* 23: 514–39.

Marx, K. (1967) *Capital*, Vols 1–3, London: Penguin.

Mauss, M. (1966 [1904]) *The Gift: Forms and Functions of Exchange in Archaic Societies*, London: Cohen & West.

Noveck, D. (1988) 'Class, culture, and the Miskito Indians: a historical perspective', *Dialectical Anthropology* 13: 17–29.

Overing, J. (1989) 'The aesthetics of production: the sense of community among the Cubeo and Piaroa', *Dialectical Anthropology* 14: 159–75.

Overing Kaplan, J. (1975) *The Piaroa: A People of the Orinoco Basin*, Oxford: Clarendon.

Rivière, P. (1984) *Individual and Society in Guiana: A Comparative Study of Amerindian Social Organization*, Cambridge: Cambridge University Press.

Sahlins, M. (1972) *Stone Age Economics*, Chicago: Aldine.

Sherzer, J. (1998) *Verbal Art in San Blas: Kuna Culture through its Discourses*, Albuquerque: University of New Mexico Press.

Suarez, J.A. (1983) *The Mesoamerican Indian Languages*, Cambridge: Cambridge University Press.

Taussig, M.T. (1980) *The Devil and Commodity Fetishism in South America*, Chapel Hill: University of North Carolina Press.

Urban, G. (1988) 'Ritual wailing in Amerindian Brazil', *American Anthropologist* 90: 385–400.

Weiner, A.B. (1976) *Women of Value, Men of Renown*, Austin: University of Texas Press.

Chapter 5

The value of working and speaking together

A facet of Pa'ikwené (Palikur) conviviality

Alan Passes

Ask a Pa'ikwené person about work, any work, and you are likely to be told that it is *mahiko*, i.e. 'hard and difficult'. This evaluation coexists, however, with another, in which the process of work and productivity is held to be enjoyable, even joyful, and an activity as rewarding in terms of the emotions and communication as in material ones. This chapter is largely about Pa'ikwené work, then; and is to be seen as a contribution to the conversation on the 'everyday' aspects of Lowland Amerindian life. Insofar as it explores the oral dimension of work, the chapter may also be said to be about conversation itself, both in the literal sense and the figurative, that of society being conceived as a 'dialogue' between its members. More fundamentally, it is about the daily and very ordinary process of people speaking and working together: the interaction of, and value placed on, these twin behaviours (cf. Alès, Overing, this volume); and how, in a Pa'ikwené context, their joint practice can be said not only to generate sociality but a sociality of a particular type, namely conviviality.

The Pa'ikwené (the self-appellation of a nation more commonly known in the literature as the Palikur) are a clan society belonging to the Maipuran (Arawak) language group. Today numbering around 1,600 people, they straddle the river Oyapock which is the frontier between Northern Brazil (Amapá state) and Guyane (French Guiana). Extensively missionised by various fundamentalist Protestant sects since the 1960s, they have increasingly formed themselves into large multi-clan 'single-denomination' communities. Deuxième Village Espérance, where I carried out my fieldwork during 1993–5, and which is situated by the small Créole town of St Georges, had a population of some 160 inhabitants and was predominantly Evangelical-Pentecostalist; Premier Village Espérance, the even bigger settlement next-door, mainly Seventh Day Adventist. As with many other groups, the lifestyle of these converts, a mixture of 'traditional' and modernist, combines a 'subsistence economy' with an increasing participation in the Western 'market economy'.[1]

A defining principle of 'economic' production in Amazonia, as revealed by Goldman's research (1979: 66) on the Cubeo and Overing's (1989) on the

Piaroa, seems to be that work is a group activity and, as such, a pleasurable, satisfying and recreational one. It was my observation that, for all the Pa'ikwené's constant reference to and complaining about the unpleasantness of the physical side of work, a similar situation applies to them. For they too greatly prize sociability as a vital component of the productive process. This they do primarily in terms of the cheerfulness and agreeableness of the people involved. The more one can interrelate in a friendly manner with one's co-workers, and chat, joke, laugh and, thus, relax while working (no contradiction in terms intended), then the more the experience seems to be enjoyed and valued. And the more, too, one's physical productivity increases rather than the reverse; or at least, because I could not have cared less about measuring it objectively, so it appeared. The more cheerful one is, the more companionable the atmosphere; and the more dialogic the event, the greater one's zest for work itself seems to grow, and the longer one keeps at it.

But while it was work it was more than just work. For, as is clear, it was social living as well. 'Work' and 'social life' were not regarded as discrete and mutually exclusive modes of behaviour for the Pa'ikwené as they can often seem to be for us; and in this intrinsically social act, which was consti- tuted by sociable working, their production did not only turn out 'economic' products. In a very concrete way, it seemed to me and, I believe, to the Pa'ikwené themselves, society itself was being produced at the same time, and performatively so, in and through the process of work. Ultimately, this was not only recreational in Goldman's sense of virtually amounting to a 'leisure activity'. It is also to be seen, I suggest, as having the ability directly to re-create, through its very sociableness, the sense and state of sociality itself. To clarify what I mean, I will resort to an incident from my fieldwork involving the processing of the manioc crop.

First, though, I would like to expand on something I have just said: that in Pa'ikwené existence the spheres of one's work and one's social life are not dis- tinct, separate and opposed as occurs – or as tends at any rate to be perceived to occur – in a certain common Western perspective. And speaking, as an essential sign, not to say constituent, of social life, is not renounced or repressed or put on hold during the periods devoted to work, as Christian Protestant, and especially Puritan, morality would dictate. Weber, for instance, examines (1971: 157–8) how this ethic enjoins the individual to work in silence and in, or as if in, isolation on the ideological grounds that congenial verbal activity is inimical to work and therefore immoral insofar as it is equated with the 'deadliest of sins', time-wasting, that is, not working, and thus failing to direct one's energies and thoughts to the deity: 'Loss of time through sociability [and] idle talk . . . is worthy of absolute moral con- demnation . . . [since] every hour lost [in this way] is lost to labour for the glory of God' (Weber, ibid. See too pp. 260–1, notes 10, 14).

For a Pa'ikwené on the other hand, notwithstanding present-day con- version to Protestant fundamentalism, such dialogic abstinence, such self-imposed mutism whilst working is inconceivable, not to say impractical. This applies even in hunting situations, where you might think silence a pragmatic necessity. Hunters talk not only among themselves but with their prey, such 'conversations' being seen as a crucially productive aspect of the enterprise (Passes 1998: 60–75). While one Western world-view holds that work has value to the extent that it is orientated to God, another, the Marxist, judges it on the basis of the 'labour-time' incorporated in it (Marx 1978: 423–4). Again this is not a concept shared by the Pa'ikwené, who instead see the value in terms of the knowledge, technical skill, artistry and emotion involved, and also, as I shall argue, that of the speech which is integral to these factors.

The Pa'ikwené call work '*anivit*'. Their typology of *anivit* ranges from the manual and physical activities which we would normally qualify as 'economic' (e.g. hunting, gardening, gathering) and 'domestic' (e.g. cooking, cleaning) to things like childcare, healing and being chief. As noted, *anivit* is commonly described as '*mahiko*', that is to say, hard, difficult, painful; an assessment which at first glance would appear to corroborate the claim, famously attacked by Sahlins (1974), that work in 'subsistence' economies is unmitigated drudgery.

But while Pa'ikwenés may speak of the actual activity of work as something particularly burdensome, if necessary, it does not automatically follow that they also consider it ungratifying. For, at both the personal and collective levels, there is very real pleasure to be had, and to be observed, in it. I think especially of the joy most Pa'ikwené, women as well as men, seem to take in fishing, and also of the fun characteristically experienced and expressed when out gathering. And here I do not distinguish between enjoyment and satisfaction associated with and ensuing from the physical, mental and technical sides of the activity (e.g. the keenness of eye, manual adroitness, the various knowledges involved, the 'tool use'), and pleasure and satisfaction deriving from the social side (i.e. the companionship, joking, laughter, mutual reliance and interdependence, and also friendly rivalry).

The social and affective states which comprise *anivit* – the joint conditions of work almost as a game (on the ludic in everyday Amerindian life, see Overing, this volume), of communality, amicability and high spirits, of physical labour and physical exuberance and technical expression – evoke and correspond with Illich's notion of conviviality, referred to in the Preface and presented in his critique of industrial society (1973). That is, conviviality as, precisely, a 'way of being' typified by these selfsame attributes of friendship, joy, productive playfulness and pleasurable sociality accruing from and dependent on the individual's autonomous, unregimented and creative use of their tools. I will return to Illich later; for the moment I want to concentrate on the *anivit* of the manioc processing, from harvesting the plant, which the Pa'ikwené call *kaneg*, through all the different stages involved in turning it into various foods, the main ones being flour, *púveyé* (or *kwak*, the common term for it in Guyane), bread, *búgút*, and beer, *wonska* (now banned under the Protestant fundamentalist regime adopted by many Pa'ikwené).

This type of work, which is invariably labelled, and epitomised, as not merely *mahiko* (hard and difficult) but *kainsima mahiko*, that is, 'very hard and difficult', is at the same time a particularly highly congenial, convivial, almost archetypically 'communal activity'.

Kaneg (manioc) itself is for the Pa'ikwené, like a good many other Lowland Amerindians, not only a dietary staple but a highly prized article in another sense, being invested with much emotional and symbolic power. It is reckoned as one of the key defining signs, second perhaps only to their language (Pa'ikwaki), of their culture and of their identity as a people, first specifically as Pa'ikwené and then more generally as 'Indians' (cf. Campbell 1995: 50 apropos the Wayapi). It is, I believe, significant that *anivit* itself is similarly one of the few select other markers, or conferrers, of a distinctiveness at once personal and 'ethnic'. For instance, Susana, an informant, cited 'Pa'ikwené work' as one of the three things she teaches her children in order that they should always remember who they were, that is to say, Pa'ikwené people. The other two were cooking and eating Pa'ikwené food (especially manioc) and speaking Pa'ikwaki. Like manioc and their language, then, *anivit* , and the *anivit* of the manioc in particular, not only represents but embodies, and in a sense determines, Pa'ikwené-hood. To quote Susana directly:

> I can learn, and I can do, other [i.e. non-Pa'ikwené] ways of cooking and working and speaking, but I am still Pa'ikwené and will remain Pa'ikwené because I was born Pa'ikwené and remember the Pa'ikwené things my parents taught me.[2]

To come back to the manioc processing. This work activity demands a particularly heavy commitment from individuals in terms of effort and time, with the whole operation taking up to some four or five days, and draws on the wide range of technical knowledge and skills of all the participants; that is, basically, the members of the household whose crop it is together with those of the other (related) families which collaborate in the manufacturing and are thus entitled to part of the finished product in return. The solidary unit formed by this coming together for the manioc processing (or almost any other *anivit*) tends to be non-coercive and unconstricting; each worker is free to come and go, to take part or withdraw their services as and when they wish. People frequently drop out when bored, tired or discontented, or if they consider there is something more worthwhile to pursue; to do so is legitimate and acceptable. As in many other Lowland groups, a strong sense of community coexists with an equally strong ethos of personal autonomy (cf. e.g. Alès, Kidd, Rivière, Rosengren, this volume). Although people who do not join in a task are sometimes called lazy, this tends to be in a teasing rather than an accusatory way. Granted, the first could in some contexts be construed as pressurising as the second. However, somewhat similarly to the Cubeo attitude to laziness described by Goldman (1979: 53), the Pa'ikwené seem to regard the condition less as a moral failing than an indication of being out of sorts, a symptom of social disaffection or sadness.

While the Pa'ikwené used at one time to categorise manioc processing and flour making as 'woman's work' (Nimuendajú 1971 [1926]: 24), as many other Lowland groups apparently still do (cf. e.g. Overing Kaplan (1975: 37) on the Piaroa; Goldman (1979) on the Cubeo; Campbell (1995: 49–57) on the Wayapi; Rivière (1983–4, 1984: 92–4) on the Trio and more generally), today the task is virtually ungendered. Rivière's suggestion, that in connection with the manioc production, the exclusive use of the scarce resource of women's labour provides the political-economic means for their exploitation and control by men in otherwise highly egalitarian societies, did not seem to apply (cf. Campbell, op. cit., p. 50; Santos-Granero 1986; Overing's critique 1983–4). In Deuxième Village Espérance, which was itself strikingly egalitarian, the only aspect of the manioc processing which, as far as I could see, was presently considered 'female' concerned the making of the bread itself, inasmuch as it took place under the rather informal supervision of the woman head of the household. This aside, the men are involved in all areas of production: harvesting, toting, peeling, washing and detoxifying, grating, pressing, grinding, sifting, tending to the oven, toasting.

Another key phase might be said to be the talking that goes on. I will not call it an accompaniment to the work, or a backdrop, for I believe its character and role to be more central than that – and intrinsically and vitally part of the work, just as the two of them, the work and the speech, are integrally aspects, and generative ones at that, of the actual state of conviviality and general social-ness expressed through the process of working the manioc. This particular economic task, then, is nothing if not also simultaneously, and in a directly and equally socially productive manner, a linguistic and intercommunicative one – intensively so.

How to begin to convey this communal, manual, oral, emotional event? Picture, to start with, the 'collective effervescence', the truly party atmosphere, of the process itself: the participants high, as it were, on themselves, on their being together, on the united release of their energies; their ceaseless joining in and dropping out as if on a whim; the picnicking 'on the job'; the laughter and banter, good-natured grousing and teasing and gossip, the recounting of past times and swapping of tales – work as play. And, too, work as a play, as 'performance':[3] the 'ensemble work' involved: the seemingly haphazard yet actually well-integrated choreography. The intense, intent interplay as though somehow at once spontaneous yet at the same time following known lines of previous practice and custom. The 'organised chaos', in short, of a dozen or so men and women and assorted children gathering together for the best part of a week for the *anivit* of preparing several months' supply of *kwak* (flour), and a smaller one of *kayút* (tapioca), *búgút* (bread), and other gastronomic delights such as various *matchit*, that is, mashes, purées and creams, from a vast mound of manioc tubers which first had had to be picked then carried back home the considerable distance from the 'garden', before undergoing all the above-mentioned stages which progressively transform them from poisonous plants into food. Each step requires a specific implement and technique, and people's skill in them. A crucial aspect of the process seemed to be that while the tools were with but very few exceptions the communal property of the household, the control over their use and the technical knowledge entailed remained the individual user's at the same time as they were deployed toward a collective end, and for the 'common good'. The tool, be it machete or grater, press or oven, and one's use of it were not only, it seemed to me, the instruments of a set of social relationships; they in practice, by their very use, continuously brought the relations into being. Likewise with the speech one very loudly (in typical Pa'ikwené style[4]) engaged in during the work event – the jokes and repartee, the exchange of news and views, the storytelling, singing, instructing and plain general chatter.

I was present one day when the Brazilian pastor of the fundamentalist (Assembleía de Deus) church which was established in the village, dropped in on the family I lived with as they, together with a group of relatives and friends, were hard at work processing their own manioc crop. He proposed that Karinai, the household head, invest in a machine which could turn the raw product into *farinha* (flour) in a single day instead of the several back-breaking, labour-intensive ones the operation now took. Karinai and the others with him flatly turned down the suggestion. I was surprised, for I well knew their, and most other Pa'ikwené's, appreciation for labour-saving devices like rifles, outboard motors and chainsaws.[5] Why, I asked, given both this predilection and indeed passion for other Western technology and the constant grumbles about the drudgery of *anivit*, did they regard the idea of a manioc-machine so unfavourably? Karinai explained that although it could certainly do the work faster than the Pa'ikwené, it did not do it 'as well'. This turned out to mean that what he really did not want to lose, and feared that the apparatus would threaten and possibly destroy, was the communality and congeniality characteristic of the 'old' way of manioc processing: the singing, joking, laughing, talking, eating and drinking together which (as I am trying to describe) are an integral and defining aspect of the work, and of the interpersonal relations embedded in and underpinning it. Campbell (op. cit., p. 50) has similarly speculated on how a 'futuristic manioc-processing machine' would probably have a negative impact on the social and cultural life of another Amazonian group, the Wayãpi.[6]

I am suggesting that for Karinai, and his people in general, work was seen not so much as an economic and technical activity as, fundamentally, dialogue and sociality itself in action; and was valued as such. This is not to say that such a view is just an Amerindian or 'preindustrial' one. Philippe

Meyer, for instance, reports (1993: 62) a similar attitude among fishermen in the French port of Sète on the introduction of imperishable nylon nets in the 1970s. This innovation did away with the age-old practice of tarring nets as a protection against rot, presumably a messy, time-consuming task. It also made redundant the everyday ritual of gathering together and doing the work in common on the quayside. The fishermen therefore decided to carry on as before and tarred their new nets regardless: obviously a useless exercise technically and economically. But in their eyes, it would seem, a useful one socially, for they did not want to stop their daily reunions and intercourse (the chatting and gossiping) and to lose, in short, the socialising which that specific job gave rise to.

These, then, are the two issues I am trying to get a fix on here: the link between working and speaking, and the perception that productivity results in more than just material products; that it can itself ultimately, essentially, and just as tangibly, constitute self-realising society.

In the first place, the case of the manioc processing bears out something which I constantly observed with the Pa'ikwené, but about which I was unfortunately never able to get an explicit statement from them. Namely, that work and dialogic situations did not merely coincide or provide actors with the opportunity for an alternative and 'secondary' activity whilst getting on with the 'main' one, whichever it happened to be. Rather, and at the risk of repeating myself, in everyday Pa'ikwené life work and words formed a unitary process in terms of the interconstitutive and social nature of 'economic' and communicational productivity – one in which people's speaking (and just as importantly, though I have not the time to go into it here, their listening[7]) played as intrinsic, important and creative a role as their muscle power, technical knowledge, manual dexterity or good humour, and was as cherished (cf. Alès, this volume).

Some Amazonian cosmologies conceptualise words and speaking (and listening) as procreative agents of the cosmic order in the human sphere. Perhaps the richest example is Isacsson's material (1993) on the Embera, who see verbal intercourse in terms of an alliance marriage system, and words themselves as embodying divine seminal force with the power to recreate social life. Basically, the daily reproduction of society is ideologically believed to depend on people speaking together. While Pa'ikwené metaphysics does not, or does not appear to, propose such an explicit paradigm, there is an origin myth telling how Kaúmaïyé, the creator spirit and first lone Pa'ikwené, brought his people into existence through singing (and dancing). More than this, however, they demonstrated a practical awareness, and openly expressed an understanding, of the manifest ability of speech to both generate and incarnate social relations.

I am claiming that from my perspective it was clear that the Pa'ikwené place a value on words and exchange of words. Yet according to some authorities, outside of the strictly technical senses attributed to it by linguistics, i.e. 'a precise meaning and signification' and 'exchangeability factor' (Saussure 1966: 115), this value is non-existent, or at best dubious. Lévi-Strauss, for instance, takes a somewhat equivocal position. On the one hand he asserts (1986: 61) that words are without value in that they are just signs, 'pure signs'. He stresses the word's complete and utter 'sign-ness' in order to make the analogy and contrast with woman, who in the process of woman-exchange is purportedly jointly a sign and a value.

This occurs in his thesis about the language-like quality of kinship systems and marriage rules, where he argues that the exchange of words between the individual members of a group is essentially identical to the exchange between the subgroups of its most precious values, the women. Each of the two exchanges is a 'type of communication' (ibid.), and the items being circulated are, in linguistics terms, signs – the women no less than the words. But, he specifies (ibid.), that women unlike words cannot be reduced to pure signs only since they are also values and themselves, moreover, producers of signs (words). What seems less well known is that, despite this insistence on the word as purely a sign which is necessarily opposed to the woman as both a sign and a value, Lévi-Strauss also allows, if in a somewhat self-contradictory way, that the word is not in fact bereft of value after all, even if, it transpires, the value in question is more a matter of history than present actuality. Consider the point he makes when establishing this opposition between the dual quality of the one term and the single quality of the other: 'In contrast to words, which have wholly become signs, woman has remained at once a sign and a value' (Lévi-Strauss 1969: 496).

Now what is obvious, or strikes me as obvious, from this quotation, is the implicit ambiguity of Lévi-Strauss's opinion about the very thing which, in the context and for the validation of his thesis, he requires to be a sign and nothing but: namely, the Word. For by saying, almost parenthetically, that words have wholly *become* signs, rather than that they wholly are signs, is he not conceding that their perceived non-value is not their natural original state but the result of evolution; and that, like women, their prior, and pre-structuralist, condition should actually be reckoned in terms of value as well as sign? He does in fact avow this overtly when he says that, yes, value can be attached to words, but only in the context of the past, for that value no longer exists (apparently): today, he writes, 'poets are practically the only ones who know that words were also once values [i.e. not just signs]' (1986: 61). He enlarges on this elsewhere:

> The very nature of the linguistic symbol prevented it from remaining for long in the stage which was ended by Babel, when words were still the essential property of each particular group: *values as much as signs* . . . But, to the extent that words have become common property, *and their*

signifying function has supplanted their character as values, language, along with scientific civilization, has helped to impoverish perception and to strip it of its affective, aesthetic and magical implications, as well as to schematize thought.

(Lévi-Strauss 1969: 496, my stresses)

But why this emphasis on the past, that words were values once upon a near prehistoric time, and the inference that they have now ceased to be? And why the rejection of the clearly observable fact of the survival of 'words as values' in cultures, like the Pa'ikwené's, free, or as relatively free as is possible, from the thought processes of that (Western) 'scientific civilization' and 'perception-impoverishing' language? Why indeed these assumptions about evolution and entropy, if but not for the sake of his logic (woman:word:: value:sign[8]).

As if to confuse things even more, Lévi-Strauss then admits such a destruction of value is, despite everything else he has said, not a real one at all: '[O]ne should keep in mind the processes whereby phonemes and words have lost – even though in an *illusory* manner – their character of value' (1986: 61, my stress). That is, words are still values as well as signs after all, and not (though he does not state this) just in 'primitive' societies.[9]

The linguistic–structuralist premise of the Lévi-Straussian argument in regard to kinship and marriage rules – i.e. the values that are women act in place of words (Lévi-Strauss 1986: 61) and are therefore 'treated as signs' (Lévi-Strauss 1969: 496) – is, needless to say, an imposition of a certain Eurocentric concept about both women and words on societies which more than probably do not share it. And who, some of them, might in fact just as hypothetically – or, as the Pa'ikwené would seem to, in practice – pose the equation the other way round: that words are treated as women, that is as equally highly valued values. But women and woman-exchange are not my real concern here, and I should push on with my consideration of the value of words, speech, interlocution.

But just what, first of all, is this value? On the one hand, and again according to Lévi-Strauss, it is, or at least was, somehow or 'something' connected with power. For, back in the pre-Babel times when words were, as I have already quoted, 'values as much as signs', they were consequently: 'jealously preserved, reflectively uttered, and exchanged for other words the meaning of which, once revealed, would bind the stranger, as one put oneself in his power by imitating him' (Lévi-Strauss 1969: 496).

Also, since there is a stress placed on the semantic and transactional dimensions of the dialogue, Lévi-Strauss's understanding of verbal value concurs in some measure with those peculiar to linguistics, referred to above. And then, like a partial, and tantalising, clue to his other, alternative ideas on the subject there is his aforementioned contention, implicitly posed more in terms of aesthetics and emotion (and 'magic'), that nowadays almost no one knows that words were once values as well as signs except for poets – and I suspect he just means Western ones. To relegate this recognition to the past and limit awareness of it virtually to a single (and specialist) class neglects, however, the fact that the word's value seems still to exist today for lots of ordinary people, Meyer's Mediterranean fishermen and the Pa'ikwené villagers among them.

Though, again, what the value might actually be defined as, I find it hard to pinpoint. It is an almost ineffable thing, though one plainly allied to ideas of preciousness, well-being and intimacy, and evocative, or invocative, of the strongest positive feelings. In a work context, these, if I may continue to speculate, are related to an understanding of words as a dynamic, inalienable part of work, and one in which speech is seen as a producer of the sociability which is both a concrete product of collective work and a major factor in the production of community. Accordingly, in such a perspective, is it illogical to regard speech itself as a value of work, in the same way as are the knowledge, skill and artistry which also constitute it? Granted, this assumes an evaluation of work very different from the Protestant and Marxist ones mentioned earlier.

The correlation between words, work and sociability in Pa'ikwené life that I have been talking about, seems to fall within the parameters of the aesthetics of Amerindian production proposed by Overing (1989). In it, the sense of community underlying Native notions and practice of work is predicated on two factors eminently present in 'my' own manioc-processing group: the good mood and self-autonomy of each member, which are the key agents of the style of social action which is, morally and politically, 'conducive to the creation of community' (ibid., p. 159). Which brings me back to Karinai and the others' dismissal of the pastor's proposal: that they dump their old exhausting, dirty and, it seemed to be implied, inefficient and gossip-ridden, time-wasting way of dealing with the manioc in favour of a time-saving, labour-economising machine. For, as I have tried to make clear, it was my 'educated' impression that, from the indigenous point of view, words uttered when working are far from 'idle' chatter; and that, particularly when working together, speaking together (sharing information, stories, jokes and songs, etc.) is valued, morally and affectively, as an industrious, socially productive agent in its own right (cf. Alès, this volume, on the importance of talking in Yanomami sociability and creation of community).

Staying with the emotional side of the affair for a moment, I also believe it reasonable to propose that, for Karinai's family and their helpers in the process of translating the household crop of manioc into foods, speaking *and working* together contributed to a collective mood of the kind Malinowski (1930: 315) calls 'phatic communion', in the very same way as he considers 'speaking together' on its own can do. 'Phatic communion' he describes as 'a type of speech in which ties of union are created by the mere exchange of words' (ibid.). Specifically, it is a verbal intercourse which serves, by means of the 'give and take of . . . [the] ordinary gossip' (ibid.) constituting it and through the convivial sentiments this engenders, to establish and maintain social contact and to express sociability rather than specific meaning. Speaking-and-working together seemed to fulfil, and embody, this condition for the Pa'ikwené; as for the meaning, or (alleged) lack of it, being conveyed, the people involved definitely acted as if the joint activity possessed a deep if non-semantic one of and by itself (for a more recent, and important, exploration of the relationship between language, emotion and daily social life, see Lutz and Abu-Lughod 1990).

Another major Malinowskian premise (op. cit., pp. 311–12) about language in 'primitive societies' is that inasmuch as it is, in his words, a 'mode of action, [and] not an instrument of reflection', its prime function is to serve 'as a link of concerted human activity' which is 'mixed up with and *dependent upon* the course of the activity [generally pragmatic and/or economic] in which the utterances are embedded' (my stress). According to this concept, 'primitive' language is essentially a facilitator of, and imparter of information about, the 'job at hand', whatever it might be; and its use strictly, inescapably bound up with and determined by the particular character of the practical and physical activity in progress: a very utilitarian and, again, non-Pa'ikwené way of looking at speaking together.

There are some grounds for thinking that the special interrelationship between language and work brought about human social relations in the first place. It has been argued that speech developed out of the need to communicate among prehistoric hominids banding together to pool their labour for collective tool making and use; over time their inarticulate vocalisations transformed into syllables, words, language (Isaac 1976; Montagu 1976; Hewes 1993; Toth and Schick 1993). This is quintessentially the view encapsulated in Engels's statement: 'First labour, after it and then with it, speech' (1968: 361). These are, he asserts, the two stimuli by which the ape mutated into the human being and human society evolved (ibid., pp. 358–68).

By contrast, Reynolds (1993) offers a 'complementary theory of language and tool use' which does not so much consider speaking a function of tool use as suggest a co-evolutionary correspondence between them. He proposes that the latter activity entails 'heterotechnic cooperation', that is, the contemporaneous use of different tools and skills by different people, making for a complementarity of social roles. Such heterotechnic activity is universally manifested by a distinct form of social organisation, 'defined by the shared intention to transform matter and energy through the cooperative and complementary use of tools and tool-using skills by a group of people in face to face *contact*' (ibid., p. 413, his stress). Pa'ikwené manioc processing, where at any given moment each participating individual and subgroup does a specific task together with the other individuals and subgroups forming the cooperating work-group, exemplifies this type of social structuring. For

Reynolds, such a base parallels linguistic exchange, wherein each inter-locutor's action is complementary to, and supportive of, the other's.[10]

The Pa'ikwené's own combined use of speech (both technical and non-technical) and of technology in the manioc processing (or in any other activity) leads to my second concern. This is the indigenous understanding of how such use within the social field of *anivit* effectively generates not just the necessary products for the maintenance and well-being of society but, just as substantively, the society itself. For my reading of the data (the manioc pro-cessing and its participants' firm repudiation of the idea that it be modernised and mechanised[11]) convinces me that my co-villagers were fully aware that one of the things – and conceivably the most important – that their joint and, as far as they were concerned, peculiarly Pa'ikwené tool usage and speaking produced, was the state of social-ness. And a social existence of a characteristically Native Amazonian kind it was at that: one which is, as Overing (1999) has already pointed out with regard to the Piaroa, defined by conviviality – that is, etymologically, but also ethically, aesthetically and affectively, a distinct manner of living together.

Illich (1973) has assumed a contemporary 'Western' degradation of con-viviality due to the industrial mode of production which he judges inimical to that condition's aforementioned intrinsic properties of friendly joyfulness and creative playfulness in personal relations (pp. xii–xiii): the very qualities which I perceived to be representative of, and have tried to illustrate, if sketchily, in relation to Pa'ikwené working life in general, and the informal celebration which is the manioc processing in particular. According to Illich (p. 11), the unconvivial industrial universe, from which the above traits are signally absent, is one where people, through being historically dispossessed of and alienated from their 'tools for conviviality', are like prisoners in that they lack either control over their environment or creative input into its con-struction. Instead, their status is reduced to that of mere consumers without effective say in the various 'commoditised' areas of their own lives (education, health, communication, food production and so on). By contrast, the 'convivial society' is one in which 'technologies serve politically interrelated individuals rather than managers' (p. xii), and where there exists 'autono-mous and creative intercourse among persons, and the intercourse of persons with their environment; . . . I consider conviviality [writes Illich] to be indi-vidual freedom realised in personal interdependence and, as such, an intrinsic ethical value' (ibid., p. 11).

The construction of a 'convivial' society, Illich maintains, depends on a person's rightful and free access to, and autonomous, creative manipulation of, the community's tools: that is, not only manual and mechanical imple-ments but the 'productive institutions' which produce 'tangible com-modities', from breakfast cereals to electricity, and 'intangible' ones like education, health, knowledge and 'decisions' (p. 20). The 'convivial society' itself he further defines as one which would 'allow all its members the most autonomous action by means of tools least controlled by others' (ibid.).

Crucially, in this paradigm, 'everyday language', the interlocution of ordinary people within and as part of the process of constructing and maintaining such conviviality, itself amounts to one of the tools in question inasmuch as it, too, essentially possesses a 'convivial function' (ibid., p. 91).

It seems to me that Illich's interpretation of 'conviviality' and of 'tools', which many will judge as hopelessly utopian, is in fact not so far-removed from the 'traditional' Pa'ikwené reality (as I saw it) in respect both of technology and their own society, and of the perceived threat to it posed by the invasiveness of an alien technology, as exemplified by the manioc-machine, beyond a certain practically and ethically acceptable level. To quote him again, Illich proposes that, '[in a] convivial society . . . [p]eople feel joy . . . to the extent that their activities are creative; while the growth of tools beyond a certain point increases regimentation, dependence, exploitation, and impotence' (ibid., p. 20) and, it follows, a proportionate decrease of that joy.

I suggest that Karinai's dismissive reaction to the suggestion of modern and apparently 'better' technology illustrates that both acts, the (traditional) tool use and the talking, and one no less than the other, were understood by the Pa'ikwené to counterweigh and, in a real, practical sense, nullify the indisputable drudgery and sheer hard physical slog involved in many everyday 'economic' tasks. The two behaviours were appreciated, rather, as determining and interactive factors of the condition of shared enjoyment, amicability, excitement and fun: the state of pleasurable – and productive – sociality, in short, that I have glossed as 'conviviality' and that constitutes the group's engaging in the act of *anivit* , which in this case happened to be the manioc processing.

To conclude. We seem to have got into the habit of judging the value attaching to work principally in terms of its products, their so-called use- and exchange-values, and that connected with productivity in terms of the labour and time expended,[12] and the money these are reckoned to be worth. For the Pa'ikwené, on the other hand, the productive process is valuable in the same way and for the same reasons as words and speech, i.e. its inter-communicative and sociable features and the fact that, though physically exacting, it is as fruitful emotionally and socially as it is materially. Thus they appear to understand that the joint action of words and work is itself not just intrinsic to but generative of sociality.

Acknowledgements

My fieldwork was funded by the Economic and Social Research Council, the Emslie Horniman Scholarship Fund (RAI), and the Central Research Fund (University of London). I am also particularly indebted to Karinai

(Felisberto) and Susana Labonté and their family, my hosts in Deuxième Village Espérance.

Notes

1 For detailed information on the Pa'ikwené/Palikur, see Nimuendajú (1971); Fernandes (1963); Arnaud (1968, 1970, 1984); Dreyfus (1981); Grenand and Grenand (1987); Montout (1994); Passes (1998).

2 The link between skills and personhood seems not uncommon in Amazonia, e.g. Thomas notes it (1982) among the Pemon; according to Overing (personal communication) the Piaroa also make it.

3 Cf. Schnechner (1988) on the 'dramatic' quality of everyday acts.

4 On the Pa'ikwené's distinctive 'loud-and-strong' manner of speaking and the loudness of their village life, see Passes (1998: 29–33, 56–7) (contrast Rivière on the soft-spoken Trio, this volume).

5 It seemed to echo the encounter, as perceived by Julio Cortázar (1967: 105), between technology and the so-called common man: 'Exactly where one would imagine a cultural shock, there is, on the contrary, a violent assimilation and enjoyment of the progress.'

6 It would entail, Campbell concludes, the disappearance of 'all sorts of aspects and nuances of art, ceremony, technological knowledge, role activity and daily rhythms' (1995: 50).

7 See Passes (1998, chapter 4).

8 Except, that is, and as already mentioned, in the specific situation of woman-exchange when she herself is also a sign.

9 A repudiation of the (notional and historical) separation of value and sign in respect of words seems to have been made by, among others, Bourdieu (1991: 35–89). However, his thesis is not that words are jointly values and signs, but that in the 'economy of linguistic exchange' utterances in themselves signify value. That is, their 'power' as signs is threefold: they are not only signs of communication, to be deciphered and understood, and of authority, to be believed and obeyed; no less intrinsically, 'they are also *signs of wealth*, intended to be evaluated and appreciated' (p. 66, his stress).

10 For another interesting and anthropologically relevant view of the linkage between speaking and technology, see Ingold (1986: 144ff, 202–3, 244–92; 1993). He posits (1993: 442), among other things, that in opposition to the Western notion of tools as the means whereby mankind achieves mastery over nature in the purported struggle of the social world of persons against the material world of things, the hunter–gatherers' use of technology aims at 'drawing nature into the nexus of social relations' as in a 'dialogue' with it. But this is a whole discussion in itself which I have not the time to enter into here (see Passes 1998: 60–75).

11 This is not to imply an indigenous resistance to Western technology *per se*. As mentioned, the Pa'ikwené are greatly attracted to aspects of it, such as chainsaws and outboard motors. What is at issue here is, as Stephen Hugh-Jones, among others, has stressed (1992), the capacity of Amazonian people to make reasoned decisions in respect of Western goods and the market economy. Far from being the latter's passive victims, Amerindians act as fully conscious agents in their relationship with it, and are as aware of its dangers as of its seductiveness. For a particularly perceptive account of the indigenous agency involved in the *selection*

and incorporation of Western items, both material and non-material, see Butt Colson (1985, especially p. 144).

12 What Marx describes (1978: 423) as its value considered independently of its usefulness.

References

Arnaud, E. (1968) 'Referências sôbre o sistema de parentesco dos índios Palikúr', *Bol. Mus. Par. Emílio Goeldi Nova Ser. Antropol., Belém* 36: 1–21.

—— (1970) 'O Xamanismo entre os Índios da região Uaça', *Bol. Mus. Par. Emílio Goeldi Nova Ser. Antropol., Belém* 44: 1–22.

—— (1984) 'Os Índios Palikur do Rio Urucauá: tradição tribal e protestantismo', *Publ. Avuls. Mus. Emílio Goeldi, Belém* 39.

Bourdieu, P. (1991) *Language and Symbolic Power*, ed. J.B. Thompson, Cambridge: Polity Press.

Butt Colson, A. (1985) 'Routes of knowledge: an aspect of regional integration in the circum-Roraima area of the Guiana Highlands', *Antropologica* 63–4: 103–49.

Campbell, A.T. (1995) *Getting to Know Wai-Wai*, London: Routledge.

Cortázar, Julio (1967) 'The gates of heaven', in *Blow Up and Other Stories*, pp. 97–113, New York: Pantheon Books.

Dreyfus, S. (1981) 'Le Peuple de la rivière du milieu – esquisse pour l'étude de l'espace social palikur', in *Orients pour Georges Condominas*, pp. 301–13, Paris: Sudestasie/ Privat.

Engels, F. (1968 [1895]) 'The part played by labour in the transition from ape to man', in *Karl Marx and Frederick Engels: Selected Works*, pp. 358–68, London: Lawrence & Wishart Ltd.

Fernandes, E. (1963) 'Parincur Iené', in C.M. da Silva Rondon (ed.) *Índios do Brasil dos cabeiceiras do rio Xingu, dos rios Araguaia e Oiapoque*, Vol. 2, pp. 283–92, Rio de Janeiro: Imp. Nacional.

Goldman, I. (1979 [1963]) *The Cubeo*, Urbana: University of Illinois Press.

Grenand, F. and Grenand, P. (1987) 'La Côte d'Amapa, de la bouche de l'Amazone à la baie d'Oyapock à travers la tradition orale palikur', *Bol. Mus. Par. Emílio Goeldi Ser. Antropol. Belém* 3(1): 1–77.

Hewes, G.W. (1993) 'A history of speculation on the relation between tools and language', in K.R. Gibson and T. Ingold (eds) *Tools, Language and Cognition in Human Evolution*, pp. 20–31, Cambridge: Cambridge University Press.

Hugh-Jones, S. (1992). 'Yesterday's luxuries, tomorrow's necessities: business and barter in Northwest Amazonia', in C. Humphrey and S. Hugh-Jones (eds) *Barter, Exchange and Value: An Anthropological Approach*, pp. 41–74, Cambridge: Cambridge University Press.

Illich, I. (1973) *Tools for Conviviality*, London: Calder & Boyars.

Ingold, T. (1986) *The Appropriation of Nature*, Manchester: University of Manchester Press.

—— (1993) 'Tool use, sociality and intelligence', in K.R. Gibson and T. Ingold (eds) *Tools, Language and Cognition in Human Evolution*, pp. 429–45, Cambridge: Cambridge University Press.

Isaac, G.L. (1976) 'Stages of cultural elaboration in the Pleistocene: possible archeological indicators of the development of language capabilities', in S.R. Harnad,

H. Steklis and J. Lancaster (eds) *Origins and Evolution of Language and Speech*, Annals of the New York Academy of Sciences 280: 275–88.

Isacsson, S.-E. (1993) 'Transformations of eternity: on man and cosmos in Embera myth', unpublished Ph.D dissertation, University of Gothenburg.

Lévi-Strauss, C. (1969 [1949]) *The Elementary Structures of Kinship*, trans. J. Bell, J. von Sturmer and R. Needham, London: Eyre & Spottiswoode.

—— (1986 [1958]) *Structural Anthropology 1*, trans. C. Jacobson, Harmondsworth: Penguin.

Lutz, C.A. and Abu-Lughod, L. (eds) (1990) *Language and the Politics of Emotion*, Cambridge: Cambridge University Press, Paris: Maison des Sciences de l'Homme.

Malinowski, B. (1930) 'The problem of meaning in primitive societies', in C.K. Ogden and I.A. Richards (eds) *The Meaning of Meaning*, pp. 296–336, London: Kegan Paul and Trench Trubner.

Marx, K. (1978 [1857–67]) 'The economics', section lV, in D. McLellan (ed.) *Karl Marx: Selected Writings*, Oxford: Oxford University Press.

Meyer, Ph. (1993) *Dans mon pays lui-même*, Paris: Flammarion (Livre de poche).

Montagu, A. (1976) 'Toolmaking, hunting and the origin of language', in S.R. Hamad, H. Steklis and J. Lancaster (eds) *Origins and Evolution of Language and Speech*, Annals of the New York Academy of Sciences 280: 267–74.

Montout, E. (1994) 'De Rokawa à Kamuyene. Approche de la mutation sociale et magico-réligieuse du peuple palikur', unpublished draft of paper presented at Université des Antilles et de la Guyane, Cayenne (8 December).

Nimuendajú, C. (1971 [1926]) Unpublished French translation by Cl. Jousse of *Die Palikur Indianer und ihre Nachbarn*, Götesborgs Kungl. Vet. Vitt. Handligar Vol. 31, 2.

Overing, J. (1983–4) 'Elementary structures of reciprocity, a comparative note on Guianese, Central Brazilian and North West Amazon sociopolitical thought', *Antropologica* 59–62: 331–48.

—— (1989) 'The aesthetics of production: the sense of community among the Cubeo and Piaroa', *Dialectical Anthropology* 14: 159–75.

—— (1999) 'Elogio do cotidiano: a confiança e a arte de vida social em uma comunidade Amazônica' (In praise of the everyday: trust and the art of social living in an Amazonian community), *Mana* 5(1): 81–108.

Overing Kaplan, J. (1975) *The Piaroa*, Oxford: Clarendon Press.

Passes, A. (1998) 'The hearer, the hunter, and the agouti head – aspects of inter-communication and conviviality among the Pa'ikwené (Palikur) of French Guiana', unpublished Ph.D dissertation, University of St Andrews.

Reynolds, P.C. (1993) 'The complementary theory of language and tool use', in K.R. Gibson and T. Ingold (eds) *Tools, Language and Cognition in Human Evolution*, pp. 407–28, Cambridge: Cambridge University Press.

Rivière, P. (1983–4) 'Aspects of Carib political economy', *Antropologica* 59–62: 349–58.

—— (1984) *Individual and Society in Guiana*, Cambridge: Cambridge University Press.

Sahlins, M. (1974) *Stone Age Economics*, London: Tavistock.

Santos-Granero, F. (1986) 'Power ideology and the ritual of production in Lowland South America', *Man* 21(4): 657–79.

Saussure, F. de (1966 [1915]) *Course in General Linguistics*, trans. W. Baskin, New York: McGraw-Hill.

Schnechner, R. (1988) *Performance Theory*, London: Routledge.

Thomas, D. (1982) *Order without Government, the Society of the Pemon Indians of Venezuela*, Urbana: University of Illinois Press.

Toth, N. and Schick, K. (1993) 'Early stone industries and inferences regarding language and cognition', in K.R. Gibson and T. Ingold (eds) *Tools, Language and Cognition in Human Evolution*, pp. 346–62, Cambridge: Cambridge University Press.

Weber, M. (1971 [1904–5]) *The Protestant Ethic and the Spirit of Capitalism*, trans. Talcott Parsons, London: Unwin University Books.

Chapter 6

Knowledge and the practice of love and hate among the Enxet of Paraguay

Stephen W. Kidd

One day during my fieldwork in Paraguay,[1] Alejandro, a member of the community of San Carlos, began to dismantle his house so that he could move to the nearby community of Alegre. On bumping into him I asked him why he had decided to leave. He replied that the blame rested with his wife's brother and neighbour Miguel whom he accused of having attacked him with a knife. 'He became angry and hated me and now I want to live among those who love me so that I can once again be tranquil.' The image of Miguel as a knife-wielding maniac contrasted markedly with my own experience of him as both pleasant and friendly, though somewhat shy. I determined to find out his version of the story and later that day paid him a visit. As we sat by the fire chatting, he explained to me that, the previous evening, Alejandro had been drunk and had begun to beat his wife. On hearing the commotion, Miguel had picked up a knife and run next-door to protect his sister. 'It was Alejandro who caused me to be angry', he said, 'and he is leaving because he is ashamed of what he did.' He explained that no one in the community loved Alejandro any more and that they were pleased that he was leaving so that tranquillity would, once more, return to the village. Furthermore, he continued, if Alejandro did not leave then Miguel himself would move away since he no longer wanted to live where he could 'be caused to be angry'.

Alejandro and Miguel are members of the Enxet indigenous people, a group of some 12,000 individuals inhabiting the Chaco region of Paraguay. The above description is a typical example of the type of conversation I engaged in with the Enxet whenever they tried to explain to me aspects of their social behaviour. Such discussions were characterised by a stress on the use of emotion words and I gradually gained the impression that the Enxet understood daily social practice to be intimately tied in with notions of personhood. The aim of this chapter is to begin to explain this understanding by attempting to create a picture of how the Enxet themselves explain human behaviour. In particular, I will focus on an organ of the body known as the *wáxok* which, in Enxet philosophical thought, is recognised as the cognitive and affective centre of the person. In addition, it is also an individual's social centre and a salient feature of the Enxet explanation of their social relations. A central theme of this chapter will be to examine how the *wáxok* is constructed and to describe how its development is associated with becoming knowledgeable. Knowledgeable people possess the ability to act in a socially appropriate manner and specific behaviour is expected of those who are knowledgeable as well as of those who lack knowledge. This behaviour is understood around the opposition of love and hate which, as among the Amuesha people, is a meaningful paradigm in Enxet thought and practice (cf. Santos-Granero 1991: 45). However, Enxet discourse on appropriate and inappropriate behaviour is not without its ambiguities. It will be seen that the Enxet explain many aspects of people's behaviour by reference to extraneous influences, focusing especially on the consumption of alcohol. Nevertheless, such explanations need to be seen in context. Ultimately, the stress is upon the individual's personal responsibility and the ability of knowledgeable people to control their actions.

Defining the *wáxok*

The *[-]wáxok*[2] is both a physical and metaphysical organ of the body that is located in the region of the stomach. On the one hand it is conceived of as hollow and as part of the digestive process; as such, it is the organ of the body most prone to invasion by malevolent spirits and other objects that are sent by enemy shamans to make people ill. However, it is also the cognitive and affective centre of the person, and the encapsulation of both cognitive and affective processes in the *wáxok* is illustrated by a series of linguistic expressions that make use of the term in their construction. For instance, affects are often expressed by reference to physical states of the *wáxok* such as: 'the *wáxok* spreads out' and 'the *wáxok* is sweet', which suggest happiness and content-ment; 'the *wáxok* is heavy' and 'the *wáxok* really leans over', which indicate sadness; and 'the *wáxok* shivers', which is one way of describing fear. In contrast, terms associated with cognition ascribe agency to the *wáxok*. For example, thought is expressed by terms such as 'the *wáxok* mentions', 'the *wáxok* searches' and 'the *wáxok* says', while other terms that indicate the agency of the *wáxok* include 'the *wáxok* despises', 'the *wáxok* makes fun of' and 'the *wáxok* turns around and goes back to where it came from' (which suggests a change of mind).

However, despite its physical and metaphysical qualities, the *wáxok* cannot be fully appreciated outside the context of social relations. It is, essentially, a social concept, and by developing *wáxok*s that are 'knowledgeable' and 'understanding' – both of which are expressed by the term *[-]ya'ásekyak*[3] – people learn how to relate to others in an appropriate manner (cf. Palmer 1997: 162). As I will show, each individual is taught how and when to practise both love and hate but, before discussing this in more detail, I will first of all describe how the Enxet conceive of the development of the *wáxok*.

Constructing the *wáxok*

Although the *wáxok*, as a physical organ, is present in newborn babies, it is still, in a metaphysical sense, undeveloped. Babies, therefore, are regarded as lacking in knowledge. In a sense, they are still wild and a baby's temper tantrums are described in terms reminiscent of animal savagery. As a child grows it is expected to develop knowledge and a *wáxok* that is 'good/beautiful'. Indeed, one way of expressing the raising of a child is to use the term 'to cause to be good/beautiful' and the creation of 'good/beautiful' people is essentially dependent on the construction of 'good/beautiful' *wáxok*s (cf. Overing 1989a: 87ff; McCallum 1990: 417; Gow 1991: 159ff; Belaunde 1992: 93–4, and this volume). However, the construction of the *wáxok* is not regarded as an innate ability of the child but, instead, as an achievement of those who raise it (cf. Belaunde, Gow, Lagrou, Londoño-Sulkin, this volume).

Speech is understood as a key element in the creation of knowledge and, to a certain extent, the process of gaining knowledge is conceived of as somewhat mechanical. People 'speak to' children who 'hear' and, in fact, the verb 'to speak to' can also be expressed by the term 'to cause to hear'. Indeed, hearing is often commensurate with knowledge and understanding in that, when someone asks 'do you hear?' they can also mean 'do you understand?' (cf. Palmer, op. cit., p. 163; Passes 1998: 51). Children, therefore, are considered to be passive learners while agency is placed with the adults who 'speak to' them. Their 'words' stay in children's *wáxok*s, literally 'filling them up', and a transformation occurs in the children as they gradually attain knowledge.

The importance of speech can be observed in many other aspects of child-raising. When misbehaving, children are 'spoken to' and it is not uncommon for adults almost to plead with children not to do something, frequently without success. I have even seen a young child who wanted to pick up a hot cinder and refused to listen to his parents pleadings to leave it (cf. Grubb 1911: 108). Eventually, he was allowed to take it and suffered the consequences. Disobedient children are described as being 'without ears' and the same expression can also be used in an ironic fashion to describe adults who, after a decision has been made in a community meeting, refuse to conform. Such people can be said to be 'like children'.

The stress on 'speaking to' is also apparent in the general abhorrence of corporal punishment (cf. Regehr 1987: 167; Overing 1989a: 92). It rarely occurs, and I became fully aware of the Enxet view on the matter during a community meeting in one of their settlements. One of the leaders, Papito, was speaking about the problems they were experiencing with young people and, referring to his own troublesome children, declared: 'You know the difficulties that I have with them but whenever they act wrongly I hit them'. The sudden silence that descended on the meeting reflected people's shock at Papito's admission but, realising that he was in danger of irretrievably damaging his reputation, Papito quickly clarified his position by explaining that he was not, of course, referring to a physical beating but, rather, to 'hitting them with words'. It was an elegant attempt to wriggle out of a tight corner but, since I had once witnessed Papito forcefully slap his grandchild on the head, it implied a certain economy with the truth.

Corporal punishment is believed to harm rather than build up a child's *wáxok* and, therefore, the most common method used to control children is speech. Adults use a threat from the outside to try to frighten disobedient children and so, for example, if children are prone to wander away from the house, they are often warned that, if they do so, a spirit may attack them (cf. Guemple 1988: 137; Regehr, op. cit., p. 168; Belaunde, op. cit., p. 98; Palmer, op. cit., p. 65). Missionaries are another commonly used threat, especially nurses who, children are told, will vaccinate them if they are disobedient.

Comparable conceptions of how children are taught by being spoken to are found elsewhere in Lowland South America, while Overing (1988: 179) has discussed the pedagogical value of myths among the Piaroa (cf. Belaunde, op. cit., pp. 94ff; Palmer, op. cit., pp. 161ff; Passes, op. cit., p. 57). Since their myths are nowadays rarely remembered and infrequently told, it is difficult to know whether this also used to be the case among the Enxet. However, church sermons appear to fulfil a similar function and in many communities there are at least two or three services per week which are well attended by children.[4] During the sermons stress is placed on encouraging people to relate to fellow community members in an appropriate manner.

As people become adults they are regarded as more capable of consciously controlling their own behaviour. For instance, in sermons preachers frequently express the exhortation that 'we should make our *wáxoks* good/ beautiful'; this would seem, in part, to be the result of listening to 'good speech', thereby gaining greater knowledge. Certainly, within the context of Christian teaching, people are told that they will 'make their *wáxok* "good/ beautiful"' by listening to the preaching of 'God's words'. In addition, a *wáxok* can be made 'good/beautiful' by allowing God, Jesus or the Holy Spirit to enter and dwell within. While such ideas are clearly derived from evangelical theology, they have been accepted much more literally than ever intended by the missionaries. Given that the Enxet believe that malevolent spirits can invade the *wáxok* to cause illness, madness and antisocial behaviour, it is but a small step to conceive of Jesus and the Holy Spirit – which is often said to have the physical form of a dove – as entering.

The agency of people as 'listeners' to 'good words' contrasts with the passive hearing that characterises the learning of a child. Listening implies that people permit words to enter the *wáxok* while hearing suggests much less control (cf. Palmer, op. cit., p. 163; Passes, op. cit., p. 64). It would seem that, as people gain knowledge, they become increasingly active participants in their own learning and the creation of 'good/beautiful' *wáxok*s.

Being knowledgeable about love

Knowledge is an eminently social attribute and knowledgeable people are those who know how to practise love appropriately or, as Overing (1996) puts it, possess the capabilities to live a harmonious life. 'Love' – *[-]ásekhayo* – is understood by the Enxet to be at the very heart of proper social relations. While, in 'Western' folk concepts, love is defined as an emotion or bodily feeling, the Enxet notion of love is much wider, going beyond a feeling to encompass both a moral principle and a mode of behaviour. In effect, love is associated with what Western moral philosophy defines as the 'other-regarding virtues' which are essentially those that express a concern for the well-being of others (cf. Overing 1988: 178). Therefore, when the Enxet exhort people to love others, they are talking about a way of living. Those who love should be generous and share their produce and possessions with others so that, in essence, those who love, give, while those who give, love (cf. Santos-Granero 1991: 202; Overing 1993b: 54). Love also implies helping others and encapsulates a way of talking so that only 'good speech' is directed towards those who are loved. In effect, love is conceived of by the Enxet as something that is done – in other words, the practice of sociality – and, if it is not manifested in actions, it does not exist.[5]

As a moral value, love should characterise any interaction between those who consider themselves to be in a sociable relationship. Consequently, the concepts of kinship and love are mutually implicated so that kin can be defined as those we love, while those we love are often referred to as kin. Another expression that is commonly used to describe a loving relationship is the phrase 'to look at someone'. Those who 'look at us' are those who love us by, for example, sharing their property, spending time with us and being willing to eat and drink our food. In other words, they want to develop a sociable relationship with us.

Knowledgeable people are said to have good 'thoughts' and, as I illustrated earlier, 'thinking' itself is understood to be an action of the *wáxok* as an agent. The voluntary sharing of food with others is a clear expression of love and is, in fact, said to be a thought, in other words, 'a mentioning of one's *wáxok*' (Kidd 1999: 192ff). A greeting is expressed by the same term and, since greetings are manifestations of a person's desire to create or re-create a relationship, the description of them as thoughts is particularly pertinent. Furthermore, people who express a desire to help others can be said to have 'good thoughts' which is expressed by the term 'one's *wáxok's* searching is good'.

Another way of describing a knowledgeable and loving person is by the term *hápek [-]wáxok*. The essential meaning of *hápek* is 'to be soft'. It can, for example, describe a football that is somewhat deflated or, alternatively, two objects that have been stuck or glued together but which come apart easily. In this latter sense of weak bonding, *hápek* can also describe a door that is 'unlocked'. The possession of a 'soft/unlocked' *wáxok* is regarded by the Enxet as an ideal since such a person practises love and shares food and possessions with kin and those in need. In addition, such people are compassionate. For instance, old men have told me that when, during the Chaco War of 1932–6, they were issued with rifles by the Paraguayan army and told to hunt down and shoot Paraguayan deserters, they could not do it. Their 'soft/unlocked' *wáxok*s caused them to weep with compassion when they saw the state of the deserters. The concept of compassion is usually expressed by the term 'the poor/suffering person that one looks at'. Since 'looking at' someone is, as I have explained, commensurate with the acknowledgement of a social relationship predicated on love, compassion could be described as the recognition of another person's poverty and suffering. An individual with a 'soft/unlocked' *wáxok* should practise love towards such a suffering person (cf. Alès, Gow, Jamieson, Lagrou, Londoño-Sulkin, this volume).

A further key form of behaviour associated with being knowledgeable is to act with *[-]ennawagko*, a term that is somewhat ambiguous. On the one hand, it can mean 'timidity' or 'shyness' and is described by the Enxet as similar to 'fear' (cf. Belaunde, Gow, Rivière, this volume). Thus, for instance, if, in a game of football, the members of one team seem wary of tackling their opponents, they could be accused of being too timid. Similarly, someone who is reticent to speak in public could be said to be shy. However, the Enxet themselves often translate *[-]ennawagko* as 'respect', which suggests that it is much more than an emotion. In fact, as with love, it also implies a moral value and an other-regarding mode of behaviour (cf. Belaunde, this volume). In this context, it can best be translated by the term 'restraint' (cf. Belaunde, Gonçalves, Lagrou, Overing, Rivière, Rosengren, this volume). In normal daily life, unless a relationship is particularly close, such as between members of the same household, people should treat each other with restraint and, in this sense, it is regarded as a virtue. By acting with restraint, one avoids harming the *wáxok*s of others. One should not, therefore, ask others for food, disturb them if they are otherwise occupied, deny requests, abuse community property, nor do things that are against the will of others. Furthermore, 'bad speech' – which includes criticising people to their face or speaking when angry – should be avoided. Consequently, the practice of restraint is regarded as constitutive of love and as derived from a knowledgeable and 'soft/unlocked' *wáxok*.[6] It is, therefore, associated with an aesthetics of controlling one's emotions, especially the wild, antisocial impulses – such as anger – which are an integral part of being human (cf. Grubb 1911: 200; Alvarsson 1988: 135; Overing 1989a: 91, and this volume; Belaunde, op. cit., p. 104, and this volume; Palmer, op. cit., p. 162).

Knowledge is also associated with the ability to live tranquilly and, indeed, a desire for tranquillity is a key aim of many indigenous peoples of Lowland South America, as many of the chapters in this volume describe (cf. also Overing 1989a: 79; 1993b; Belaunde, op. cit., p. 105). The Enxet are no different and express personal tranquillity by the term 'there is nothing happening in one's *wáxok*'. It describes a knowledgeable *wáxok* in a state of calm and motionlessness, one that is not suffering the intrusion of extraneous, pathogenic objects and which, to all intents and purposes, is at peace (cf. Gow, this volume). It portrays a person who is emotionally comfortable and whose *wáxok* has not been disturbed by such things as breaches in social relationships and misfortune (cf. Goldman 1963; Overing 1989b: 163; Ellis 1997: 12). It is a state that is not incompatible with certain other agreeable conditions of the *wáxok* such as 'sweetness' – which suggests contentment – and a *wáxok* that 'spreads out' – which is indicative of happiness.

The ideal of 'nothing happening in the *wáxok*' contrasts strongly with a *wáxok* that is 'in motion' or 'disturbed' and, in effect, is experiencing negative or disagreeable emotions such as anger, shame, shock, fear or sadness. Invariably, these affective states have causes that are extraneous to the individual, such as conflictive social relationships, attacks from the spiritual beings of the invisible world, or simply misfortune (cf. Belaunde, this volume). As I described earlier, emotions are often expressed by terms that combine the *wáxok*, as subject, with a verb. However, the effect of outside influences on an individual's affective state can be expressed grammatically by changing the *wáxok* from subject to object and adding a causative suffix to the verb. For example, 'one's *wáxok* falls down' could be transformed to 'it made one's *wáxok* fall down', thereby identifying the cause of the emotion.[7] Similarly, specific events can become the subject so that the emotion term highlights both the event and its effect on the *wáxok*. For instance, 'it kills/hits one's *wáxok*' can describe an event, such as a theft of property or bad news, that shocks or traumatises a person while 'it really squeezes one's *wáxok*' refers to a situation that causes a person to be very sad.

People continually strive to retain or regain tranquil *wáxok*s and are aware that their personal affective comfort is dependent on harmony in their social lives. They aspire to live in tranquil communities and, although people are concerned to maintain peaceful *wáxok*s of their own, they realise that this requires the *wáxok*s of other people, especially co-residents, to be similarly tranquil. One should, therefore, practise restraint and love when dealing with others and should only speak to others when one's own *wáxok* is tranquil so that only 'good speech' that 'causes others to be good/beautiful' is used. If each individual is tranquil, the chances of the community as a whole being tranquil are greatly enhanced.

Lacking knowledge

However, in reality, daily community life is pregnant with possible sources of disharmony and the presence of even one or two people who act without knowledge and 'good thoughts' can cause tremendous disruption within a community (cf. Gonçalves, Rivière, Rosengren, Santos-Granero, this volume). A variety of terms can be used to describe persistently antisocial individuals. For instance, such people can be known as *ayasaxma*, which means, literally, 'lacking in knowledge/understanding', or could be described as possessing a 'bad/ugly' *wáxok*. Alternatively, people can be said to be 'without a *wáxok*' and an old man once used this term to describe young men who walked straight past him without 'looking at him'. 'They are like snakes or dogs,' he added, suggesting an association between a lack of *wáxok* and an animal nature. Similarly, the term 'really missing a *wáxok*' describes those who are excessively proud and look down on others whom they refuse to treat as equals. Indeed, this term is used to describe those missionaries who prefer to keep their distance from the Enxet, appear uncomfortable when visiting their homes and refuse to eat and drink with them.

Antisocial, 'unknowledgeable' people are those who, instead of practising love, exhibit *[-]taknagko*, a term that I will translate, in shorthand, as 'hate' since it is, effectively, the opposite of love. As with love, hate is not just a feeling but is a way of acting, in effect a denial of a social relationship and a refusal 'to look at other people'. It is associated with a *kayhek [-]wáxok*, a term that characterises a selfish, egotistical person who is lacking in compassion. *Kayhek* is, essentially, the opposite of *hápek* ('soft/unlocked') and can mean 'to be strong' (as in a 'strong person'), 'to be hard' (like a fully inflated football), or 'to be tightly stuck' (as in two objects that are glued together). In this latter sense, it is also used to refer to a locked door. People with 'strong/hard/locked' *wáxok*s do not practise love, refuse to look at people with compassion and seek to benefit themselves without thinking of others. For instance, when someone refuses to share they could be accused of having a *wáxok* that is 'hard/locked'. Furthermore, those who hate us can be described as 'opponents/enemies' and can seek to harm us, perhaps by using malevolent shamanism. Although non-kin are not necessarily hated, hate should not characterise a relationship between kin.

Those who lack knowledge also act without restraint. They demand things of others, give orders and use 'heavy' or 'strong' words in conversation which can harm the *wáxok*s of the listeners. Indeed, people who behave without restraint are often said to have 'strengthened/locked' their *wáxok*s so that they can act in this antisocial manner. The most extreme lack of restraint is said to be 'anger': *[-]ló*.

Anger is regarded as the gravest form of antisocial behaviour and is viewed as almost synonymous with hate (cf. Santos-Granero 1991: 220; see also Alès, Belaunde, Londoño-Sulkin, Overing, Rivière, Rosengren, this volume). In fact, as was illustrated by the conflict between Alejandro and Miguel, the two words are frequently expressed in almost the same breath, as in 'he was angry with me; he hated me'. Anger should, therefore, be totally avoided in inappropriate situations such as with kin, co-residents and, in general, with those who are loved. In fact, anger and love are effectively incompatible.

The Enxet relate anger to violent behaviour such as shouting, other unacceptable forms of speech which are subsumed under the notion of 'heavy words',
and fighting. Indeed, the fact that anger can be expressed without reference
to the *wáxok* suggests that the focus is on the visible aspects of anger as manifested in behaviour. Nevertheless, it goes without saying that an angry
person also has an angry *wáxok*. Although anger is rarely thought of as
hidden, it is possible to use the expression 'the *wáxok* is angry' to refer to someone who has managed to conceal their true feelings.

So abhorrent is anger that, unless people are drunk, it is rarely observed
(cf. Grubb 1911: 200). Indeed, the self-control that is implied by the term
'nothing happening in the *wáxok*' is mainly concerned with the avoidance of
anger. Those people who have a tendency to anger easily can be called
'savage', and, since savagery is characteristic of the more dangerous wild
animals, the description effectively underscores the lack of knowledge of such
people.

Knowledge and the ability to hate

Although I have suggested that knowledge is associated with love and a lack
of knowledge with hate, it would, in fact, be more accurate to say that being
knowledgeable implies having an understanding of when and how to act
appropriately. Therefore, the relationships between knowledge, love and
hate are more ambiguous than I have hitherto suggested and, in contrast to
the Amuesha, who 'see love as permeating every aspect of human interaction'
(Santos-Granero 1991: 201), the Enxet conceive of the requirement to love
as contextual. Although they stress practising love, this does not imply a blan-
ket condemnation of hate and so people are taught not just who and how to
love but also who and how to hate (cf. Overing 1989a: 82f). While one
should love those considered to be in the in-group, it is acceptable to hate
those on the 'outside'.[8]

Therefore, although acting with a 'strong/locked' *wáxok* is usually condemned within one's own in-group – which the Enxet describe as comprising
'those of us who love each other' – when a leader meets with White people on
behalf of the community he should have a strong *wáxok* and show no fear.[9]
He need not show restraint but should be strong and prepared to use 'heavy'
speech. A leader who, when dealing with outsiders, demonstrates a 'soft/
weak' *wáxok* is regarded as useless since his *wáxok* would shiver and he would
remain quiet, too scared to speak up for his community. Such leaders are
accused of being too 'restrained/timid,' with the stress clearly placed on the
side of timidity.

Anger can even be considered appropriate behaviour in the right circumstances. While it should never be expressed in a relationship predicated on
love, it may be acceptable when the need to practise love is irrelevant. This

is clearest in the action of the shaman who, to save a patient, must fight with malevolent shamans and other dangerous beings of the invisible world. It is anger that causes shamans to harm people and the healing shaman must meet anger with anger in the battlefields of the cosmos and try his best to kill the enemy shaman. The *meteymog* revenge magic is also provoked by a mixture of sorrow and anger at the loss of a loved one. If a person's death is thought to have been caused by a shaman, before burial a red-hot stone, known as a *meteymog*, can be placed into an incision in the cadaver (cf. Grubb 1904: 42ff, 128; 1911: 160ff; Susnik 1977: 22; Chase-Sardi 1981). The stone shoots off into the sky to seek out the murdering shaman and burn him to death, and his demise is a cause of rejoicing. Leaders could also use anger to confront missionaries, politicians or government officials if, by doing so, they can acquire material advantages for their communities. Anger, therefore, when directed towards the outside, can be productive of social life (cf. Alès, this volume).

The above examples indicate that many Enxet emotion words tend to have multiple meanings and can be used in apparently contradictory and creative ways depending on the context. While a 'soft/unlocked' *wáxok* can be used positively to praise a generous loving person, the same term can be used to condemn someone regarded as cowardly. And, although a person who refuses to share can be denounced as having a 'strong/locked' *wáxok*, in another context the same expression can indicate courage. Indeed, different people can use similar words in conversation but lend quite distinct meanings to them. For instance, if, in a meeting, someone takes the initiative to confront a wrongdoer to his face, those who support the speaker may speak favourably of his strong *wáxok* – in other words, his courage – while those on the side of the person attacked could use the same expression to criticise the speaker's lack of restraint. Although such apparent contradictions may be confusing to outsiders, the Enxet themselves experience no difficulty in understanding their meaning, interpreting them according to the specific context.

Indeed, individuals can even be said to exhibit two quite different characters and the term 'two *wáxoks*' can be used to describe such people. They may, for example, demonstrate knowledge by acting in a loving, responsible manner but, at times, could comport themselves as if they were without knowledge by becoming angry and fighting with others.

Temptation and the tempter

The *wáxok* should be understood as encapsulating an individual's character or personality, although always within the context of relations with others (cf. Loewen 1966). Yet, there remains the question of the degree to which people are regarded as responsible for their own behaviour. Clearly, the notion of individual responsibility has been implied by my description of a correlation between antisocial behaviour and a lack of knowledge; for example, a person's 'savage' behaviour can be explained by the term *[-]témakxa* which means, essentially, 'that is how he/she is' or 'that is what he/she always does'. At other times, though, antisocial behaviour can be explained by reference to the invasion of the *wáxok* by an outside agent that causes a person to act inappropriately.[10] One of the most frequently mentioned culprits is Satan who is often referred to by the term *Segyepkeynma*.

Segyepkeynma is derived from the verb *[-]yepkeynma*, which means 'to tempt' or 'to test', and can be understood as 'he who tempts us'. Its origin would seem to be the story of Jesus' temptation in the desert during his forty days of fasting and may be a translation of an alternative name for Satan, 'the Tempter'. While the Tempter is said to encourage people to act in a wrong or self-indulgent manner, Satan is not the only being that is a source of temptation. Other spirits can tempt us and, indeed, when people become insane, they can be said to have been seduced by spirits: men fall under the spell of 'wild women' spirits, who have the appearance of beautiful White women, while women become attracted to the guardian spirits of the water who look like short Paraguayan soldiers. Foreign 'pop' music is believed to have a spiritual master that can 'take hold of' the *wáxok* of those who dance and 'speed them up' so that they behave towards others without restraint. They could, perhaps, become excited, talk in an unacceptable or insulting manner, have sex with other people's spouses, or even become angry and fight. Even humans can be described as tempters and a leader of the Enxet Anglican Church once complained to the missionaries that I was one. He was not accusing me of possessing a demonic nature – at least, I hope not – but was alleging that I encouraged the Enxet to return to their traditional dances which had been banned by the Church many years earlier.

Often, people say that they are tempted into doing 'things that they like', in other words, behaving in a selfish and self-centred manner so that their own pleasure is placed before the well-being of those they love or should love. However, although the concept of temptation could be used to argue that people's behaviour is determined by outside forces, I believe that, instead, it provides evidence to support the suggestion that individuals who have been taught to be knowledgeable are, in fact, personally responsible for their own actions. People may be tempted, but each individual can choose whether to succumb or resist.

An explanation for why people are responsible for their antisocial behaviour can be obtained by focusing on the dual concept of the 'soft/weak/unlocked' and the 'hard/strong/locked' *wáxok*. People talk of a door to the *wáxok* and, although the term may be figurative, it certainly implies that the *wáxok* can be locked shut. Furthermore, other terms suggest that individuals are active agents in locking and unlocking their own *wáxok*s. For example, when people are faced with an outside temptation or the possibility of an outside force entering the *wáxok*, they can be encouraged to lock their *wáxok*s and impede entry. Certainly, within a Christian context, those who, for example, resist the temptation to dance, drink and commit adultery are said to have 'strong/locked' *wáxok*s. In contrast, those who succumb possess 'weak/unlocked' *wáxok*s since they allow temptation and other outside forces – such as the Tempter – to enter. Once inside, these outside forces can influence the *wáxok* and cause people to behave antisocially.

I suspect that it is knowledge that enables people to 'lock' their *wáxok*s when required, and it is probably for this reason that young people – who are less mature – are more liable to behave antisocially. Nevertheless, as I have indicated, the notion that people are incapable of resisting outside influences is a continually recurring theme in daily discourse, and its inherent contradiction with the concept of human agency and responsibility is never adequately resolved. However, for the concepts to work as explanations of human behaviour and social relations it is not necessary for these contradictions to be resolved, and, indeed, the ambiguities permit a greater latitude and freedom whenever individuals explain their own behaviour and that of others. For example, when people act antisocially, the option exists either to blame them personally by referring to their 'weak/unlocked' *wáxok*s and lack of knowledge or, alternatively, to claim that they were blameless and were overcome by powerful outside forces that were almost impossible to resist.

The causative suffix is frequently used to indicate that a person's failings have an outside source and a common example is the word for anger. When it is expressed in conjunction with the causative suffix the motive for any anger is highlighted and, in addition, located outside the person in a similar way to temptation.[11] Often, the actions of other people are identified as causing anger so that, for example, someone who is mistreated could use the causative suffix to indicate that their anger is justified because it has been caused by the actions of another person (cf. Belaunde, this volume). Even inanimate objects could be said to cause anger: communal money, for instance, is often said to make people angry if it is not distributed equally.

The use or non-use of the causative suffix usually depends on the perspective and motives of the speaker: does he/she want to criticise the errant individual or, alternatively, absolve him or her by shifting the responsibility for any aberrant behaviour to an outside force? Distinct explanations can, therefore, be attributed to a single act by different people. Certainly, when people explain their own antisocial behaviour, the tendency is to minimise their own role and to blame an outside influence. Similarly, the decision to add or omit the causative suffix can depend on the speaker's relationship to the angry person. When referring to close kin it is likely that the cause and the justifiable nature of the anger will be stressed; in contrast, when talking about a rival or someone who is hated the causative suffix may well be omitted. However, this point should not be over-stretched, as the use of the causative suffix can be little more than a grammatical device. Even if a person is caused to be angry, he or she is angry nevertheless and, therefore, ultimately responsible.

Alcohol and anger

Alcohol is recognised as the main cause of anger and its role in provoking anti-social behaviour is a good illustration of how the Enxet understand outside influences (cf. Rivière, Rosengren, this volume). Yet drink presents something of a paradox. On the one hand, it is an essential component of festivals and community celebrations and its consumption is viewed as generative of informality, enjoyment and sociality (cf. Grubb 1911: 180ff; Goldman 1963: 202ff; Gow 1991: 127–8; Viveiros de Castro 1992: 119ff; Belaunde, op. cit., p. 17; Ellis, op. cit., pp. 153–4). Yet the consumption of alcohol has also been noted as a major cause of fighting among indigenous peoples[12] and it is rare for an Enxet dance to pass without some sort of conflict (cf. Grubb 1911: 184). Although this is normally limited to shouting and fist fights, I know a number of men who have suffered knife wounds. Usually, though, knives are drawn with little intention of their being used, as if drunks are convinced that they can enhance the spectacle of their anger by brandishing a knife while shouting out their grievances.

Why should alcohol promote such paradoxical behaviour in that it is both productive and destructive of sociality (cf. Rivière, this volume)? The Enxet describe drunkenness as, literally, 'alcohol killing/knocking out someone', and this suggests that the consumption of alcohol brings about a temporary reduction in knowledge. In other words, people become less aware of how to act towards others. They begin to lose their self-control and behave with less restraint but, as long as this reduction in restraint is limited, it can stimulate greater openness and fluidity in social relations and encourage people to talk, joke and, in general, be more intimate (cf. Ellis, op. cit., p. 153). If, however, the loss of restraint is excessive, it can end in the ultimate disrespect of anger.

At another level, though, the Enxet also stress the agency of beings of the invisible world. One shaman explained to me that people drink because the spiritual owner of Paraguayan rum sings its song which is so beautiful that men, who hear it in their *wáxoks*, are attracted to the source – usually a shop – where they feel compelled to drink.[13] In this sense, alcohol is a temptation. However, I was also told that fighting occurs because spirits can pour their 'medicine' into the alcohol that people are drinking. As a result, it enters their *wáxoks*, turning them temporarily crazy so that they act without knowledge and are, therefore, prone to anger (cf. Ellis, op. cit., p. 154).

Because they recognise the power of the outside, people are, in general, tolerant of drunks who become angry, and one shaman told me that we should hate the drinking rather than the drunk. In contrast, a person who becomes angry when sober is likely to be much more harshly condemned although, as I mentioned earlier, any judgement on people's anger is always dependent on the perspective and intentions of the speaker.

However, even when drunk, people are, ultimately, still regarded as individually responsible for their own actions since they could have refused drink by 'strengthening/locking' their *wáxok*s. Similarly, those who want to give up drink must learn to lock their *wáxok*s against temptation, and this can be achieved by being spoken to by others. Such people often say that they have come to a 'realisation' that they should give up drink, and the verb 'to realise' is expressed literally by the term 'to arrive at knowledge'. The change of behaviour is, therefore, explained by gaining knowledge through listening to others. Interestingly, very few Enxet women drink alcohol and their abstinence is explained by their possession of 'strong/locked' *wáxok*s (cf. Grubb 1911: 184).

When drunks who have been angry eventually sober up they usually 'realise' what they have done, and one common reaction is to experience 'shame'. In a sense, shame could be described as the result of 'arriving at a knowledge/understanding' about one's behaviour; in other words, it is a 'realisation' that one has behaved inappropriately and without due love and restraint. One common reaction to experiencing shame is to leave a community and this often happens after drunken men have beaten their wives. In fact, shame is often described by the Enxet as if it were a social regulatory mechanism.

An Enxet perspective on personal autonomy

Although it has only occasionally been explicitly referred to, a central theme of this chapter – as with others in this volume – has been the notion of personal autonomy, a value that has been widely noted as characteristic of Lowland South American indigenous societies.[14] Yet, as a number of authors have stressed, this autonomy should not be confused with a rampant, ego-centred and asocial individualism that finds an echo in certain strands of Western thinking (cf. Overing 1989b: 162–3; Santos-Granero 1991: 254; Ellis, op. cit., pp. 12–13). While, as Overing (1989b: 162) has pointed out, 'the antipathy between the principles of community and personal autonomy is salient to a major strand of Western individualism', among many indigenous peoples autonomy is understood to be grounded in the social totality (Ingold 1986: 223). Rather than undermining social life, personal autonomy underpins and reproduces the community and should be regarded, in effect, as a social and cultural quality (cf. Thomas 1982: 236; Myers 1988; Overing 1989b: p. 162; Ellis, op. cit., p. 13).

The Enxet discourse on personal autonomy corresponds perfectly with the wider picture from Lowland South America and is always expressed within the context of an individual's relationship with intimate others. Rather than centring uniquely on a person's own freedom and fulfilment, it is conveyed through a series of ideas on how one should treat and respect others. As Overing (1996) states for the Piaroa, it is necessary 'to conjoin the conscious, intentional I with skills for both social and customary action'. For the Enxet, these skills are intimately related to the concepts of the *wáxok* and knowledge. They repeatedly use phrases such as: 'we must present only good/beautiful *wáxok*s to our kin', 'we should only speak to our kin when nothing is happening in our *wáxok*s' (i.e. when tranquil) and 'we should cause our kin to be good/ beautiful'. Alternatively, people can stress the need to avoid 'harming the *wáxok* of others' and care should be taken in only using 'good words' when speaking to each other. Central to this aesthetics of interpersonal relations is the notion of restraint and its implication that people should not impose themselves on others (cf. Forrest 1987: 325). Such behaviour is an essential aspect of loving one another.

As Overing (1996) remarks concerning the Piaroa: 'The responsible, reflective "I" from the start is a social "I": one's own autonomy is dependent upon the autonomy of others – and vice versa.' If, within a community, there is mutual respect among the members for the autonomy of all others, the community will prosper and love will be engendered. The key, as Thomas has noted for the Pemon, is to extend 'autonomy as a prerogative *of the other*' (op. cit., p. 237, Thomas's emphasis) so that, rather than giving priority to one's own independence, stress is placed on upholding the well-being of others. However, as always, this is only relevant within the appropriate context, in other words among those who love each other.

The Enxet discourse is, however, distinct from that of the Piaroa who, if a person is questioned about a personal decision, is most likely to answer with a phrase that can be understood as: 'what I do is *my* business, and not yours – nor anyone else's' (Overing 1996; see Rivière, this volume). This is probably the most commonly heard expression among the Piaroa and is described by Overing (op. cit.) as 'an emphatic statement of personal autonomy or purpose'. Quite apart from the fact that the Enxet rarely question each other's personal decisions, such a self-centred comment would be anathema to the Enxet. In contrast, a very similar term – *[-]teme [-]agkok [-]agko* – is employed as a criticism of those who act in a selfish, individualistic manner. It could be translated as 'one does one's very own thing' and implies a sense of 'acting on one's own behalf' or 'in one's own interests'. Such an accusation suggests a lack of restraint and love, and when individuals act in an egotistical manner others will often say, 'Let him do his own thing'. It is rarely said to the faces of errant individuals – since this would require the speaker to have a 'strong' *wáxok* and to practise a concomitant lack of restraint; instead, it is directed towards those who are thought to share the same opinion. The statement is a condemnation of selfish behaviour yet, at the same time, it expresses a continued respect for the autonomy of others, irrespective of their errors. It is similar, perhaps, to the Piaroa expression 'too much individualism' which Oldham (1996) has reported as being used to criticise egotistical leaders.

Conclusion

In this chapter I have illustrated how the Enxet make salient use of 'emotion words' to explain their own behaviour and social relations. Key to their thinking is the dichotomy between love and hate; yet, while these words may express affective states, they are much more than this. They also reflect an aesthetics of practice and appropriate behaviour which is learnt in childhood through a process of constructing a knowledgeable *wáxok*, the organ of the body that is the social centre of the person. However, the translation of these and many other 'emotion words' that reflect cognitive and affective states of the *wáxok* is not a straightforward task. Instead, meaning is dependent on factors such as context and the perspective and motives of the speaker, as well as being frequently contested. In one context a word may have a very positive valuation whilst, in another, it may have quite the opposite. Yet, rather than viewing these apparent incoherences, contradictions and ambiguities as problematic, they should be understood as an integral element of the use of language. Indeed, it is only by dwelling on the ambiguities of language that we can obtain a fuller appreciation of its true significance.

Notes

1 Research for this paper was, in part, financed by research grants from the Economic and Social Research Council and the Emslie Horniman Fund of the Royal Anthropological Institute.
2 *[-]wáxok* is always used with the addition of a prefix to indicate the person, such as *éwáxok* which means 'my *wáxok*'. However, in this chapter I will use the shorthand form *wáxok*.
3 Although *[-]ya'ásekyak* encompasses both knowledge and understanding, in my discussion I will express them both by the shorthand term: knowledge.
4 The Enxet were originally evangelised by Anglican missionaries belonging to the South American Missionary Society. The Mission commenced in 1888 and Anglican churches can still be found in a small number of communities.
5 Similar ideas about the relationship between knowledge and sociable behaviour are held by other Lowland South American peoples. See, for example, Overing (1988), Belaunde (1992: 94ff and this volume) and Palmer (1997: 161ff).
6 The restraint practised by the Enxet is distinct from the 'restraint/respect' reported for other indigenous peoples by Henley (1982: 131), Forrest (1987: 325) and Belaunde (1992: 128ff). In these examples 'restraint/respect' characterises the behaviour of younger people to older people. Among the Enxet, even parents should practise restraint with their children and this is one explanation for the aversion to corporal punishment. Cf. McCallum (1989: 209) who refers to reciprocal restraint between neighbours and kin.
7 *Teyekmek éwáxok* means 'my *wáxok* falls down' while 'he causes my *wáxok* to fall down' can be written as *aptegkese éwáxok*.

 8 See Kidd (1999: 225ff) for a discussion of the problematic concept of inside/
    outside among indigenous American peoples.
 9 A 'strong' *wáxok* is, therefore, associated with courage (cf. Palmer 1997: 160).
10 Antisocial behaviour can, therefore, be presented as a form of physical illness
    caused by the presence of extraneous objects within the person. Cf. Overing
    (1985b: 270–1).
11 By adding the causative suffix, the verb *[-]ló* – 'to be angry' – becomes *[-]lókáso* –
    'to cause to be angry'.
12 See Goldman (1963: 216ff); Siskind (1973: 127); Kracke (1978: 22, 105, 170);
    Thomas (1982: 162); Brown (1986: 319); Myers (1986: 119); Gow (1991: 128);
    Belaunde (1992: 105); Viveiros de Castro (1992: 128); Harvey (1994: 53); Dean
    (1995: 93) and Peters (1998: 207). It should be noted that Ellis (1997) suggests
    that the Tsimane of Bolivia are an exception to the generally accepted correlation
    between alcohol and antisocial behaviour among indigenous American peoples.
    She states that the consumption of alcohol allows the normal underlying Tsimane
    potential for anger to be temporarily subsumed by the shared intimacy of drinking
    (ibid., p. 154). See also Forrest (1987: 300ff).
13 The 'owner' of Paraguayan rum is the 'owner' of the sugar-cane plant from which
    the rum is produced.
14 See, for example, Goldman (1963: 253); Buenaventura-Posso and Brown (1980:
    111); Thomas (1982); Rivière (1984: 4); Santos-Granero (1986: 108); Renshaw
    (1986: 13, 272); Forrest (1987: 325); Overing (1988, 1989a, 1989b, 1993a,
    1993b, 1996); McCallum (1989: 241); Belaunde (1992: 20) and Viveiros de
    Castro (1992: 109ff). Personal autonomy has also been noted as characteristic of
    many hunter–gatherer societies (cf. Woodburn 1980: 106; Ingold 1986: 222ff).

References

Alvarsson, J. (1988) *The Mataco of the Gran Chaco: An Ethnographic Account of Change and
    Continuity in Mataco Socio-economic Organization*, Uppsala Studies in Cultural Anthro-
    pology 11.
Belaunde, L.E. (1992) 'Gender, commensality and community among the Airo-Pai
    of West Amazonia (Secoya, Western-Tukanoan speaking)', Ph.D dissertation,
    University of London.
Brown, M.F. (1986) 'Power, gender and the social meaning of Aguaruna suicide', *Man*
    (n.s.) 21: 311–28.
Buenaventura-Posso, E. and Brown, S.E. (1980) 'Forced transition from egalitarian-
    ism to male dominance: the Bari of Columbia', in M. Etienne and E. Leacock (eds)
    Women and Colonization: Anthropological Perspectives, New York: Praeger.
Chase-Sardi, M. (1981) *Pequeño decameron Nivaklé: literatura oral de una etnia del Chaco
    Paraguayo*, Asunción: Ediciones NAPA.
Dean, B. (1995) 'Forbidden fruit: infidelity, affinity and brideservice among the
    Urarina of Peruvian Amazon', *Journal of the Royal Anthropological Institute* (n.s.) 1:
    87–110.
Ellis, R. (1997) 'A taste for movement: an exploration of the social ethics of the
    Tsimanes of Lowland Bolivia', unpublished Ph.D dissertation, University of
    St Andrews.

Forrest, L.A. (1987) 'Economics and the social organization of labour: a case study of a coastal Carib community in Surinam', unpublished Ph.D dissertation, University of London.

Goldman, I. (1963) *The Cubeo: Indians of the Northwest Amazon*, Urbana: University of Illinois Press.

Gow, P. (1991) *Of Mixed Blood: Kinship and History in Peruvian Amazon*, Oxford: Clarendon Press.

Grubb, W.B. (1904) *Among the Indians of the Paraguayan Chaco*, London: Charles Murray.

—— (1911) *An Unknown People in an Unknown Land: an account of the life and customs of the Lengua Indians of the Paraguayan Chaco, with adventures and experiences met with during twenty years' pioneering and exploration amongst them*, London: Seeley.

Guemple, L. (1988) 'Teaching social relations to Inuit children', in T. Ingold, D. Riches and J. Woodburn (eds) *Hunters and Gatherers 2: Property, Power and Ideology*, New York and Oxford: Berg (Explorations in Anthropology series).

Harvey, P. (1994) 'The presence and absence of speech in the communication of gender', in P. Burton, K.K. Dyson and S. Ardener (eds) *Bilingual Women*, Oxford: Berg.

Henley, P. (1982) *The Panare: Tradition and Change on the Amazonian Frontier*, New Haven, Conn. and London: Yale University Press.

Ingold, T. (1986) *The Appropriation of Nature: Essays on Human Ecology and Social Relations*, Manchester: Manchester University Press.

Kidd, S.W. (1999) 'Love and hate among the people without things: the social and economic relations of the Enxet people of Paraguay', unpublished Ph.D dissertation, University of St Andrews.

Kracke, W.H. (1978) *Force and Persuasion: Leadership in an Amazonian Society*, Chicago: University of Chicago Press.

Loewen, J.A. (1966) 'Lengua Indians and their "innermost"', *Practical Anthropology* 13: 252–72.

McCallum, C. (1989) 'Gender, personhood and social organization amongst the Cashinahua of Western Amazonia', unpublished Ph.D dissertation, University of London.

—— (1990) 'Language, kinship and politics in Amazonia', *Man* (n.s.) 25: 412–33.

Myers, F.R. (1986) *Pintupi Country, Pintupi Self: Sentiment, Place and Politics among Western Desert Aborigines*, Berkeley: University of California Press.

—— (1988) 'Burning the truck and holding the country: property, time and the negotiation of identity among Pintupi Aborigines', in T. Ingold, D. Riches and J. Woodburn (eds) *Hunters and Gatherers 2: Property, Power and Ideology*, New York and Oxford: Berg (Explorations in Anthropology series).

Oldham, P.A. (1996) 'The impacts of development and indigenous responses among the Piaroa of the Venezuelan Amazon', unpublished Ph.D dissertation, University of London.

Overing, J. (1985a) Introduction, in J. Overing (ed.) *Reason and Morality*, ASA Monographs 24, London and New York: Tavistock.

—— (1985b) 'There is no end of evil: the guilty innocents and their fallible god', in D. Parkin (ed.) *The Anthropology of Evil*, Oxford: Basil Blackwell.

—— (1988) 'Personal autonomy and the domestication of the self in Piaroa society', in I.M. Lewis and G. Jahoda (eds) *Acquiring Culture*, London: Croom Helm.

——— (1989a) 'Styles of manhood: an Amazonian contrast in tranquillity and violence', in S. Howell and R. Willis (eds) *Societies at Peace*, London: Tavistock.

——— (1989b) 'The aesthetics of production: the sense of community among the Cubeo and Piaroa', *Dialectical Anthropology* 14: 159–75.

——— (1993a) 'Death and the loss of civilised predation among the Piaroa of the Orinoco Basin', *L'Homme* 126–8, 33(2–4): 191–211.

——— (1993b) 'The anarchy and collectivism of the "primitive other": Marx and Sahlins in the Amazon', in C. Hann (ed.) *Socialism: Ideals, Ideologies and Local Practice*, London: Routledge.

——— (1996) 'Under the sky of the domesticated: in praise of the everyday', Inaugural Lecture for the Professorship and Chair of Social Anthropology, University of St Andrews, 4 December.

Palmer, J. (1997) 'Wichí goodwill: ethnographic allusions', unpublished Ph.D dissertation, University of Oxford.

Passes, A. (1998) 'The hearer, the hunter, and the agouti head – aspects of inter-communication and conviviality among the Pa'ikwené (Palikur) of French Guiana', unpublished Ph.D dissertation, University of St Andrews.

Peters, J.F. (1998) *Life among the Yanomami: The Story of Change among the Xilixana on the Mucajai River in Brazil*, Peterborough, Ontario: Broadview Press.

Regehr, V. (1987) 'Criarse en una comunidad Nivaclé', *Suplemento Antropológico* 22: 155–202.

Renshaw, J. (1986) 'The economy and economic morality of the Indians of the Paraguayan Chaco', unpublished Ph.D dissertation, University of London.

Rivière, P. (1984) *Individual and Society in Guiana: A Comparative Study of Amerindian Social Organization*, Cambridge: Cambridge University Press.

Santos-Granero, F. (1986) 'The moral and social aspects of equality among the Amuesha of Central Peru', *Journal de la Société des Américanistes* 72: 107–31.

——— (1991) *The Power of Love: The Moral Use of Knowledge amongst the Amuesha of Central Peru*, London: Athlone Press.

Siskind, J. (1973) *To Hunt in the Morning*, Oxford: Oxford University Press.

Susnik, B.J. (1977) *Lengua-Maskoy: su hablar, su pensar, su vivencia*, Lenguas Chaqueñas VI, Asunción: Museo Etnográfico 'Andrés Barbero'.

Thomas, D.J. (1982) *Order without Government: The Society of the Pemon Indians of Venezuela*, Urbana: University of Illinois Press.

Viveiros de Castro, E. (1992) *From the Enemy's Point of View: Humanity and Divinity in an Amazonian Society*, trans. C.V. Howard, Chicago and London: University of Chicago Press.

Woodburn, J. (1980) 'Hunters and gatherers today and reconstruction of the past', in E. Gellner (ed.) *Soviet and Western Anthropology*, London: Duckworth.

Chapter 7

Anger as a marker of love

The ethic of conviviality among the Yanomami

Catherine Alès

This chapter, which explores how the Yanomami[1] achieve conviviality, grew out of an initial endeavour to analyse Yanomami 'tools of concord', or of agreement,[2] in order to unfold an important facet of their sociality other than the fighting and bellicosity for which they have for so long been (in)famously caricatured.[3] I will concentrate particularly on the means through which the construction of conviviality is realised, or attempted, by the Yanomami both intracommunally and in their intercommunity relations. In the process of this exploration, I wish to point to the possibility that what we as anthropologists may consider to be an indigenous attachment to 'informality' and 'intimacy', rather than rule and obedience, can actually be, for the people themselves, considered as practices that are both formal and obligatory, and which therefore serve as the general 'rule' with regard to their creation of sociable groups and relationships. We are the ones who have categorised the sociality of Amazonian peoples as 'informal' and 'intimate', and this is because they appear to pay no attention whatsoever to the *type* of formality and *form* of rule with which we are familiar, i.e. the concepts of rules and regulations as they have been formulated in anthropological theory. However, I think the issue is more complicated than our 'formal' versus 'informal' distinction allows. To begin with, I do not think the Yanomami recognise a conceptual division between 'formal' and 'informal' behaviour, and it is for this very reason that, at first glance, we tend to see them as an anarchical people, lacking order and strong rules. In reality, however, what we *ourselves* observe as 'simpler' attitudes, such as those expressed in everyday relations and 'spontaneous' actions, as in chatting or conversing with one another, are in fact – for the Yanomami – not merely the consequence of obligation and formality; they are at the same time constitutive of their sociality, and therefore one of the important ingredients of their 'tools of conviviality'.

Any Western discussion on what we can call 'communitarian values' is linked to its contrary, the Western values of individualism, freedom and autonomy, a triad linked in its turn to the notion of contractual power, a principle ultimately based on the acceptance of the necessity of coercive force. According to the feminist moral philosopher, Annette Baier (1985, 1986, 1987), the individualistic triad of values are male obsessions, which should be balanced by the more communitarian principles of care and trust, which are the female values. Like Overing (1999a, 1999b), I do not consider this kind of gendered opposition to be applicable to Amazonian societies, where in contrast to a prevalent modern Western division of moral concerns which separates men from women, the men of Amazonia share with the women a set of communitarian values premised upon a high evaluation of personal autonomy, in which (certainly in the Yanomami case) the value upon collectivity encompasses individualism and its acceptance of a 'necessary' coercive force (contrast Rivière's and Rosengren's respective discussions in this volume of the Trio and the Matsigenka, both peoples who appear to privilege in the end personal autonomy over collectivity). To explore this discussion of moral concerns with respect to the Amazonian cases provides us with a chance to reconsider what in fact one means when describing these societies as ones that place a special value upon personal autonomy. The philosopher Baier is following the cognitive psychologist Gilligan (1982), who developed a clear distinction between 'ethics of care' and 'ethics of justice' as initially described by Kohlberg (1981) in a denigration of the female high evaluation of care and family concerns. For Kohlberg, justice, not care, is the final end of moral development. He is here following Rawls (1971), for whom justice is the most important political principle.[4] In such an argument, as Meyers (1998) has pointed out, 'care' then lies outside the political, and not within it. This leads us to ponder whether this is indeed true of Amazonian societies, and I have chosen the Yanomami as a pertinent example for seeking how to reconcile, leaving gender considerations aside, the ethics of care with the sociopolitical life.

Sadness, to be in pain and anger

All the themes discussed below are essentially associated with the passions, and it is with the Yanomami understanding of emotions that this chapter is concerned. Yanomami people pay considerable attention to each others' feelings and 'psychological' states. Each person strives systematically to make their relatives 'feel well and happy', pufi toprao (vital principle glad). The states they contrast with 'being happy' are those of 'sadness' and 'anger', both expressed by the single formula, pufi hushuo (vital principle sad–angry), a serious condition in which to be. The pufi, as vital principle or 'soul', is the centre simultaneously of one's motor-system, physiology, senses, emotions and thought (cf. Jamieson, Kidd, Lagrou, Rivière, this volume). Thus, when someone feels sad or angry, the whole community is affected and as a result mobilises on the unhappy individual's behalf. Each co-resident feels obliged to behave in such a manner as to calm the affected person, in order to enable him or her to become reintegrated with a balanced state of tranquillity (*ononowë*). The aim is that he or she regains the 'beautiful soul' (*pufi riyëhëwë*, vital principle beautiful) that they have lost. The members of the community must help the person return to their state of health, happiness and propriety. He or she must emerge from the affective state of 'bad soul', which is a state of sickness, anxiety and hostility. An enraged person has to regain a 'quiet soul' that is neutral and free of anger, a *pufi okewë* (soul neutral – neutral contextually taking the sense of safe, inefficient, insipid, non-aggressive) (cf. Kidd, this volume). The main idea is that one should not be suffering and in pain, *nï preaï*, nor should one allow a co-resident to remain in such a state.

Since the term *nï preaï* designates both emotional and physical pain, it applies to a wide semantic domain. It can, for instance, refer to the suffering of the pain of work. The general rule of thumb is to prevent a person from becoming *nï preaï* and therefore having to endure the pain of solitude (cf. Gow, this volume). This concern underlies most of the economic activities within a group, where people aim to share the pain and effort of labour (cf. Passes, this volume), thereby ensuring that no one undergoes it alone. The collective nature of working and fighting activities allows people to share the 'suffering' of toil and, consequently, to quell it. Yanomami men prefer doing their brideservice at the same time and place as one or more of their brothers, as the fact of suffering together serves to make the experience individually less painful. Nothing affects a Yanomami more than working without success, and thus having 'suffered' for nothing. On the other hand, one is also proud of toiling toward the end of feeding one's close relatives and peers, and to obtain through gathering, hunting or gardening the means of providing them with happiness and well-being. Many actions of a person, in the give and take of everyday life, are thought of in terms of how 'not to suffer'. For example, a person asks for a machete so as 'not to suffer' when gardening. The same rationale applies to all other similar requests.

The Yanomami make judgements about the validity of actions in terms of the predictability of 'suffering'. Thus if a man takes a wife who is too young, he will incur many problems, or so it is assumed, since the girl will probably run away; or if he is lazy in gardening he will later suffer hunger. Similarly, if a person commits adultery or non-lethal sorcery or steals from another's garden, his or her entire family circle will suffer from the resulting conflict and troubles. All these kinds of situations would work against a community's health and well-being. Thus, whatever causes suffering to close kinspeople is to be feared: a Yanomami takes pains to avoid everything that can cause suffering to relatives during his or her lifetime and, especially, after his or her death. This is why they do not want to leave behind something 'perennial' – *parimi* – of themselves, as this reminder would inevitably sadden their kinsfolk.

The strong desire to prevent suffering is also the key to understanding why a strong taboo is placed on pronouncing personal names after puberty. The individual's name needs time to be forgotten because if it, or the root(s) of the word from which it is made up, were to be used after their death, their close relatives would be *pufi hushuo*, sad and angry. Relatives, and people who are friendly with one another, therefore take care to respect this prohibition. By contrast, enemies repeatedly pronounce the name of the person they want to kill, as a means of inducing suffering in the designated victim's 'vital principle' (*pufi*) and thereby ensuring their eventual death. In circumstances both banal and serious, then, close kinspeople and friends must mutually avoid making one another suffer, be it in the here and now or after death. This is why one has to give happiness to, and be generous with, one's peers; it is also the reason why the Yanomami evaluate avarice so negatively. Consequently, it is difficult to refuse to satisfy someone who is lacking tobacco, food, or an implement – or company, or a wife. No stone will be left unturned in satisfying the needs and wishes of a kinsperson, affine or friend. All these actions are marks of attention, affection and amity; they are constructive of everyday life, sociality and conviviality.

The ethic of care in Yanomami society is directly associated with a retaliatory system which sustains an agonistic logic and confrontation. How does this seemingly paradoxical (at first glance) logic work? When a Yanomami man is angry it is because he has been despoiled, offended or, worse, because one of his relatives has died as the result, putatively or actually, of warfare or lethal sorcery practices. He is, therefore, suffering. To ease such suffering, his relatives, co-residents and allies will take retaliatory action, proportionate to the offence, until such time as will be thought sufficient for him to feel well again and recover the state of being without anger, *pufi okewë*, as described above. The objective goal of revenge is to inflict at least an equivalent pain or amount of suffering (*nï preaï*) on the adversary. This is a principle that applies equally to all types of retaliatory situations, from quarrels between men and women to the conflict between shamans who have strangled each other's children by means of spirits. During a war, killing the young adult men of your enemy causes suffering to their older relatives, who will express their sadness intensely and at length. The degree of anger for an offence itself varies in relation to the degree of genealogical, spatial and social proximity or distance of the individuals involved which in turn determines the means of compensation which will be used.[5] Each form of revenge works to calm the anger felt by one particular member of the collective, in the knowledge that this anger is immediately communicated to all its solidary parts and will, with each successive act of revenge, spread through and escalate among both sides throughout the length of the conflict. The Yanomami are very conscious that this logic of retaliation entails an increase of suffering on both sides, but the objective of destroying the other is said explicitly to be more valuable than one's own personal suffering. Thus the Yanomami always want to inflict more destruction than the pain they have themselves endured (two or three people must be killed to avenge one dead relative), although, in the end, the obligatory reciprocity involved makes for a draw. As the ritual treatment of the ashes of the dead who are to be avenged remains incomplete for as long as retaliation is not carried out, parity is the only model that will allow for the cessation of hostilities. It is these acts of solidarity with, and compassion for, the anger and pain of relatives, affines and friends – which demand reciprocity – that cement the coalitions for 'regular' (formal) fighting against allied communities, and for sorcery and bellicose expeditions against enemy communities (see note 5).

Likewise, when a relative is sick, everybody will try to find the cause and ask to fight against it in order for the person to regain health and cease suffering. The identical logic used for dealing with local, neighbourhood conflicts also operates in respect of everyday problems, such as those that arise in difficulties and disappointments of work, love or domestic life. At each level, the collective and solidary groups come into play when a person is suffering, sad or angry. And it is through all this concern with affectivity, and its comfort, that solidarity and conviviality, and thus an ethic of care, are achieved between co-residents and neighbours.[6]

Thus it is clear that the Yanomami's ethics of care and aesthetics of conviviality are integrally connected with their politics. I will now consider this linkage of care and the political in more detail, by exploring how the notions of amity, solidarity and love, expressed by the verb *nofimaï*, work on distinct levels of society, and how they are also associated with the notion of trust.

The construction of trust and solidarity at the different levels of social interaction

To attain a more general idea of Yanomami political philosophy, it is necessary to understand that the apparent autonomy of individuals, and their liberty, is encompassed in a wider sense by a principle of collective solidarity.

Inside a community, the leader does not constitute the figure of a strong chief in the sense of deploying coercive force, and we find that the element of trust is crucial to the acceptance of his authority. Leadership is more a matter (as is so often the case in Amazonia) of social and political authority being devoted more to the common interest than one of self-seeking and personal power.[7] From this perspective we have to focus on the fact that it is a system in which leaders exercise authority without practising authoritarianism (Alès 1995). In general, a leader, called *pata*, or 'elder', a term referring to the senior age group, is a mature individual of superior experience and intelligence. There can be more than one within a single collective house, each acting as a 'protector' or 'defender' of the house segment they represent. Theirs is the responsibility for the harmonious relations between the members of a communal house, as well as with the other neighbouring communities. Essentially, their role is to stimulate the economic, political and ceremonial activities of the group. They promote and initiate the daily collective tasks to be completed, and in their pre-dawn discourses take charge of the moral education of the young people. They also arbitrate conflicts and pronounce themselves for war or peace.[8]

This system works not by force but by preference, adherence and the recognition of the leader's 'protective role': his followers must know that their leader likes them and wants to shield them. It is because they understand he strives to protect and sustain tranquillity, harmony and peaceful relations, inside as well as outside the community, that they in the end listen to him when, in loud shouting tones, he forbids the actions of some of their number. Moreover, in that the *pata* suffers as a result of the inadequate behaviour of the young, people must please him in order to assuage his anger and anxiety, and to enable his *pufi* (vital principle) to regain a tranquil state. People's trust in the elder's unconditional solidarity with them is the mainspring of the efficacy of his moralising discourses. It is through the same mechanism that he can obtain the co-residents' endorsement of some economic task, for instance, hunting game or gathering wild fruit, or a political one, like waging war, and also of a ritual one, such as carrying out a hunting expedition for a ceremonial feast.

It is more by suggestion than command, then, that the leader stimulates and coordinates the activities of his village, and curbs its members' transgressions. Talking nearly every night towards daybreak, his voice awakens the residents of the communal house (it is not good to sleep too long after dawn as one will wake feeling bad and thus be unable to work). His announcement of the tasks he considers judicious for obtaining edible products, and his commentary of all news of collective interest, instil reassurance and optimism for today and for the future among the group. People normally respond with a short, firm, enthusiastic expression of agreement, 'Yes! Yes!' This is the moment speakers reserve for providing detailed accounts of the previous day's hunting trip (something the Yanomami relish above all, if successful) or any particular event able to stimulate the co-residents. The speakers' intonation, their way of cutting the words and repeating parts of the sentences, and the overall style of delivery are special to these speeches and require much skill on the part of the orator. They like to end with a hackneyed joke – very often relating to some sexual affair they supposedly had with a woman in their youth. This will undoubtably make the younger members laugh; they will wake in a happy frame of mind and consequently full of energy for producing plenty of food, which in turn represents satisfaction for the co-residents and thus tranquillity. The logical counterpart of this sequence is that if they wake in a sad mood then they will feel bad like a sick person and stay at home, and thus be without ardour for work. The *pata* public discourses make people feel that they are not alone; as an important daily component of the practices of conviviality, such verbal art communicates the feeling of belonging to a community.

This discourse also calls on the collective responsibility of the co-residents of immature age to desist from behaviour likely to endanger the community and its relations with neighbours, notably theft of garden produce, repeated sexual propositioning of married women and gossip. If leaders focus on these behaviours it is because they can be predicted to provoke internal or supra-local conflicts, and to lead inevitably to a disruption of tranquillity and the onset of troubles, raging from verbal disputes to 'regular' fights, internal fission or separation between neighbours, sorcery practices, and thus, in cases of serious injuries, belligerency. If Yanomami elders harbour a dream, it is that of living tranquilly and peacefully (no matter how impossible this might seem). They explicitly want to stay in the same area as long as possible, an intention expressed by the statement 'to live [at the same place] quietly', *përïaï onowë*. The Yanomami do not like being obliged to flee because of conflict or war, an action synonymous with fear, instability and dependence on other communities. It is the reason why the shouting and angry moralising monologues the leaders direct to their communities are so specifically protective.

If people have things to complain of concerning co-residents or neighbours they themselves shout during the day. The repetition of such speeches can lead to the dispersal of the community. 'They sound bad', i.e. 'because they shout', is a regularly evoked motive for a communal house fission. And leaders have to work hard, on a repetitive and daily basis, to develop their skill at persuading community members not to provoke trouble. In order to translate properly the Yanomami concepts involved in their leaders' maintenance of cohesion and tranquillity, we need to note that the leaders are 'conciliating' (*wasïï*, to win someone over from doing some action) rather than censuring or forbidding, and that they are 'delegating' (*shimaï*), i.e. soliciting the collaboration of someone to do something, which can be translated more directly by 'to send someone to do something', but not in the sense of giving orders to be obeyed.

As I have argued elsewhere (Alès 1995), leaders take charge of and discuss group affairs in public, but do not have the power of decision. All important problems are collectively discussed. Individual autonomy is preserved in the sense that all are free to give or withhold their agreement and solidarity with the decisions taken. But in reality things are not quite that simple. While people can do what they want, if they repeatedly fail to concur with collective decisions and do not participate in important collective activities, such as raiding parties for example, they will have to split from the others, and to live alone or join another village.

The Yanomami cultivate individual autonomy, then, but it is encompassed in a superior principle of collective responsibility realised at the level of the community and, beyond that, in respect of a situation whereby each residential unit is integrated in a wider nexus of solidarity and reciprocity with the other neighbouring local groups. The social link is thus produced by the fact that individuals sacrifice at least part of their personal autonomy both at the first level of collective organisation, the community, and at the second level, the alliance or association with the neighbours' houses.[9]

In this context, the Yanomami construct on an ongoing daily basis the relations of solidarity and trust through the density of the exchanges of services, food, words and fun. In particular, they conceptualise all these exchanges in terms of 'company' (*rurupou*, to accompany) and friendship. The idea is that of being close to, frequenting, visiting; this signifies liking the company of someone and, hence, sharing love and amity.

This notion can be illustrated first with some salient points that define affection and thus trust between members of a family or real affines. The relation between children, parents and the community is best defined by the way children acquire their sense of community. The spirit of collective membership and collective responsibility is taught to children through their increasing participation in the economic and ritual system. They notably perform the role of dealers in the daily exchanges of cooked food. Children have to cooperate with each other in all the daily work activities, and a special severity is manifested towards a child who refuses to go gathering or gardening with its relatives. A child's refusal to participate can provoke immediate retaliation from the mother, elder sister or brother: 'You will not be fed if you don't accompany us.' It is noteworthy that merely accompanying other people gives you the right to a part of the produce. 'To accompany' (*rurupou*) is conceived as a form of participation in the work: one toils (*nï preaï*) by accompanying and, thereby, helps by sustaining morally and affectively the worker who is thus spared having to toil in solitude. Participation, be it apparently even only passive, through one's mere presence at the economic, domestic and ritual tasks, is highly valued by the Yanomami. This elementary solidarity is at the root of the forging of trust and relations of affection.

Children have to learn very early to protect and defend their brothers in any situation. Parents teach children they have to take their brothers' side in all circumstances; they also inculcate a spirit of systematic revenge. From the Yanomami point of view, male and female siblings constitute a same 'side' (*mashi*). The systematisation of the idea of the solidarity of the male-sibling sets corresponds to the basis of the composition of the collective houses. Mothers want at least four sons and two daughters, the main reason given for this preference being that each mother seeks to ensure the safety of her sons by giving them enough brothers to defend them in case of conflict and attack and in times of fighting.

It is daily repetition that gives permanence and weight to the relations of mutual care. Children learn they must help and take care of the elders, pay attention to those who share their life, labour for them and take care of them. Unlike in modern Western education, which gives the impression that it is the parents alone who give and are responsible for the children, Yanomami children are socialised at a very early age to participate in group activities and responsibilities, in order to obtain the morality of collective responsibility.

Among spouses, it is important that a wife be at home when her husband returns, for her absence will be taken as a provocation and she could be beaten. A husband likes a wife to go gardening or gathering with him: indeed it is among a bachelor's key criteria for choosing a wife, since a wife is supposed to accompany her husband when he is engaged on certain garden-ing tasks which women do not do. Hence, it is common to see a wife sitting in the garden, unoccupied save for cooking some plantains and tending to the children: she is there just to provide company (*rurupou*) for her husband, and in so doing she is participating in the work process. This scene, so apparently intimate and personal, is in reality a valued model of the husband-and-wife relationship.

A son-in-law has, for his part, constantly to prove his ability to feed his wife, by giving all his produce and work to his in-laws for a very long time. He has to show how he loves them, and the parents-in-law have to demon-strate how they care for him like a son, and his brothers-in-law like a brother. Symmetrically, sisters-in-law must display the same care for their brother's wife as for a sister. Between parents- and children-in-law the obligations of demonstration of affection never really end, even after death, particularly through the funerary rituals. Problems arise when an ally has divergent and conflicting obligations with two factions: a son-in-law normally has to stand alongside his brothers-in-law and father-in-law; in case of war, he may have to renounce his wife, and if he does not join in a fight, he will forever be reproached by both sides, putting him in a very embarrassing position.

Between the *yafitheri*, or members of the same *shapono* (communal house) and of a very close neighbourhood, the key concepts are named as, 'to sit' (*roo*), 'to discuss' (*wayou*) and 'to make friendship' (*nofimou*). Each and every day, once the most demanding preoccupation, the alimentary, has been dealt with, it is social and affective relationships which absorb the Yanomami, especially in the late afternoon. This is the moment of groupings, of male assembly on the plaza for shamanic sessions, followed later by visits to one hearth or another; of meetings of women outside the house; of children playing.

In the general milieu of lascivity and leisure that dominates a Yanomami *shapono*, the movements of people, such as male visits and news exchanges and female discussions, body painting and delousing before sunset, seem very natural and informal. However, to analyse the phenomenon with more precision, all such actions are to be seen as components of a very formalised process of sociability.

The visiting activity where one 'sits' (*roo*) near somebody is particularly characteristic of the fact of cohabiting. From a pragmatical point of view, people can sit and discuss regularly and frequently with somebody only if they live together or very close by; for the Yanomami all this activity of frequenting has to be intense. It is thus by everyday neighbourly contact and chatting that the social cement is created and maintained.

As all the social frequenting constitutes an indispensable, unavoidable amity marker, the practice of friendship takes distinct forms according to the spatial distance between groups and individuals. The measure of amity weakens according to the order of distance between two residences, thereby providing the idea of spatial structure as a kind of relational universe metaphor.

Frequent visits between very close communities are made possible by their proximity. They can even come to visit as often as co-residents do so between themselves. These are relations of the 'to sit' type (*roo*). Up to a certain point, close neighbours are assimilated in the co-residents category (*yafitheri*); they form what I call a 'neighbourhood group' (Alès 1984) or an 'extended local group', in which they enjoy similar preferential exchanges of marriages, and economic, military, shamanic and ritual solidarity.

Between slightly more distant friendly communities (*nofi thë pë*) there is a correlative spacing of visits. Theirs are not really simple visits of the 'to sit' type (*roo*) but ones already designated by the more formal term, 'to visit' (*famamou*, to have the visitor behaviour). There will be a food gift and, generally, a precise motive, some particular information or request, underlying the visit. The length of the visit is limited, the visitor leaving the same day, normally in order to arrive home before dusk. These communities also weave between themselves intensive relations of matrimonial exchanges and of economic, military and ritual solidarity; they correspond to an 'extended neighbourhood group', as viewed from the perspective of more distant groups.

On top of this, visiting activity for individuals who have kinspeople in another community is very general and frequent. Daughters, married in another village, shuttle back and forth between the two communities, and the sons-in-law commute periodically with their wives for shorter or longer stays with the wife's parents (this is true whatever the distance).

Apart from these individual visits that express and regenerate amity, the ceremonial funerary feasts (*reafu*) provide the opportunity for jamborees, when the majority of the members of a community are invited into another one. This action is described as 'to congregate', *kõkamou*. During these feasts people can mark friendship (*nofimou*), have discussions (*wayou*) and hold ceremonial dialogues. Between close communal houses, this kind of reciprocal invitation is relatively frequent, both parties being involved in a wide complex of ritual complementarity as privileged feasting partners. Nevertheless, these people do not sleep in the host's house: the weaker the social distance, the less pronounced the formalisation of the amity activity.[10]

Producing and maintaining friendship between more distant allied neighbours is not easily realised. The mode is more formal and the amity between the protagonists is said 'to make friend like that' (*nofimou pëtao*), that is to say, the amity is not a really deep one. Sojourning in order to be fed (*thaõ*), visiting (*famamou*) and inviting (*shoaï*) are the most important values.

These are the three forms of gathering between these kinds of communities. The first one occurs when a community comes to live near another in order 'to be fed or sustained' (*thaõ*). This consists of the visiting party installing itself in a forest camp to live for a period (from two to four weeks, for example) in a state of economic dependency. This can take the form of an invitation from the host community to share in the plentiful produce of its garden, or to exploit a particularly abundant wild resource. It can also result from an invitation which the visitors have sought in order to overcome a food shortage or a spell of hostile relations with a third community. In this context of lengthy spatial proximity, friendship relations are expressed in the same way as between co-residents and near neighbours. This kind of meeting (*kõkamou*) draws groups together socially and allows the production, confirmation and conservation of the ties of amity.

The second form of gathering – *famamou*, 'to behave as a visitor' – consists in carrying out distant visits to communities based one day's walk away or more. The arrival of visitors from afar is a considerable event for the Yanomami, with respect to the surprise entailed, the pleasure and the inter-ruption of the daily routine. Once the arrival protocol is over with, the visitor must receive a large amount of food – not to give it would signal that he is unwelcome; then he will visit the different hearths of the house in turn, an action for which there is a special term: *rimïmou*. During his round he will discuss (*wayou*), 'make friendship' (*nofimou*) and ask for goods (*matofi narei*). The category of people who are visitors – and whom one consequently visits – is in fact called *rimïyë thë pë*, 'the ones who go from one hearth to another in turn'; they are said to be *fama uprao*, 'standing up as visitor', an expression referring to the erect, immobile, formal pose visitors have to adopt when entering the plaza.[11]

These relations often have a basis in a kinship relation with some member of the visited community that allows for the creation of exchange partnerships with more distant people. Those with parents living in a remote place, some three or four days' walk away, like to visit them at least once if not more during their lifetime, and to make a long stay. They can thus forge links with the whole community through relations which are those of a co-resident. This kind of long-stay visit is undertaken as much by young men as older ones, as well as by divorced or widowed women.

Since one cannot visit somewhere without a precise motive, a specific demand for goods frequently serves as a pretext.[12] In this context it is a parti-cularly serious matter to refuse to give something, to feed visitors badly, or to otherwise mistreat them. Such behaviour systematically signifies a rejection of friendship, alliance refusal, and thus hostility – and a possible *casus belli*, as I myself noted to be the case with the groups I have studied.[13] The important thing to understand is that it is not a question of material exchange. What is being played out through the process of amicable communication is the creation of social relations. The symbolic conditions for the exchange of goods are an exchange of words, via formalised dialogues, and an affirmation of amity embodied in the participants' behaviour (Alès 1990b).[14]

The third element conducive to encounter and congregation (kõkamou) between distant allied communities is that of the invitations for a ceremonial feast (reafu), which I have already mentioned in connection with the nearest allied communities. This is an occasion for enjoyment through dances, beverages, games, songs, shamanic sessions, oratory jousts and all the other things allowing the expression of sociability which, in other words, provide one with the opportunity to discuss, exchange news and goods, to amuse one-self, laugh, make friends – which between young people involves mutual physical touching and tickling (upayou) – finding sexual partners and so on. Correlatively, meetings between people and communities are the occasion to exchange accusations, arguments and even blows (cf. Kidd, Rivière, Rosengren, this volume). Demonstrations of amity and accusations of hostile behaviour effectively go hand in hand. This underlines the fragility of alliance, which one is called upon endlessly to reconstruct, resecure and test. All invitations to a feast are formally reciprocal, an invitation one way being automatically followed by another the opposite way.

Direct encounters with more distant communities that one does not frequent are only initiated when it is opportune or strategically advantageous to do so. The first encounter is achieved through the 'visits channel', with each age group and gender having its specific role to play in the process of establishing alliance relations between groups, or of re-establishing them after periods of hostility (Alès 1990b, 1995).[15] However, visits should only be paid if there is a valid reason for doing so, or the visitor will be immediately suspected of malevolent intentions. When visitors leave a house in the early morning, they need to receive some warm words from their hosts signifying that they will be welcome next time. Without them, it would not be very prudent to return.

Thus, it should be underlined that the instruments of concord are physical frequenting and association, and that these provide the possibility for con-cretely manifesting friendship. They permit one to measure the conviviality and the degree of amicable social relations within a community and between two communities.

Discord is the negative version of this scheme of amity relations. To behave in a hostile way (napëmou, 'to behave as an enemy') is manifested on the spatial plane by fissions and displacements, and on the social plane by arguments, duels and battles, lethal sorcery, armed raids, aggressive shamanism or 'animal-double attacks'. Each of these modes of conflict or aggression regula-tion is defined in accordance with different interconnected criteria relating to the parties' degree of spatial and genealogical proximity or distance, and to the category of sociopolitical relations between them (cf. Alès 1984,

1990a). Amity exchange, as we have seen, is as much an exchange of hostility as a dynamic mechanism of social reproduction. There are two sides to the system, and we cannot present one without the other. Neither of the aspects, aggression and amity, should be thought of in isolation.

Relations of trust and distrust

All positive relationships are counterbalanced by negative relationships at each level of social interaction. Solidarity is therefore largely constructed in such a way as to defend the group against the transgressions and attacks of neighbours, and also when any of its own members provoke aggression and attacks from co-residents or neighbours. Male solidarity is mainly based on two kinds of problem: the collective control over their rights – which includes rights over women – and the collective control over the health and physical integrity of their peers.

This results in solidarity groups of young men against unfaithful or absconding wives and against wife thieves – groups in which women participate as helpers. Purely female solidarity groups against men exist at the local level, in cases of abduction of a single woman, of retrieving an upset wife and of serious injuries to a wife.

The prime unit of solidarity consists of a nucleus of kinspeople backed up by 'real allies'. Groups of brothers and their children or of fathers with theirs are the main line along which the solidarity groups are formed. Depending on any given level of conflict, this base is enhanced by co-residents, cognates and in-laws and, thereafter, by unrelated friends who can be near or distant neighbours.

Trust is the result of proofs of solidarity and, for family members, co-residents and friends alike, trust is created as much through acts of solidarity in everyday life as in times of misfortune, dispute, conflict and war. Whatever the context, people have to give each other proof of their affection, cooperation and alliance, and to affirm their amity repeatedly. As unstable matter, solidarity has constantly to be generated, maintained and reproduced to be effective. It would be an understatement to say that, for the Yanomami, 'trust' constitutes a permanent matter of doubt.

All the positive exchanges at play in the reproduction of trust implicitly evince a trust in the fact that lethal practices such as sorcery will not be implemented within one's own sphere of proximity, or, in others words, between co-residents, close neighbours and even near-neighbourhood groups. Effectively, without this mutual agreement of non-aggression – which has permanently to be demonstrated through convivial behaviours – life would be impossible for the residents of the different houses. Were the threat of lethal aggression from their nearest neighbours permanently to be hanging over them, the Yanomami would not be able to circulate in the minimum of

territory required for hunting, gathering or gardening; they could not produce and live peacefully.

The circulation areas, the visits to other communities or the avoidance of
other communities by individuals are always determined in terms of a relative
security, that is to say, as a function of the fear of being the subject of patent
or occult aggression. According to their intentional agency system of death
and sickness, the Yanomami live permanently at a very high level of fear.
The smallest visit is always the object of a lot of advice from others not to go,
with the direst consequences being predicted.[16] This phenomenon particularises the circulation of each individual and community within the territory
(Alès 1984).

This is also the reason why conflict in a collective house results in a division
into separate units, and why 'regular' battles or the outbreak of war between
very close communities necessarily compels flight and relocation, entailing a
large spatial distancing of one to three days at least between hostile houses.[17]

In sum, for the Yanomami, who live in a sociopolitical relational climate
that does not permit the free circulation of individuals and communities
through the territory, all the exchanges of food, visits, feasts, words, goods
and marriage partners – together with the economic, shamanistic, ritual,
political and military solidarity – create, maintain and reproduce the
relations of trust between neighbouring communities.

In this climate of chronic suspicion of manifest or dissimulated aggression,
the Yanomami are obliged to establish firm local and circum-local solidarity,
and strategically to construct or reinforce, according to circumstance, more
distant alliances. Simultaneously, they must also cultivate a wide experience
of appropriate distrust, not only, naturally enough, about their enemies, but
about their friends and official non-enemies. A lot of energy is spent discussing
and informing one another about the multiple relations in a given nexus of
interaction. The Yanomami are ever ready to spread rumours of hostility, to
believe in them and to react against their cited adversaries.[18]

The Yanomami are very aware of the betrayal of supposed friends and
allies. There exists a very famous and dangerous form of treachery called
nomohorimou. In wartime, aggression is generally effected through ambushes
or house raids. But another form of attack exists that requires the betrayal of
one's own allies who are at the same time conniving with the enemy. This
strategy is realised through the use of an intermediary who is simultaneously
allied with both sets of combatants. The intermediary, generally helped by
his peers, can himself kill his friends' enemies, after having treacherously
invited them to his house, by a mortal blow delivered with a weapon. He can
also, being more able to approach them and circulate freely in their territory,
steal something personal from them (such as the remains of a meal, tobacco
or the earth containing traces of their footprints) in order to kill them by
lethal sorcery, an act carried out either by himself or by his friends.

In the building of trust, it is particularly interesting to note that homicide has a lot to do with the principle of delegation (a myth of the origin of war refers explicitly to this principle). This form of transaction, in which a third party acts as another's agent, and which can be described as a fiduciary relationship, is an essential and powerful concept in Yanomami moral and political philosophy. This category of action simultaneously creates relations of trust between those who commissioned the crime and those who committed it, and, symmetrically, relations of appropriate distrust between fragile friends, as well as reinforcing a general morality of suspicion and distrust.

It is important to specify that the Yanomami notion we commonly translate as 'betrayal' is in reality more subtle. It is related to the idea of 'wishing to fight'. This corresponds to the idea of the rupture of a previously amicable commitment; the same term can be used, for example, to describe those who refuse to give up a woman promised in marriage. It is the contriving of a deliberate provocation in order to be confrontational and to fight.

Betrayal is the most powerful instrument an enemy has because the ruse is even more violent and effective than war with undisguised enemies. As a war tactic, perfidy, as expressed through an unexpected attack by an unsuspecting foe, has to do with failure of alliances and trust relations. This signifies a displacement of trust: in other words, one was not suspicious enough. Pragmatically, betrayal makes it possible to kill more people than is usual during a single attack. Effectively, the only way to kill somebody among the Yanomami is when their guard is down and they forget to be 'alert' (*moyawë*). It is only when they become unsuspicious – that is, when their mind and volition, that is to say their vital principal, *pufi*, have been paralysed – that their enemies are able to kill them.

The versatility of amity, so pivotal to Yanomami social life, is linked with a special concept as to what constitutes 'true friendship'. The only friendship in which one can believe, and that is considered trustworthy, is a war friendship; for the friendship which exists between battle companions is seen as 'real friendship'. As the Yanomami explain, only the elders have many friends because they are the generation that long ago obtained partners to go to war with. The elders are the ones who, in past wars, made alliances and got other Yanomami to join with them in order to share their 'anger' and help them fulfil their revenge obligations. They have created solid links of mutual assistance. Thus, adult coalition members can be said to be real friends in that they have achieved a relationship of trust with 'others' (i.e. with distant kinspeople) which has allowed them to reinforce their group. By contrast, the younger adults say they will not be able create real friends outside the local group, or develop real amity with the external houses, until their fathers die. The youngest ones, even if they go on raids, do not possess friends; these will appear only when they are eventually attacked, and will consist of those who will rally to their side.

All the aforementioned practices of *rapprochement* between distant communities, in which the younger males participate, are a step in the direction of future alliance in case of eventual war. But they will only be confirmed by real engagement in a war, as proof of a true trusting relationship.

This pathology of political alliance – which can be described as the lability, flexibility and reversibility of positive as well as negative relationships, which lie at the core of the Yanomami system of factionalism – does not allow for the possibility of a large stable union. The Yanomami are an example of a limited trust system which, although possessing but temporary or context-related efficacy, imparts considerable dynamism to their social relations.

This is precisely why amity and acts of solidarity are so important to the whole social system. The 'affective' character of the Yanomami can probably never be stressed enough. Certainly they have already acquired a solid reputation for 'fierceness', and as a conflict-ridden and belligerent people. But what is far less well known is their capacity for melancholy and sadness after the death of one of their number (cf. Gow, this volume). Their ability to feel distress – mythically associated with the apparition of death, homicide and war (Alès 1995) – over someone close[19] is proportionate to their capacity for 'hatred' of others, the enemy. Non-friends, unrelated people, can never be trusted. From the Yanomami perspective, their violence is directly determined by the pain inflicted on their peers and the love they have for them. Love, amity, sadness, anger and enmity exist in a continuum. It is euphemistic to describe the Yanomami as a very affectionate and sensitive people, deeply attached to those who are close to them. The excess of 'love' is inseparable from the diametrically opposite excess of 'anger' and the 'violence' which ensues when something bad happens to one's kinspeople and friends. Therein lies the explanation for their recourse to the retaliation system. In such a formal complex of strong passions and emotions, to manifest their amity to those closest to them, they have of necessity to manifest hate towards their enemies so as to demonstrate their willingness to fight and kill for a kinsperson or ally.

Notes

1 The Yanomami live on both sides of the Venezuela–Brazil frontier, and with their different sub-groups, the Sanïma, Yanam and Yanomam, number around 21,000 people.
2 I would like to thank both Luc Boltanski and Laurent Thévenot, as well as Joanna Overing and Alan Passes, for their help and stimulating discussions.
3 See e.g. Chagnon (1968, 1988); Harris (1979).
4 For an interesting discussion of this debate, see Meyers (1998); cf. also Flanagan and Jackson (1987), Okin (1989), Cannold *et al.* (1995).
5 The Yanomami dispose of a wide range of graduated means to confront their adversaries, from verbal to physical fighting (Alès 1984, 1990b, 1995). There exist several types of 'regular' fights with 'friends' and allies, i.e. those who are

not lethal enemies, ranging from duels to pitched battles. Within local, neighbourhood and friendly communities non-lethal sorcery is commonly practised for personal ends (jealousy, spite, love, hate). Lethal attacks are resorted to against enemies, i.e. those against whom one must take revenge for an earlier death, by means of various kinds of sorcery or weapons. All forms of confrontation, verbal and physical, are scrupulously reciprocal. As sickness and death are frequently attributed to occult aggression, they consequently tend to lead to lethal retaliation. War begins the moment a person is, actually or supposedly, intentionally killed. Beyond the physical-interaction level Yanomami practise shamanical war and 'animal-double' revenge (on the Yanomami sociopolitical model, their aggression system and the different forms of fighting, see Alès 1984).

6 The same thinking justifies violence towards women. The Yanomami consider that, as a man 'suffers' considerably in respect of his brideservice in order to obtain a wife, any overly inattentive or offensive act on her part (e.g. infidelity, refusal of sexual relations, desertion) legitimately constitutes a provocation of the husband's anger and lays her open to reprisals (see Alès 2000).

7 Political power in this type of society cannot be posed, as by Clastres (1974), for example, in terms of coercive power. For one thing, the political embraces a much wider field of social relations which include, among other things, cosmic ones (see note 9). Moreover, the definition of the political cannot be limited to a theory of power (Alès 1995).

8 The *pata* plays an important role in relation to the native principle of generosity and the 'good life'. His garden is generally bigger than his co-residents' and he ensures the output of a greater quantity of foodstuffs in order, notably, to allow the production of numerous ceremonial feasts (*reafu*) in his house.

9 The Yanomami system can be defined as being composed of a myriad of independent and sovereign communities, equivalent one to the other. On the supralocal level, each is joined in political, economic and ritual association with neighbouring communities, in order to guarantee the defence and rights of its inhabitants. At a higher inclusive level, the local groups are linked within the framework of a shamanic system and within one of animal doubles. There is thus a certain degree of sociopolitical integrality among the groups, which are encompassed within a society understood as a sociocosmical 'whole' (Alès 1995; see also 1984, 1990a, 1998).

10 The ceremonial context of the encounter relates to the ritual treatment of the deceased's ashes or personal effects. Different participants will, on departure, receive a part of the *reafu*, a food gift which closes the ceremony. Depending on the distance separating visitors and hosts, the feast takes place in a single day, or else over one or more nights.

11 These expressions distinguish them from *yafitheri*, co-residents and, by extension, near neighbours, and from *napë thë pë*, enemies. They are equivalent, in this context, to the category, *nofi thë pë*, friends, non-enemies.

12 A visitor may come quickly during the day to hold a formal daytime dialogue (*himou*) in connection with a specific matter. Visits to distant communities, however, imply an overnight stay. In such situations, ceremonial nocturnal dialogues (*wayamou*), lasting till daybreak, occur between visitors and hosts. During them visitors ask for the goods they desire, and state their identity through a gift of the names of the places once inhabited by their ancestors. They also answer for any grievances their hosts may have against them (see Alès 1990b, 1995).

13 To deny conviviality is equivalent to causing 'suffering' (*nï preaï*), and as a behaviour is the epitome of hatred.

14 Young people may also accompany their elders and pay visits on their own to other youths who have invited them to stay in their community. This form of conviviality makes it possible to initiate new relations, to reinvigorate relations which may have grown cold and also to re-establish relations after a war.

15 One cannot visit without an invitation, which is generally delivered through the mediation of messengers who frequent both communities, such as young men (see previous note) and out-married women. It is they who facilitate the establishment or re-establishment of peaceful relations after a war. The older men can then visit one another to exchange peace dialogues, in which they affirm their friendship, reassure each other that they will no longer be aggressive, state that they are weary of fearing to be attacked, hungry and desirous of sleeping in peace.

16 It is not uncommon for visitors or raiders to turn back before reaching the community they are making for.

17 The spatial dimension, which is determined and manipulated by the groups themselves, would seem to be a basic structural element of Yanomami social organisation. For a given community, identity and alterity are determined as functions of the relations of kinship, residential proximity/distance, alliance and hostility (Alès 1984: 77; 1990a: 75–7, 95); the resulting combination is more or less frequently redrawn and particularises individual and collective relations between the communities.

18 They have numerous modes in which to do so, see note 5.

19 Besides crying for their dead, regularly and at length, every time they remember them, the Yanomami openly exhibit great sadness in various contexts such as the absence of close kin or friends (cf. Lagrou, this volume). They weep at the departure of close visitors; the women cry when separating from their parents, husband and children. Mourning, as a manifestation of affection, a proof of the measure of one's love, has a great value which calls for reciprocity and generosity.

References

Alès, C. (1984) 'Violence et ordre social dans une société amazonienne. Les Yanomamï du Venezuela', *Etudes Rurales* 95–6: 89–114.

—— (1987) 'The forms of accord', paper presented at the Ecole des Hautes Etudes en Sciences Sociales (EHESS) seminar, organised by L. Boltanski and L. Thévenot, Paris, April.

—— (1990a) 'Chroniques des temps ordinaires. Corésidence et fission Yanomami', *L'Homme* 113, 30(1): 73–101.

—— (1990b) 'Entre Cris et chuchotements. Représentations de la voix chez les Yanomami', in C. Alès (ed.), *L'Esprit des voix. Essais sur la fonction vocale*, pp. 221–45, Grenoble: La Pensée Sauvage.

—— (1995) 'Función simbólica y organización social. Discursos rituales y política entre los Yanomami', in C. Alès and J. Chiappino (eds), *Caminos cruzados. Ensayos en antropología social, etnoecología y etnoeducación*, pp. 219–60, Caracas: Monte Avila Editores/IRD.

—— (1998) 'Pourquoi les Yanomamï ont-ils des filles?', in M. Godelier and M. Panoff (eds), *La Production du corps*, pp. 281–315, Amsterdam: Overseas Publishers Association, Editions des Archives Contemporaines.

—— (2000) 'Ethnologie ou discours-écrans? Fragments du discours amoureux yanomami', in B. Masquelier and J.-L. Siran (eds), *Pour une Anthropologie de l'interlocution: les rhétoriques du quotidien*, Paris: L'Harmattan.

Baier, A. (1985) 'What do women want in a moral theory?', *Nous* 19: 53–65.

—— (1986) 'Trust and antitrust', *Ethics* 96: 231–60.

—— (1987) *Moral Prejudices*, Cambridge, Mass.: Harvard University Press.

Cannold, L., Singer, P., Kuhse, H. and Gruen, L. (1995) 'What is the justice–care debate really about?', *Midwest Studies in Philosophy* 20: 357–77.

Chagnon, N.A. (1968) *Yanomamö. The Fierce People*, New York: Holt, Rinehart & Winston.

—— (1988) 'Life histories, blood revenge, and warfare in a tribal population', *Science* 239: 985–92.

Clastres, P. (1974) *La Société contre l'État*, Paris: Editions de Minuit.

Flanagan, O. and Jackson, K. (1987) 'Justice, care, and gender: the Kohlberg–Gilligan debate revisited', *Ethics* 97: 622–37.

Gilligan, C. (1982) *In a Different Voice*, Cambridge, Mass.: Harvard University Press.

Harris, M. (1979) 'The Yanomamö and the causes of war in band and village societies', in M. Margolies and W. Carter (eds), *Brazil: An Anthropological Perspective. Essays in Honor of Charles Wagley*, New York: Columbia University Press.

Kohlberg L. (1981) *Essays in Moral Development*, San Francisco: Harper & Row.

Meyers, P.A. (1998) 'The "ethic of care" and the problem of power', *The Journal of Political Philosophy* 6(2): 142–70.

Okin, S.M. (1989) 'Reason and feeling in thinking about justice', *Ethics* 99: 229–49.

Overing, J. (1999a) Introduction to the Conference *Appropriate Trust and Inappropriate Trust*, CIASE, University of St Andrews (8–9 May).

—— (1999b) 'Elogio do cotidiano: a confiança e a arte de vida social em uma comunidade Amazônica', *Mana* 5(1): 81–108.

Rawls, J. (1971) *A Theory of Justice*, Cambridge, Mass.: Harvard University Press.

Chapter 8

Homesickness and the Cashinahua self

A reflection on the embodied condition of relatedness

Elsje Maria Lagrou

Talking about emotions

It was during a conversation about the desirability or undesirability of home-sickness that Antonio Pinheiro, one of my main Cashinahua interlocutors, said: 'He who doesn't miss his kin in the same way as one craves water when thirsty, is not a person but a *yuxin* [a rootless, kinless, wandering spirit].' The Panoan-speaking Cashinahua of Western Amazonia use the same verb, *manu-*, to express the feeling of having *saudades*, the nostalgia provoked by the absence of close ones, and that of being thirsty for water. The passion that causes lovers to suffer, on the other hand, is called *manu-name-aii*: the mutual craving for each other.

The statement that a lack of yearning for close ones makes someone non-human says a lot about Antonio's ideas on proper community life and the feel-ings which are supposed to go with it. For him, a proper human being was not only characterised by human agency but, pre-eminently, by feelings of belonging. According to this view a person so resents the absence of those who 'made' and looked after him or her, that were that person to live without them, he or she would no longer be the same but might become transformed into a stranger (*nawa*), a spirit (*yuxin*), or an animal. Paths followed, experi-ences shared and food eaten mould a being into what it is, an identity which nonetheless has its ephemeral side.

The Cashinahua stress the fact that emotions are incorporated into a person's body, and that is the reason why it is the thinking and feeling body which is spoken of when one talks about positive and negative feelings. Feelings are forces which, so to speak, transform the person's body, bodily fluids, smell and appearance. 'Emotion talk', therefore, involves images of bodily attitudes, such as the aforementioned one of 'thirst' to express the feel-ing of missing close relatives (*manu-*). Another is that of passion and desire, expressed in terms of wanting to swallow the beloved one (*mia xeakatis*, 'want-ing to swallow you'). By contrast, hatred and rage against a person are phrased in terms of 'wanting to eat you' (*mia pikatis*) as opposed to 'offering food' (*mia pimaikiki*), the standard way of receiving people well. Anger is principally expressed by means of a denial of dialogue (*miki sinataki, hamakidi besua dakamiski mia hantxauma*, 'he is angry with you, turns away his face and refuses to talk to you') (cf. Alès, Kidd, Rivière, Rosengren, this volume). Jealousy (*sinadaw*, also translated as 'anger'), on the other hand, provokes sadness (*nui*, also translated as 'suffering'), a feeling that brings about a 'slowness to the heart' (*huinti pês*) and 'tiredness', or 'sadness to the veins' (*punu nuka*). This emotional state is expressed by a total lack of energy and initiative; one is said to feel lazy and listless (*en txikix ikai*). As Antonio explains, when one thinks too much about something (*mia xinai*, 'all the time thinking of you', or *mixinain-*, 'thinking very much', translatable also as 'sad', 'jealous'), one does not want to work. Sad people withdraw from social interaction, go for lonely walks in the forest or lie in their hammocks, with the mosquito net pulled down.

If gossip is to be believed, discreet extramarital affairs are not uncommon among the Cashinahua (cf. Kensinger 1995: 53–82). Affairs seem to be considered fairly innocuous in theory, though not necessarily in practice. I was repeatedly told that a happily married woman is healthy and fat, 'because her husband never talks about his affairs' and does not openly 'play' with or provoke other women. To jokingly tease people of the opposite sex is understood as foreplay to a love affair. Young couples can be frequently seen in public, playing around and laughing at each other's provocation. People will pay little attention to them or comment with a smile that they are at the stage of 'working at their child'. Conversely, almost all collective rituals have teasing between cross-cousins of the opposite sex as their central feature. This sexual joking implies physical as well as verbal provocation. Depending on the ritual, men and women will attack each other in groups with sticks, corn cobs, burning leaves or miniature arrows, or (during the increase ritual only) collectively insult each other's genitalia through ingenious metaphors (cf. McCallum 1989a, 1989b; Kensinger 1995; Lagrou 1998).

It is noteworthy that the code of decorum with regard to talking about the delicate theme of extramarital affairs appears not so much to stress their prohibition, as the impropriety of discussing them. What is at stake is the well-being of loving people living closely together which one takes care never to disturb. Thus a man who decides to take a second wife will strive not to neglect his first one. According to several Cashinahua I heard on the subject, sisters married to the same man do not tend to be jealous of each other, whereas cousins do. As Edivaldo, married to two sisters, explained:

> If you start the night in the hammock of your first wife, you will end it in the hammock of your other wife. The next day, you reverse the order. If not, there will be jealousy. You have to treat them well, both of them.

The Cashinahua, then, seem to disapprove not so much of extramarital affairs *per se* as of a lack of tact in talking about them. It is ostentation, comparison and lack of sexual generosity towards partners that provoke crises of marital jealousy, as illustrated by the following episode involving a young woman who had been beaten by her husband because of her affair with a man from another village. Her father, from whom I learned of the incident, was sad and strongly disapproving of his son-in-law's behaviour, but understood his anger. 'One should not want to know', the father said as he explained that the real mistake had been committed by his daughter's lover when, motivated by vanity and pride, he had spoken about the affair to his own wife. The father was upset, then, not because the young man had seduced his daughter, but because he was so selfish as to boast about it to his spouse, who then informed the father's son-in-law.

Thus a good husband, capable of keeping his wife satisfied and fat, never provokes her jealousy or uses violence (*hawen ain deteamaki*), and is an industrious worker and dedicated hunter. Being a good person (*duapa*) is synonymous with being generous, a quality that, in turn, expresses 'good or healthy thoughts' (*xinan pepa*). The quality of *duapa* implies for both men and women not to be *yauxi*, stingy, the infamous opposite of the appropriate social behaviour of a capable person. As a responsible adult, a person must offer food to visitors when they enter the house. The stingy host or hostess offers you nothing, thereby showing a disinterest in establishing any sort of sharing relationship. Since it is women and not men who give food to visitors, and taking into account the fact that men never give orders to women, the men's role as generous hosts depends for its success on the women's attitude.

To be stingy is the archetypical trait of all strangers. The Cashinahua myth of the origin of humanity links the achievement of sociality and humanity to the overcoming of the power of stinginess. It tells how the undifferentiated protohumans engaged in a war against Yauxi kunawa ('the Stingy Enemy'), the owner of cultivated plants and fire, who had repeatedly refused to share his knowledge and goods with them. The theft of fire and cultivated plants produced the differentiation between animals and humans, marking each of the former with a sign of the quality of their participation in the fight. Thus Xane, 'little blue bird', who gave his name to the title for village leader, *xanen ibu* (father or leader of the *xane* birds), acquired the marvellous colour of his bright blue feathers by bathing in the Enemy's bile. After he set the example, others followed, but not enough bile was left to paint their whole body. Xane's exceptional beauty can therefore be seen as the emblem and reminder of his courageous attitude. Furthermore, Xane always knows where to find food, and the other birds follow him, which is also why, according to Edivaldo, the village leader is 'the one who goes first'. For he too is expected to possess a disposition to take the initiative in work and play, thereby manifesting an attitude and way of speaking capable of infecting others with his enthusiasm, without ever giving orders (cf. Alès, Overing, this volume). A leader who speaks loudly to his people is considered to be *sinata*, an 'angry person', and criticised accordingly, as is one who is unsharing; both behaviours can cause a leader to lose his following.

The opposition between stinginess and generosity does not only regulate relations between a leader and his village, or hosts and their guests; it is also a crucial factor in the regulation of relations between husband and wife. Here the meaning of the concept *yauxi* is more complex than the straightforward translation of 'stinginess' can convey. *Yauxi* is a heavily loaded term in the Cashinahua's moral vocabulary and stands, in most cases, for antisocial behaviour. In respect of marital relations, however, the meaning of the word is more ambiguous. To say that a husband is stingy with his wife does not mean that a generous man judges it all right for his wife to have affairs. Rather, a stingy husband is a paranoid, obsessive husband, someone who mistrusts his wife all the time, keeps watch on her every movement and beats her when he suspects unfaithfulness. Beating is always publicly condemned and can lead to major political shifts and village fission.

In her turn, a woman is said to be stingy with her husband when she tries to prevent him from travelling alone or refuses to accept his wish for a second wife. As for women who refuse to have sex, they are said to be stingy with their vagina (*hawen xebi yauxi*). The expression refers primarily to virgins who won't let men come close: girls who do not want to marry yet and are afraid of becoming pregnant. Another context for its use is during fertility rituals, when male cross-cousins collectively provoke and challenge a group of women, calling them stingy. The women answer by ritually insulting, in a high-pitched song, male genitals. Vaginal stinginess can also manifest itself at childbirth: when a woman's labour is excessively long, her vagina is said to be stingy with the child (McCallum 1996).

In contrast to the withholding attitude of the *yauxi* character, generosity generates movement and enthusiasm. Thus, at the daily meetings held at dawn in front of his house, the village leader induces motivation for work with his encouraging words, while the song leader produces enthusiasm in nature and its animating forces through his propitiating songs. The creation of a positive disposition for work through words and songs is called *benimai*, 'to make happy'. The *nixpupima* initiation ritual, for instance, is composed of a long series of *benimai* songs intended to gladden the different beings (stars, animals, plants and their (spirit) 'owners') involved in the ritual reshaping of the initiates.

During the regularly held fertility rituals (*katxanawa*) it is through teasing and playful fights between the sexes of opposite moieties, jokingly and openly arousing sexual desire, that the *yuxin* (invisible) powers of fertility are invoked. 'When we ask for the fertility of plants and for abundance in our gardens', explained Milton Maia to me, 'we are asking at the same time for the fertility of our people. A happy village is a village where many babies are born.' The same image of the birth of many babies being representative of high village morale was used by Manuel Sampaio, the young leader of a new village:

> When people knew the use of poison and shamanising, kinsmen killed kinsmen. When people started to die from white man's illnesses, we lost a great amount of people. We decided that we needed to grow in number, if not we would disappear. We had already diminished very much. Now our villages are growing. Many new children have been born and the Cashinahua nation has become big again. In this new village, which is celebrating its third birthday today, eighteen children have been born and only two have died. This is so because our village is a happy village. Nobody should ever kill kinsmen again. Today the Culina still kill their own people with *duri* [shamanising]. They also kill our people with *duri*. Our old people still know the poison which can kill but nobody knows how to take away *duri*.

The foregoing declaration links the decline of the use of shamanism and poison to the need for population growth (cf. Erikson 1996, on the Matis). To be productive and create new bodies, a stronger emphasis on the fabrication and use of sweet (*bata*) products at the expense of bitter (*muka*) ones, related to shamanism, was required. As among other Panoan-speaking people (ibid.), the opposition between sweet and bitter is used in discourse about bodily as well as emotional states and character. Thus someone with a 'sweet liver' (*taka batapa*), or a 'liver that knows a lot' (*hawen taka unahaida*), is generous and sociable, an internal state expressed outwardly by a sweet face (*besu batapa*) (Kensinger, op. cit., p. 243). Sweetness is especially attributed to women, while generous and sociable men are more often said to be *duapa*, 'good', 'with brilliance' (*dua*) and 'with a shine on their face'. The first case associates a psychologically pleasant state with the palate, the second with an aesthetic pleasure for the eye. Although women are said to be warm, and men cool, and despite coolness of the heart being recommended for men (to be hot means to lose one's temper), the bitter/sweet duality seems much more salient in Cashinahua emotional and corporeal discourse, as well as in those on health and power, than the hot/cold opposition (on the latter, see Londoño-Sulkin with reference to the Muinane, this volume).

However, there is always a note of ambiguity to such dichotomies, and, as with all cognitively important concepts in Cashinahua style of thought, their meaning and value depend upon context. Thus, people in general are said to need some amount of bitterness in their body because it hardens it. Men, though, need more than women, and when women feed babies the latter initially require only sweet and neutral food as their bodies are still soft, malleable and vulnerable.

At the other extreme, a shaman is imbued with bitterness, as indicated by his name, *mukaya* ('the one with bitterness'). In this instance the quality stands for power and should not be understood in the Western metaphorical sense of having a 'bitter heart'. The shaman's heart is bitter, but so are his blood and flesh and even his palate. He is so suffused with bitterness that for him all meat tastes like beeswax (*bui*), and as a consequence he loses all desire for it. This is an example of the relation of symmetrical inversion between speaking and eating: as indicated above, those with whom you speak you do not eat, and vice versa. However, while the shaman is unable to eat and kill animals (because they would speak to him before he was able to kill them), he can nonetheless help hunters by playing tricks on the game, seducing them into his garden through the promise of 'plenty of rotting plantains'.

The prolonged and systematic use of tobacco powder (*rapé*) combined with rigorous fasting (no meat, sweet food, salt or spices) is another way of acquiring a bitter and thus strong body, that of a shaman. The story of the mythical shaman hero, Tene Kuin Dumeya ('Tene himself [the proper one] with tobacco'), is an epic account of his successive victories over *yuxibu*, monsters that made the forest paths unsafe. Tene's flesh became so strong that it was as bitter as poison. When he dived into the water to bathe, all the fish died as if they had been killed with fish poison (*puikama*). However, in that he did this after killing his wife and her lover, it is not clear from the myth whether the poisonous quality of his skin was due solely to the bitterness of the tobacco or also to the state of being a murderer, who, through his act of killing, absorbs the blood and *yuxin* (soul) of his victims.

Knowledge and the body

The definition of a body is to be alive: to be a thinking, social being that perceives, moves and speaks. When the *yuda,* the thinking body, is active and completely healthy, all its *yuxin* (souls) are with the person. *Yuxin* only exist as distinct entities, that is they are only named and perceived when separated from the body. This explains why knowledge is said to belong not to a person's *yuxin* ('soul') but *yuda* ('body'). Knowledge of how to bring about desirable effects in the world is embodied knowledge. Both its acquisition and its manifestation need the right setting to be efficacious and meaningful. Since words and deeds out of context are empty and without direction, the Cashinahua conception of knowledge does not insist on representation, distance and objectification of praxis to gain an understanding of a phenomenon. Rather, for knowledge to acquire meaning, a familiarity with performance and the acting out of techniques that embody both content and purpose are necessary.

The importance given to context, embodiment and the enactment of knowledge in the ongoing creation of a meaningful world that 'works' and fits is neither unique to the Cashinahua (as other contributions to this volume testify) nor specific to oral cultures. The association of concept and action and of concept and body has long been a topic for discussion and reflection in philosophy, the cognitive sciences and psychology.[1] In these different fields of inquiry into the workings of the human mind, the necessity to overcome the limitations of Cartesian dualism is often acutely felt, and scientists are beginning to realise that as long as the role of the body and emotions in cognitive performance is not taken into account, we will continue to be under the spell of false problems. Non-Western ontologies throw new light on old questions, and can thus be helpful in stimulating our reflection about the human condition through a change of perspective.[2]

Apropos the Cashinahua, Kensinger (op. cit.) has identified a number of particular knowledges all linked to the body and the senses. They include hand knowledge (*meken una*), eye knowledge (*bedu una*), ear knowledge (*pabinki una*), liver knowledge (*taka una*) and skin knowledge (*bitxi una*), as well as genital knowledge (relating to the testicles in the case of men – the location of female genital knowledge not being specified).

> One learns about things like the sun, wind, water, and rain through the sensations they produce on the surface of the body. It is in this sense that knowledge of the natural world is skin knowledge, *bichi* [*bitxi*] *una*, that is, knowledge gained through and located in the skin.
>
> (Kensinger, op. cit., p. 240)

Knowledge of the surrounding world, which is acquired through the eyes, is said to be 'knowledge about the jungle's body spirit' (ibid.). A person whose whole body knows is a wise person, *unahaida* ('knows strongly').

The body *yuxin* is called *yuda baka yuxin* ('body shadow' *yuxin*). It is a shadow, a person's reflection in water or in a mirror, or the image captured in a photograph of persons and things. Both during the day and at night the world known by the eye *yuxin* is a world of images. For something to become embodied and therefore adequate knowledge, the other senses have to help root this perception of the surrounding world through the skin, the ears, the hands, the body.

Accordingly, the capacities that make someone a good hunter are varied. There is eye knowledge to point the arrow, knowledge of the hands to control the technique of shooting and skin knowledge to sense the environment, the capacity to smell game and to produce the smell to seduce it with herbs, as well as whistles and songs to attract it. Hunters are said to imitate the hunting techniques and qualities of the boa much more than those of the jaguar. The boa is famous for seducing its prey, attracting it through the emission of a high-pitched sound and the hypnotising power of its eyes, and also through its charm (*dau*), incorporated in the design on its skin.

Weaving, women's knowledge, is a knowledge of both eyes and hands, and is manifested in the capacity to visualise an unseen pattern while manually progressing thread by thread. To acquire such knowledge, a girl needs the patience to sit and look at a master weaver for hours. After a while she is given the chance to try plain weaving, then she progresses to stripes, and finally weaves simple designs by herself. While part of the girl's initiation consists in methodical observation and practice, another part is intended to act directly on the incorporated memory itself. Thus she will be systematically treated with eye drops to induce dreams involving design patterns and the Master of Design, Sidika, the female boa, who appears to her in the form of an old lady and shows her all kinds of different weaving patterns, each accompanied by the appropriate weaving songs.

An embodied notion of self

It is important to stress the cognitive and emotional significance of the embodied notion of self for the Cashinahua, whereby the self is a thinking body, whose state, shape and texture are the concern of all. Equally central is that the idea of the actual identity of this self depends on, and is circum-scribed by, the network of relations that give it its place to rest and come home to. That is the meaning of the statement quoted above, 'He who doesn't miss his kin in the same way as one craves water when thirsty, is not a person but a *yuxin*.' *Yuxin* are free-floating beings without a fixed form or abode. People can turn into them if they lose their constitutive links with others and start to eat all manner of other foods, share thoughts, songs and words with all sorts of other beings and continue changing places and relations until they forget those who modelled and shaped them when they were still living among kin (cf. Gow, this volume).

A glimpse of the importance of interpersonal links for the identity of a person was revealed to me when, a few days after my arrival, I had a bout of sadness and homesickness. As I was living in the village leader's house, I could think of no other way to retreat from social intercourse than to with-draw into my hammock and pull down my mosquito net. This was my first visit to the Cashinahua and I had brought along a transparent nylon net, thinking that its only purpose was to protect me from insect bites. A mosquito net, however, fulfils several other functions among the Cashinahua, including that of providing privacy by hiding one or several persons from the view of others. That is why the Cashinahua's nets, which look much more like little tents, are made of cotton. Since mine was transparent, two women present in the house could see me taking a small bundle of photos out of my bag. They knew these photos already, as I had repeatedly been requested to show them, over and over again, to almost every newcomer or visitor. The two women stood up, came to my hammock, took me by the arm and made me follow them to the central place of the house. There they made me sit down and show my photos, one after the other, asking me with ritual patience, 'Who is this?', 'Your mother?', and then, repeating to each other, 'This is her mother'. 'And this?', 'Your husband?', 'This is her husband'. Slowly they went over the photos, reconstituting the whole network of my relations. When no photos were left to be commented on, they asked me to sing the song of my father, followed by that of my mother, sister and brother. After this domestic ritual of remembering I was considered cured of my homesick mood and the two ladies took me with them to their gardens.

This incident drew my attention to the Cashinahua's positive valuing of the feeling of homesickness, a feeling that is not to be neglected but healed through careful remembering. The expression of my feelings of longing and missing struck a chord of recognition in the two women, since this actualisation of my relatedness and belonging somewhere else in a way similar to theirs was for them a proof of my humanity. That the contrary was also possible became clear to me when, one day, a white-bearded Brazilian appeared in the village to be greeted by the women's screams: *yuxibu, yuxibu!*, which means 'spirit monster'. The women fled into their houses, afraid to be seen by the *yuxibu*, who was in reality a lone itinerant preacher well known to the Cashinahua. His solitary and strange habit of coming and going without greeting or farewell, and his wanderings without apparent purpose or destiny were considered by the Cashinahua to be a behaviour proper for *yuxibu* spirits who travel with the winds, but not for human beings.

The same idea of the importance of incorporated habit is also expressed in the word *yudawa*, 'to get used to', or, literally, 'to make the body'. One becomes used to a place when the intervention of others upon one's body – through food sharing, body painting and herbal baths – has changed that body in such a way that it has been made, or, better, transformed to be, in a certain way, similar enough to others to be able to live well in the new environment and without bodily discomfort. The Cashinahua are very explicit about this in regard to receiving visitors. One is advised not to rebuff the people or the food; to do so would result, it is said, in becoming ill. Illness is here understood as a part of the process of 'othering'; it is a person's reaction to the invasion of strange elements in the body. According to the Cashinahua, illness is obviated or avoided when the body (and that includes one's mind and thoughts) has become used to the influences and treatments to which it is exposed. This 'becoming used to' implies elements of taste as well as affection and is considered to be an attitude, a state of mind which, in Cashinahua terms, is a state of the body, or a state of being.

The body is held to be the result of a constant modelling of its forms by other people. The foetus is fashioned by the father through repeated sexual intercourse and 'cooked' by the mother in her womb. After birth, the child's features are considered still malleable. Accordingly, the woman who picks up the child and cuts the umbilical cord also moulds its face, flattening the little cheeks and straightening the nose. She will thus transform the child's appearance, transmitting some of her own features to the child through her moulding (cf. Londoño-Sulkin, this volume). Laura, one of my fellow co-residents, had asked me to perform these functions during the delivery of her child, and afterwards playfully told me, while looking at her baby's face, 'You gave him your body! Look! He has little blue-green eyes and his hair is the same colour as yours.'

The same idea of interpersonal transmission of qualities through physical contact and ritual song is expressed by a short domestic ritual performed after the umbilical cord has fallen off. At this stage the child is considered to be ready to leave the mosquito net and be exposed to the sunlight and the sight of people who do not belong to the circle of close relatives. A hard-working and knowledgeable close relative, or the song leader himself in the case of a male child, will, while singing a ritual song, dye the child black with genipa and paint a design on its forehead. The song sung during the painting invokes the dark skin of monkeys and the feathers of black birds. The painting protects the body, making it invisible to *yuxin* predation. Further measures for counteracting the harmful influences awaiting the child outside the mosquito net include herbal baths and the burning of fragrant herbs under its hammock. The Cashinahua seem to make explicit the continuity and per-sisting links between the child's body and its human and non-human environ-ment; thus smells, fluids and sounds are held to influence the child's shape and bodily abilities (e.g. being a quick or lazy learner), the quality and texture of its skin (all sorts of eggs are held responsible for pimples and skin problems), its dreams and the quality of its sleep.

The hands, sweat and words used in ritual are believed to transmit their character, power, *dau* (charm, medicine, good luck) and *dua* (brilliance, health) to the person receiving them. The ritualised speaking, the blowing and the touching also pass on an experienced person's thoughts (*xina*) and knowledge (*una*) to the recipient. Thus not only the body but all aspects of the person are simultaneously modelled. The body is not perceived as a bounded independent entity, separate from other bodies. Both its shape and state of being are the result of collective modelling and fabrication, and are of concern to all close kin (cf. Belaunde, Gow, Kidd, Londoño-Sulkin, this volume).

This collective responsibility for the well-being and state of other bodies also explains why, once I had been accepted in their houses, the Cashinahua wanted my body to be in a desirable state of health and beauty to be shown to my real kin, once back home. I was repeatedly told, 'We want you to be fat and healthy when you return to your family', for the state of my body would be the most eloquent testimony of the way I had been treated. Someone who is sad loses their appetite and someone who is socially excluded will not be offered much food. Thus thinness is considered almost always a sign of unhappiness. When a couple are constantly fighting, for example, the woman will lose weight. Consequently, the size of someone's body is the object of social comments and concern.

Thinness is also a sign of *yuxin* ('spirits') interference. Such interference in the life of a person only occurs when his or her normal social links are not strong enough to prevent the parasitic *yuxin* from occupying the place of close kin or from taking their victim with them to live in the forest with the forest beings, *ni yuxin*. Examples are: when a close relative (a child, wife or husband) dies and the mourning person cannot recover; when someone is living in a village without close kin; or when, whether belligerent, isolated, angry or jealous, they may start to spend most of their time lying down and crying softly in their hammock, or going for lonely walks in the forest (cf. Gow, this volume). The *yuxin*, hearing their cries, understand that this person 'wants to die' (*mawa katiski*) – that is when they strike. Small children, because of their weak bodies and young unfixed souls, are especially exposed to the nightly calls of *yuxin* (invisible beings), and babies frightened by *yuxin* get a high fever and are inconsolable in their crying.

Along with small children and unhappy people, it is the old who are most vulnerable to the call of *yuxin* beings, or, in other words, to the call of the dead. It is not uncommon to hear old people complain that they miss their dead kin and are the only ones left over from their generation. This mood can be translated as 'homesickness' for the past, and people say that person 'wants to die'. The old person misses their youth, the people of days gone by and the old lifestyle.

When an ailing person becomes unconscious, all close kin are summoned to gather around his or her hammock. Thus, when the song leader Augusto suffered a stroke in the middle of the night, almost the whole village, children and adults alike, was awakened to collect around him to cry and ritually wail. The event resembled a ritual combat between two communities, the living and the dead, fighting over the right to have their beloved one living with them. Augusto's son-in-law, the village leader Edivaldo, shouted in his ear: 'Look, father-in-law, listen! Here is your wife, here are your children, look at her, she is calling you!' Fragrant leaves were burned to repel the *yuxin* who had come to take him with them. Augusto told his audience what he was seeing: *pupu yuxibu* (owl *yuxibu*) announcing his death, his dead sister offering him corn soup, several of his dead relatives arriving and calling him. But this time the living cried louder and Augusto's eyes 'came back'. His son-in-law was shaking him; he opened his eyes and could see again. 'They were all there,' he whispered to his wife.

The destiny of the *bedu yuxin* (*yuxin* of the eye) is the land of the dead, the heavenly village of the *Inka* (the cannibal god of the dead). The ill person's *bedu yuxin* is said to know he or she will die and starts to explore the pathways leading to the divine village in the sky. Sudden and unprepared deaths, like those of Whites from shootings or knife fights, are problematic, Edivaldo told me, because these souls lose their way, whereas death from illness and ageing helps both the dying person and their kin to prepare themselves properly for the separation.

Self and other in a transformational universe

The idea of an embodied self embedded in a network of relations which constitutes a person's mental and corporeal frame of reference is expressed in Cashinahua phenomenological discourse, myth and ritual through the basic question of the relation between fixed and unfixed form.

In Cashinahua imagery about identity and difference, the idea of 'stranger' or 'enemy' (*nawa*) can easily be subsumed under the rubric of 'free-floating being without a fixed abode', or, in other words, spirit beings (*yuxin* or *yuxibu*). What interests the Cashinahua is reminiscent of what chroniclers tell us about the first encounters between Amerindians and colonisers: if the latter were puzzled as to whether the Amerindians had a soul or not, they for their part tried to discover if the Whites had a 'real' body, that is, a body subject to putrefaction, or, in other words, a body similar to theirs (Lévi-Strauss 1973: 384; see Mason, this volume).

Cashinahua ideas on similarity and difference focus on the body and the mode of its production or 'fabrication'. Ethnic identity and difference will therefore be expressed in terms of how one lives and how one's body is modelled by others through conviviality and the sharing of thoughts and substances with those one lives with or encounters when travelling. As noted, wanderers are people who virtually lack the prerequisites for humanity, since they seem to live without any relatedness or interwovenness with close others. They appear rootless and without any social feeling of belonging; neither do they have people for whom to live. This brings them very close to the invulnerable and solitary powerful spirit beings, *yuxibu*, who, like wanderers, know no fixed abode. In Cashinahua ontology the ideas of fixedness of form and of dwelling place are intimately linked (cf. Belaunde and Gow, on the Airo-Pai and Piro respectively, this volume).

The decision to live alone, far from one's relatives, is what turns kinspeople into strangers, say the Cashinahua. Identity is thus understood as a process inscribed in and on a person's body. The community of close kin with whom one lives is called 'our body' (*nukun yuda*). This is because people who live close ultimately end up 'belonging' to the same collective body as a result of the experiences, memories, food and bodily substances that have been exchanged and shared among them. The frequency with which collective meals are organised (whenever there is game available), along with a systematic sharing of goods and productive activities, creates the strong consciousness of interdependence responsible for the idea of one's community understood in terms of 'our body'.

People with a similar social practice and alimentation are said, then, to have a similar body (cf. Gow, Jamieson, Londoño-Sulkin, this volume). Depending on the entity to which the comparison refers, the speaker can either include in this category just the people constituting his or her community, or extend it to cover all the Cashinahua, or all other Panoans and, if contrasted with Whites and city life, even all indigenous peoples known to one (cf. Gow, this volume). This flexible use of categories of sameness and differ-ence, or of inclusion and exclusion, again reveals the importance of context in Cashinahua classificatory thought. We could even say that the principal endeavour is not so much to classify beings in closed and well-defined classes as to situate and circumscribe them in relation to the perspective from which they are being observed (cf. Viveiros de Castro 1998).

This perspectival approach allows for a constant awareness of the possibi-lity of role inversions, and of changing perceptions that depend on a modifica-tion of position or intention, either on the part of the perceiver or the perceived. Many factors can be held responsible for a modification in the relation or perception one has of another being with whom one is engaged in an exchange relationship. This shifting ground for classification reveals a profound awareness of the intricate interwovenness and intrinsic or potential equality in agency and power of all animated beings, each of whom has their equivalent or *yuxin* side which can at some point reveal itself and invert the positions in a given hierarchical relationship. The hunter can suddenly become game; kinspeople can become transformed into strangers or other beings (animals or *yuxin*); and strangers or enemies (like the *Inka*) can become the representatives of everything that is most proper to and valued by the community of humans. An acute awareness of the interdependence of all living beings is effectively translated into a cosmology that sets transfor-mational processes at the centre of philosophical reflection. Thus the question of what it means to be similar or different is transformed from a classificatory device into a philosophical paradox. All categories or concepts that refer to 'others' are conceived in such a way that they always end up referring as much to the category of otherness as to that of self.

This ambivalence also holds for the difference between humans and non-humans. Thus, human beings are bodies but can produce (and become) *yuxin* spirits as soon as the integrity or activity of their body is placed in danger, or as soon as it is at rest. The *yuxin* and *yuxibu* spirit beings, on the other hand, can also have a body, although their relation to it is different from that between a human person and his or her body. In contrast to the human self who *is* his or her body, the relationship between a *yuxibu* and its body is much more transitory. It is this transitory character of its relation to the fixed shape of a solid body that marks the crucial difference between a spirit, *yuxin*, and a human being.

Ritual praxis and the importance of the cooking process

Against this cosmic context of constant effacement of the frontiers between different kinds of beings and phenomena, Cashinahua ritual praxis reveals an obsession with the fixation of forms. If the spirit world is inhabited by powers of 'excessive fertility' and fluidity, the human world and the bodies produced by human agency manifest an opposite tendency. A human body is characterised by its heavy, fixed and slow-growing form, and, as we have seen, is gradually moulded by the constant intervention of other thinking and caring bodies, which seek to shape it to their own image. This is why experienced and successful adults are asked to massage, bathe, or paint a child's body. Through their hands they are said to pass on their bodily knowledge to the child. To enhance the effect of this sharing of qualities, those who have been requested by parents to perform the protective ritual will rub their hands in the sweat of their brow and armpits in order to relay it to the child (a ritual also performed on weak or sick adults).

The cooking process constitutes the principal means of bodily transformation employed by the Cashinahua during all the crucial stages of transition in a life cycle. It is used to fix the multiplicity of forms inhabiting the world of images, a world of *yuxin* that reveals the many suggestions of other possible worlds and bodies to be lived, created and visited in the cosmic space inhabited by kin as well as by strangers. The image of cooking, along with that of the collective remoulding of the initiates' bodies, is at the centre of ritual activity connected with *nixpupima*, the rite of passage for children, both female and male.

The ritual reshaping of children's bodies during *nixpupima* works simultaneously on their teeth, bones and skin. The bones, the invisible vital structure sustaining the body, are symbolised by the teeth, the central focus of ritual attention. Only children who have already shed their milk teeth partake in the ritual. While bones and teeth are strengthened, the bodily posture is shaped. The sculptural effect of the collective ritual intervention on the child's body is understood to have long-lasting effects: if a child should lie crooked in its hammock while sleeping during the central phase of the ritual operation, the four days of jumping and swinging crowned with the teeth-blackening treatment, its body would stay bent for ever.

The treatment given to children's skin is as important as the attention paid to the sculpting of their bones. The child's body is covered with *nixpupima* painting, broad black lines forming a 'broad web of design'. This has the function of absorbing the prayers and the medicinal qualities of the liquid with which experienced elders bathe the child, whose body is considered to be 'open' to receive the bodily knowledge transmitted by adults renowned for their industriousness and knowledge. This openness stems from the loose-mesh motif of the design, which leaves large portions of the body unpainted. The ritual situation of the *nixpupima* initiate's body contrasts with that of a baby, which is totally closed off by the black genipa paint covering its whole body, as described earlier. It also contrasts with the bodies of adults, which are but partially open and protected by a fine network of interconnected lines that form a web, filtering influences from the outside. The young initiate's body is also more naked or open because it lacks the thin layer of red achiote paint that serves as a base for the adult pattern.

The operation enacted by the community on the initiate's body is that of a symbolic recooking. For the Cashinahua, the cooking process, whose importance is stated in the above-mentioned myth of the creation of humanity through the theft of the cooking fire from the 'Stingy Enemy', would appear to be the quintessential operation productive of all transformative processes. The crucial role of cooking as a vehicle for the transformation of beings and bodies is encountered in many contexts of daily and ritual practice. First and foremost, all legitimate food is cooked food, and no meat should ever be eaten raw or with any blood left in it. Secondly, human beings are themselves created by means of a process of cooking: as noted above, the mother cooks the child in her womb, while the father sculpts its form.

The same image of collaboration between male and female reproductive capacities is represented during the ritual reshaping of the child, when the jumping around with the children, alternating with the drinking of huge quantities of maize soup, can be seen as an allusion to the intra-uterine modelling of the bone structure by the father's penis and semen. Each activity (repeated sexual intercourse and repeated jumping around with the children) is understood to model and remodel the child's bodily structure.

On the eve of the child's ritual bathing, its mother swings its hammock the whole night through, while the father dances around the fire. The fire is considered to be a gift of the *Inka*, cannibal god of the dead. It is a luminous force during the night, a producer of heat when it is cold, and a power that transforms all matter which it touches. The transformative power of fire is referred to in song through such invocations as 'the fire of work', 'of knowledge', 'of design' and 'of game'. In this way the men keep the fire alive with their song, while the mothers cook their hammock-wrapped children. The 'hammock swinging song' is called *kawa*, which also refers to the banana leaf in which food is cooked on the fire. Thus we can see the clear association between the cooking of small game enveloped in a banana leaf and the child swathed in its hammock, swung by the mothers as the men fan the flames.

Because a new body is the product of a transformation carried out on raw matter through the process of cooking, the body can be said to be real 'food-to-be'. To become edible, however, it will have to be transformed further, again by means of cooking. The result of the symbolic cooking of the child during gestation and the initiation ritual is a living body, while the result of real cooking is not a body but food. Thus the joining of liquid and fire during the transformative processes of cooking has two possible opposite outcomes: either a new amalgam arising from the fusion of previously separated substances, or its dissolution back into separate parts.

The corpse, locus of physical relatedness and memory, and point of reference for the body soul (released after death but still emotionally attached to its dead body), needs to be dissolved through the transformational process of cooking. This will disengage the *yuxin* (souls), still permeating and inhabiting the flesh, from the bodily remains that need to become transformed into mere meat. After twelve hours of cooking, the flesh is held to have become meat, to have released all its *yuxin*, and to have thus become less dangerous. It is, however, never consumed on its own but accompanied with cooked vegetables, for despite now being free of *yuxin* and so no longer a corpse, it is still very strong food that needs to be neutralised.

Since a person's body is the result of a lifelong incorporation of substances and care shared with others, the corpse, as a painful reminder and incarnation of these combined influences and memories, must disappear for the people to let the dead person go (cf. Conklin 1995: 86 on the Wari). Concomitantly with the ritual actions performed to dissolve the body, songs are sung to encourage the soul to acquire a new body by clothing itself with the robe of the *Inka*. The ritual intervention on the body, nexus of the person's human identity and uniqueness, is intended to undo both the fascination of the body soul for its lost body and lost kin, and the fixation of the living with their lost relative (cf. Alès, Gow, Jamieson, this volume). What is striking in this ritual intervention is the active role given to close relatives in the transformation of their kinsfolk's bodies. A body that has been collectively constructed and cared for, will also have to be collectively and ritually dissolved to liberate both the living and the soul of the deceased, in order to start a new life.

Conclusion

In this chapter I have tried to demonstrate how emotions and knowledge are conceived of by the Cashinahua as embodied processes. Among all the positively valued emotions, the cultivation of 'homesickness' (or more accurately 'kinsickness') is stressed as the defining feature of humanity, a moral judgement that reflects a notion of self embedded in relations of mutual caring. Without a systematic cultivation of feelings of belonging and of mutual craving for each other, sentiments expressed through the telling of stories about absent relatives and invoked as the prime motivating force justifying travel, a person's identity is considered to become weak. A drastic loosening of the links that tie a person to his or her relatives is held responsible for the initiation of a process of change capable of turning that person into a non-person, a *yuxin* spirit, an animal, or a stranger. Death too is understood to be the result of a radical process of 'othering'. To illustrate how ritual underpins this Native theory of personhood as an embodied condition of relatedness, the chapter synthesises some of the principal procedures of the collective 'remodelling' of the body and the self during the *nixpupima* rite of passage for girls and boys and the traditional funeral ritual.

Notes

1 In philosophy this discussion goes back to Heidegger, Wittgenstein (1981) and Gadamer (1984). What hermeneutics, phenomenology and existentialism have in common with reference to Cartesian dualism and Kantian 'pure reason' is their critique of the decontextualisation of thought and, in Heidegger's words (1996), 'an amputation of the being from Being'. The pre-existence of a background that delineates the figure of the individual implies history, human and non-human environment, emotions, body, values and motivation. Thought processes and knowledge systems can only be understood when taking this background into account as a constitutive, intrinsic part. A clarifying account of the discussion of the importance of body and setting in the field of cognitive psychology can be found in Shanon (1993). In the field of philosophy, Jakob Meløe's Wittgenstein-inspired 'praxeological' approach to knowledge applies the association of concept and action to fields close to anthropology. With examples taken from the daily life of Saami reindeer herders and Norwegian fishermen, he demonstrates how an active participation in the landscape and the mastering of techniques mould the perception of, respectively, landscape and boat (Meløe 1983, 1988).
2 In relation to this question, Jackson (1996) chooses the Cashinahua case to illustrate new ways of approaching different forms of knowledge, as well as to demonstrate why and how other, non-Western ontologies need to be taken seriously by scientific and philosophical thought.

References

Conklin, B. (1995) 'Thus are our bodies, thus was our custom: mortuary cannibalism in an Amazonian Society', *American Ethnologist* 22(1): pp. 75–101.

Erikson, P. (1986) 'Altérité, tatouage et anthropophagie chez les Pano: la belliqueuse quête du soi', *Journal de la Société des Américanistes* LXXII: 185–210.

—— (1996) *La Griffe des aïeux: marquage du corps et démarquages ethniques chez les Matis d'Amazonie*, Louvain and Paris: Peeters.

Gadamer, H.-G. (1984) *Truth and Method*, New York: Crossroad.

Heidegger, M. (1996 [1927]) *Being and Time (A Selected Reader)*, sections 31–4, edited by K. Mueller-Vollmer, Cambridge: Cambridge University Press.

Jackson, M. (1996) 'Introduction: Phenomenology, radical empiricism, and anthropological critique', in M. Jackson (ed.) *Things As They Are. New Directions in Phenomenological Anthropology*, Bloomington: Indiana University Press.

Kensinger, K. (1995) *How Real People Ought to Live: The Cashinahua of Eastern Peru*, Prospect Heights, Ill.: Waveland Press.

Lagrou, E.M. (1998) 'Cashinahua cosmovision: a perspectival approach to identity and alterity', unpublished Ph.D dissertation, University of St Andrews.

Lévi-Strauss, C. (1973) *Anthropologie Structurale II*, Paris: Plon.

McCallum, C. (1989a) 'Gender, personhood and social organization amongst the Cashinahua of Western Amazonia', unpublished Ph.D dissertation, University of London.

—— (1989b) 'Vampire bats and tortoise necks: a reanalysis of rituals of sexual antagonism in Amazonia', ms.

—— (1996) 'The body that knows: from Cashinahua epistemology to a medical anthropology of Lowland South America', *Medical Anthropology Quarterly* 10(3): 347–72.

Meløe, J. (1983) 'The agent and his world', *Praxeology* 13–89, Oslo: Universitets-forlaget.

—— (1988) 'The two landscapes of Northern Norway', *Inquiry* 3: 387–401.

Shanon, B. (1993) *The Representational and the Presentational. An Essay on Cognition and the Study of Mind*, London: Harvester Wheatsheaf.

Viveiros de Castro, E. (1998) 'Cosmological deixis and Amerindian perspectivism', *Journal of the Royal Anthropological Institute* 4(3): 469–88.

Wittgenstein, L. (1981 [1953]) *Philosophical Investigations*, Oxford: Basil Blackwell.

Chapter 9

'Though it comes as evil, I embrace it as good'

Social sensibilities and the transformation of malignant agency among the Muinane

Carlos David Londoño-Sulkin

On 'living well'

According to the rhetoric of Muinane[1] elders, the ultimate purpose of their everyday labours, numerous rituals and other practices congruent with proper knowledge is to bring about the 'multiplication of people', that is, the propagation of their own lineages and clans and those of their ritual allies. Successful propagation is conditioned on the community's and the individual's attainment of health, material productivity and proper social relations with others. These conditions are intricately interrelated. For the Muinane, health includes not only people's bodily vigour and fertility which enable them to be productive and engender children, but also the sensibility that leads them to act in a properly sociable manner. Proper sociability – a uniquely human quality – ensures the support of kin and others in the labours and rituals which are necessary for production and health. In turn, abundant production of foodstuffs, tools and ritual substances enables people to satisfy their own and their communities' needs, and to carry out rituals for health, social well-being and further production.

The combination of generalised good health, proper social relationships between the members of a community, and an abundance of food and ritual substances, constitutes what the Muinane refer to in Spanish as '*vivir sabroso*': to live well, or to live pleasurably.[2] The Muinane classify the bodily and (for lack of a better word) mental conditions which lead to living well as 'cool', and those that lead to the destruction of health and of convivial social relations as 'hot'. They place particular stress on the cool thoughts which people must experience and make manifest in order to live well: among other things, they should love their kin, be wary of improprieties and danger, be respectful of others according to certain prescriptions, be willing to work hard, and, especially, be tranquil and of good temper in everyday behaviour. Achieving coolness for the group is a manifestation of the morality and knowledge of its members and its leaders. Hot anger, envy, violence and social atomisation, on the other hand, are specifically morally devalued as manifestations of evil and lack of knowledge (cf. most other chapters in this volume).

Though pleasurable, living in a cool fashion is also an arduous task. The Muinane often rehearse the hardships and dangers of leading a life of moral action. They speak much about the fact that it involves a permanent, knowledgeable watchfulness against evil. Such evil is conceived of as the ill-will and power of the many malevolent agents in the cosmos who wish to harm people. Evil beings (mostly animals) strongly threaten the uniquely human capacity to achieve the bodily health and proper sensibilities that are necessary for the maintenance of the community. They destroy people's health and supplant their tranquil, loving, conscientious thoughts with those agents' own antisocial, misanthropic motivations. People must carefully guard their 'Cool Speech' – that is, their tranquil thoughts and peaceful disposition – against the hot anger-mongering of animals. Otherwise, the malevolent beings would cause people to quarrel and eventually stop supporting each other through the work and ritual practices of everyday life. Mutual anger and suspicion would escalate, social atomisation would ensue and witchcraft and violence would proliferate, all in the end creating a hot chaos of disease and death. In time all social life, that engendering of a healthy and prolific existence, would disappear.[3]

The Muinane's emphasis on coolness is part of their complex theory of sociality, selfhood and the experience of thoughts–emotions. The mythic narratives which they put to use in their rituals involve an articulation of this theory. Central to these narratives is an assumption that people's manifest actions stem from their thoughts and emotions. Moral actions stem from moral thoughts, and immoral actions from immoral thoughts. Another assumption is that these thoughts and emotions stem from certain substances. Most of the key ritual substances produce cool, moral sensibilities in people, while the substances of animals make anybody bearing them experience inappropriately angry or otherwise socially destructive thoughts. Thoughts–emotions can be manipulated to some extent as if they were material substances or objects themselves. For the Muinane, many of their activities – gardening, hunting, small healing rituals, the construction of houses and the great dance rituals, to mention a few – constitute just such manipulations. These everyday activities are understood to transform the hot, evil substances and agencies that cause diseases, antisocial thoughts and other kinds of tribulations into the very substances that sustain a peaceful, loving, properly human way of life (I will return to this below; see Echeverri, this volume).

The moral existence which the Muinane desire does not always – or even often – coincide with their own judgements of others' behaviour. Whether a person or a community indeed lives well is very much a matter of opinion, and in fact is often contested. Along with the rhetoric that underscores the need for a tranquil and caring lifestyle, Muinane people also engage in an ongoing flow of mostly negative moral evaluations of others. Siblings and other kin and affines, but especially members of other clans and ethnic groups, were pointed out to me as thieves, gossiping liars, ignorant browbeaters, witches or whores, and therefore responsible for damaging community life. The Muinane often make sense of misbehaviours and other troubles which hinder their achievement of a desirable way of life in terms of their cosmological construal of a world pervaded by hostile non-human agents. In this dangerous cosmos, the morally sociable Muinane seek to establish a productive, peaceful lifestyle in the face of the obstacles set forth by misanthropic animals and other beings that lead less moral lives. In the following section, I discuss some aspects of the Muinane's theory of selfhood and thoughts–emotions which partially explain the agential power of human beings, and address particular forms of the danger which the antagonistic cosmos holds for them.

Constitution and tribulations of the agential self

The ontological constitution of the human self as the Muinane construe it explains both the powerful agency that they attribute to moral human action and the assumed vulnerability of humans to the evil machinations of other beings in the cosmos. Let me dwell upon this briefly, not with the intention of exploring exhaustively a notion of 'self', but rather to present a picture of the human agent which fits into this project of achieving peaceful conviviality and successful reproduction against such heavy odds.

Modern, neo-Kantian dichotomies do not quite apply for the Muinane: the body is not 'natural' as opposed to 'cultural'; and nature – that is, the non-human – is not lacking in a 'culture' of its own, as my presentation below of the Muinane's human–animal relationships will show. They also dispense with the distinction between 'emotions' and 'thoughts': they have a single term which they translate into Spanish as *pensamientos* ('thoughts'), but which includes experiences such as love, sadness, anger and so on. Such thoughts are not merely aspects of the inner life of an individual, but are held to originate outside the bodies of the people that experience them.

Muinane elders often portray human beings as constituted in a somewhat Christian dualistic fashion: there is a body made of flesh which houses an *espíritu*, a spirit. Further exploration of the composition of the self, however, multiplies its elements and sheds critical light on any presuppositions of its unity and continuity across a range of behavioural manifestations. This makes the word 'self', with its connotations of sameness, identity and singularity, slightly inappropriate for the task of making sense of the Muinane's rhetoric. They treat the individual body as potentially a component of different selves, without, however, treating the non-corporeal aspects of the self as if they constituted something akin to an essential Ego. For the purposes of this chapter, I shall focus basically on two of the several basic aspects that are important in (my interpretation of) the Muinane's view of the self: bodies and Speeches.

Speeches

According to the Muinane's cosmological rhetoric, if people are alive, aware, articulate and morally agential, it is in great part because their 'baskets of knowledge' – roughly, their thoraces – are the temporary resonating chambers of extrinsic 'Breaths' and 'Speeches'. These Speeches are the proper thoughts which the Muinane's ritual substances – tobacco and coca foremost among them – generate inside people. They are also the moral talk that people produce as a result of experiencing such thoughts. Muinane *mambeadores*, that is, men who consume *mambe*, a pulverised mix of toasted coca leaves and incinerated *Cecropia* leaves,[4] describe this in terms of the Speeches of substances speaking inside or *through* a body. These substances speak in a 'truthful' way, constituting the normal moral awareness and dispositions of people who 'live well'. The thoughts which people experience as love for kin, their judgements when they correctly distinguish between good and evil behaviour, and their strong willingness to assuage conflict are examples of the Speech of some of these substances sounding inside the body. In Muinane rhetoric, there is no essential Ego-like entity which pre-exists the Speeches of ritual substances and perceives them; rather, the moral self is constituted by the aggregated Speeches of these substances inside an individual body.

The most commonly used ritual substances are tobacco paste[5] and *mambe*. Most rituals are carried out in the *mambeadero*, the exclusively male ritual coca circle usually found in the centre of the *maloca* or traditional house. They always involve the consumption of tobacco and *mambe*, and sometimes of other substances as well (cf. Candre 1996). For the purposes of this chapter I focus my discussion mainly on tobacco, which along with *mambe* receives the most attention in Muinane rhetoric. However, I must note that fire, water, axes, sweet manioc juice, hot chillies, certain herbs, at least two hallucinogenic mixes and other substances and material objects also play different and important roles in the Muinane's understanding of thoughts–emotions and agency.

Tobacco is the substance that is most often linked to proper Speeches. Juan, a Muinane elder, explained to me that the love of kin is nothing other than the extrinsic, divine Speech of Tobacco sounding through one's body. When one addresses kin properly with care and compassion, it is the tobacco speaking through one. Juan's explanation of love linked it to the notion of the consubstantiality of the kinship group. 'They [the members of one's patriline and clan] are one's own body; they are made with the same tobacco with which one is made', he told me. Juan was speaking about the fact that he and the members of his clan had been bred and raised by elders who used tobacco paste made from the clan's single strain of tobacco plants, in the numerous processes and rituals involved in making, rearing and protecting children. To care for his clanspeople, he said, was therefore to care for his own body.

He added that an elder may speak of his children as the arms of his body, or mention pain in his fingers and fingernails when slightly more distant kin are ill (cf. Jamieson, this volume). The image of kin as parts of the body is also used in exhortations of what I can only call empathy: prescriptions demand that people be aware that others feel pain akin to theirs when beaten or wounded, and *mambeadores'* exegeses of these prescriptions explain that the same applies to the anger, grief and indignation felt when kin is attacked (cf. Alès, this volume). Furthermore, because of the link between thoughts and substances, the consubstantiality of kin also entails, ideally, that kinspeople all 'have the same thoughts', and can collaborate without contradictions or contestations (cf. Gow, this volume).

The extrinsic origin and material base of the Speeches of which proper subjectivity is constituted also allow for the possibility of the disruption of such a subjectivity. There is ever the possibility of the proper self being impinged upon by the evil Speeches of Animals that might sound through the person's body. Such an attack would result in a spurious self who is incapable of relating properly to other people or of working productively. This is one of the main threats of these hostile forces – the taking away of the capacities of the self for achieving a true, tranquil and productive sociality. Let me discuss this briefly.

The Muinane's cosmological narratives depict an agent-filled cosmos where animals, birds, fish, trees and other beings of the jungle, rivers and various layers of the universe lead social lives in certain ways similar to those of Real People (i.e. humans, basically the Muinane), but which are fundamentally flawed in ways prototypical of the undesirable. The ritual substances of animals – their dialogues, tools, houses, marriages, cultigens and so on – are but imperfect or perverse caricatures of the ideal human forms, when not absolute deviations from them. As the myths describe and explain, at the time of creation, the creator god[6] made several attempts to fabricate human beings. The results of one such attempt were animals, who were initially shaped like Real People. The creator gave them his 'Speech of Tobacco' (simultaneously a substance, an animating breath and the capacity for speech). This tobacco was to provide them with awareness, and motivate and empower them to behave in the manner the deity prescribed. The myths reiterate often that animals behaved immorally, misusing the tobacco and disobeying the prescriptions of the Speech. They did not behave with the love, respect, humility, persistence, discipline and productivity which the creator had attempted to instil in them, and so they ruined the tobacco that endowed such virtues. Infuriated by the disobedient transgressions of his creations, the deity transformed them into animals, and their tobacco into spurious versions of tobacco. He rebuked them, and told them that thenceforth they would be 'fruit' to be eaten by Real People, the sole creation which used his Speech of tobacco correctly. He gave each animal its name, and stated that its original undesirable behaviour and false tobacco would remain with it for ever, and that with it the animal would cause people to have disease or other problems.

Since then, to quote a Muinane elder, 'the tobaccos of animals have no sense'; they motivate the animals' immoral behaviour (e.g. incest) and empower their destructive intentions. *Mambeadero* rhetoric states that some animals claim to be or else to possess true tobacco, or true fire, or true axes, which are all material things which constitute moral human agency, and which in fact animals lack.[7] For example, the teeth of an agouti are its 'axe', yet this axe does not enable it to fell the forest and plant a garden, in a proper moral way. The hair of a red deer is its fire, yet this false fire cannot cook food to remove its pathogens and disgusting flavours, nor burn up the slashed forest so that people can plant their seeds in fertile ashes. The jaguar's tobacco is strong and enables it to hunt, but does not allow it to distinguish between its prey and its kin, and so the jaguar cannot live in a properly sociable manner. At times animals are said to perceive themselves as human; at others, they are aware of their non-human status in the face of true humanity. Whatever the case, they feel animosity towards Real People. They are envious of the products and way of life which Real People enjoy thanks to the agency of true tobacco and coca, as opposed to the miserable existence which animals' own spurious substances bring about. Their envy is malevolent, and motivates them to destroy what they themselves cannot have. Animals also fear and resent the predatory agency of humans, and constantly seek therefore both to pre-empt human predatoriness and to avenge past human predations upon them. To achieve their misanthropic aims, they sabotage the social capabilities of Real People by causing them to experience antisocial emotions, and they enervate their bodies by causing diseases, accidents and even death.

The hot Speeches ensuing from animals alter people's sensibilities so much that they do not perceive or act as Real People. Their unique capacities for moral human endeavours are thwarted. Some particular 'uncool' thoughts can be attributed to particular animals. For example, when I asked an elder about the thoughts that stem from a jaguar, he answered, 'That one does not say, "This is my brother".' In other words, when a jaguar's Speech sounds through a person, it is experienced by them as indiscriminately angry thoughts against their own kinspeople. The improper jaguar affects displace the person's proper Speech, which would normally make them think, 'This is my brother' (and therefore not an enemy or an animal to be attacked). Such proper thoughts would normally lead the person to act with love and compassion towards the sibling. The person with the jaguar's Speech inside behaves viciously and destructively towards their own relatives, much as a cannibalistic jaguar would towards *its* kin. In a certain myth, jaguars do appear as cannibalistic murderers who kill and devour their own kinspeople. Similarly, the Speech of the coati can be the abusive anger of a man against his wife, or else his general surliness. Juan explained to me that the owners of this Speech, large male coatis, battle any member of their species they meet, and do not stay together with their mates for very long for this reason. He attributed similar behaviour – and the Speech of the coati – to a local leader who was rather tyrannical, and who was therefore losing his following.

Another evil Speech is that of the mythic figure of the False Woman. This Speech makes people experience jealousy, perverted sexual desire or vanity, and behave in purposeless ways. In mythical times, this feminine spirit bore a penis-shaped tobacco container, the contents of which made her desire sex uncontrollably and indiscriminately. She was beautiful and vain, but too lazy, incompetent and libidinous to produce the food and ritual substances which were her responsibility as a woman. She attempted to seduce her own brothers, and therefore the creator banished her to the outskirts of the land of moral Real People.

Whatever the sources of evil Speeches – a tapir, a jaguar, an oropendola, an agouti, or others – they threaten health, personal well-being and the peaceful, mutually supportive relationships between people. If not dealt with, they can eventually lead to the extinction of the kinship group. Part of their insidious danger lies in the fact that with another's body they constitute a counterfeit self: an immoral false self that is persuaded of its own authenticity. Several *mambeadores* told me that it is for this reason that people who mis-behave often do not recognise their own faults, and protest vigorously when discerning elders point out their misdemeanours. In Juan's words, 'When they deny their culpability, it is the disease speaking. The real person would admit to the mistake.'

The Muinane's rhetoric on proper and improper Speeches sounding through bodies is partially but powerfully and intimately constitutive of their daily interpretations and experiences of emotions. It is a frequent occur-rence for them to attribute Speeches of Animals to each other, and even to themselves, and they take for granted that their Speeches in the nightly *mambeadero* sessions stem from the tobacco they have licked throughout their lifetimes. Perhaps the clearest example I can provide of the constitutive character of this rhetoric came from Manuel. He told me that at one time he had suffered from the 'disease' of jealousy, and used to mistreat his wife con-stantly because of it. After inflicting much abuse upon her and ruining life in his household, he had discovered through a ritual that his jealousy was being caused by the False Woman, the above-mentioned evil mythical being against whom the myths warned. He explained to me:

> She is the one who makes one say, when one's wife laughs, that she is laughing at one; she makes one say when one sees her speaking to herself, that she is speaking about one. It is all lies! I told her I did not wish to lick her tobacco, for I have my own.

According to his autobiographical narrative, Manuel had experienced the False Woman's jealous Speeches *as his own inner speech,* that is, as his own thoughts–emotions. He claimed the ritual made him aware that it had not been his true Speeches which he had experienced, and that it simultaneously transformed his jealousy into an animal. Since it was already game, that substance-like thought could therefore no longer be in him. He therefore stopped abusing his wife. My interpretation is that his new awareness – made possible only by the narratives of his people, which establish the plausibility of perverted thoughts and feelings of extrinsic origin – changed how he perceived the situation, and therefore how he felt (I dare say) and behaved.

Bodies

According to the elders, only the tangible or visible results of a person's efforts constitute evidence that the person had spoken True Speech when carrying out the rituals in which they made explicit the plan to carry out a productive endeavour. If a person makes such plans public but these do not 'dawn', that is, they do not bring about the proposed results, others may claim afterwards that the person had spoken the persuasive but false and ineffective Speech of some animal. A person who speaks beautifully of hard work and production but who is too lazy or physically incompetent to carry it out is not speaking True Speech, but Lying Speech. To avoid this happening, people have to develop tough, vigorous, disciplined bodies. Competent bodies in combined action with moral Speeches can be truly agential in a properly human way.

The Muinane do not view Real People's bodies as 'natural', or as 'innate givens' in a biological sense, because they understand them to be produced by the purposeful action of kin, not merely through the act of sex but also through diverse everyday actions such as eating, drinking, sleeping and consuming ritual substances. The proper behaviours of kinspeople confer upon the bodies they produce their beauty and capability for moral endeavours, whereas their immoral actions misshape them. During their early development in particular, the bodies of people are malleable and therefore vulnerable. Their own and their kinspeople's misbehaviours may distort their bodies. For example, the dietary behaviour of a child's parent's before its birth determines whether it will be bald or hairy, light-skinned or dark-skinned, ugly or beautiful. After birth, the child is further moulded by the kneading of the midwife or other female kin to correct any birth defects and ensure that the face and body are set correctly for growth. When I inquired about this kneading of newborn babies, a woman pointed out her different children to me, and called my attention to the fact that those whom she herself had 'fixed' all had flat abdomens and shapely faces, while those whom her aunt and her oldest daughter had kneaded were pot-bellied and less handsome of face. She claimed that her better performance was due to the fact that as a young woman she had followed the strict dietary prescriptions pertaining to this particular skill (cf. Lagrou on baby-kneading among the Cashinahua, this volume).

In childhood and adolescence, a child's body receives further shaping from its elders, but its own diet, bodily discipline and ways of relating with others all become more determining influences. For example, regular bathing early in the morning in the cool waters of a stream will make a child's body strong, its skin tough, its state of health excellent; in short, it will help it become a competent, productive, fertile adult. On the other hand, constantly touching its own body and head instead of maintaining a disciplined stillness may make a child age quickly or become diseased (cf. Belaunde, this volume). Growing healthily requires also that a child be respectful, for otherwise it may awaken the animosity of others and in consequence fall victim to disease. In short, a disciplined, convivial child grows well and healthily, while an undisciplined, disrespectful, antisocial one may easily become sickly, unproductive and barren.

A greater danger to bodies stems from evil beings who cause diseases by placing deleterious substances in them such as false fires or fevers which 'cook' people's hearts, and thorns, darts or pieces of ceramic that cause pains, debilitated states, interruptions in bodies' inner paths and so on. Many diseases are treated in rituals as attempts by animals to prey upon human victims. For example, muscular pains are said to stem from having fallen into the perverse hunting traps of animals, or from being wrapped in their invisible but pathogenic carrier cloths. Some visceral afflictions are the result of being eaten inside by worms or grubs. Some forms of infertility are thought to stem from a mythical turtle biting into the scrotum of a male victim. Whatever the cause of bodily disabilities, with few exceptions their effect is to interrupt the moral endeavours which are people's duty. As a result, disabilities impede the 'multiplication of people' and the tranquil, pleasurable lifestyle which Real People seek to achieve.

Transformations of evil

The predatory transformational agency of tobacco

The material character which the Muinane attribute both to their own proper thoughts and to detrimental diseases and tribulations is central to their view of agency in the world. The different agencies which the ritual substances provide largely involve the transformation and movement of substance-like emotion or of sentient materials. The agency of several of the ritual substances is predatory. Tobacco's action, for example, usually consists of the transformation of some 'useless' or 'evil' material object or negative substance-like emotion into nourishing food or some other desirable substance, including moral substance-like thoughts. The transformative action more often than not involves the death of some evil causal agent. The predatory agency of tobacco is established in the mythical narratives, which portray the tobacco as a sentient cultigen/person immersed in a dangerous world full of animals intent on preying upon him or her (the gender of the substances depends on the clan of the narrator). Tobacco's salient attributes in these narratives are that it initially appears to be very fragile, but then turns out to be a potent and invulnerable predator that feeds upon its attackers without being harmed by their particular pathogens.

The Muinane depend on what I call 'instrumental Speeches' to make proper use of the agency of ritual substances. The instrumental Speeches constitute the *conocimiento propio* ('our own knowledge'), a knowledge the Muinane consider peculiar to themselves as opposed to the knowledge of other local indigenous groups and of White people. Instrumental Speeches, such as the Speeches of Apprising (myths), of Healing (chants and recipes), of Work, of Maloca Construction and others, spring from tobacco, *mambe* and other substances, and are the very words of the deity sounding through people. However, they differ from the innate Speech that animates people in that it has to be acquired by each person in their lifetime, through demanding learning processes and the consumption of many ritual substances. These Speeches also differ from other moral thoughts in that they involve certain formulaic articulations. They constitute the discursive elements which direct the different agencies of the ritual substances to transform evil and thereby to bring about a proper way of life.

In the *mambeadero*, the men describe many of their everyday activities as righteous assaults upon evil agents through physical work and ritual Speeches. The latter direct the predatory transformative agency of the ritual substances, ensuring performatively that the attacks bring about the proposed results. For example, common acts such as felling the forest for a garden, hunting, fishing and healing the sick are understood to involve tobacco's action against evil trees, animals and fish. The processes of production of some of the ritual substances are themselves examples of predatory transformations. They involve removing or modifying the useless, undesirable or dangerous components of some original plant substance and keeping the pure, empowering elements (cf. Echeverri, this volume). The premise is that in unprocessed stuffs there is evil, contamination, or at the very least, something useless such as the 'pulp'. Fire – another predatory substance – plays an important role in several of these processes by 'eating' pollutants or cooking the raw. Tobacco's own predatory agency and invulnerability become proper human agency by means of a process of cooking and filtering.

The extraction of the vegetable salt to be mixed with tobacco paste is a particularly clear example of a predatory, purifying transformation. It involves the burning of certain palm trees or other plants, an action which the Speeches describe as the incineration of dangerous thorns, itchy bark fuzz, poisonous snakes and scorpions, among other dangerous stuffs. The ritual Speech (needless to say, empowered by tobacco) that is instrumental in effecting one aspect of the transformation at one point takes the form of a commonsensical question rooted in what is portrayed as a matter of fact:

> Given that here the True Fire of Life is eating the false fires, destroying
> the thorns, the snakes and the scorpions, why should I be bitten, why
> should I be stung? Why should my children, my people, be bitten, be
> stung? Why should we feel itchy? We will not be, for I am consigning
> such thorns, saps, fuzzes, scorpions and snakes to the fire, that I may
> then lick good tobacco.

The stings, animal poisons, itches and so on have tangible referents whose
potential for bodily harm the Muinane very much wish to pre-empt; however,
the Speech also treats them as sources of unpleasant, antisocial thoughts and
actions. The fire turns the plants with their itchy fuzz, bitter saps and sharp
thorns into ashes which can then be subjected to filtering. Water is poured on
the ashes, where it dissolves the salts and then drips through into a receptacle.
The resulting salty water is evaporated over fire, leaving only the vegetable
salts, ready to be mixed with the tobacco paste. By transforming and incorporating the very substance of evil into salt, this preparation pre-empts some
of the evils that keep people from living well, namely, stings, cuts and bites,
but also anger, envy and jealousy. Furthermore, the substance of evil is not
only rendered harmless to people, but made into a properly agential
substance in its own right, and one which makes tobacco paste tasty (cf.
Echeverri, this volume, on salt).

Healing as a predatory transformation

Another example of the predatory agency of tobacco is to be found in healing
rituals which deal with the 'diseases' which affect people's bodies and their
subjective states. In several healing rituals I attended, the healer and a conversation partner or 'what-sayer' (Echeverri 1997: 29) licked tobacco and
coca in order that their thoughts would become 'open' and perspicacious,
and that their Speeches would have 'strength'.[8] The healer then narrated or
alluded to the mythical events that dealt with the different origins of the
disease which affected the victim, trying to pinpoint which particular animal
or other evil agent had attacked him or her. The what-sayer interspersed
comments or assenting expressions regularly, establishing with the healer a
typical *mambeadero* dialogue characterised by its rhythm and singsong intonation. In some of the rituals, they discovered the causal agent because a
sudden silence, or an explosion in the bonfire, or a particular sound in the
jungle, signalling the culprit's culpability, would happen to occur at the very
point in the narration of the Speech of Apprising where its name would be
mentioned. As the healing rituals continued, the dialogue addressed different
beings: the deity or deities, the guilty animals, or the leaders of animals, and
scolded them, denounced them, cajoled them, or persuaded them. Then
healer and what-sayer performatively rejected the disease by means of
Speech formulae in which they claimed to be sweeping it away, blowing it

away, proscribing it; or else they described in an equally performative manner how the creator deity rid them of it. Afterwards, on those occasions in which the victim soon healed and game was caught, the rituals were pronounced successful. The elders claimed that the tobacco had transformed the improper thought or disease into game, in a manner to which they referred as 'making [the problem] dawn', or else, more clearly predatorily, as 'grabbing' the culprit, 'snaring' it , or 'placing it in the [hunter's] path'. Another way in which they stated it was that the tobacco had sent the animal's own evil back upon it, killing it. Whatever the case, the destructive disease or affect had been transformed into nourishing meat, and was understood thereby to be removed from the person.

In his autobiographical accounts, Manuel presented in a similar fashion his dealings with the beings who had made him an angry, drunken, violent person in the past. He attributed great importance to a ritual which he claimed saved his life and made him a properly behaved person. Through that ritual his father had shown him, years before, those evil beings whose Speeches had made him misbehave, without his being aware of their presence in him. In that very ritual he 'saw' a possible future in which his diseased actions caused by those Speeches would lead to the destruction of his marriage, the dispersal of his patriline, and his own death. In the process of the ritual, however, he and his father transformed those false Speeches by means of their own true Speeches and tobacco. After the ritual, he spent months hunting intensely for the causal agents. The edible game he killed he ate with his family, and others he used for his animal-tooth necklace. He claimed that afterwards he never again misbehaved in the same fashion, for he had rid himself of the Speeches of Animals by making them – their substance – 'dawn' (i.e. become manifest) as game. He considered his necklace to constitute a domestication (in Muinane, a 'bringing into the *maloca*') of those animals: a transformation of their misguided predatory capabilities into an object of beauty and of proper predatory agency which he could direct for the defence of his family.

Preying upon the jungle

Another context for predatory transformations is the garden. Making a garden is presented as the destruction of the inedible fruit of animals, and their replacement with proper human stuffs. Felling the jungle appears in Speeches as a 'war' which redirects the anger in people so that they attack trees instead of other people. The felling process is also likened to a meal in which the axes and machetes 'eat' itchy, pathogenic trees, saplings, vines and so on. Afterwards, the flattened jungle is left to dry out before it can be burned and made adequate for planting. According to some Muinane elders, proper drying is achieved by means of Speeches that instruct the deity of the Summer to smoke (in the culinary sense) the chopped trees and vines etc., telling her (or him, depending on the clan of the narrator) that the felled plants are a meal placed there by the garden owner for the deity's satisfaction. The Muinane also use Speeches to deceive game, ants and insects by telling them that in the garden they have made a sleeping place for them, and instructing them to go and sleep there. Finally, when everything is dry, the owners of the garden set fire to it. The burning is also a meal in which the True Fire of Life 'eats' the ugly, polluting, dry matter of the forest, as well as any unwary insects trapped in the garden. The fire then vomits them up again as fertile ashes from which nourishing foodstuffs and ritual substances will grow.

On one occasion I helped Manuel to prepare a new garden. Together we felled a section of the forest, and a month or so later, we burned it to prepare for planting. When we had finished he said to me, 'We will now heal . . . If anything bothers us now, it is but a lie.' As I understood him, we had effectively transformed the active substance of any threat into fertile ashes, and any new tribulation would have no 'substance', and thus no agency, to truly harm us.

The great transformative rituals

Dance rituals too are understood to transform evil by means of tobacco's hunting power. For some of the dance rituals, the host or 'owner' of the ritual delivers tobacco paste to his 'Men of the Speech of Tobacco' – his formal ritual partners from other clans – as a means of demanding that they and their families come to sing and dance at his ritual. This tobacco is also meant as a request that the guests bring game with them. Before delivering the tobacco, the owner of the dance ritual prepares it by means of a Speech of Incantation in which he instructs the tobacco paste to make all envy, anger and disease attacking the group fall as game. An old man once explained to me what one such incantation was about. Pointing to a little yellow bird, he said, 'Look. It stands on its perch . . . looks around . . . and flies and catches its prey close by. It does not need to go far, to catch its prey!' Indeed, the little bird did not fly more than a few metres from its perch before snapping up some insect in midair and returning to its branch. The old man continued,

> That is why it is named in the Speech of Incantation to prepare tobacco for dances . . . So that the people who hunt game to bring to the dance will not have to hunt far afield . . . they will just sit in their coca circle, lick the tobacco and look around, and next day they will kill nearby, in the garden or on the path.

This 'looking around' is a spiritual search for the causes of tribulations in the communities involved; the game killed is the product of a transformation of those causal agents, and thereby of the tribulations.

An elder explained to me that if the dance owner's Speeches are true, that is, if his knowledge has been morally implemented, this conjured tobacco will restore the diseases and detrimental emotions to their animal originators, and will place the latter in the path of the hunting guests. People's incapacitating illnesses and their angry, brooding or envious thoughts convert into[9] the fortifying flesh of game animals. Freed of such impediments, people recover their health. They no longer brood, but, rather, experience properly sociable thoughts concerned with dancing, eating and consuming ritual substances, activities which make people fertile and sociable. The meat, a nourishing product of the transformation of evil, is redistributed by the ritual's owner so that his own group and that of the dancers may gain strength from it. With that strength, and with the added power of the drinks and ritual substances consumed in the dance itself, they can all work, produce more food and ritual substances, and have children.

The construction of a *maloca* also brings together numerous transformations of evil. When Juan built his *maloca*, he first delivered tobacco paste to his 'Men of the Speech of Tobacco', to invite them to help him construct the house. In the ritual dialogue he held with them at the time of delivery, they all enthusiastically described the whole process of building as a salutary endeavour that would bring health to all and ensure the proper raising of the youths and the successful growth of all the clans involved. Their dialogue was premised on the material character of diseases, undesirable emotions and potential troubles; for them, these could therefore be pre-empted by means of transforming them into elements of the *maloca*. Juan explained to me that building a *maloca* took care of numerous tribulations. For example, the owner could use a Speech that said,

> Given that the pillar holds upon its back the weight of so much wood, and his back does not hurt, why should my people's backs hurt? I place that backache upon the pillar, who does not suffer from it. Why should it make me suffer, make my family suffer, when it is already there?

According to the elders, any tribulation can be transformed in the process of *maloca* construction: undesirable restlessness and diarrhoea, colds and disrespect for elders, speechless anger and blindness, and so forth. Novel threats also find their way into the *maloca's* structure: Juan's brother once told me that when there was a jail sentence pending for some kinsman, a Speech could be used which would transform it into a knot of the kind that ties several rafters together. 'How then', he asked, 'can the person be jailed, if the sentence has already been transformed into a knot?'

A common phrase used in the *mambeaderos*, the ritual coca circles, syn-thesises the Muinane's optimistic view of their own capability to transform evil: 'Though it comes as evil, I embrace it as good.' Diseases, anger and all kinds of tribulations become, from this perspective, the necessary elements from which to draw the good substances necessary to live well.

Conclusion

The Muinane are profoundly persuaded by the reality postulates which inform their narratives, rituals and interpretations of behaviour, concerning the materiality of subjectivity and agency, the constitution of the self and the principles of proper human action. I witnessed many debates contesting the order of events or the names and natures of participants in particular versions of incantations and myths; however, their postulates were never points of debate. They were matter-of-factly taken for granted. Similarly, sometimes my conversation partners among the Muinane would contest other people's particular interpretations of a behaviour; however, both the contesting and contested interpretations were usually based on the plausibility of these postulates, and never on their denial.

The Muinane's self-depictions partake of these postulates. They enable the Muinane to experience very particular thoughts and emotions which other people who do not share these postulates and narratives – and therefore their self-depictions – cannot. I would claim that the Muinane's articulations of the substance-like materiality of their thoughts and of the qualities of proper sociality, are what makes it possible for a Muinane individual to *be* a Real Person of a certain clan, marked off from others by the tobacco that consti-tutes him or her. These articulations also make it possible for a person to realise that their proper Speech has been supplanted by an animal's, and to feel and act differently because of that realisation. They make the Muinane painfully aware of the impropriety and danger of antisocial thoughts, and make the project of 'living well' a deeply motivated one.

I must note, however, that the Muinane do not appear to make use of either the narratives or their postulates to make sense of certain events. Sometimes they explain particular actions and thoughts with arguments that do not take into consideration the causalities which involve transformative sub-stances, Speeches or animals, but, rather, seem to fit into a more essentialist, Ego-attributing theory of selfhood akin to a modern Western one. I do not interpret their acceptance of mutually contradicting accounts in terms of oppositions such as that between the ideal and the real. I would rather limit my claim to stating that on different occasions the Muinane make sense of events by reference to different sets of postulates concerning the workings of the 'self' and the canons of proper social life. Despite the contradictions – which are sometimes more of a problem for the logician's 'Speech' sounding through me, the anthropologist, than for my Muinane friends – these opposed orientations form part of their depictions at particular times, and, as such, are also constitutive of their lived experiences.

Notes

1 There are approximately 150 Muinane in the Medio Caquetá region of Colombia today, distributed in four or five 'Muinane' (i.e., most of the men are Muinane) and mixed communities. They are organised in patrilineal clans and lineages which trace their origins to different ancestors in the mythical past. The Muinane's language belongs to the Bora linguistic group along with the Bora and the Miraña languages (Landaburu 1996: 86).
2 In their high valuation of productivity and of peaceful co-residence with supportive kin, the Muinane converge with other Amazonian groups (see e.g. Belaunde 1992; Descola 1994; Gow 1991; Overing 1993; Santos-Granero 1991).
3 The purpose of animals is to destroy humanity; their motivation is envy and the desire to pre-empt or avenge human predation upon them. It does not seem to be a case of animals' preying on other species in an attempt to gain individuals for their own species, as described by Vilaça (1992) for the Pakaa Nova.
4 To consume *mambe* is referred to in Spanish as '*mambear*' (hence, 'to *mambe*').
5 Tobacco paste is a thick, dark extract of tobacco mixed with vegetable salt. It is kept in containers known as 'apprising cumare nuts', and consumed by licking small amounts from a twig inserted into the container. Only men possess such containers, but women and children also lick tobacco paste (cf. Echeverri, this volume).
6 In this chapter I refer to the creator as a male figure linked to tobacco, following the preferences of the Cumare and Pineapple clans. However, there are differences between Muinane clans concerning the number, gender and names of deities.
7 The *mambeadores* sometimes make a similar claim to predatory agency and invulnerability: 'I am fire, I am water, I am tobacco, I am the axe.' Sometimes they speak of themselves as possessing rather than being these substances.
8 In the following section I discuss the agencies of some of these substances. Sometimes particular instances of substance consumption are understood to empower Speeches which people already possess, and sometimes to actually generate Speech inside the consumer. Having the alternative makes 'phenomenological' sense, for people are undoubtedly aware that they know chants, invocations and songs and can repeat them without using ritual substances. They simply find these 'powerless' if not made agential by substances.
9 The Muinane explain antisocial thoughts and actions as caused by the presence of an animal, or the ritual substance of an animal, or the Speech of an animal inside a body. They do not pay much attention to the distinctions between these causal explanations. In turn, the transformations which rid people of these antisocial thoughts and behaviours are indifferently portrayed as a reversion of the evil substance to the animal, who dies of it, or as a transformation of the disease or affect into an animal.

References

Belaunde, L.E. (1992) 'Gender, commensality and community among the Airo-Pai of West Amazonia (Secoya, Westen-Tukanoan speaking)', Ph.D dissertation, University of London, currently preparing for publication.

Candre, H. (1996) *Cool Tobacco, Sweet Coca: Teachings of an Indian Sage from the Colombian Amazon*, translated from Uitoto and with a commentary by J.A. Echeverri, London: Themis Books.

Descola, P. (1994) *In the Society of Nature: A Native Ecology in Amazonia*, Cambridge: Cambridge University Press

Echeverri, J.A. (1997) 'The people of the center of the world: a study in culture, history, and orality in the Colombian Amazon', unpublished Ph.D dissertation, New School for Social Research, New York.

Gow, P. (1991) *Of Mixed Blood*, Oxford and New York: Oxford University Press.

Landaburu, J. (ed.) (1996) *Documentos sobre lenguas aborígenes de Colombia del archivo de Paul Rivet: Vol. I*, Lenguas de la Amazonía colombiana, Bogotá: Ediciones Uniandes.

Overing, J. (1993) 'Death and the loss of civilized predation among the Piaroa of the Orinoco Basin', *L'Homme* 126–8, 33(2–4): 191–211.

Santos-Granero, F. (1991) *The Power of Love: The Moral Use of Knowledge amongst the Amuesha of Central Peru*, London: Athlone Press.

Vilaça, A. (1992) *Comendo como gente: Formas do canibalismo Wari*, Rio de Janeiro: Editora UFRJ.

Part II

Conquest and contact

The historical failure of convivial relations

Chapter 10

Pretty vacant

Columbus, conviviality and New World faces

Peter Mason

Conviviality and transcendence

> His eyes looked red-rimmed and blinking, his cheeks mottled and sodden, his hair tangled and dirty. He had one hand to his forehead, and groaning with the corners of his mouth lamentably drawn down, exhibited a shocking and salutary picture of the consequences of excessive conviviality.

As the above quotation from Wilkie Collins's *Hide and Seek* (1981 [1854]: 260) shows, conviviality – in the particular English sense of 'having a good time' described in the Preface to this volume – can be carried to excess. However, the equivalents in other languages (Sp. *convivencia*, Fr. *convivialité*) are more general in scope, referring to living with one another in harmony – the kind of societal relations that Ivan Illich had in mind in his *Tools for Conviviality* (1973) – in other words, the good life, a life which, arguably, can never be carried to excess. Most of the contributions to this volume focus on relations of conviviality within a specific group or culture, conforming to a mode of interpretation of which anthropologist Nicholas Thomas has written (1997: 189):

> interpretation has until recently emphasized the position and resonance of particular meanings within totalities, rather than processes of explication provoked by cross-cultural contact and contest. That is, despite their great diversity, ways of talking about culture in anthropology have proceeded by relating particular metaphors enacted in ritual, mythic idioms, forms of behavior, notions of relatedness, to some more general set of values, dispositions, key symbols, or structures.

But when the object of analysis involves the enhanced possibilities of misunderstanding implied by any situation of cross-cultural contact, the notion of 'conviviality' is itself open to multiple interpretations or translations – a problem on which Joanna Overing has concentrated in a number of articles (e.g. 1987, 1998).

Awareness of this risk of semantic sliding informs the present chapter, which concentrates on the long moment of cross-cultural contact between European travellers to and observers of the New World, on the one hand, and the Native peoples of the American continent, on the other. If there was to be any kind of conviviality between these different human groups, it would be based not only on mutual interaction and practical behaviour, but also – and previously – on the mental frameworks with which each side viewed the other, and on the resonances of these frameworks. Todorov (1982: 191ff) broke down discussion of knowing or understanding the other into three levels: the *plan axiologique* or level of value judgements; the *plan praxéologique*, or level of distance from the other, ranging from acceptance of the other to assimilation of the other; and the *plan épistémique*, or level of knowledge of the other's identity, with its varying degrees and modalities. However, it should be evident that each of these levels exerts an influence on, and receives the influence of, the others. Passing judgement, acquiring knowledge and devising a *modus convivendi* are mutually related activities. The remarks that follow, though primarily directed at the epistemic level, should therefore be read as bearing on value judgements and practical arrangements for living together too. They follow a strategy somewhat resembling that of Thomas in seeking to explore how 'the community that is imagined is not simply conceived of in its empirical complexity; its singularity and distinctiveness is understood, rather, through particular resonant practices and characteristics' (Thomas, op. cit.).

Many of these resonant practices and characteristics can be found at work in Michel de Montaigne's essay 'Des Cannibales' (Montaigne 1962 [1580]: 200–13), a work that is all the more topical in the present context, given the important role played by cannibalism in present-day discussions of love and violence in Amazonia (cf. Lagrou, this volume).[1] Moreover, it offers two instances of conviviality. The first is internal to the Old World, between Montaigne and a manservant. For a long time, Montaigne writes, he has had a 'simple and crude' (*simple et grossier*) man with him who has spent ten or twelve years in 'that other world' (*cet autre monde*) discovered in the sixteenth century, that the French called *La France antartique*.[2] This man provides the second instance of conviviality, but in his case it takes a New World–Old World turn: his experiences with the cannibals who live in Brazil qualify him as an authority on their doings. Their acts are transmitted via the words of the manservant into Montaigne's text. Two forms of conviviality, two risks of distortion: between the cannibals and the manservant, and between the manservant and Montaigne.

Montaigne is well aware of this risk of distortion. He prefaces his manservant's story with a triple refutation of other authorities: common opinion, the views of Plato and Aristotle in antiquity and the unsubstantiated claims of contemporary travellers (he probably has André Thevet in mind) who expatiate beyond the limits of their own experiences. The claim to veracity of the manservant's account is thus predicated on his simple-mindedness; his lack of familiarity with letters and literary ruse is supposed to confer a disingenuous, 'savage' transparency on his words, rendering them as 'savage' as the wild fruits enjoyed by the Brazilian cannibals without the intervention of any human artifice.

But Montaigne is being very sly here, for his account of the cannibals in fact draws quite heavily on the writings of at least Gomara, Osorio and Thevet. The figure of the 'simple and crude manservant' functions as a smoke-screen to divert attention away from these textual borrowings.

Still, let us go along with Montaigne a bit further, suspending our disbelief for the time being. If the tricks of language serve to distance or obfuscate the lived experience of the other, Montaigne has something to offer in its stead: the tangibility of contact with the material object. In his castle, his collection enabled visitors to admire:

> the form of their beds, their ropes, their swords and the wooden armbands with which they cover their wrists in combat, and the large canes, open at one end, which they use to beat out the rhythm of their dances.
>
> (Montaigne 1962: 206)[3]

Moreover, Montaigne had tasted Brazilian cassava – he had ingested a bit of America. It is in this framework that his manservant assumes full significance: as someone who had 'been there', who had been in direct physical contact with the cannibals, he – in the materiality of his body – can bear witness to them, can become an authority on them. The illiterate author – an oxymoron very close to Montaigne's heart – can in turn be 'read' by Montaigne, whose text thereby becomes the written record authorised by the proximity of the manservant, a man who had lived with, been convivial with, the cannibals of Brazil. Contrast the passage at the end of 'Des Cannibales' where Montaigne claims to have personally met one of the Brazilians who had travelled to Rouen and to have had a long talk with him. One might have expected this face-to-face encounter with a representative of the New World to have provided Montaigne with a wealth of detail. Yet he has little to relate from this talk (cf. Greenblatt 1991: 148 n.2).

Like so many of Michel de Certeau's writings, his essay on 'Des Cannibales' (1981) is full of brilliant insights. And, as in so many of his other writings, he continually has recourse to the notion of writing and reading bodies, whether they be the bodies of the cannibals, the body of the manservant, or Montaigne's own body, to name but a few.[4] Indeed, as Mary Fuller points out (1993: 224), 'de Certeau's discussion places a kind of transcendent value on the body, in particular the "savage" body. . . . It would appear that the savage body guaranteeing language is, in fact, a body of writing.' By a clever ruse, then, Montaigne tries to get the reader to believe in the existence of proximate bodies as bearers of authority, even though their very materiality seems to be little more than the materiality of the very text above whose authority they are elevated. Indeed, a number of scholars have gone so far as to call the historicity (and thus materiality) of his manservant into question. Thus Stephen Greenblatt notes (op. cit., p. 148) that the servant is primarily a rhetorical figure of transparency in Montaigne's text; outside of the essays in which he appears, there is no firm evidence that the servant ever existed. And if he never existed, his account is not based on any New World–Old World conviviality either. But whether he existed or not, Montaigne's dialogue with his manservant is, as mentioned above, internal to Old World relations. In that sense, the dialogue is a European monologue. As we shall see at the end of this chapter, this is a regular pattern in Old World inter-pretations of the New World.

If the bodies to which de Certeau refers seem to vanish before our gaze, a similar fate lies in store for his notion of 'reading'. Montaigne himself, it should be noted, does not used the word 'to read' in this sense in 'Des Cannibales'. De Certeau's usage has more to do with the 'textualisation' of the world which dominated French literary studies in the 1970s and 1980s than with Montaigne's usage. All the more reason, then, to look more closely at the question of what it means to 'read' a body, and more particularly a New World body, in the sixteenth century. Consideration of the issues this raises might offer us insight into how European observers interpreted the people they saw in the New World, with all the consequences that this entails for the possibility of their living together in any form of conviviality.

Reading the body

> *Pero nada que toque a Colón puede ser simple y diáfano* [But nothing bearing on Columbus can be simple and diaphanous]
>
> (Gil 1984: lvii)

Let us start with Columbus. To start with Columbus is to recognise that the history of contact between the Old World and the New is punctuated by his presence. In the same way that the Greeks started their history with the foundation of the first Olympic Games in 776 BC, the years 1892 and 1992 were both marked by large-scale celebrations to reinscribe 1492 as the foundation of the story of the American continent, even if its name was taken not from Columbus but from Amerigo Vespucci. Given the tremendous persistence and influence of the Columbian vision on later images of the New World, this is more than a historical exercise, for it is at the same time an archaeology of present-day conceptions. Images are not secondary, derivative illustrations of something else; they have a force of their own, capable of submerging and then re-emerging over extremely long durations of time. The interest of the following remarks on sixteenth-century practices of reading is not antiquarian; on the contrary, some of the ways of 'reading bodies' and the forms of (non-)conviviality based on them may prove to be surprisingly familiar.

Let us start, then, with Columbus and his comments on the inhabitants of different Caribbean islands in his Letter to the Sovereigns of 4 March 1493 Announcing the Discovery: 'In the Westernmost part [of Cuba], in one of the two provinces I did not cover, which is called Faba, everyone is born with a tail. Beyond this island of Juana, still within sight, there is another . . . where all the people are bald.'[5] These look like straightforward, unambiguous remarks which say no more than what they say. But just the mention of a tail is enough to evoke the *homines caudati* to which the first-century AD encyclopaedist Pliny refers in his *Historia Naturalis* (VII, 30), and which recur in a series of texts stretching from the beginning of the Christian era down to Columbus's time.[6] These were one of the monstrous human races that were believed to live in the Orient. So the mere use of the word 'tail' by Columbus is enough to suggest that he has reached Asia. This, in turn, will enable him to interpret other phenomena he encounters from the same perspective, thus setting in motion an 'Oriental' reading of America.

Or let us take Columbus's first words on the people of the New World: 'Then they saw naked people,' which he further elaborates as 'They all go about naked as their mothers bore them'.[7] At first sight this seems to be an objective recording of a fact: that the people wore no clothes. But the theme of the lack of clothes could be interpreted in two ways. As a celebration of natural innocence, it is a topos of European representations of the Golden Age, particularly popularised through the account in the *Metamorphoses* of Ovid. On the other hand, when it symbolised closeness to nature and the lack of knowledge to protect oneself, it could be used to signify bestiality and a lower stage of cultural development (a view propounded by the Latin poet Lucretius, for example).[8] Hence Columbus's use of the single epithet 'naked' already frames the inhabitants of the New World as a people who live in a primitive state resembling either the mythical Golden Age of the past or a brutish condition awaiting social and technological advance.

At work behind the words of Columbus's account, then, is a hermeneutic of the other in which the eye that perceives interprets at the same time. Even the apparently simple act of the perception of one human body by another is already caught up in this process of conferring meaning.

It is not the purpose of the present article to add to the already considerable literature on the different bodies of knowledge which observers of the New World could and did bring to bear on the interpretation of what they saw.[9] Tzvetan Todorov in particular has stressed the way in which Columbus's perceptions were (over)determined by his preconceptions, the way in which he only took note of what he considered would confirm what he already 'knew'.[10] Much of this literature, however, focuses on language – both the written word and the spoken word, both (mis)communications between Europeans and Native Americans and what those Europeans recorded in writing about their encounters. Columbus looks and writes, and for Stephen Greenblatt there is a tension between 'the visual and the verbal, seeing and reading' (Greenblatt 1991: 87).[11] In the present chapter, however, this tension is absent, as the focus is on how New World bodies were simultaneously perceived and read in the sixteenth century. In the course of the inquiry, I hope to show that there is no need to write 'read': the act of reading the body was not metaphorical. Though a phrase like 'reading the body' may look suspiciously late twentieth century, it is no anachronism to apply it to sixteenth-century perceptions.

Bodies that speak

Admiral Columbus presents the following picture of a Ciguayo Arawak whom he encountered near Las Flechas, towards the end of the first voyage, on 13 January 1493:

> The admiral says that he was more ugly in appearance (*acatadura*) than any whom he had seen. He had his face all painted with various colours; he wore all his hair very long and drawn back and tied behind, and then gathered in meshes of parrots' feathers, and he was as naked as the others.
>
> (Colón 1984: 114)

This man was different from the Natives Columbus had already met, and in Columbus's eyes he was uglier than the others. What conclusion does he draw? 'The Admiral judged that he must be one of the Caribs who eat people.' To confirm this deduction, Columbus redefined the neighbouring gulf that he had seen the day before as open sea; in that case, he had now reached an island, and since it was known that the Caribs lived on an island, his hypothesis was confirmed. By the time of the fourth voyage, Columbus has become more adept at drawing snap conclusions: 'I came across other people who ate men: the ugliness of their features (*gesto*) shows it' (Colón, op. cit., p. 326). '*Gesto*', like '*acatadura*' above, refers to facial expression. The face is here the privileged seat of information, but it is taken to provide information about a figure endowed with subhuman qualities.

According to the physiognomical tradition, the face could not lie. Thus Charles de Rochefort, whose history of the Antilles was first published in 1658, assumes a transparency of the Native peoples of the Caribbean to the French when he states that 'in the face of the whole crowd, you can clearly read [*lire*] the satisfaction they have at seeing you'. Yet only a few years earlier, Father Jacques Bouton, whose *Relation de l'Etablissement des Français depuis l'an 1635 en l'île de la Martinique* (1640) was based on a stay of only a few months in the islands, was complaining about the lack of transparency: 'you can never be sure among these savages, no matter what a face they put on'.[12]

The stress on the head as an index of humanity was a standard part of medieval thinking about human form.[13] True to his medieval forebears, Gonzalo Fernández de Oviedo y Valdés warns of the dangers of striking Native Americans on the head – their skulls are so thick that a sword can be broken on them. He continues: 'And as they have thick skulls, they likewise have a bestial and evil (*mal inclinado*) understanding.'[14] The violence of this form of direct reading is undisguised.

It is not just the face itself which is open to interpretation, but the hair too. In the Letter to Luis de Santangel, Columbus contradicts claims that the Plinian monstrous races are to be found in the Americas: 'So far I have not found any monstrous people in these islands.' However, he makes an exception for the island of the Caribs:

> which is populated by a people who are held on all the islands to be very fierce, who eat human flesh. They have many canoes, with which they travel to all the islands of India, steal and take what they can. They are no uglier than the rest, except that they have the habit of *wearing their hair long like women*.
>
> (Cólon, op. cit., p. 145, emphasis added)

This passage contradicts Columbus's statement earlier the same year that the Caribs were uglier than the rest; this discrepancy is absent from the Letter to the Sovereigns of 4 March 1493 Announcing the Discovery, where the reference to their ugliness has been replaced by the statement that they go about naked like the others (Zamora 1993: 8). But both the Letter to Santangel and the Letter from the *Libro Copiador* agree on comparing the long hair of the Caribs to that of women. Behind this detail of men with women's hair emerges the spectre of gender confusion, and this confusion is compounded by the introduction of the Amazon-like women of the island of Matinino who behave like men. Anthropophagous Carib males and warrior-like females exert a mutual attraction on one another, not only in Columbus's text but in the situation he imagines to exist in the Caribbean, for the description of the Caribs in the Letter to Santangel is immediately followed by reference to the 'women of Matinino' with whom the Carib males have intercourse. It is also relevant in this connection that women, particularly old women, were believed to show a particularly keenly developed taste for human flesh (cf. Bucher 1977).[15]

In addition to face and hair we can consider the presence of marks on the body. On 12 October 1492, after commenting that the Arawakan Lucayans are generally tall in stature, good-looking and well-proportioned [*de buena estatura de grandeza y buenos gestos, bien hechos*], Columbus continues: 'I saw some who had the marks [*señales*] of wounds on their bodies, and I made signs [*señas*] to them to ask what they were, and they indicated to me [*amostraron*] how people came from other islands that were near and wished to capture them and they defended themselves' (Colón, op. cit., p. 31). As the words *señales*, *señas* and *amostraron* indicate, communication here is visual and by gesture. These signs have nothing of the arbitrariness of the Saussurian signs about them; on the contrary, the marks of wounds are taken to tell the story of the relations of the Lucayans with their allegedly anthropophagous neighbours. Ironically, Columbus continued this entry in his *Diario* with a statement of his intention to take six of the Lucayans back to Spain: it was not their allegedly anthropophagous neighbours, but the European intruders, who were destined to capture them and carry them off, initiating a tradition of kidnapping and displaying others that continued down to the twentieth century (cf. Mason 2000).

Columbus's logic of deduction based on his observation of a Ciguayo Arawak is summed up by Peter Hulme: 'The Native was *different* from those already met, and ugly to boot, *therefore* he was a man-eating Carib' (1978: 131). Cannibalism might be supposed to render the features of its practitioners ugly, but the reverse position – that people who are ugly are therefore cannibals – is untenable. Columbus's logic of deduction is a *non sequitur*, for there is nothing in the man's appearance, especially in view of Columbus's own confusion on whether the Caribs are ugly or not, to justify the conclusion that the Admiral draws. What he assumes is a connection between inner nature and outer appearance. But what he cannot prevent is that this process will run wild. Lacking the rigidity of a frame, Columbus's 'wild hermeneutic' lacks direction.

We can gain some idea of the effects of the presence of a rigid frame from a comparison between Columbus and the Jesuit Joseph François Lafitau, author of a large-scale two-volume work entitled *Mœurs des sauvages amériquains comparées aux mœurs des premiers temps* (1724), in which he systematically compared the practices of Native Americans (Lafitau spent five years in Canada among the Algonquin, Huron and Iroquois) with those of antiquity.[16] This scheme was his frame: if he encountered a Brazilian *maraka* or a North American *chichikoué*, he compared them with ancient instruments like the Egyptian rattle of Anubis. Moreover, the same process took place at the visual level: in the engravings to his work, artefacts from the New World are compared and contrasted with artefacts from the Old World.[17] Lafitau's frame compels the reader to follow a certain direction: from the New World to the Old. Columbus's hermeneutic, by contrast, lacks direction because it lacks a frame.

The spectre of men with women's hair opens up the alarming possibility that effeminisation might have gone even further in the New World. We can gauge some of the responses to this from the reactions of the conquistadores to the practice of the berdache. In a study of the institution of the berdache in the Americas (1995),[18] Richard Trexler has argued that it contains three distinct elements: the sodomisation of one male by another; the dressing of the sodomised male as a woman; and the violent nature of this practice of subordination. The relation between the first two admits of two possible causalities: is the transvestite subjected to sodomisation because of his female dress, or is he dressed as a female because he is sodomised?

Both cases can be found in the historical record: Oviedo, for example, offers an eye-witness description of the berdache as practised in Cueva (Panama) in 1526: after penetrating a boy, his master went on to dress him as a girl. On the other hand, a so-called Chichimeca, captured and executed in 1530, confessed to having dressed as a girl from childhood in order to attract active homosexual clients (Trexler, op. cit., pp. 90–1).

The issue of the alleged prevalence of sodomy in the Americas formed a bone of contention between Oviedo and the defender of the Native Americans, Bartolomé de las Casas. While they were agreed that cross-dressing was widespread, they diverged on the question of whether its prevalence should be taken to imply the prevalence of sodomy. No doubt it was easy for Europeans who conventionally associated cosmetics with women to assume that all Indians were sodomites (Trexler, op. cit., p. 67), but accusations of sodomy must often have been based on no more than the presence of men in women's dress performing certain non-sexual female activities.

It is interesting to note that in the last quarter of the sixteenth century the debate was being conducted in the same terms in a completely different context, that of the conventions of the Elizabethan stage in England. In a heated controversy that was conducted primarily through a pamphlet war, the question of the wearing of female clothing by male actors was vigorously debated. Would male actors who wore female clothing gradually become effeminised by it, as if clothes had a quasi-magical ability to convert the nature of the person who wore them? Or did the vice precede the clothing, with the theatre offering a pretext for male homosexuality (cf. Lavine 1994)? As in the case of Columbus, the reversibility of the argument is due to a lack of direction.

Since it is unlikely that many of the Iberians actually witnessed acts of sodomy, most of their claims are no more than allegations based on deductions, as they deduced sexual practices from appearances. Some observers were cautious in making such deductions. Jean de Léry, for instance, notes the use of the word *tyvire*, 'bugger', as a term of abuse, from which 'one can conjecture . . . that this abominable sin is committed among them', but he underlines the fact that this is mere surmise by adding the words 'for I affirm nothing'.[19] Not everyone was so cautious. Take the notorious case of the forty or so transvestites torn to pieces by mastiffs on the orders of Vasco Núñez de Balboa in Quaraco province, Panama, in 1513. According to our source, Peter Martyr d'Anghiera, the 'evidence' of their sodomy consisted of nothing more than their female dress and the reports of neighbours (in Eatough 1998).

The issue had far-reaching political ramifications. Transvestism, however reprehensible it might be, was not a just title of conquest, but if the indigenous civil authorities were tolerating sodomy, this gave the Iberians the right to intervene. On the other hand, if it could be shown that 'the Incas were Limpid of the Nefandous Sin and of Other Dirtinesses that are Found in other Princes of the World', as Cieza de León attempted to show, this too could prove useful to Iberian attempts to legitimate their actions through an appeal to the Inca past. Moreover, the argument that women's interests were damaged by sodomites – Cieza de León could not understand why men went in for sodomy when they had access to beautiful women – could also be used by the Europeans to profile themselves as defenders of women and castigators of the men who maltreated or neglected them. How observers 'read' Native bodies could therefore have profound implications for how they acted towards or on those same bodies.

One of the most sinister expressions of this attitude towards Native American bodies can be found in the biographical portrait of Francisco Pizarro by the French cosmographer André Thevet. Cynically, he claims that the conquistadores would have been shrouded in obscurity had they not made a name for themselves by their feats during the conquest. This does not mean to say, he hastily adds, that the Europeans gained their skills from these Americans. On the contrary, he holds that: 'the latter [the Americans] served merely as a paper, bronze, or marble upon which to inscribe the immortal memory of their deeds'.[20] As Lestringant drily comments, 'a topical metaphor, but one with particularly sinister consequences!' (1990: 236 n.5). A more toned-down version of the metaphor is used by Peter Martyr in a letter to Pope Leo X, where the naked peoples of the Americas are compared to 'writing tablets scraped clean' (*rasae tabellae*)[21] which 'easily put on the clothing of our religious rites, and through commerce with our people shake off the uncivilized savagery which is Native to them' (cited in Eatough, op. cit., p. 21).

The transition from reading to inscription and engraving is only one step away from Kafka's monstrous machine in *In the Penal Colony*. But there is no need to move away from the Americas to Central Europe to find other examples of this work of inhuman engraving. In a letter to the Council of the Indias, Vasco de Quiroga wrote:

> They are branded with iron on the face and their skin is inscribed with the initials of the names of their successive owners; they are passed from hand to hand, and some have three or four names, so that the faces of these men who were created in the image of God have been transformed into paper by our sins.[22]

Going round in circles

The succinct, 'I came across other people who ate men: the ugliness of their features shows it' combines perception and interpretation in a single moment. The act of reading is instantaneous. Moreover, there is no directionality, starting-point or frame: in other words, no privileged point of access. An ugly facial expression, the wearing of a female item of clothing, the use of the single word 'bugger' – each of these is enough to lead the observer to draw an immediate conclusion. These bodies have simple forms. They are immediately legible and transparent.

   This notion of transparency that Columbus applies to perceptions of others is also a characteristic of his own self-perception. This can be seen at work in his various attempts to situate his endeavour within a much larger time-frame, going back to the prophecies of the Old Testament and texts from Greco-Roman antiquity. (The *reason* why he did so is that, by his time, the Christian community that saw itself as the culmination of history 'had to direct all visionary projection into temporal distance towards the past'.)[23] In her excellent discussion of 'the imaginative landscape of Christopher Columbus' (1992), Valerie Flint has suggested that Columbus may have regarded his first voyage as modelled on the journey of the Argonauts; moreover, she argues (ibid., p. 86), within such an imaginary drama Columbus could have pictured himself as playing the Jason to Isabella's Medea. We can be sure that Columbus was familiar at least with the version of the myth of the Argonauts as narrated in *Medea* by the first-century Roman philosopher and statesman Lucius Annaeus Seneca, as is clear from the quotation of a passage from this Roman tragedy in the *Libro de las Profecías*. In modern editions of the play, the text in question runs:

> *venient annis*
> *saecula seris, quibus Oceanus*
> *vincula rerum laxet et ingens*
> *pateat tellus Tethysque novos*
> *detegat orbes nec sit terris*
> *ultima Thule*
>
> (Seneca, *Medea* 374–94)[24]

However, it is certain that this was not the text which Columbus knew.[25] A passage from the *Libro de las Profecías* (folio 59v) – 'and a new mariner, like the one who was Jason's pilot, called Tiphys, will discover a new world'[26] – indicates that the name that Columbus read in his Seneca was not Tethys, the bride of the sea, but Tiphys, the helmsman of the Argo.[27] In other words, the first half of Flint's theory is unobjectionable, for Columbus evidently did pattern his voyage on that of the Argonauts. But the role he chose was not that of Jason, the leader of the enterprise (and *a fortiori* Isabella was no

Medea), but that of Tiphys, who had been taught the art of navigation by the goddess Athena. It was Tiphys, like Columbus, who was to discover the new world. Moreover, Columbus's rendering of the Latin plural *novos orbes* as the singular *nuebo mundo* also serves to bring his discovery of a single continent into line with ancient predictions. Once again we come up against a notion of reading that implies transparency: when Columbus reads his Seneca, he has no difficulty in assuming that the text is actually about himself.

Given the lack of a privileged starting-point, the observer can single out any item for comment in an arbitrary fashion. This is because, within the European imaginary, many of the alleged characteristics of the Native Americans were symptoms of the same thing: whether they engaged in non-conventional sexual practices, wore non-conventional dress, or ate non-conventional food, the message was the same on each occasion – they failed to draw the correct distinctions between edible and inedible, between nudity and dress, between appropriate sexual partners and promiscuity. What they lacked was the ability to discriminate, and it was this inability that served as a marker of their lack of civilisation (cf. Pagden 1982: 80–90).

There is a name for the rhetoric practised by Columbus and his contemporaries: tautology. The alleged primitiveness of the Native Americans is 'read off' from – their observed primitiveness. Each symptom of that primitiveness conveys the same message, namely that they are primitive. So this hermeneutic of the other ends up as a tautology of the same. Moreover, this transparency is in fact an opacity,[28] for the simple act of revelation fails to reveal anything that was not already 'known'. In a certain way, this form of production of knowledge that is at the same time a non-production recalls Michel de Certeau's classic discussion of Jean de Léry's *Histoire d'un voyage fait en la terre du Brésil autrement dite Amérique*. In a chapter entitled 'Ethnographie. L'oralité, ou l'espace de l'autre: Léry', de Certeau set out to demonstrate (1975: 237) that the structure of Léry's work is that of a return to a single source of production by reducing the other to the same.

The act of interpretation, then, presents itself as a tautological movement in which the meaning of what is observed is immediately laid bare in its transparency as the common condition of Native American peoples. Yet precisely in the production of an imaginary 'savage', in its failure to genuinely engage the other (de Certeau's project of heterologies), this tautological hermeneutic runs up against an opaque, unreadable body.[29] In concentrating on the signs they produce as a reality in their own right (for the message they convey is the same each time), Columbus and the European observers of Native America invest their intellectual capacity in the sign at the expense of its referentiality. In this process, the sign itself becomes dense and opaque.[30] And it becomes easy to follow Peter Hulme in concluding that, if Columbus's 'understanding' was based on the answers he wanted to hear, on the expectations that he brought with him, then the inescapable conclusion is that 'the supposed "communication" between European and Native was in effect a European monologue' (Hulme, op. cit., p. 119).

What kind of a conviviality does this imply? Within the oppositional process in which 'a variety of dominant and dominated groups reify the attributes both of others and themselves in a self-fashioning process' (Thomas, op. cit., p. 189), the resulting relation will be an asymmetrical one. The difference of the other is construed as vacancy, awaiting inscription of its blankness by those who wield the power to confer meaning. Columbus's epistemology anticipates the non-conviviality of the *Conquista* and the resulting genocide.

Notes

1 The following discussion is heavily indebted to Michel de Certeau's essay on 'Des Cannibales' (1981: 187-200).

2 Throughout the sixteenth century, it should be noted, images of America were primarily and predominantly images of Brazil. The way in which native Americans from other parts of the continent tended to be subsumed under the by now familiar representations of the Tupinamba of Brazil – the process of 'Tupinambisation' – has been most thoroughly documented by William Sturtevant (1988).

3 On the presence of objects from the Americas in European collections, see Feest (1993) and Mason (1994a).

4 See especially de Certeau (1979: 3-14).

5 I am here following the version of this letter taken from Columbus's 'copy book' (*Libro Copiador*), edited by Antonio Rumeu de Armas, 2 vols, Madrid, 1989; English version in Margarita Zamora, 1993. For the parallel passages in Columbus's Letter to Luis de Santangel of 15 February 1493, see Colón 1984, p. 143 ('where the people with tails are born') and p. 145 ('Another island . . . in which the people do not have any hair').

6 Claude Lecouteux (1982, vol. II, p. 14) refers to several texts of the Alexander tradition, the *Liber Monstrorum*, Gervais of Tilbury's *Otia imperialia*, Jacques de Vitry's *Historia Orientalis*, Thomas of Cantimpré's *De natura rerum*, Vincent de Beauvais's *Speculum naturale* and the travels of Marco Polo. For a monograph on *homo caudatus*, see J.D. Penel (1982). See too the discussion in Mason (1990: 104).

7 '*Luego vieron gente desnuda*' and '*ellos andan todos desnudos como su madre los parió*' (Colón op. cit., p. 30).

8 For the persistence of this negative connotation in images of the human past, see Stephanie Moser (1998).

9 See e.g. Anthony Grafton, April Shelford and Nancy Siraisi (1992); Marinella Pregliasco (1992); Adriano Prosperi and Wolfgang Reinhard (1992); Peter Mason (1994b); Karen Ordahl Kupperman (1995).

10 See the chapter entitled 'Colon herméneute' in Todorov (1982). As Stephen Greenblatt points out (1991: 88 n.5), however, this is a tendency, not an invariable habit of mind.

11 In a later article, however, Greenblatt does refer to 'a language in and of the body itself, independent of any particular forms of speech' (1997: 223).

12 The passages from Rochefort and Bouton are both cited by Dominique Bertrand (1998: 425).

13 John B. Friedman (1981: 181) cites the fourteenth-century Peter of Abano on *monstra*: '*Et scias quod maxime decernitur in figuracione capitis: si aliquid animal debet dici*

nostrum genitum' [You know that it is to be seen especially in the form of the head if an animal ought to be said to belong to our race].

14 See the proem to Gonzalo Fernández de Oviedo y Valdés, *Historia General y Natural de las Indias, Part I, Book V* (1959 [1526]).

15 On the theme in Léry, see Léry (1990, chapter XV).

16 For a fuller discussion of Lafitau, see Peter Mason (1998, chapter 5).

17 Many of the latter were taken from Bernard de Montfaucon's *L'Antiquité expliquée et représentée en figures* in five volumes, published in Paris five years before Lafitau's work.

18 This controversial work led to an exchange between Trexler and myself in the pages of the German anthropological journal *Anthropos* (see Mason 1997; Trexler 1998; Mason 1999; Trexler 1999).

19 Jean de Léry (1990: 153). For French text, see Léry (1992: 166).

20 In Roger Schlesinger (1993: 23); the French original is in André Thevet (1584, f. 374v).

21 Cf. S. Greenblatt (1990: 17).

22 Cited in Tzvetan Todorov (op. cit., p. 143); cf. Peter Mason (1988).

23 For a full discussion of Columbus's relation to this typological schema, see Djelal Kadir (1992).

24   (An age shall come, in later years,
                            when Ocean shall loose creation's bonds,
                            when the great planet shall stand revealed
                            and Tethys shall disclose new worlds
                            nor shall Thule be the last among lands.)

25 For other cases of inexact translation and the selection and amalgamation of data from ancient texts to bring them into line with ideologies relating to the discovery of the New World, see M. Mund-Dopchie (1990).

26 '*Y um nuebo marinero, como aquel que fue guía de Jasón, que obe nombre Tiphi, descobrirá nuebo mundo*' (Colón, op. cit., p. 287).

27 The so-called A class of manuscripts of Seneca, the group most widely employed by Renaissance editors, gave the name as Tiphys. As James Romm has pointed out (1994), this change enabled Columbus to read the Senecan passage not only as a prediction of new discoveries but also as a celebration of the single, heroic individual who would reveal them: Tiphys–Columbus, a reading that was confirmed by Columbus's son Fernando. See also Diskin Clay (1992: 617–20). On the problematic nature of oceanic travel in Seneca's tragedies and in his philosophical writings, see James Romm (1992: 165–71).

28 On opaqueness as the result of translation in the work of Jean de Léry and André Thevet, see Peter Mason (1996, esp. p. 141).

29 For this ambivalent representation of the captive, compare S. Greenblatt (1991: 112).

30 On '*le signe opacifié*', see Michel de Certeau (1982: 200–8).

References

Bertrand, D. (1998) 'Verbal et non verbal dans les relations entre européens et caraïbes: Echanges réels et imaginaires', in F. Lestringant (ed.) *La France-Amérique* (xvie–xviiie *siècles*). Actes du xxve colloque international d'études humanistes, pp. 419–31, Paris: Honoré Champion.

Bouton, Father J. (1640) *Relation de l'Etablissement des Français depuis l'an 1635 en l'île de la Martinique*, Paris.

Bucher, B. (1977) *Le sauvage aux seins pendants*, Paris: Hermann.

Clay, D. (1992) 'Columbus' Senecan prophecy', *American Journal of Philology* 113: 617–20.

Collins, W. (1981 [1854]) *Hide and Seek*, New York: Dover.

Colón, C. (1984, 2nd edition) *Cristóbal Colón. Textos y documentos completos*. Prólogo y notas de Consuelo Varela, Madrid: Alianza Universidad.

de Certeau, M. (1975) *L'écriture de l'histoire*, Paris: Gallimard.

—— (1979). 'Des outils pour écrire le corps', *Traverses* 14/15: 3–14.

—— (1981) 'Le lieu et l'autre Montaigne: "Des Cannibales"', in M. Olender (ed.) *Le racisme: mythes et sciences: pour Léon Poliakov*, Brussels: Complexe.

—— (1982) *La fable mystique XVIᵉ–XVIIIᵉ siècles*, Paris: Gallimard.

Eatough, G. (1998) *Selections from Peter Martyr*, Repertorium Columbianum, Vol. V., Turnhout: Brepols.

Feest, C.F. (1993) 'European collecting of American Indian artefacts and art', *Journal of the History of Collections* 5(1): 1–11.

Flint, V.I.J. (1992) *The Imaginative Landscape of Christopher Columbus*, Princeton, NJ: Princeton University Press.

Friedman, J.B. (1981) *The Monstrous Races in Medieval Art and Thought*, Cambridge Mass.: Harvard University Press.

Fuller, M.C. (1993) 'Ralegh's fugitive gold: reference and deferral in *The Discoverie of Guiana*', in S. Greenblatt (ed.) *New World Encounters*, pp. 218–40, Berkeley, Los Angeles and Oxford: University of California Press.

Gil, J. (1984, 2nd edition) Introducción, *Cristóbal Colón. Textos y documentos completos*, prólogo y notas de Consuelo Varela, Madrid: Alianza Universidad.

Grafton, A., Shelford, A. and Siraisi, N. (1992) *New Worlds, Ancient Texts: The Power of Tradition and the Shock of Discovery*, Cambridge, Mass. and London: Belknap Press.

Greenblatt, S. (1990) *Learning to Curse*, London: Routledge and New York: Chapman & Hall.

—— (1991) *Marvelous Possessions. The Wonder of the New World*, Oxford: Clarendon Press.

—— (1997) 'Mutilation and meaning', in D. Hillman and C. Mazzio (eds) *The Body in Parts*, pp. 221–241, London: Routledge.

Hulme, P. (1978) 'Columbus and the cannibals: a study of the reports of anthropophagy in the journal of Christopher Columbus', *Ibero-Amerikanisches Archiv*, Neue Folge 4(2): 115–39.

Illich, I. (1973) *Tools for Conviviality*, London: Calder & Boyars.

Kadir, D. (1992) *Columbus and the Ends of the Earth. Europe's Prophetic Rhetoric as Conquering Ideology*, Berkeley, Los Angeles and London: University of California Press.

Kupperman, K.O. (ed.) (1995) *America in European Consciousness 1493–1750*, Chapel Hill and London: University of North Carolina Press.

Lafitau, J.F. (1724) *Mœurs des sauvages amériquains comparées aux mœurs des premiers temps*, two volumes, Paris: Saugrain & Hochereau.

Lavine, L. (1994) *Men in Women's Clothing. Anti-Theatricality and Effeminization, 1579–1642*, Cambridge: Cambridge University Press.

Lecouteux, C. (1982) *Les monstres dans la littérature allemande du moyen âge* (three volumes), Göppingen: Kümmerle Verlag.

Léry, J. de (1990) *History of a Voyage to the Land of Brazil, otherwise known as America*, trans. J. Whatley, Berkeley, Los Angeles and London: University of California Press.

—— (1992) *Histoire d'un voyage fait en la terre du Brésil (1578)*, edited by F. Lestringant, Montpellier: Max Chaleil.

Lestringant, F. (1990) *Le Huguenot et le Sauvage*, Paris: Aux Amateurs de Livres.

Mason, P. (1988) 'De la ponctuation. Refléxions sur quelques races pliniennes', *Circé* 16–19, *Les monstres dans l'imaginaire des indiens d'Amérique latine*, textes réunis par Edmundo Magaña, pp. 161–72, Paris: Lettres Modernes.

—— (1990) *Deconstructing America: Representations of the Other*, London: Routledge and New York: Chapman & Hall.

—— (1994a) 'From presentation to representation: *Americana* in Europe', *Journal of the History of Collections* 6(1): 1–20.

—— (1994b) 'Classical ethnography and its influence on the European perception of the peoples of the New World', in W. Haase and M. Reinhold (eds) *The Classical Tradition and the Americas*, Vol. 1, Part 1, pp. 135–72, Berlin and New York: Walter de Gruyter.

—— (1996) 'On producing the (American) exotic', *Anthropos* 91(1): 139–51.

—— (1997) 'Sex and conquest. A redundant copula?', *Anthropos* 92(2): 577–82.

—— (1998) *Infelicities. Representations of the Exotic*, Baltimore and London: Johns Hopkins University Press.

—— (1999) 'Reply to Trexler', *Anthropos* 94(1): 315.

—— (2000) 'En tránsito: los fueguinos, sus imágenes en Europa, y los pocos que regresaron', in P. Mason and C. Odone (eds) *Mundos fueginos. Nuevos ensayos sobre las culturas nativas de Tierra del Fuego*, Santiago de Chile: Ediciones Cuerpos Pintados.

Montaigne, M. de (1962) *Œuvres complètes*, edited by A. Thibaudet and M. Rat, with introduction and notes by M. Rat, Paris: Bibliothèque de la Pléiade, Gallimard.

Moser, S. (1998) *Ancestral Images: The Iconography of Human Origins*, Stroud: Sutton Publishing.

Mund-Dopchie, M. (1990) 'L'Extrême-Occident de l'Antiquité classique et la découverte du nouveau monde: une manipulation de textes à des fins idéologiques', *Nouvelle Revue du Seizième Siècle* 8: 27–49.

Overing, J. (1987) 'Translation as a creative process: the power of the name', in L. Holy (ed.) *Comparative Anthropology*, pp. 70–87, Oxford: Basil Blackwell.

—— (1998) 'Is an anthropological translation of the "unhomely" possible, or desirable?', in M. Bal *et al.* (eds) *Intellectual Traditions in Movement. Brief. ASCA Yearbook*, pp. 101–16, Amsterdam: ASCA Press.

Oviedo y Valdés, G.F. (1959 [1526]) *Historia general y natural de las Indias*, Madrid: Atlas.

Pagden, A. (1982) *The Fall of Natural Man: The American Indian and the Origins of Comparative Ethnology*, Cambridge: Cambridge University Press.

Penel, J.D. (1982) *Homo caudatus. Les hommes à queue d'Afrique centrale: un avatar de l'imaginaire occidental*, Paris: CNRS.

Pregliasco, M. (1992) *Antilia. Il viaggio e il Mondo Nuovo (XV–XVII secolo)*, Turin: Einaudi.

Prosperi, A. and Reinhard, W. (eds) (1992) *Il Nuovo Mondo nella conscienza italiana e tedesca del Cinquecento*, Bologna: Il Mulino.

Romm, J. (1992) *The Edges of the Earth in Ancient Thought*, Princeton, NJ: Princeton University Press.

—— (1994) 'New World and "novos orbes": Seneca in the Renaissance debate over ancient knowledge of the Americas', in W. Haase and M. Reinhold (eds) *The Classical Tradition and the Americas*, Vol. 1, Part 1, pp. 77–116, Berlin and New York: Walter de Gruyter.

Schlesinger, R. (ed.) (1993) *Portraits from the Age of Exploration. Selections from André Thevet's 'Les Vrais pourtraits et vies des hommes illustres'*, trans. E. Benson, Urbana and Chicago: University of Illinois Press.

Sturtevant, W. (1988) 'La Tupinambisation des Indiens d'Amérique du Nord', in G. Thérien (ed.) *Les figures de l'Indien*, pp. 293–303, Ontario, Université du Québec à Montréal.

Thevet, A. (1584) *Les vrais pourtraits et vies des hommes illustres*, Paris: J. Kervet & G. Chandière.

Thomas, N. (1997) *In Oceania. Visions, Artifacts, Histories*, Durham, NC and London: Duke University Press.

Todorov, T. (1982) *La Conquête de l'Amérique. La question de l'autre*, Paris: Seuil.

Trexler, R. (1995) *Sex and Conquest. Gendered Violence, Political Order, and the European Conquest of the Americas*, Cambridge: Polity Press.

—— (1998) 'Rejoinder to Mason', *Anthropos* 93(2): 655–6.

—— (1999) 'Rejoinder to Mason', *Anthropos* 94(1): 315–16.

Zamora, M. (1993) 'Christopher Columbus's "Letter to the Sovereigns: Announcing the Discovery"', in S. Greenblatt (ed.) *New World Encounters*, pp. 1–11, Berkeley, Los Angeles and Oxford: University of California Press.

Part III

The delicacy of Amazonian sociality

Chapter 11

The convivial self and the fear of anger amongst the Airo-Pai of Amazonian Peru

Luisa Elvira Belaunde

To outsiders, daily life in the kindred-based Airo-Pai[1] community of Huajoya provides a striking example of conviviality in action. People visit one another freely, bringing gifts of food at any time of the day. Neighbours work side-by-side, discussing their dreams, sharing decisions and opinions, chatting and laughing. Heavy work, such as building gardens and houses, is done communally with the help of large amounts of manioc beer and good humour. One soon realises, however, that such harmony is not automatic, but actively fostered by each person. The Airo-Pai are extremely sensitive to conflict and indeed they think of themselves as people who are, as they say, easily inclined to anger. Achieving a highly desired state of communal well-being, which they describe as 'living well', is only possible if men and women learn to fear both their own and other people's anger (cf. Kidd, Lagrou, Overing, Rosengren, Santos-Granero, this volume).

Taking my cue from the anthropological study of 'emotion talk' and its contextualisation within social and embodied practices (e.g. Rosaldo 1980; Lutz and Abu-Lughod 1990; Csordas 1994; Leavitt 1996), I relate Airo-Pai anger talk to daily behaviour and ethnopsychology, especially as manifested in the indigenous approach to child rearing. Following Overing (1985, 1988) and Howell (1988), I place my discussion of the social self within the wider framework of the cosmology and ideas about humankind.

The main thesis of this chapter is that, for the Airo-Pai, 'anger' (*goapëine*) is not solely an emotional state, but a transformational force of key sociological and cosmological significance. It is synonymous with death and acts as an operator of radical alterity. It is also the main drive behind sorcery (cf. Smith 1977; Overing 1985; Ellis 1997; see also Rivière, this volume). So powerful are the meanings and bodily experiences attached to anger, that it is said to dehumanise people and transform their perception of reality so as to make them into murderers. An angry person quite simply is not a true person or a kinsman, but an enemy, a monster, a predator who fails to recognise his or her own kind and therefore treats them as though they were prey. Although amoral *par excellence*, anger is inherently interactional. It is said to be provoked by other people's behaviour and to spread easily from person to person, causing each other anger (cf. Kidd, Overing, Rosengren, this volume). One of the main preoccupations of all adults, therefore, is to teach their children to 'live well' like themselves, fearing and avoiding anger. This is the source of their daily conviviality.

The fear of anger

That man has no heart. He has been badly brought up. He is angry without purpose. Against his own kinsfolk he is angry without purpose.

These are typical words said by Airo-Pai men and women to vent their exasperation with troublesome kinsfolk. Agusto,[2] a father of four married to a non-Airo-Pai, was often the object of such reproaches. As a child, he was taken away from his people and brought up to be a servant by a Spanish-speaking trader in forest products. His loud bossy manners meant that he was generally disliked. Yet people put up with his offensive behaviour with astonishing detachment and kept away from him when he was in a bad mood.

'How could he behave well now that he is grown up if he did not learn as a child?', explained Cornea to me. '*Cadaye*', she exclaimed thinking about him. She followed her words with a typical facial expression, as though she had eaten something very sour. *Cadaye* is a complex feeling which is experienced physically and expressed in words meaning fear, shame, shyness and repugnance. In Spanish, the Airo-Pai translate it as 'fear' (*miedo*). In general, they uttered the word '*cadaye*' whenever they were confronted with culturally inappropriate behaviour and anything which may generate an angry response in themselves or others.

Amongst relatives, anger is always said to be in vain or purposeless, even when one allegedly has a good reason to be upset. This is built into the language. The prefix *goa-*, meaning 'without purpose' and 'bad' (Johnson and Wheeler 1987: 113), is added to the verb 'to be angry' (*pëine*) to form the typical expression, 'to be angry without purpose' (*goapëine*). An angry person is one who says: 'I want to kill' (*huasi'i*), and 'mortal enemies' (*pëinequë*) are literally described as 'the angered ones'. A murderous desire defines their cultural understanding of enmity. By contrast, the desire to 'live well' (*deoye paiye*) defines kinship. No matter the circumstances, amongst people who regard themselves as relatives and truly human, anger is always purposeless and amoral.

Anger, however, is conceived as inherent to social existence, and even individuals fully brought up in the Airo-Pai ways are held to be fallible. In most cases, people are willing to accept their own and other people's failings and make explicit efforts to overcome their grievances. Nevertheless, small outbursts of exasperation towards male and female kin are quite common amongst individuals of all ages and made manifest in verbal complaints.

When gifts of food are not reciprocated, for instance, women complain to their children and close relatives – but very rarely to the offender in person. They speak in a high-pitched voice, only audible to the people standing next to them. Typically, they use the causal voice (cf. Johnson and Wheeler, op. cit., p. 82; also Kidd, this volume) as follows: 'She causes me to be angry without purpose. I always give her meat stews and now she has prepared a whole pot and given me nothing.' Anger is conceived as emerging from social interaction and being provoked by others. For this reason, people are always aware that they may even involuntarily impinge upon and provoke others (cf. Ellis, op. cit., p. 122). Complaints are usually very short-lived because people tend to quickly remind themselves of the need to fear anger and utter a typical expression as follows: '*Cadaye*. I am angry without purpose. I should better not be angry.' As they say these words, they characteristically nod and smile, as if to chase away bad and inappropriate feelings.

Such an explicit 'emotion talk' and bodily feelings are revealing of how community members deal with culturally defined expressions and psychic states in the process of maintaining conviviality (cf. Lutz and Abu-Lughod 1990; Leavitt 1996). Although a person's anger is caused by others, he or she is responsible for controlling it once it is felt. The management of emotional life is articulated upon key formulaic expressions which are used, first, to recognise, and then, to disperse feelings of upset. Rather than to search for explanations, apologies or compensation from others, the Airo-Pai overcome their own feelings by verbally reminding themselves, and the others around them, that anger means death. The psychic act of purposefully chasing away angry feelings is expressed physically by nodding the head and changing one's facial expression into a smile. People who fail to do so are said to be badly brought up. According to Airo-Pai social philosophy, the good outcome of daily life rests on having learned culturally appropriate dispositions throughout childhood. Ultimately, as elsewhere in Amazonia, upbringing is the cornerstone of personhood and kinship.

Learning fear and thought

The Airo-Pai notion of 'upbringing' (*ai deoye*) means 'transforming into the beautiful and good' (cf. Kidd and Lagrou, this volume). As a child is brought up, he or she is said 'to learn how to think' and acquire a *joyo*, a concept which the Airo-Pai translate in Spanish as 'heart' – although this differs from the physical organ. The 'heart' is the centre of one's 'thoughts' (*cuatsaye*), which are understood as both conceptual and emotional meanings rooted in bodily experience. The 'heart' is the container of one's personal memories and social knowledge, which is sanctioned by Airo-Pai ancestral tradition. This knowledge is acquired from lived experience through the senses and always involves practical situations and social interactions of learning.

In that babies and young children do not know how to think, they are said to have very little 'heart'.

Mario, a man in his fifties, explained about his baby grandson as follows: 'He does not yet know how to think. He touches everything he sees and then throws it away without consideration for the person to whom it belongs. He goes after whatever his eyes perceive, but just in vain.' The ideas expressed here are shared by men and women. Infants ramble and act without regard to others. Adults feel pity for a baby's helplessness (cf. Gow, this volume), but they also fear their inclination towards anger and the reaction this might provoke.

During my stay in Huajoya I was puzzled by the way men and women tease babies: whenever they visit a household where there is one, the visitor holds the baby's fists and repeats several times in a baby voice: 'I am angry without purpose!'; and everybody laughs at the bemused-looking child.

Not only are babies thought to be easily angered when unhappy, they are also said to cause others to become angry. Parents in particular fear their baby's crying, which might end in the violence of a death. In Airo-Pai mythology, there is an episode of a crying baby that managed to infuriate its mother to the extent that she got so angry that she threw her child into the fire. This is the story behind the birth of the sun, a crying baby rising from the flames of his own fury and his mother's exasperation (Cipolletti 1988: 65).

Parents do everything possible to prevent young children from crying, feeding them on demand and entertaining them constantly. Older children are systematically taught to recognise and avoid their own anger. Whenever a child is particularly difficult, he or she is warned that their shouts will attract spirit monsters who feed on human souls. Invariably, the child calms down of his or her own accord at the thought of such a terrifying prospect. In this way, children learn to control themselves and fear the deadly consequences of their bad mood.[3] Adults are acutely aware that children imitate their behaviour, and for this reason they never hit or shout at them. They understand that if they did so, the child in following suit would learn how to be violent and bad-tempered.

As long as a child is unable to understand well, he or she is allowed to move around freely, but under the protective eye of the mother or an elder sibling. After 3 years of age, they are exhorted to imitate their same-sex parent and acquire gender-specific handicraft skills and knowledge. Formal instruction is given in well-structured 'pieces of advice' (*yëhuoye*). Such advice, which is said to be housed in the 'heart' of the young person, constitutes the bedrock through which he or she may autonomously make correct decisions in life. On a daily basis, parents give advice to their children before dawn, in the privacy of the hearth. Advice is also given during the teaching ceremonies of puberty and marriage. Young adults are no longer given advice by their parents because they are expected to have developed their own thoughts which grew from their elders' wisdom. The following is an example of advice given just before dawn by a couple to their children aged 16, 13, 10 and 6.

> How do you think? One must live slowly. One must live well. Think ahead. Do not think behind. Do not speak quickly about other people. Think knowledgeably to make many useful things. Do not wait for other people to work for you. Do not touch other people's things. You will cause them to be angry at you. Having knowledge, you can make all sort of things by yourself. Behave like the good bird, sitting still. Do not behave like the crazy bird which goes from branch to branch. This is how my elders advised me. Listening to them, I have lived tranquilly until this day.

This piece of advice stresses the need for children to become self-reliant, respect others' belongings, avoid causing anger in others and develop a peaceful attitude. Children are also encouraged to be still 'like a cooking pot' – 'sitting on its bottom' – 'not like a vine swinging in the air, letting the wind take it from one side to the other'. This attitude of centredness is epitomised amongst both sexes in erectness of posture and physical endurance (Belaunde 1994: 106). A thoughtful person is therefore someone whose conceptual and emotional life is manifested in a calm and secure bodily disposition. The erectness and stillness of posture encapsulate the values of personal autonomy and sociability which, as Overing (1988) has demonstrated, are characteristically Amazonian, and which are also exemplified amongst most of the other peoples studied in this volume. Cultural values are experienced and internalised in people's 'hearts' and exteriorised in their physical embodiment.

Other formal instruction assumes a harsher tone and warns young people about death and the after-death alienation anger creates.

> Young man, young woman, do not live with your tongue hanging out of your mouth. Do not live in this way saying bad things about others.
> You say: 'Such and such a person has said such a thing.'
> Do not speak in this way.
> You say: 'I want to kill!'
> Do not speak in this way.
> If you speak in this way the worms will be asking for your skin. Your heart will be lost. It's bad.
> If you are angry, people will kill you and then your own kinsfolk will drag you to the forest and abandon you there to be eaten by worms. The worms will be working in your body.
> When I was a young man I heard these words of advice from my elders.

Thus, the desire to kill paradoxically ends up in one's own death and, more significantly, the deprival of a proper burial. This is the worst form of abandonment and breakdown of kinship. Deprived of a proper funerary ritual, a deceased person would be unable to undergo the transformations which would lead to their rebirth in the upper world amongst their dead relatives and the divine beings (cf. also Cipolletti 1987).

The harsh warnings of this piece of advice contrast with the detached attitude of men and women in daily life towards the rare people who actually act out their anger, such as Agusto whom I mentioned earlier. One villager explained to me that although they disliked Agusto and avoided dealing with him as much as possible, they did not consider him a real threat. Having been taken away from his kin in childhood, he had been deprived of his elders' advice. He had therefore been unable to grow a solid human 'heart' and lacked the fear of anger. Nevertheless, his bad mood was only occasional, and particularly evident when he was drunk, which was relatively rare, because in Huajoya drinking was limited to occasional working parties and never involved strong commercial alcohol.[4] Most importantly, Agusto had not been initiated into shamanic practice as a teenager. Consequently, he could only kill physically, which his kin knew to be very unlikely. From their point of view, the important thing was that, lacking a spirit companion, he could not kill with sorcery, and was therefore relatively harmless (cf. Overing 1985). Only individuals who had been fully initiated into the Airo-Pai ways, and specifically its shamanic practices, and yet possessed an angry personal character, were held capable of sorcery.

The idea that asocial behaviour is exceedingly destructive when associated with spiritual powers is shared by many cultural groups. Amazonian people do not have a 'natural' idea of death independent of a notion of spiritual causation, and all death and serious illnesses are attributed to sorcery. As Overing (1985: 274) has shown for the Piaroa, murderous sorcery results from uncontrolled knowledge of spiritual matters. Great emphasis is put upon distributing and restraining the learning of spiritual powers in order to prevent shamans losing control over a knowledge beyond their capacities. Smith (op. cit., p. 103) argues for the Amuesha that sorcery is also triggered by anger. 'A witch works by meditating angrily about his enemy.' To be angry with someone and to bewitch someone are interchangeable ideas expressed by the same term. In a similar vein, Ellis (op. cit., p. 107) demonstrates that amongst the Tsimane, 'the invariable equation of angry behaviour and sorcery is frequently drawn'. These and many other ethnographies suggest that there is a need to go beyond an emotion-based approach to the question of anger in order to look at the indigenous cosmology and aetiology of death (cf. Gow and Jamieson, this volume).

The monster of people's hearts

The emphasis on tranquillity and fixity for teenagers of both sexes goes hand in hand with the fact that during puberty boys and girls learn to deal with spiritual beings called *huati*. Contact with these spirits is necessary to conduct adult social life, to reproduce and to look after oneself and others. However, they are also dangerous. The *huati* are pure strength, moving air – whirlpools of power – and their visible shape, when manifested, is monstrous: two heads, burnt skin, extreme hairiness.

When a woman has her first menses, it is said that she has a *huati* inside which is causing her vagina to rot and bleed – thus enabling her to carry a child. If the girl moves around, it is understood that she could die of a haemorrhage. She would also become as unsettled and roving as a red deer, which, according to the Airo-Pai, 'jumps from one side to the other and goes nowhere'. This animal epitomises the idea of craziness and boredom – restlessness – typical of women who have not learnt to think well. It is repulsive and its meat is never eaten. The Airo-Pai say that women can even kill men when they are menstruating, because menstrual blood causes damage to a man's head and lethal nose bleeds. A woman who knows how to think fears the *huati* of her menstruation and keeps it at bay by respecting the menstrual confinement.

Young men[5] also enter into contact with *huati* at puberty, during the ritual of their initiation into shamanism, when they take powerful hallucinogenics such as *Banisteriopsis caapi* and *Brugmansia* (Vickers 1989: 168). There are many types of *huati* in the Airo-Pai cosmos, but the most feared by far are the kind called '*huati* of people's hearts' (*pai joyo huati*), which accompany shamans. Young men inherit their spirit companions from a dead relative, through dreams. The '*huati* of people's hearts' is said to look like a person but to have a transparent chest like a glass window, through which one can see all the internal organs moving and the heart beating. I was told that the most terrifying vision is when the monster opens the window of its chest and takes its heart in its hand.

The destructive power of anger is fully displayed when associated with the practice of shamanism, as stated in the following pieces of advice.

> When a young man does not know how to think, when he is an angry person, he should not drink [the hallucinogenic] *yaje*. If he should take *yaje*, his *huati* will approach him to keep him company. The *huati* will tell the boy: 'Come with me. Let's go hunting birds [i.e. from the spirit's perspective, people] with my blowgun.' If the boy does not know how to think, he will accept and send illness and death to his own kin. When a young boy knows how to think he does not allow the *huati* to come too close to him. He refuses his invitation and tells the *huati*: 'Go back to your house, do not stay here.'

The blowgun mentioned in the dream is a spirit weapon, part of shamanic paraphernalia. Sorcery is described as a mystical form of hunting birds. These 'birds' are the sorcerer's victims who are said to be killed with a mystical dart. These images are drawn from a rich cosmological fund of shamanic metaphors. Elsewhere (Belaunde 1994), I have demonstrated that Airo-Pai shamanism plays upon multiple scales of perception of reality. Each different being in the cosmos is held to have a different point of view on the world. For instance, living people are seen as birds by the spirits. A similar idea of 'perspectivism', as Viveiros de Castro calls it (1998), has been reported for many other Amazonian groups (cf. Gow, Lagrou, this volume). Amongst the Airo-Pai, cosmological perception is loaded with moral implications. The bird shape of people, for instance, signifies the human's capability for caring for offspring.

Men and women are associated with two different species of birds. Men are related to the oropendola (*Icteridus chrysocephalus*) and women are linked with the green parrot (*Amazona farinosa*). Both species are intensely social but differ in their natural habits of nesting, feeding and defence. Oropendolas weave fibre nests, pierce through fruits and insects and defend their nests with the help of associated insects, such as wasps and ants. Parrots root in cavities, grind seeds and protect their young by remaining quietly vigilant inside their nests. Like the oropendola, Airo-Pai men produce fibre woven objects, such as hammocks and baskets. They hunt and protect their families with shamanism, using spiritual darts. Women are like parrots in that they harvest and transform crops, carrying their babies inside themselves or in a sling wherever they go. According to this imagery, both genders have equal responsibilities towards their young but their procedures differ. Each is autonomous and responsible for his or her own work. In marriage, the spouses unite their capabilities and complement each other's fertility. Their idea of conviviality is understood as the union of gendered and autonomous persons who raise their children together.

These metaphors are used to guide and teach people and to transform them into the human replicas of these beautiful birds. They also express an aesthetic sense in social relations that the Airo-Pai attempt to realise in their lives. At the same time, these images give expression to people's vulnerability. Birds that are breeding are an easy prey for hunters; and such is also the fate of peaceful humans. The *huati* spirits feed on human 'birds'. Nevertheless, these spirits can carry out their murderous deeds only if in association with a sorcerer. This is conceived of as involving a spiritual temptation and fall. The spirits 'invite' a shaman to 'hunt'. If he accepts, he is said to adopt the spirit's interests as his own, and hence loses sight of a proper human point of view on reality. He therefore sees his own kin as his prey. It is understood that anger motivates a shaman's acceptance of sorcery and a view of the world from a man-eating perspective. Cosmologically, such a transformation signifies that a radical alienation of kinship is being acted out through sorcery.

Death through either intentional or inadvertent sorcery is treated very seriously. Despite Airo-Pai efforts to render people fixed and thus capable of controlling the power of their spirit companions, sometimes the individual *huati* is far too strong, its air considered too powerful. For this reason, men are advised to refuse the spirit companions of dead sorcerers. The following is an account of a dream which Mario had as a young man. His dead grandfather, whom he had never met when he was alive, came to him in a dream to offer him his spirit companions. The grandfather was a sorcerer of renown who intimidated his in-laws and had accumulated five wives. He was murdered by his brothers-in-law.

> One night when I was very ill, my grandfather came nicely dressed with necklaces of beads and a crown on his head. He had a small gun in his hand, a very red and small gun. 'You have called me, this is why I have come,' said my grandfather. 'What's going on, grandson?,' 'Nothing,' I answered. Then he shot his gun in the air and it made a loud noise, like when you pour water into hot frying fat. If I had taken his gun, I would have taken his *pai joyo huati* ['*huati* of people's hearts'], and I would have become a sorcerer like him. If I had accepted, I would have died young because people would have murdered me as well in retaliation for my sorcery.

Once again, it is clear that to kill is to bring about one's own death, for to accumulate too much power will cause one's demise. As Mario explained, he preferred to abstain from shamanism rather than exposing himself to the danger of becoming the object of sorcery accusations.

Until recently, retaliations against perceived sorcerers were usual, although it is difficult to assess how many actually took place. All adults know of two or three cases which they vividly narrate, describing how not only the sorcerer but also his immediate kin were mercilessly put to death. Such retaliations were exacerbated during the recurrent epidemics of disease, such as flu, measles and yellow fever, which are an ongoing cause of morbidity amongst the Airo-Pai communities (Belaunde 1997: 132). Although the aetiology of contamination is understood, the ultimate causality of death is held to be that of sorcery, for which a shaman is always held accountable. The idea that epidemics are created by intense sorcery activity against one's own people is fairly common in Amazonia (Ireland 1988: 168; Erikson 1996: 208). Amongst the Airo-Pai, psychology, morality and cosmology come together in the cultural understanding that death is produced by the radical alienation of angry relatives. With this view in mind, we can better appreciate their efforts to create a convivial community, that is, a place where people fearful of anger can 'live well' and raise their children together.

Conclusion

As White and Kirkpatrick (1985: 221) argue, in agreement with Briggs (1970) and Le Vine (1980) amongst others, a heightened perception of the fragility of infants is associated with a highly elaborated developmental phase of infancy and puberty. Like many forest hunters, in both Amazonia and other regions, the Airo-Pai are acutely aware of children's affective and cognitive growth and its influence upon adult sociability. This is also the case with other Amazonian groups examined in this book. The Uitoto's poetical instruction of youth in handicrafts and sociability (Echeverri, this volume) strongly echoes the Airo-Pai's giving of advice. The Cashinahua concern with moulding young people through designs and fixity (Lagrou, this volume) elaborates upon a similar stress on spiritual empowerment, personal growth and the creation of true kinship.

It has often been claimed that tropical forest peoples have an exogenous idea of anger and sorcery – as something that belongs outside the community of equals. This is the case for Howell's (1988) analysis of the Chewong, who see anger in their Malay and Chinese neighbours but reject it among themselves, inside their own Chewong 'truly human' society. As with many other Amazonian peoples, the Airo-Pai perceive outsiders as dangerous, and their influence is seen as harmful, especially with regard to children. Nevertheless, the art of dealing with anger is at the same time an intrinsic part of daily community living for all kinsfolk (cf. Smith, op. cit.; Ellis, op. cit.; Overing 1988). Like other Amerindian peoples who figure in this book (cf. Kidd, Lagrou, Overing, Rosengren), the Airo-Pai conceive of anger as relational, and they stress the moral responsibility of both the one who causes anger in others and the one who becomes angered by others, with the greater emphasis upon the former. This is true for situations I observed such as the giving and receiving of food. Moreover, at a deeper level, the fear of anger is rooted inside the social group itself, since it is Airo-Pai shamans – and not foreigners – who are held responsible for diseases and death in their communities.

We need to go beyond a theory of the cultural construction of emotions and take into account the indigenous morality and cosmology in order to arrive at the full significance of anger. More than an emotion, anger is a transformational force which lies at the core of their understanding of human nature and death. The Airo-Pai convivial self is socially produced through childhood and enacted every day in practices of self-control through which the character of adults is traced back to their upbringing. If fear is an expression of one's thoughts – that is, an expression of one's purposeful listening to the advice of elders which is embodied in feelings and physical posture – then anger is, by contrast, the negation of thought and the destruction of human companionship. As Leavitt (1996: 523) argues, emotions are both conceptual, having meaning that can be expressed through talk, and also felt, and as such experienced in people's bodies. This idea of affective life also holds for the Airo-Pai, but it is necessary to go one step further to truly see the full picture. Anger is understood as a deeply rooted desire to kill which can be satisfied either through physical murder or through sorcery. It is the ultimate cause of all death amongst fellow human beings. So powerful are the meanings and embodied feelings associated with anger that it is conceived as having a performative power that can transform people's perception of reality, alienating them from their relationships and altering their social and cosmological identity. Anger draws the boundaries of alterity. Angry people, as the Airo-Pai say, 'are not people, they have no heart. They are *huati* spirits.'

Notes

1 The Airo-Pai are a Western Tukanoan-speaking people who are also known as the Secoya. There are approximately 400 Airo-Pai living in the Alto-Napo region of Amazonian Peru. There are seven nucleated villages, most of which have a Spanish-speaking primary school and basic medical care, but no other institutional infrastructural development. Their hunter–horticulturalist subsistence economy is supplemented with occasional paid labour in local agricultural and forestry businesses. The data for this chapter was collected during an intensive period of fieldwork in the community of Huajoya in 1988–9, which had a population of approximately seventy people.
2 All names have been changed.
3 Children who have recurrent tantrums are considered to be ill and are cured with shamanism.
4 At the time of my fieldwork, Evangelical Christianity had gained some acceptance in Huajoya, and several men had decided to stop taking hallucinogenic drugs. However, they continued to drink home-brewed manioc beer for special occasions. As Vickers reported (1989: 193), when heavily drunk men and women tend to argue and sometimes exchange blows over past grievances, especially those involving infidelity and unreciprocated love.
5 Some women learn shamanism after the menopause.

References

Belaunde, L.E. (1994) 'Parrots and oropendolas: the aesthetics of gender relations among the Airo-Pai of the Peruvian Amazon', *Journal de la Société des Américanistes* 80: 95–111.
—— (1997) 'Looking after your woman: contraception amongst the Airo-Pai (Secoya) of Western Amazonia', *Anthropology and Medicine* 4(2): 131–44.
Briggs, J.L. (1970) *Never in Anger: Portrait of an Eskimo Family*, Cambridge, Mass.: Harvard University Press.
Cipolletti, M.S. (1987) 'The visit to the realm of the dead in Ecuadorian Amazon. Mythologies of the Siona and the Secoya', *Journal of Latin American Indian Literatures* 3(2): 127–56.
—— (1988) *Aipë Koka. La Palabra de los Antiguos. Tradición Oral Siona-Secoya*, Quito: Abya-Yala.
Csordas, T. (1994) *Embodiment and Experience: The Existential Grounds of Culture and Self*, Cambridge: Cambridge University Press.
Ellis, R. (1997) 'A taste for movement: an exploration of the social ethics of the Tsimanes of Lowland Bolivia', unpublished Ph.D dissertation, University of St Andrews.

Erikson, P. (1996) *La Griffe des aïeux. Marquage du corps et démarquages ethniques chez les Matis d'Amazonie*, Paris: Peeters.

Howell, S. (1988) 'To be angry is not human; to be fearful is', in S. Howell and R. Willis (eds)*Societies at Peace*, London: Basil Blackwell.

Ireland, E. (1988) 'Cerebral savage: the whiteman as symbol of cleverness and savagery in Waura myth', in J.D. Hill (ed.) *Rethinking History and Myth. Indigenous South American Perspectives on the Past*, pp. 157–73, Urbana: University of Illinois Press.

Johnson, O.R. and Wheeler, A. (1987) *Gramática Secoya*, unpublished draft, Limoncocha, Ecuador: Summer Institute of Linguistics.

Leavitt, J. (1996) 'Meaning and feeling in the anthropology of emotions', *American Ethnologist* 23(3): 514–39.

Le Vine, R.A. (1980) 'Anthropology and child development', in C. Super and S. Harkness (eds) *Anthropological Perspectives on Child Development*, San Francisco: Jossey-Bass.

Lutz, C.A. and Abu-Lughod, L. (eds) (1990) *Language and the Politics of Emotion*, Cambridge: Cambridge University Press.

Overing, J. (1985) 'There is no end of evil: the guilty innocents and their fallible God', in David Parkin (ed.) *The Anthropology of Evil*, pp. 244–78, Oxford: Basil Blackwell.

—— (1988) 'Lessons in wizardry: personal autonomy and the domestication of the self in Piaroa society', in G. Jahoda and I.M. Lewis (eds), pp. 86–102, *Acquiring Culture*, London: Croom Helm.

Rosaldo, M. (1980) *Knowledge and Passion: Illongot Notion of Self and Social Life*, Cambridge: Cambridge University Press.

Smith, R.C. (1977) 'Deliverance from chaos for a song: a social and religious interpretation of the ritual of Amuesha music', unpublished Ph.D dissertation, Cornell University.

Vickers, W. (1989) *Los Siona y Los Secoya. Su Adaptación al Medio Ambiente*, Quito: Abya-Yala.

Viveiros, de Castro E. (1998) 'Cosmological deixis and Amerindian perspectivism', *Journal of the Royal Anthropological Institute* 4(3): 469–88.

White, G.M. and Kirkpatrick, J. (eds) (1985) *Person, Self and Experience. Exploring Pacific Ethnopsychologies*, Berkeley: University of California Press.

Chapter 12

The delicacy of community

On *kisagantsi* in Matsigenka narrative discourse

Dan Rosengren

Emotions are intimately associated with the person being affected, but as human beings are eminently social beings this means that others are also influenced. It is from this social perspective that I examine here the Matsigenka concept *kisagantsi*,[1] which is commonly translated as 'anger', and the role which the public manifestation of this emotion plays as an indicator of the degree to which social cohesion and communal solidarity are threatened (cf. Belaunde, Kidd, Overing, Rivière, this volume). In the study of emotions anthropologists often analyse these as 'terms and concepts' which are subsequently located within 'webs of significance'. As a consequence the focus tends to become lexical and the studies frequently constitute meta-semantic exercises. Accordingly, it has been argued (Rosenberg 1990: 171) that the contextualisation of emotive terms and concepts really amounts to nothing but a reduction of situated discourse to a discourse about situations which eventually may even end up in a discussion on the appositeness of particular terms in given situations. To avoid such 'linguistic reductionism', I will heed Wittgenstein's suggestion that to understand the meaning of a concept it is necessary to understand its use within natural discourse.

In relation to the Matsigenka's attitude towards anger this may, at first glance, seem a problematic point of departure since 'anger' is not something which they freely discuss. Rather, particularly in relation to specific persons, it is a subject that Matsigenka people by and large avoid talking about. Myth as a narrative genre constitutes, however, an exception in this respect. In myth the mention of anger contributes to enhancing the realism of the described social ambience in which the main plot is set. Hence, Matsigenka myths do not depict an inversion of 'real life' in the way that, for instance, Pierre Clastres (1977) argues that the Chulupi employ myths, that is, as a means for symbolically handling and overcoming dangers by reducing them to something laughable. In Matsigenka myth, 'anger' tends to be associated with people who in some way stand apart from the community. This relationship between 'anger' and detachment is not a simple causal relation as the one is as likely to provoke the other as vice versa. Moreover, it should be noted that Matsigenka do not consider mythic narratives as moral lessons

and they do not look to myth for moral guidance (Rosengren 1998). At narrating sessions myths are received by the ordinary Matsigenka audience in
the same way that we read an exciting and thrilling crime novel. Before reading the story you already know that you are not supposed to kill people; thus
this is not something you learn from your reading of this particular book.
Similarly, you know that Professor Moriarty, Cardinal Mazarin and Karla
are the 'baddies', while Sherlock Holmes, d'Artagnan and George Smiley
are the 'good guys'. In the same way most Matsigenka above a certain age
are familiar with the principal characters who appear in myths and they
know what kind of behaviour to expect from them. Myth therefore contains
a moral dimension, but as social life is moral this dimension is part of the
naturalistic description of the background against which the plot develops
and against which it acquires either its credibility or its absurdity. Myths
consequently describe plainly what happens when anger breaks out in public
but, being part of the social logic, the manifested effects are something the
audience realise will happen. There is thus no guidance in the myths; it
would seem instead to be a matter of restating the dominant moral system.
Accordingly, rather than arguing that myths provide moral lessons I would
say that myths, at least in regard to those dimensions presently under discussion, are created to conform to certain fundamental assumptions about
society and culture. As a consequence, where the Matsigenka are concerned,
the avoidance of displaying anger in public is an important factor behind the
limited attention that this emotion is given in myths. Hence, it is only to one
not familiar with the common norms of behaviour or with the characters
involved, that these stories may provide important insights on the pre-
dominant conceptions of morality.[2]

To inquire into how the emotional state of *kisagantsi* is dealt with in
Matsigenka narratives I have reviewed some twenty myths arbitrarily
chosen from those recorded during several years of intermittent fieldwork.[3]
No myth explicitly concerns emotive states nor do any of them have emotions
as a major theme. Some do not even mention emotions or emotive states – a
condition which should be noted. In the narratives in which emotions are
mentioned, they constitute part of the general setting, the description of
which is consonant with the general Matsigenka ethos. Thus the articulation
of emotions in these myths conforms to the expected behaviour of ordinary
everyday life, and their particular expressions do not require further explica-
tion as they are taken for granted and therefore appear to be self-explanatory.
This is part of the narrative economy according to which there is no need to
deal with already well-known phenomena that do not further contribute to
the understanding of the plot. In this sense, myths provide an indication of
how the Matsigenka spontaneously talk and think about anger when not
specifically reflecting on this affective state. From this perspective myths can
be considered as constituting a form of natural discourse in the Wittgen-
steinian sense referred to above.

In reviewing the selected myths a couple of conditions immediately stand out. First, it is obvious that emotions do not constitute a big theme or motif in Matsigenka mythic discourse; second, when reference is made to emotions, in the overwhelming majority of instances it is what is denoted as *kisagantsi* that is mentioned. This may seem strange since the expression of anger in public is suppressed; in thinking back, I cannot remember having seen any Matsigenka being really angry when sober apart from the brief outbursts of irritation that children may provoke in adults. The relative importance given to anger in myth, and its suppression outside the household[4] in everyday life, is significant as it indicates a deep concern for maintaining peace and harmony within the community. Moreover, it is at the same time an implicit acknowledgement of social harmony being the result of a precarious balancing act which may easily be disrupted, since Matsigenka life (like that of most of the other peoples described in this book) is also influenced by a strong ethos of personal freedom to act according to one's own wishes.

Before commencing the analysis of the selected myths, I will briefly place the Matsigenka within their sociopolitical setting. The Matsigenka live in the *montaña* or Andean foothills of south-eastern Peru. Although geographically at the periphery of the tropical rainforest area, they conform to the general Amazonian mode of economic organisation. Matsigenka society is atomistic and outspokenly individualistic in nature. Social organisation is 'loose' and flexible, lacking permanent groups such as unilineal descent groups and moieties. Settlements generally consist of a number of single households dispersed in the forest, each often within ten to fifteen minutes' walking distance of the closest neighbours. The households are commonly made up of an extended family of some five to fifteen persons. From the individual's perspective, the social core of Matsigenka society consists of his or her household whose relations with the external world are like concentric circles: in principle they extend indefinitely outwards but the closer to the centre the stronger they are (cf. Rosengren 1994). As a consequence of the requirements of brideservice and a preference for uxorilocal post-marital residence, a number of households form around a core of matrilaterally related women, which together frequently constitute the neighbourhood groups. Since the Matsigenka tend to conceive of these local groups from an ego-centred perspective, the constitution of the actual groups also depends on each ego's set of relations, with the result that the individually conceived groups are usually overlapping. Moreover, a group exists as such only in the moment of interaction. This means that the members that constitute the group are not necessarily fixed from the perspective of the individual (cf. Gow, Lagrou, this volume).

In accordance with the weak organisational integration of the neighbourhood groups, the coherence of the larger cluster of households that constitutes the more comprehensive settlement group is even more frail and, from an individual's point of view, ephemeral. At the same time, however, each group is also an aggregative collectivity rather than a mere congregation of individuals. Thus the peace and harmony that most people are prepared to make an effort to maintain requires a tolerant acceptance of fellow community members. Although this may seem inconsistent with the importance given to personal autonomy, it is so only from the perspective of the community being one that requires conformity and disallows difference. But from a Matsigenka perspective, that is, stressing sociality and allowing for difference, it is the person who tries to dominate and impose uniformity who is breaking up the collectivity. This attitude is consistent with a communal decision-making process in which decisions are considered to be taken not collectively but individually and to apply only to those who accept them. Consequently, they can be disregarded by those who take exception to them without this creating serious disruptions within the local community (cf. Alès, this volume).

Political leadership at community level is correspondingly weak. Until recently it consisted of informally recognised men who principally based their position on social prestige supplemented by a certain control over daughters and their husbands. With the establishment of reservations, so-called *comunidades nativas*, a process starting in the late 1970s, a formalised political structure was introduced for the first time. There is still no formal system for the resolution of community conflicts, but residents are commonly, and literally, prepared to go to great lengths in order to avoid them. When tensions increase, members – individually or collectively – leave the place where they live either temporarily, for longer or shorter periods of time, or permanently if the divergence is felt to be sufficiently acute (cf. Alès, Gonçalves, Kidd, Rivière, Santos-Granero, this volume). Where people go depends largely upon whom they are in disagreement with. If it is a conflict between members of the same household, one of the contending parties usually moves to a close relative's household in the vicinity. If it is a conflict between members of different households, the resolution of the conflict is usually considered to be more difficult, and the distance that people move therefore increases. Accordingly, there is a relation between social distance and the distance people move when they are in disagreement. There is also, most probably, a temporal dimension to this, that is, the more distantly related the contending parties the longer the time of avoidance.[5] The gravity of the conflict must, however, also be taken into consideration and if a conflict is felt to be sufficiently serious this may lead to a definitive rupture of all relations even between close relatives. Divorced couples is one instance of this, but such a breaking off of relations can also be found between close kin.

The present focus on anger, and the withholding of it in public, must not give the impression that the Matsigenka generally are a dour, withdrawn people. On the contrary, they are commonly known as a smiling and laughing people who uninhibitedly demonstrate joy, contentment and calmness. As among other conflict-avoiding Amerindian peoples (cf. Overing 1989;

Belaunde, Gonçalves, Kidd, Lagrou, Rivière, Santos-Granero, this volume),
the Matsigenka approve of virtues focusing on sociability, such as generosity
and tolerance, while they disapprove of those which socially detach the individual, such as anger, fearlessness and aggressive bravery. However, at
times, some men take to violence and they are generally feared as 'assassins'
(*kogapakori*). The antisocial behaviour of such individuals includes the presentation of self as aggressively brave, a stance stressed in the repertoire of 'killer
songs'[6] which were formerly sung before attacking an enemy. These songs
are all structurally similar: various birds are repetitiously invoked, the singer
telling them what he is about to do. When these birds are seen behaving in a
particular manner it is interpreted as an omen of imminent and violent
death. The song to the *keshíto*, a variety of toucan (*Andigena hypoglauca*), may
serve as an example of such a killer song:

> *Keshíto, keshíto*
> Toucan, toucan
> *Mángori, mángori, mángori, mángori, mángori*
> Mángori, mángori, mángori, mángori, mángori [an unidentified bird]
> *iragaigakatyo*
> those who are about to be attacked and killed are crying
> *Keshíto, keshíto*
> Toucan, toucan
> *Mángori, mángori, mángori, mángori, mángori*
> Mángori, mángori, mángori, mángori, mángori
> *kenkiseireakatyo*
> those who will be attacked are sad
> *Keshíto, keshíto*
> Toucan, toucan
> *Mángori, mángori, mángori, mángori, mángori*
> Mángori, mángori, mángori, mángori, mángori
> *Nopotsopotsotáro manataribótsote*
> I paint myself with the 'killer design'
> *Nomatimatikakonatiri manataigankicharira*
> I am singing to those who are threatened
> *Keshíto, keshíto*
> Toucan, toucan
> *Mángori, mángori, mángori, mángori, mángori*
> Mángori, mángori, mángori, mángori, mángori

The singing of these songs was associated with danger not only for the
intended victims but also for the performer who would shortly be killed himself if he failed to carry out his threat. These aggressive men had thus to be
very conscious of what they were about to do. In the conception of these
songs' efficacy there was accordingly a built-in restraint for those who were

violently inclined that inhibited excessive violence[7] – an important feature because it was believed that if these killers were not restrained they would go on killing indiscriminately. Besides this inhibition the only means for people to put a stop to a killer was to take his life. From accounts of such cases this measure appears, however, to have been taken only reluctantly when the killing had already reached excessive proportions. The reason for this reluctance is complex, and fear was probably only a part of it while, for instance, tolerance and lack of accountability (being a consequence of individualism) may also have had some influence.

Matsigenka sociability in its most diverse forms consequently respects individual idiosyncrasies and freedom while minimising authoritarian and hierarchical relations outside the household. Social control is largely replaced by individual control of the self, and self-restraint is accordingly crucial for social cohesion. The dispersed settlement pattern is sometimes stated to be a consequence thereof because such a mode of habitation means a relaxation in the demands on the moderation of behaviour in relation to those outside ego's own household. The centrifugal and fragmenting forces in this society are consequently strong. As a counterbalance, visiting is important and men in particular often spend their afternoons socialising with neighbouring households. Occasionally people come together in bigger groups at drinking parties when large quantities of *masato*, or manioc beer, are consumed. These drinking parties constitute critical events in Matsigenka communal life: while they principally function to smooth social relations they are also the occasions during which public outbreaks of anger are most likely to take place (cf. Kidd, Rivière, this volume). Usually this is explained as a consequence of alcohol's erosive effect on people's control of their emotions, which is probably the physical effect in most cases. However, drunkenness is also seen as a state in which people can come in contact with their own true selves (*noseire*) which means that the social restraints set by the generally shared sense of community may be discarded in order to let the suppressed self take over and dominate. This aspect of self-focusing contained in drinking and drunkenness is clearly expressed in the following drinking song:

Nobiekakyempara shitea
I am going to drink *masato*
oga shitea oshinkitanakena
this *masato* makes me drunk
makena shitea
bring me *masato*
noshinkitanaka
I am getting drunk
oga oseiretaganakena noseire
she [the *masato*] makes me think of my true self/my thoughts/my 'soul'

In summary, there are no formal relations of authority outside the limited household sphere. On the contrary, ideals and sentiments of individual independence and personal freedom are strong. From the perspective of the expressed radical individualism, the mere existence of Matsigenka society may even seem enigmatic.

Returning to the myths, I will in the following analyse the instances in which the concept of *kisagantsi* appears in the selected narratives in order to approach its pragmatic meaning. This can be accomplished from a number of perspectives and here I will principally discuss how the particular feeling of *kisagantsi* is described, how those described as affected by *kisagantsi* are socially characterised, whether any salience in regard to particular social roles can be elicited from the myths' attention to anger, how the social consequences of outbursts of *kisagantsi* are described and, finally, what it is in the myths that provokes *kisagantsi*.

Before considering the usage of the concept I will first dwell on a few aspects relating to its translation. A condition which immediately strikes one when examining the ways in which *kisagantsi* is translated is the wide range of the affective field covered by the concept, that is, in comparison to Western languages, *kisagantsi* can be seen as quite unspecific. This can be contrasted with Signe Howell's (1989: 208) suggestion, in relation to the Chewong of Malaysia, that 'one manifestation of the suppression of emotions is the limited psychological vocabulary'. However, among the Matsigenka not all emotions are suppressed as they are among the Chewong. Another aspect of the Matsigenka vocabulary relating to emotions is that the range of the affective field covered by the different terms is as a rule much wider, or more unspecific, than that connected with corresponding Western terms. Thus, for instance, *shinétagantsi* was during the translation sessions alternatively translated as 'love', 'happiness', 'contentment', etc., and *kamétikʸa* as 'good', 'calm', 'harmony', etc. Also, *kisagantsi* is a gloss that covers a field of emotional expressions that in Western psychology is generally treated as being constituted by several distinct kinds of emotions (cf. below).

In the selected narratives the stem *-kisa-* appears in 13 of the 20 myths and 58 times altogether. Since Matsigenka is a highly polysynthetic language it is found in no less than 39 different grammatical combinations, as verb, noun and adjective. In these different combinations *-kisa-* is translated in a variety of ways: 'to be angry,' 'to anger', 'to treat badly', 'to hate', 'to frighten', 'to scold', 'to blame', 'to fight', 'maltreatment' and 'bad/evil person'. Moreover, *-kisa-* is the only gloss encountered in the revised myths that is translated as 'anger' or with a cognate expression. When translated the word is used as if it were self-explanatory. However, while 'angry' and 'anger' are the most frequent forms of translation, it is obvious that to the translator the concept formed part of a more comprehensive semantic dimension in which anger is more than a mere emotion. Thus, in discussing the significance of *-kisa-* the translator accordingly explained that it stands for 'evil, criticising, slander-ing, fighting, arguing'. Hence the concept also, and perhaps principally, denotes a particular form of social relation, and as such constitutes part of a notion of sociality in which, I will argue, the collective good takes precedence over the individual good in a society which is otherwise such an individualistic one.

It is in line with the concept's wide range of meaning that there are no descriptions in the selected myths of how this emotional mode is articulated: no one is fuming, exploding, or even stuttering. Conversely, in the narratives it is merely stated that the affected persons are, were, or become angry. In the myth about Tsosóti (an unidentified bird) a woman visiting a strange house inadvertently kills a baby boy when she is about to cuddle him. Upon this the boy's mother merely comments that the boy's father will become angry when he returns home and learns what has taken place. Whether the mother becomes angry or upset is not specifically mentioned and the women remain seated awaiting the father's appearance. When the man eventually returns he becomes angry as predicted and he tells the woman who killed his son that from now on she must stay in his house as his wife.

Apparently there is no need to elaborate or qualify the force of the feeling mentioned, nor to describe it in any kind of expressive metaphor. This lack of descriptive elaboration should not be seen as an outcome of stylistic poverty or of an unwillingness to talk about that which is best left suppressed. Rather, it is a condition that indicates, first, that *kisagantsi* is considered as absolute in the sense that it is a question of either/or, and, second, that it is not the personal experience of the feeling as such that is of importance in the narratives but the social situation of which the angry person is a part. This is furthermore very likely associated with the social importance given to the mastering of anger: when someone actually shows that he or she is angry this is of and by itself considered as highly disturbing, while expression of the modes and degrees of affect are consequently of no interest.

The personal qualities of the angry are treated in a similar manner to anger. In only a few cases are personal characteristics explicitly noted and then the persons are described as being either *ikisanti* or *tera ikisanti*, expressions alter-natively translated as 'bad' or 'angry' and 'not bad' or 'not angry' respec-tively. Although personal relations are commonly at the very core of narratives dealing with 'anger', these relations are hinted at rather than elaborately described. In the myth about Anteater (Shiani), a man describes his sister as being kind to him by observing that 'she did not maltreat me'. This statement is subsequently elaborated with the observation that the sister always made his *cushma* (i.e. a kind of tunic that the Matsigenka wear). Hereby a degree of attachment is suggested since unmarried adult men rely on the goodwill of a sister for obtaining their dress. When a sister provides a brother with his clothing he hunts and fishes for her and between the two the relationship is normally quite close and can, in this cooperative sense, be compared to that between husband and wife.

In the narratives individual qualities are accordingly paid scant attention compared to the prominence given to the social relations between those involved. At the same time, it seems to be generally held that women are more prone to show anger than men (cf. note 4). However, in the myths covered by this study there does not seem to be any significant variation to be discerned in regard to gender. In fact, analysis revealed that slightly more men (20) than women (18) become angry. In contrast, what is significant is that in almost all instances the contending parties form part of the same household. Moreover, in twenty-six cases the conflicts are between in-laws, either between spouses or between parents-in-law and their sons-in-law. There are only seven instances of conflicts pitting consanguineal relatives against each other. In five of them the disagreement is between fathers and daughters, and in the remaining two between pairs of brothers. In the conflicts between fathers and daughters, anger is caused by a variance of opinion regarding the daughters' intended husbands, and the brothers contend with one another to marry the same women (cf. Gonçalves, this volume). Thus affinal relations are also at the core of conflicts between consanguineal relatives.

The myth about Moon (Kashiri), who is one of the principal Matsigenka deities as well as an important culture hero, provides an illustration of an intra-household conflict that develops between affinal relatives. This myth is of particular interest as it discloses in its implicit treatment of 'anger' how this feeling is comprehended in general. The narrative relates how Moon settles with a family, divulges knowledge and marries the daughter with whom he has four sons who subsequently become the suns that now illuminate different parts of the universe. At the birth of the fourth son the woman dies, but Moon explains to his parents-in-law that there is no need to worry because he will resuscitate her. Moon's mother-in-law, however, will not listen to what he has to say since she is upset by the difficult births he had her daughter go through. She is so angry with him that she forces him to eat her dead daughter. In relation to the ill-fated woman's parents the narrative focuses on the mother while the father is mentioned only *en passant*. Significantly enough, though, it is observed that the father is not 'angry' and it is explicitly stated that he is not bad/evil in contrast to the mother. Accordingly, there is in this case an association between 'anger' and evil. So, one may ask, why is it that the woman's father is described as 'not angry' and 'not evil' and in what consists the evil of her mother? Is it in merely being angry? Is it in making Moon eat the daughter? Or, is it in something else that is not immediately obvious? I will return to these points below.

As in the myth about Moon, anger is frequently associated with quite drastic events, often with serious repercussions for at least one of the parties involved in the conflict. On a general level, the principal social consequence associated with the manifestation of *kisagantsi* is connected with separation in some form. In most instances this consists of the physical withdrawal of one of the parties, a withdrawal that may be either voluntary or forced. While the separation of contending parties within a household in everyday life is often only temporary, in the myths included in the study the rifts are, with but few exceptions, as permanent and as definitive as possible. Accordingly, in these narratives, separation tends to signify outright dissolution. Thus, for instance, Pareni, another principal deity, gets angry at her husband when he criticises her for serving fish that she produces from her vagina, and she therefore transforms him into a hummingbird. When Kachiborerini (Comet) prohibits a classificatory daughter-in-law from marrying his son, the woman kills both father and son through magical means. When Moon is inhibited from resuscitating his dead wife by his nagging mother-in-law he not only eats his wife, but withdraws from earth to the heavenly world which has been his abode ever since. In these cases it is the angry person that brings about the separation, either through eliminating the person causing anger as in the cases of Pareni and Kachiborerini's classificatory daughter-in-law, or by removing oneself as in the case of Moon. The definitive separation may, however, also be produced by the individual targeted by the anger. For instance, in the myth of Anteater (Shiani) a young woman does not want to marry the man her father has chosen for her since she loves Worm (Tsómiri). To escape her father's wrath she runs away into the forest where she meets Jaguar (Matsóntsori) whom she implores to devour her. Jaguar transmutes into a man and asks why she desires to be eaten and she tells him that it is because her father is angry with her.

Although there exists an obvious relation between 'anger' and separation, cause and effect is not *a priori* determined in the narratives; while *kisagantsi* sometimes causes separation, at other times separation provokes outbursts of *kisagantsi*. In one instance a woman is captured by Bear (Maeni). She tells him her parents will become angry with her if she does not return home, that is, the separation is already a fact but her family will react if it is not ended and their daughter reunited with them. In the aforementioned myth of Anteater (Shiani), the brother of the escaping woman gives chase and on finding his sister decides to take up residence with her and her husband, Jaguar. After a while the brother leaves and remains away for a long time before returning. Because of this uncalled-for absence Jaguar is angry and makes the brother stay in the household permanently. The objective of the 'angry' person in these latter situations is thus to reconstitute the social group to which he or she belongs.

In some cases the separation of the parties involved is of a social nature only and does not involve any actual physical separation. In the myth about Spinning Spider (Ektó Kirikachirira), Spider Woman's mother-in-law scolds her for only spinning and weaving and not doing the other chores she ought to carry out according to the division of labour. Spinning and weaving is a chore that women are supposed to undertake when they have nothing else to do, principally during the early morning and late evening. However, here too a certain physical separation is involved in that much of women's labour is done together in groups (Rosengren 1987), while spinning and weaving are commonly done alone (Veber 1996). By dedicating herself exclusively to these chores, Spider Woman detaches herself from the other women of the household, thereby prompting the wrath of her mother-in-law. In the myth about Anteater the principal woman protagonist's preference for a worm as lover instead of the man whom her father favours as his prospective son-in-law, results in the distancing of herself from her fellow humans. She thus incurs the anger of her father, who tries to make her return to the man he has chosen for her. In both these instances the conflicts are unresolved which leads eventually to the physical separation of the contending parties.

Roy Wagner observes (1991: 37) that as emotions are subjective experiences they are lacking an object. That which is perceived is thus not distinct from the one who perceives it. Wagner consequently stresses the interconnectedness between the individual subject and the experienced emotion. In spite of the radical individualism of the Matsigenka, Wagner's perspective would be too narrow to understand their attitude towards the emotional condition of *kisagantsi*. Even though 'anger' is undeniably experienced individually, to emphasise the subjective experience would, from a Matsigenka point of view, signify a failure to take into consideration the particular social relation of which, in each case, *kisagantsi* is a part. As a mere subjective experience emotions are of no concern to anyone but the experiencing subject. Emotion acquires a more general interest only as an intersubjective phenomenon, and it is as such that it is considered in the selected narratives. Thus, in common with many other Native peoples of Lowland South America, while the Matsigenka explicitly express a radical individualism they also simultaneously entertain a communitarian view of society. Since the emotional condition described as *kisagantsi* is obviously closely connected with prevailing conditions for social cohesion and disruption, the narratives also deal with the conditions for belonging to a community: the point at which the individual and the collective converge. Even though it may seem a rather trivial observation, it must be borne in mind that when *kisagantsi* is understood not just as an expression of an individual's experience of 'anger' but as a force of disruption, it follows that this particular emotional state is conceived of as a potential threat to the continuity of the actual community.

This signifies, moreover, that *kisagantsi* is considered as a socially 'dangerous' feeling which should as far as possible be suppressed. Howell suggests (1981, 1989) that the reason for the Chewong's suppression of emotionality is the existence of numerous rules governing behaviour. Among the Matsigenka, as elsewhere in Amazonia, the corresponding rules are few in comparison. For the Matsigenka, such prescriptions with regard to conduct would be in opposition to the ideal of personal liberty and would imply a transgression upon individual integrity. Instead of rules and sanctions that structure and organise social behaviour, the ideal of individual freedom to act and behave according to one's own liking is prominent in the Matsigenka's view of social conduct. This does not mean, though, that the community is without any importance – quite the contrary. However, community is a thing of great delicacy and, with the individualistic ideal, its maintenance is the responsibility of all. The realisation of this ideal requires caution in respect of the maintenance of social relations, particularly outside one's own household where there are rarely any stronger ties of interdependence that can restrain manifestations of conflict. The dispersed settlement pattern may therefore be taken as an indication of the high valuation of community as it facilitates the avoidance of disruptive conflicts (cf. Gonçalves, Rivière, Santos-Granero, this volume).[8]

The valuation of community is expressed in the song referred to as 'Asháninka',[9] a fragment of which is presented below.

> *Antaarityo noatae kirinka kirinka kirinka*
> When I am going downriver
> *noneapakerityo noshaningate*
> I will see my 'fellows'
> *iriataerikara katongoakeityo*
> when they go upriver
> *kenkiseireakatyo kirinka kirinka*
> they are going to be sad downriver
> *kombério kombério kombério kombério*
> kombério kombério kombério kombério [an unidentified bird]
> *ogarityo natyoi natyoi*
> and my sister-in-law
> *oabetaempa katonkoakerityo*
> when she is going upriver
> *kenkiseireakatyo kirinka kirinka*
> they are going to be sad downriver
> *posankaka posankaka posankaka posankaka posankaka posankaka*
> pusanga[10] pusanga pusanga pusanga pusanga pusanga
> *iragakoterótyo niaririani posanga posanga*
> my brother is going to smear her with magic love potion
> *onkaemababagyete natyoi natyoi*
> and she is going to cry, my sister-in-law
> *kenkiseireakatyo kirinka kirinka*
> they are going to be sad downriver

In the light of this we can return to the questions raised in relation to the moral status of Moon's mother- and father-in-law. The characterisation of the mother as 'bad' can now be seen to follow from her inability to master her wrath, which leads to the death of her daughter and the separation of both her and Moon from the community, as well as to the subsequent alienation of Moon from mankind and this world. In contrast, in that the father's inactivity will not result in social decomposition, the community would have remained intact. The mother and the father thus come to constitute images of the fundamentally irresolvable contradiction between the desirable individualism and the necessary communalism that condition Matsigenka existence and make community a highly delicate state.

Notes

1 The grammatical infinitive does not appear in isolated form in Matsigenka but is always accompanied by infix. Thus, *kisagantsi* is a grammatical construction which is not found in ordinary speech where it appears only as a root in composite forms, like, e.g. *o-**kisa***, 'she is angry', *i-**kisa**-nti*, 'he is bad', *i-**kisa**-bintsabagyeta-kyémpi*, 'he treated you badly' and *pi-**kisa**-bintsabagyetakyéna*, 'how you hate me'.

2 Of course, one could argue that myths serve as a morality charter or somesuch, but then I believe that people should refer to myths or mythic sequences in ordinary conversations to morally qualify modes of behaviour which the Matsigenka do not do.

3 The myths included in this study were all recorded in Koribeni which, in terms of population, is one of the largest Matsigenka communities in the Upper Urubamba area. The myths were first recorded in Matsigenka, then transcribed and finally translated word-for-word into Spanish. During the latter stage I had the opportunity to discuss the parts I found obscure with the people then present in the translator's house. Two narrators are the source for this material: one, my principal translator, a woman of about 35 years of age who is more or less fluent in Spanish; the other, a man of approximately 60–65, also speaks some Spanish but is more comfortable in Matsigenka. He has a reputation within the community for being knowledgeable in the mythology and usually takes great pleasure in telling these stories. The woman, while a more reluctant narrator, also has a reputation for being knowledgeable in regard to myths and 'esoterica', principally because her late father was a shaman.

4 Anger is shown within the privacy of the household and it is assumed that women are more prone to show anger than men. There is a corroboration of this assumption in, for instance, the myth about Owl (Tontókoti) where a man is likened to a woman because of his outbursts of anger.

5 Since Matsigenka usually avoid talking about conflicts this relation is hard to corroborate decisively, particularly as the given motives for moving rarely include the possibility that any conflict could have had anything to do with the matter.

6 Rüegg and Baer (1997) refer to these songs as 'war songs'. However, when talking about this genre of songs, people in Koribeni described their singing as anticipatory to attacks perpetrated by single men. As war is a collective undertaking I feel 'killer song' to be a more adequate designation.

7 What is considered as 'excessive' and as 'acceptable' degrees of violence is of course relative. This was made very clear once in a conversation on the rubber boom when one Asháninka headman, who was used by a rubber company to round up Matsigenka men for forced labour, was described as a good man since 'he killed almost nobody, he only killed a few'.

8 This is an alternative explanation of the dispersed settlement pattern to the ecological argument that stresses that this mode of living is the outcome of limited or poor natural resources (cf. Baksh 1985). The explanation also accords with the Matsigenkas' own explanation that to live in this manner is a way of avoiding prying neighbours.

9 'Asháninka' does not refer here to the ethnolinguistic group known under that name but should be understood as 'fellows' or one's 'countrymen/women'. It is commonly translated into Spanish as 'mis paisanos'.

10 The generic name for magic love pastes of which the Matsigenka distinguish several kinds.

References

Baksh, M. (1985) 'Faunal food as a "limiting factor" on Amazonian behavior: a Machiguenga example', *Research in Economic Anthropology* 7: 145–75.

Clastres, P. (1977) *Society against the State*, New York: Urizen Books.

Howell, S. (1981) 'Rules not words', in P. Heelas and A. Lock (eds) *Indigenous Psychologies*, pp. 133–43, London: Academic Press.

—— (1989) *Society and Cosmos. Chewong of Peninsular Malaysia*, Chicago and London: University of Chicago Press.

Overing, J. (1989) 'Styles of manhood: an Amazonian contrast in tranquillity and violence', in S. Howell and R. Willis (eds) *Societies of Peace*, pp. 79–99, London and New York: Routledge.

Rosenberg, D. (1990) 'Language in the discourse of the emotions', in C.A. Lutz and L. Abu-Lughod (eds) *Language and the Politics of Emotion*, pp. 162–85, Cambridge: Cambridge University Press; Paris: Editions de la Maison des Sciences de l'Homme.

Rosengren, D. (1987) 'Concepciónes del trabajo y las relaciónes sociales en el uso de la tierra entre los Machiguenga del Alto Urubamba', *Amazonía Peruana* 7(14): 39–59.

—— (1994) 'Matsigenka, territory and notions of the other: conceptual contradictions and current conflicts', Paper presented at the 48th International Congress of Americanists, Uppsala (4–8 July).

—— (1998) 'Matsigenka myth and morality: notions of the social and the asocial', *Ethnos* 63(2): 248–72.

Rüegg, D.K. and Baer, G. (1997) 'Zum Liedrepertoire der Matsigenka: Notizen und Analysen', *Société suisse des Américanistes/Schweizerische Amerikanisten-Gesellschaft Bulletin* 61: 71–8.

Veber, H. (1996) 'External inducement and non-westernization in the uses of the Ashéninka cushma', *Journal of Material Culture* 1(2): 155–82.

Wagner, R. (1991) 'Poetics and the recentering of anthropology', in I. Brady (ed.) *Anthropological Poetics*, pp. 37–46, Savage, Md.: Rowman and Littlefield.

Chapter 13

A woman between two men and a man between two women

The production of jealousy and the predation of sociality amongst the Paresi Indians of Mato Grosso (Brazil)

Marco Antonio Gonçalves

> Without jealousy there is no suffering
> (Paresi comment quoted in Pereira 1986: 733)

This chapter[1] deals with narratives of 'jealousy' amongst the Paresi, an Arawak-speaking group of hunter–gatherers and horticulturalists of the Brazilian Mato Grosso. The data for this chapter were collected during ten months of fieldwork in 1981–3. Using myths,[2] interviews and narratives, it examines the social contexts in which jealousy is expressed and analyses its connections with indigenous notions of community, sociability, and the achievement of harmony in daily life.

The Paresi's social construction of jealousy (*okóati, okóa ihíye*) is pivotal to their daily life, cosmology and mythology, and it conveys meanings that extend to all areas of their existence. Jealousy is the operator of difference *par excellence* between men and women, men and men, women and women. The study of this culturally stressed emotion sheds new light on our understanding of Paresi sociality, questions of continuity and schism of residential groups, and notions of social differentiation/non-differentiation, distance/closeness, and exterior/interior boundaries of the community.

I therefore will not explore the cultural meaning of jealousy in 'substantivist' terms, but stress its structural aspects, showing how this particular emotion operates within and shapes community life and its inherent tensions. Jealousy is a consequence of the inevitable difference that installs itself in relations that should be marked by equality.

The idea of identity and difference varies from society to society. Each culture constructs this distinction, which is said by Héritier (1989) to be the purpose of all symbolic systems, in its own way.[3] Starting from this point, my aim is to examine how identity and difference are constituted through jealousy amongst the Paresi and what this implies for their symbolic system.

The question of identity and difference amongst the Paresi conducts us to key issues developed in their narratives, such as the endogamic ideal, the closing up of local groups upon themselves, the tendency towards internal non-differentiation, the notions of equality and equilibrium within a settlement, and the difference and hostility projected upon the distant other.

The question of what constitutes identity and difference for the Paresi arises within the mosaic of their social relations. The problem of establishing identity and difference can be reduced to two possibilities: between consanguines, represented by same-sex siblings, and between affines, represented by same-sex siblings-in-law.

The prototypical model of Paresi sociability is the village. Taking into account that asymmetry and symmetry are established through gender relationships (same sex: symmetrical; different sex: asymmetrical), we have two asymmetrical pairs of consanguines, cross-sex siblings, and two symmetrical pairs of affines, same-sex siblings-in-law.[4] A settlement is ideally constituted by a primary difference anchored in gender asymmetry, a brother and a sister (Costa 1985; Gonçalves 1990). Starting with this asymmetry as a principle, a man becomes connected with another man, that is, to his sister's husband, and in this way, this woman simultaneously differentiates them and makes them similar to one another. She is the sister of one, and the wife of the other. Upon this initial differentiation, brothers-in-law create an identification structured through co-residence and companionship. They have similar activities and establish a relationship based upon the equivalence of exchanges. Thus, starting from a difference created by affinity and established through a differential relationship towards the same woman, an identity is established.

The relationship between brothers works in the opposite way. Male siblings occupy the same position in relation to one woman: the spouse of one of the brothers who is in a marriageable position in relation to the set of brothers. The woman as a wife creates a difference in relation to her husband and his brother(s), a difference which is manifested through jealousy. Thus the principle of sociability is not guaranteed between brothers because they may compete over the same woman. The initial criterion of fraternity, which guarantees an identity, is undermined by the distinction established between people who should be equal: brothers. In this case, it is not the sister who is responsible for the creation of difference between brothers, but the wife.

The sister and wife of a man produce a process of differentiation between him and his brothers. Both the differentiation of same-sex siblings and the identification of same-sex affines are structured on the basis of the fundamental difference between men and women. The asymmetry of difference existing in the husband/wife and brother/sister pairs structures and produces processes of differentiation and identification. The definition of gender, the difference between male and female, is the focal point from which other differ-

ences and similarities are elaborated which in turn creates possible forms of
sociability.

It is important to stress that in Paresi society the construction of equivalence and difference deals with same-sex relations, mediated by a third
person: two men and one woman or two women and one man. Despite the
differences between male and female points of view as expressed in narratives
on jealousy, both are expressing the same question, the equivalence and
difference of people belonging to the same sex relative to a person of the opposite sex. Given this principle, a difference can be perceived in the way men
and women deal with jealousy, thus establishing the inequality of gender relationships. Inequality here means that gender relations are not symmetrically
inverse in daily life, any more than in Paresi narratives: two women can
permanently share one man without jealousy, while two men can share a
woman only until jealousy separates them.

Thus jealousy finds its strongest expression in the relationship between
brothers. In this society, same-sex siblings are expected to share their spouses
and the paternity of their children. This is seen as a sign of their disposition
to share everything they have. Therefore, when jealousy appears, it is seen as
a 'disease' (cf. Overing, this volume), something that can be acquired and
should be avoided for the well-being of social relationships. Jealousy causes
people to act unlike themselves, that is, antisocially, and it destroys community life.

Jealousy engenders a series of antisocial feelings *par excellence*, which in
turn create an internal differentiation which threatens the ideal of non-
differentiation and tranquillity achieved through living among kin. Because
of its great social significance, jealousy is the most conceptualised emotion
and appears in many narratives linked to other emotions such as respect
(*áiminisa*), shame (*zehaihaliti*) and anger (*ezeharene*).

To have respect for someone implies not provoking their jealousy. In daily
life as well as in many narratives husband and wife are reminded to respect
their respective spouses and not to seduce or let themselves be seduced by
others. The jealous person experiences shame when he or she behaves antisocially, and provokes shame in those who are the subject of his or her
jealousy. The jealous person is angry and this emotion produces other forms
of antisocial behaviour such as sorcery, gossip and revenge (cf. Alès,
Belaunde, Overing, this volume). In this sense, jealousy creates a whole
range of extremely disruptive feelings which produce an internal differentiation, threatening the publicly professed ideal of tranquillity (cf. Rivière,
Rosengren, Santos-Granero, this volume).

The place of jealousy in Paresi social organisation

The Paresi's endogamic ideology and value of commensal living has major
implications for their conceptions of proper social relationships. In their

social organisation, the high value placed on endogamy manifests itself at three different levels: subgroups, close kin (*inhinaihare kaiserehare*) and local groups. A strong emphasis on living among close kin is observed: small villages with little internal differentiation (1,000 inhabitants/30 villages). Inside the village, generosity is the rule. Almost all the food is collectively consumed after having been ritually offered by the head of the village to the god Enoré in the 'house of the flutes'.

The leader of the village is designated by the term *ezekwahare* (the one who gives) and the other villagers are referred to as *wakanehare* (those who receive). A person refers to the inhabitants of their own village as 'real kin' (*ihinaihare kaiserehare*). Habitually a village is formed by two big longhouses (*hati*) and one small one, to keep the sacred flutes which are used during special rituals.

To each house corresponds a domestic group, constituted by individuals belonging to three generations. Each village has a leader, whose main responsibility is to maintain the cohesion of the group. Leadership is transmitted from father to son, preferentially to the firstborn. Each village is politically and economically autonomous, although mutual help is offered during big enterprises such as the clearing of new gardens.

Originally, Paresi society was constituted by five subgroups (Kozárini, Waimaré, Kazíniti, Warére and Káwali). Each of these subgroups was said to occupy a specific territory. Thus, in the past, the organisation in subgroups seems to have corresponded to fixed territorial limits. The myth of origin of the Haliti (the Paresi's name for themselves) states that the subgroups are composed of the children of five ancestral brothers who married tree women. The five brothers left the underworld and arrived on earth through a hole hidden under a stone. The oldest brother, Wazáre, created the world, and named the headwaters of the rivers and the regions where his brothers and their descendants would establish themselves. A Paresi explained to me their stress upon the ideal of endogamy by saying that the mythical ancestors were brothers and that this was the reason why their descendants could not marry. The separation of the brothers coincides with the origin of the world, when the brothers left the undifferentiated world to live in a new world full of differences.

In this myth on the origin of humanity and society, jealousy appears in the context of sexual relations. At a certain point the ancestor brothers kill their wives because they discovered that they had been hiding food instead of sharing it with them. After this episode, the brothers leave their place to look for new wives. On their way they encounter a couple, their uncle and aunt, in the act of making love. The brothers ask their uncle for his permission to do the same; he answers that if they do, all of them will become jealous. Thus, a woman susceptible to be shared by the brothers produces the emotion of jealousy, and once contaminated by jealousy, the brothers lose their brotherly identity, their undifferentiated and united state.

Another narrative reinforces the idea that it is women who produce differ-ence between men who were, at the beginning, equivalent. Two brothers live together and engage all the time in the same activities together: they walk together, hunt together, cook and sing together. They are alone in the world and are happy this way, but they miss women. One night, looking at the sky, they ask the stars for women. The next day, two star women arrive at their house to live with them. From this moment on everything changes. The relation between the brothers is no longer the same. When they go hunting, one returns with game, the other empty-handed; and if one is generous, then the other is stingy. Thus it goes until one of the brothers dies in a conflict with his wife's relatives. The surviving brother decides to take revenge and kills all the star people, the wives included. In the end he is alone and unhappy. Missing his brother, he decides to transform himself into a soul to accompany him. The myth ends with the two brothers reunited, hunting, walking, cooking and singing together in afterlife in the same undifferentiated way as at the beginning of the myth. This narrative accentuates the dilemma facing the Paresi: to live in the undifferentiated state of united brothers with-out wives, or to have wives and be forced to live with the difference and conflict this choice produces.

In this context, difference seems to be translated into a manifestation of the antisocial, and in many narratives jealousy conveys the same meaning. Because jealousy produces disruption, it needs to be avoided at all costs. In this sense, jealousy brings with it the danger of having to live alone, and is associated with the impossibility of social relationships, the dissolution of marriage and the suffering produced by these social ruptures. A comment by one Paresi is clear about this point: 'without jealousy there is no suffering' (Pereira, op. cit., p. 733).

Jealousy in social life

The following case illustrates the dramatic implications of brotherly rivalry expressed through the idiom of jealousy. This real-life event took place a few years before my fieldwork and was narrated to me as follows. Three brothers and one sister with their respective spouses and children were living in the same village. The oldest brother was the headman and his firstborn boy was in fact the child of his wife and his younger brother. This boy became sexually involved with the daughter of his father's sister. His parallel cousin (and classificatory brother according to Paresi terminology), the son of the third brother, was also involved with this girl. For a while, the triadic relationship existed without problems. Eventually, the headman's son married the girl, but his parallel cousin, overcome by jealousy, killed him.

This fratricide between classificatory brothers led to another tragedy. The genitor of the boy decided to avenge his biological child. However, in the attempt to shoot his nephew he mistakenly killed his own brother, that is, the murderer's father. After this double fratricide, the village was burned down and abandoned and each of the surviving brothers created his own village. Other cases of village fission, not as dramatic, are told from the same perspective of jealousy between brothers, such as when the sexual sharing of a brother's wife produces gossip and accusations of sorcery, culminating in the separation of villages and the foundation of new ones.

These dramatic situations give rise to some important questions. The first relates to how villages die and are born (cf. Rivière, Rosengren, Santos-Granero, this volume): the process of fission of villages seems always to occur when brothers are concentrated in one and the same group, paradoxically when the intended ideal of community and endogamy has been achieved. Another important question is that at a certain stage of the development of the local group a process of differentiation between brothers is initiated over which is going to marry outside or within the village, a choice that influences the stability of the marriage, the scope of alliances with the outside and, finally, the possibility of becoming village leader. It is at this moment of differentiation in possibilities and choices that there comes into play the prerogative of the elder brother, the desires of the younger and the jealousy of both.

This problematic issue is more evident in the family of the village leader because it is the firstborn who is expected to inherit the leadership and, therefore, to marry virilocally. For the leader's son to be able to become a leader himself, he needs a stable marriage, and this means that he needs a father-in-law living in his own local group. This is the reason why his preferential marriage will be with a woman from the same village, more specifically, with the daughter of his father's sister. This prerequisite, however, turns the choice of a marriage partner into a delicate affair, for the firstborn might not find a marriageable woman of his own age in the house of his father's sister, whereas a younger brother might. Consequently, one or several brothers will be forced to leave the village to look for a wife since it is improbable that there will be enough marriageable women in the village for them all to marry. It is precisely at this point that there arises the question of jealousy and the drama of separation.

The offering of one's wife to a younger brother and the recognition of his paternity of her children, who consequently reside in the village of origin, seem to be social strategies to compensate for the inevitable separation of brothers. In this context the presence and expression of jealousy highlight the latent competition between brothers over the headmanship of the village and residence in one's own village of origin.

Conflict between brothers is latent in the very existence of a community. At the same time, their relationship is so close that they are expected to share almost everything (substance, food, house, affection), even women. Yet the sharing of women is not so fortunate as ideology might have it, since as soon as jealousy appears, it becomes the focus of conflict and the cause of frequent ruptures.

Shared women and Paresi paternity

The ideology of social coherence seems to be the reason for the implicit rule that posits the possibility of the sharing of wives by brothers (an attitude that proscribes jealousy between brothers) which is but a metaphor of a brotherly sharing of the same things that symbolises in a broader sense the ideology of a community of substance. It is a common experience to hear from Paresi men such comments as: 'This child is not mine, it is the child of my brother and my wife.' These kinds of statement have the explicit intention of affirming that jealousy between brothers is nonexistent and that both can share the same woman.

During his whole life the genitor will be identified as the child's father, though it will be educated by its pater, the mother's husband. Paresi theory of conception is so constructed as to sustain the possibility of identification between the genitor and the child. Although repeated sexual intercourse is needed to form the child, only one intercourse will produce its shape, when the semen of the genitor is mixed with the blood of the mother, giving the child its specific features. Thus, by comparing the features of the child with those of both men, it is possible to identify the genitor.

In this context, the negation of jealousy between brothers seems to be central to the definition of community, non-differentiation, and the production of difference. The following narrative on the hummingbird makes this aspect explicit:

> The hummingbird of the virgin forest was not jealous and ridiculed jealous men. And, to show that no one should be jealous, in his own life he used to exchange his wife with his younger brother's wife. Every day each stayed with the wife of the other. The hummingbird of the virgin forest used to sing the following song to his younger brother: '*Natyúisã, hityúisã swahá, nokató*' (For me, for you as well, my younger brother).

The Paresi relate this myth to the ritual practice of hunting hummingbirds and giving the meat to their children in order to prevent them from becoming jealous when adults (Pereira, op. cit., p. 733). The narrative, besides reinforcing the idea of jealousy being an acquired feeling, situates the problem of jealousy at the centre of the relationship between older and younger brothers. The hummingbird shared his wife with his younger brother, affirming and repeating the message that between them there was no jealousy, and that, as long as there was no jealousy, the ideology of sharing and non-differentiation was viable.

Asocial aspects of the jealous man

In one mythic narrative, a jealous man is depicted who beats his wife, controls her and does not let her perform any of her daily tasks. She is not allowed to go to her gardens, to prepare manioc flour, to chew manioc to prepare manioc beer, not even to take her own child to the river for its baptism. Not only do his parents-in-law intervene, trying to hide their daughter from him, but even his own parents attempt to persuade him to change his behaviour. Finally, aided by her kinspeople from another community, the wife manages to escape from her jealous husband and marries in another village. The abandoned husband, because of his reputation of jealousy, cannot find another wife to marry. He stays alone and dies, devoured by a jaguar.

In another narrative, a woman is advised by her relatives to abandon her sorcerer husband and marry his younger brother. The rejected husband takes revenge by killing all the people of the village. His wife and brother, however, he does not kill. The destiny of this couple is to wander around the world without kin. The idea of jealousy is explicit in this myth, since, when two brothers compete for the same wife (and in this case what is at stake is not sharing but substitution), a disruption which negates sociability may occur. This latent form of hostility and the negotiation over the sharing of a wife between brothers seem to be structural. Thus when no negotiation of differences occurs, in situations where jealousy emerges in relations between brothers, the result is a rupture: as the myth demonstrates, jealousy produces a couple who are alone in the world.

In yet other narratives, somebody who is jealous appears as a foolish clown, behaving antisocially and provoking everyone's laughter. Jealousy consequently appears as something that causes people to do everything in a wrong way. One Paresi commented, in the context of a narrative about a foolish jealous man, that to laugh at him would trigger heavy rains (cf. Overing, this volume). Thus one can conclude that if a jealous person's conduct is funny and risible, it is because this emotion and the resulting behaviour are considered to be quintessentially antisocial.

The following myth illustrates how jealousy can make brotherly conviviality impossible:

> Okiore was married to Kyawlo. The land turtle and Kyawlo's mother lived with the couple. The turtle wished he could also be Kyawlo's husband, but she did not like him. She only liked Okiore. The turtle was full of jealousy and he could not stand seeing Okiore sleeping with Kyawlo. One day, the turtle said to them: 'I am so upset, I cannot cope with you two always sleeping together and never separating from each other.' But Okiore and Kyawlo did not change their ways. So, one day, the turtle announced to Okiore's mother-in-law: 'I am going to live in the house of the secret flutes.'

'No, do not do that. If you go away, who is going to hunt for us?'

'I am going away!'

The turtle unslung his hammock and left. But the end of the hammock got caught in the door. The turtle pulled at it vigorously, saying: 'Let go of my hammock, Kyawlo. Go away from me. Let me go now. You never fancied me, but now that I'm leaving, you hold on to me. I am going away, never to come back. Let go of me, so I can be on my way!' And he pulled and pulled more strongly.

'But it's not me who is holding your hammock. It's stuck on the door pole. If you wish to go away, let go of your hammock and leave.'

The turtle became embarrassed. He freed his hammock and left, full of shame. He entered the house of the secret flutes, put up his hammock and slept. Early next morning, the turtle woke up, returned to his old house, and said:

'I had a very bad dream last night. Mother-in-law, go see if the manioc beer has got any dirt in it because I want to drink some. And do you know something, I am going to drink and then I am going to wander around.'

'Go see if the manioc beer's dirty, yourself!' said the mother-in-law.

The turtle got a light, checked there was nothing in the beer, drank some, took his arrows and left. Reaching the path, he began to walk here and there, this way and that. He broke one of his arrows and left it in the middle of the path, then he went back to the village. He arrived shouting. The three others heard his shout and said: 'Who's that shouting?' They went out to see. The turtle appeared and they asked: 'What happened to you?'

'I saw the arrows and footprints of the Nambikwara nearby. If they had come here they would have killed Okiore and Kyawlo with just one arrow, because those two are never apart.'

The others said, 'Let's go and see whether these are truly Nambikwara footprints.' They arrived at the path and the turtle said: 'Look at the footprints and arrows!'

'These aren't Nambikwara footprints,' the others replied. 'Nambikwara footprints aren't round like this. Yours are round. These are your own footprints and this isn't a Nambikwara arrow either, it's yours too. You came by and left this broken arrow. And besides, what would a Nambikwara do around here? All this is just your jealousy. Let's go home.'

The turtle was full of jealousy, and that's how the four of them lived together.

This narrative shows the place of jealousy within the masculine world. Here is a male who is excluded from a couple's relationship but acts as though he had sexual and conjugal rights over the woman he desires. Thus we have a woman and two men, one of whom does the most crazy things and behaves asocially; he does not want to accept that the woman he yearns for is another's wife. The tenor of the myth is that everything a jealous man does, no matter how much he tries to intervene in the life of a couple, is revealed as an expression of his jealousy, which pushes him to invent things that do not exist and make him look like a liar.

Another narrative demonstrates the relation, at once complicated and desirable, of a woman with two brothers. While the husband goes hunting, a hairy armadillo assumes the form of the husband's brother to visit and have intercourse with the wife. The husband, suspecting that someone was making love to his wife, hid himself close to the house to discover the lover's identity. When he saw it was the hairy armadillo in the guise of his brother, he decided to kill him. This myth engenders a problem: the husband wants to discover who is having sex with his wife, whether it is his real brother or someone imitating him; this means someone who uses the prerogative of being the brother to gain access to his wife. Thus the dilemma of jealousy is posed: if his wife's lover *is* his brother, a man is not supposed to experience jealousy; when the lover is not his brother, but a hairy armadillo taking the brother's place, then he is killed by the jealous husband.

Still in the context of jealousy between brothers, one myth tells the story of a solitary man who, after a long time, meets his brother with his wife. The solitary man begins to have 'bad thoughts' about his brother's wife and ends up making love to her. During the love-making, the woman transforms herself into a snake, curling up around his penis. The husband, returning from a hunting trip, witnesses the scene and without comment transforms the snake back into a woman. The husband, jealous of his brother, then secretly plots to kill him. This story shows how the possibility of jealousy is present in the relationship between brothers from the start and can culminate in fratricide.

Jealousy amongst women

An *apacamin* eagle was married. His *apacamin* mother-in-law and a female *pedreiro* bird lived with him. The *apacamin* also called the female *pedreiro* 'mother-in-law'. His *apacamin* mother-in-law was jealous of the other (fictitious) one.

> One day when *içá* birds were flying around, the *apacamin* man said: 'I am going to kill *içá* birds to give to my mothers-in-law to eat.'
> 'I am also going,' said his wife.
> 'You cannot come because there are many thorns and bamboo trees, and if you saw them you would make lots of mistakes.'
> So his wife did not go.

The *apacamin* reached the *iça*'s nest. He took some eggs home. He gave them to his *apacamin* mother-in-law. She saw it was only a little, and thought that he had given more to his other mother-in-law. Later, she had further thoughts about it, and gathered all her *iça* and put them in hot ashes to toast. As they were toasting they increased. The *apacamin* mother-in-law took some from the fire and put them on a *beiju* stone. The *iça* which she took turned into the red *iça* and flew away, making a big cloud which covered the sky. The *apacamin* mother-in-law felt like sleeping and went to sleep. The *iça* which remained in the ashes continued to burn until they turned into ashes also, and from these ashes the black *iça* flew away.

In this myth, jealousy arises between two females ascribed the same position, that of mother-in-law, by a male. The narrative also points out the difference which could be created between women by a man giving more food to one than to the other. The distinction between the two allegedly identical positions constitutes the privileged theme of jealousy.

We noted earlier in respect of men that jealousy can create difference between two individuals who occupy the same place, as in the case of brothers: in that there is always an elder and a younger brother, age introduces a distinction which jealousy deepens (a function also of the two issues, marrying within the community and accession to leadership). The foregoing narrative conversely describes the playing out of jealousy between two women, by rendering explicit the difference between an actual mother-in-law and another woman, living with the married couple, who was not really a mother-in-law but was treated as one by the husband. She thus took the same place as the real mother-in-law in relation to the man. This is a necessary triangulation for the existence of jealousy and for an understanding of what is equal and what is different. Two people of the same sex occupying a same position are differentiated through a relationship with someone from the opposite sex.

By contrast, jealousy between two sisters married to the same man seems, as a mythological theme, to be nonexistent. Rather, jealousy is linked to the appearance of a third woman who is not a sister. One can observe therefore a tendency not to put the stress upon jealousy in the relationship between sisters sharing the same spouse. There are some cases of sororal polygyny amongst the Paresi, and the ethnography shows that jealousy is apparently absent from this relationship. From a sociological point of view, women are not competing, be it for leadership or for the right to stay in the village after a matrilocal marriage. For them, the ideal of sharing is actually a possibility. In the following narrative, jealousy is rendered apparent from the point of view of women.

A man lived with his wife and his wife's sister-in-law [her brother's wife]. The man came upon his wife's sister-in-law in the forest and attempted to have sexual intercourse with her, but she did not let him. The man pulled off her skirt and threw it away. The man came back home and said to his wife: 'I found your sister-in-law in the forest and she did not allow me to have sex with her, so I pulled off her skirt and threw it away. Now she cannot come back out of shame. Take her another skirt.' The woman took her sister-in-law another skirt and she asked her upon her arrival, 'What happened?' Her sister-in-law answered, 'Your husband wanted to have sex with me and I did not let him, so he pulled my skirt off and threw it away.' After she told this, both women laughed together. 'Take this other skirt and come back home,' said the wife.

Although the two women are not equivalent, the wife does not feel any jealousy when her husband tells her he had attempted to seduce her sister-in-law in the forest. The two women behave in such a way so as to prevent the appearance of jealousy in the relationship. The myth seems to convey the message that the woman's generosity went against what one would expect. Given that the women were not sisters, they could not share the same man lest jealousy grew between them. Nevertheless, the non-equivalence of the women in this situation does not produce jealousy in the wife. We are thus confronted with an apparent contradiction. On the one hand, two equivalent women (sisters married to the same husband) are not jealous; on the other hand, according to the above narrative, two non-equivalent women (not being married to the same husband) are not jealous either. The latter example, however, seems to be an exception to the rule. It highlights significant differences in the way relationships are constructed and perceived from masculine and feminine points of view. From the male perspective, jealousy exists when there is an equivalence between men. But the same does not hold for women's perspective on the social. Jealousy can arise between women who are not equivalent, but it does not arise between sisters who share the same man.

Therefore, two sisters can be equivalent within a relationship with one man, but two men cannot be equivalent within a relationship with one woman. The relationship of two brothers with the same woman, while accepted, is only provisional and marked by conflict and the possibility of impermanence.

Let us now look at another narrative that tackles jealousy from a female perspective. Zawloré was married to Menaka and her older sister. They lived in a village with very large houses full of people. Zawloré was a good hunter and Menaka very hard-working. He always went into the forest to hunt while she prepared manioc bread and beer to eat with the meat he would bring back. In the late afternoon, the other women of the village used to meet Zawloré in the bush and take the liver, intestines and fat from the game he had killed, and Zawloré used to have sex with them. Even when he went alone to his gardens, the women went after him. His two wives used to say to each other: 'Why does our husband always bring meat without internal organs?'

> One day, Menake asked her husband, Zawloré, to prepare fish poison. He prepared it and fished and kept his catch in some leaves. Suddenly he heard the women shout, 'Zawloré, Zawloré!'
>
> Zawloré took his fish and buried them in the ground. The women came to him and did not see any fish. They told him: 'You always kill fish, where is the fish?' One of the women took hold of him from one side, and another woman from the other side and . . . they ended up stepping on the fish. Each woman took a fish for herself and returned home. Menaka saw the women coming back to the village with the fish and became very angry.
>
> Zawloré went up the river and continued fishing, but he only got small fish. He returned home in the afternoon. Menaka was preparing manioc and maize beer. Zawloré sat by the fire and cooked the small fish, put them on his lap and ate them. Menaka took from the pan a cup of hot beer. Zawloré thought that it was for him to drink. Menaka approached him and threw the beer on his head and burned all his body. The other women shouted: 'What is this? You are jealous!' They threw cold water on Zawloré, but that was worse because it made his skin fall out.
>
> Zawloré's older wife tended to him with roots for many days. When he had nearly recovered, he decided to go with his older wife, his children and his brother-in-law to the village Onetohe.

In this narrative a younger wife is not jealous of her husband's relationship with her co-wife and older sister, but of his relations with other women: a case of female jealousy which results in another instance of antisocial behaviour, for she throws boiling beer on her husband and scalds him. Her older sister reprimands her, but the jealous wife does not pay attention. In this sense, jealousy from the female point of view exists between non-equivalent women, and this in turn produces a difference between the male and the female condition in Paresi society, implying differentiated gender positions.

Conclusion

The custom of brothers sharing wives, and of sisters sharing the same man, corresponds to the Paresi ideal of total reciprocity, of living in community and sharing everything in a close relationship. It is an affirmation of the ethos of a solidarity that promotes the ideal of a community without conflict, a place of equivalences and peacefulness. Yet there also exists another side to this relation, one that surfaces as soon as jealousy appears: conflict, the possibility of fission, difference.

As noted elsewhere in this volume, it has been argued that two complementary forms of envisioning an Amerindian socio-cosmological theory,[5] have been formulated. On the one hand, there is the ideal of endogamy, the closing of local groups upon themselves, as 'Clastrean monads', that is further associated with a tendency to internal non-differentiation, and the notions of equality and of balanced relations. On the other hand, there is the 'symbolic economy' of alterity, where difference and hostility are projected onto the outside world of relationships. According to the latter conceptualisation, the exterior would circumscribe the sphere of predation, while the interior would represent the sphere of production.[6]

Depending on one's analytical point of view, and the emphasis placed respectively on production or predation, the interior can be perceived either as 'encompassed by' the exterior or, conversely, as 'encompassing' the exterior. Internal tranquillity can be seen 'to encompass' or 'to be encompassed' by external cannibalistic predation. In my view, the division of the Amerindian universe into peaceful interior and violent cannibalistic exterior, and the attempt to discern a distinction between the 'encompassing' and 'encompassed' levels, are strategies that do not seem to be the most productive paths to follow if one is to understand Amazonian sociability. For, in reality, we find that both aspects – the tranquil and the predatory – are not only concomitant but intertwined; and from the perspective of many Amerindian peoples the relations between the two levels, the interior and the exterior, are more ambiguously interrelated than any straightforward distinction between them might imply (cf. Rivière, Santos-Granero, this volume).

The lessons one can learn from the Paresi case lead to the understanding that the inside is not an island of tranquillity and peace, *opposed* to a hostile and bellicose exterior. The idea of community, which implies a sharing of substances, food and spouses, is based on the idea that the relation between brothers, the most prototypical for expressing the idea of sharing and equality, has no place for jealousy.

The jealous individual is considered to be a highly antisocial character. Not to want to share your wife in a relationship held to embody the ideal of the community through consanguinity and fraternity – the one between brothers – is so antisocial that the jealous person is transformed into a fool. Yet the very prohibition linked to the feeling of jealousy in this brotherly relation throws into relief its importance for the production of differences inside a system considered to be, in ideal terms, one of non-differentiation.

Jealousy creates a differential at the community level, distinguishing between older and younger brothers, and consequently between which will or will not marry inside his village, and will or will not assume its leadership.

Thus difference between brothers exists from the very start, that is, inside a relationship judged the most intimate and close. From this primary nucleus it emits a whole series of differences which transforms the tranquillity of the so-called 'inside' into a place of tensions and conflict, and their negotiation into the structural seed of the destruction of sociability inside local groups.

Paresi sociability is based on a contradictory logic: on the one hand, a sense of community which implies a repression of jealousy, and on the other, that of the recognition of the provisional character of all social relations which can be disrupted as soon as the inevitable jealousy sets in between close kin. Jealousy introduces difference, instigates conflict and is responsible for the birth and death of local groups. Interior and exterior are less fixed places with spatial determination (as with the local group versus the outside) than forms to deal with processes of differentiation and non-differentiation. The meaning of community for the Paresi lies in the administration of the difference which necessarily establishes itself between consanguines, without also necessarily appealing to a concept of affinity in which the stranger represents the outside. Difference makes itself felt from the start through the language of jealousy within the most prototypical kin relationship, the one between brothers. The universe of Paresi consanguinity is therefore a differential universe where violence lurks. Thus we can conclude that our data on Paresi society reveal an inside which is not an island of tranquillity and peace where the only conceivable violence comes from the outside.

For the Paresi, the above-mentioned antithetical and mutually exclusive models seem to be but two sides of the same coin. To opt for one of the two levels of 'encompassment', be it predation or production, the interior or the exterior, would lead to a partial perception of the Native model of the constitution of the social, which in contrast rests and constructs itself on the basis of this double conception, allowing for multiple combinations when the demarcation of difference imposes itself.

Notes

1 This chapter is a partial result of the project, 'Ethnography of the myth: Paresi mythology', sponsored by CNPq, and funded by the Carlos Chagas/Ford Foundation. I would like to thank Elsje Maria Lagrou, Luisa Elvira Belaunde, Alan Passes and Joanna Overing for their helpful comments and criticisms on the previous draft of this chapter; I solely am responsible for the ideas expressed in it.
2 I rely heavily on the work of Pereira (1986), a missionary who for many years collected the vast compendium of Paresi mythology, published in two volumes.
3 Héritier's works (1972, 1994, 1996) delineate the more general theoretical framework related to the symmetry/asymmetry, identical/different, brother/sister pairs used in the constitution of symbolic systems and the establishment of sociality.
4 This model of the constitution of sociability seems to be prototypical for many Amerindian societies and has become known as the 'Guianese' model. The problem raised by the Paresi finds itself situated on the same level as that suggested for the Trio and Piaroa. The debate between Rivière (1969, 1984, especially chapter 3) and Overing Kaplan (1975) initiates a discussion about the importance of consanguinity and affinity in the constitution of a village, conceived as a microcosmos

where sociability is produced. Overing Kaplan (op. cit., p. 191), in contrast to Rivière, emphasises affinity in opposition to the sibling set as a crucial factor for the viability of the unity of local groups or villages. The advantage of Overing Kaplan's concept of 'alliance based kinship groups' lies in the inclusion of alliance and affinity without excluding the idea of consanguinity. For a reflection on the applicability of this notion in the case of the Paresi, see Gonçalves (1990).

5 Clastres (1978: 36–55, 1982: 169–204), in the intention of delineating a socio-cosmological model for Amerindian societies, seems to have been the first to use, albeit not explicitly, the interior/exterior and production/predation oppositions. In his attempt to conceptualise Amerindian society, Clastres introduces ideas such as exchange necessarily occurring between three parties, thus breaking the symmetry of the two-section system; communitarian assemblages in the form of 'polidemic structures'; and the importance of residence for the constitution of kinship (1978: 47). These themes were later to be developed by other ethnologists.

6 For a more extensive discussion of these positions, see Overing (1989, 1993, 1999) on 'production' and the 'sense of community'; Viveiros de Castro (1993) and Descola (1989) on 'predation' and the 'encompassment of the interior by the exterior'. Overing (1985, 1986, 1988, 1996), on the other hand, already calls attention to the ambiguity of the inside/outside opposition and to the inevitable implication of predation in any process of production.

References

Clastres, P. (1978 [1974]) *A Sociedade contra o Estado. Pesquisas de Antropologia Política*, Rio de Janeiro: Francisco Alves.
—— (1982) *Arqueologia da violência. Ensaios de Antropologia Política*, São Paulo: Brasiliense.
Costa, R.M.R. (1985) 'Cultura e Contato: um estudo da sociedade Paresí no contexto das relações interétnicas', Dissertação de mestrado em Antropologia Social, PPGAS-MN/UFRJ.
Descola, P. (1989) 'Pensée mythique et théories de l'identité dans le monde amazonien', in *Encyclopédie Philosophique Universelle*, Paris: Presses Universitaires de France.
Gonçalves, M.A. (1990) 'Trabalhando a endogamia: o caso Paresí', *Revista Brasileira de Ciências Sociais*, ANPOCS, 14: 32–45.
Héritier, F. (1972) *L'Exercice de la parenté*, Paris: Plon.
—— (1989) 'Masculino/Feminino', in *Enciclopedia Einaudi, Vol. 20, Parentesco*, Imprensa Nacional, Casa da Moeda.
—— (1994) *Les Deux sœurs et leur mère*, Paris: Editions Odile Jacob.
—— (1996) *Masculin/Féminin. La pensée de la différence*, Paris: Editions Odile Jacob.
Overing, J. (1985) 'There is no end of evil: the guilty innocents and their fallible god', in D. Parkin (ed.) *The Anthropology of Evil*, pp. 244–78, Oxford: Basil Blackwell.
—— (1986) 'Images of cannibalism, death and domination in a "non-violent" society', *Journal de la Société des Américanistes* LXXII: 133–56.
—— (1988) 'Styles of manhood: an Amazonian contrast in tranquillity and violence', in S. Howell and R. Willis (eds) *Societies at Peace*, pp. 79–99, London: Basil Blackwell.
—— (1989) 'The aesthetics of production: the sense of community among the Cubeo and Piaroa', *Dialectical Anthropology* 14: 159–75.

—— (1993) 'Death and the loss of civilized predation among the Piaroa of the Orinoco Basin', *L'Homme* 126–8, 33(2–4): 191–211.

—— (1996) 'Who is the mightiest of them all? Jaguar and conquistador in Piaroa images of alterity and identity', in J. Arnold (ed.) *Monsters, Tricksters and Sacred Cows*, pp. 50–79, Charlottesville: University Press of Virginia.

—— (1999) 'Elogio do cotidiano: a confiança e a arte de vida social em uma comunidade Amazônica' (In praise of the everyday: trust and the art of social living in an Amazonian community), *Mana* 5(1): 81–108.

Overing Kaplan, J. (1975) *The Piaroa. A People of the Orinoco Basin. A Study in Kinship and Marriage*, Oxford: Clarendon Press.

Pereira, A.H. (1986) *O pensamento mítico do Paresí*, Instituto Achietano de Pesquisas, R.S. (2 vols).

Rivière, P. (1969) *Marriage among the Trio: A Principle of Social Organization*, Oxford: Oxford University Press.

—— (1984) *Individual and Society in Guiana. A Comparative Study of Amerindian Organization*, Cambridge: Cambridge University Press.

Viveiros de Castro, E. (1993) 'Alguns aspectos da afinidade no Dravidianato Amazônico', in E. Viveiros de Castro and M. Carneiro da Cunha (eds) *Amazônia. Etnologia e História Indígena*, São Paulo: NHII/USP/FAPESP.

Chapter 14

'The more we are together . . .'

Peter Rivière

These words occur in an old English music-hall song which continues 'the happier we will be'. I have no idea who first threw doubts on this sentiment but there is considerable evidence to suggest that it is a questionable, if not faulty, proposition. Even so it is a sentiment to which the Trio Indians of the Surinam/Brazilian border subscribe. In this chapter I want to look at this idea they have and some other emotions in terms of which they account for their behaviour, and to show how closely a number of the features of their social organisation fit with this behaviour. Before turning to do this, I wish to make some general remarks about the Guiana ethnographic region aimed at those unfamiliar with the area and then some more specific comments to set the context for what follows.

The Native peoples who inhabit the interior of Guiana, that geographical region circumscribed by the Orinoco, Rio Negro, Amazon and Atlantic, were traditionally slash-and-burn cultivators, hunters and gatherers who lived in small and dispersed settlements. Kinship and co-residence are the main organising features of these societies, political institutions are not characterised by coercive mechanisms but by personal authority and the world-view is shamanic. The population may well be in part the remnants of larger populations that found refuge in the interior following the upheavals consequent on European arrival. These groups should not, however, be seen as isolated, for non-Amerindian influences have affected even the remotest of them for centuries, if only in the form of worn metal tools. During the second half of the twentieth century, most groups have found themselves in direct and permanent contact with national populations, which, although it has resulted in a modified settlement pattern and economy, has often, even where intense evangelisation has taken place, left the ideas about the nature of the world relatively intact.

To turn to more specific points, there are two frequently reported features from the region that appear to be intimately associated. The first is the high degree of residential mobility; people move around a great deal from one settlement to another although often within a restricted geographical area, a river basin for example. The settlement pattern, the economy, social

networks, the material culture and other features make such mobility relatively easy. In the past settlements were also moved at frequent intervals,
although today, throughout most of the region and as a result of non-
Amerindian influences, settlements have tended to become more permanent.
The second point is the Native people's low threshold of tolerance for
dissension and disharmony in social relationships which is coupled with an
unwillingness openly to voice criticism or register complaints about the behaviour or actions of others. This means that gossip is rife and one of the
solutions is for those affected to go and live elsewhere. I suspect a chicken-
and-egg conundrum here, but instead of getting lost in trying to decide
which came first, it is possible to accept, without giving priority to either, the
fact that mobility allows for the dissipation of social tensions and intolerance
for social tensions encourages mobility (cf. Gonçalves, Rosengren, Santos-
Granero, this volume).[1]

These remarks are all true of the Trio who until the 1960s had only sporadic
contact with national societies and depended on trade with the Bush Negroes
for manufactured goods. The arrival of missionaries, in both Brazil and
Surinam, at the beginning of that decade, resulted in various upheavals but
not so as to have disrupted traditional sets of ideas and values when the
information on which this chapter is mainly based was collected. The Trio,
like other people in the region, viewed settlements as ideally self-sufficient
and autonomous and placed great emphasis on co-residency in defining the
closeness of a relationship. In practice, however, and more so under pre-
missionary rather than present conditions, this ideal was never achieved nor
was it achievable except for short periods of time. In the past there was a
considerable network of relationships connecting neighbouring villages and
a relatively high level of dependency among them. This interdependence
revealed itself at a number of levels. For example, although ideally endogamous, settlements, which rarely exceeded fifty inhabitants and averaged
closer to thirty, were demographically too small to reproduce themselves
insofar as not everyone was able to find a spouse internally. There was also
considerable trading between settlements, in either genuine or artificially
created scarce resources and objects. One such scarce resource was ritual or
mystical knowledge and an aspect of this, widely reported from across
Guiana, was the need for outsiders, that is people from another settlement,
to be involved for the successful completion of crucial rituals of social reproduction such as an initiation or a house building ceremony. In other words, a
latent function of ritual dependency was the maintenance of communication
between settlements that ideally saw themselves as independent and self-
sufficient.

Among the Trio, the dance festival fulfilled this role since it required the
participation of non-residents for it to be a success, and as such it was a total
social fact insofar as it embodied social, political, economic and ritual aspects.
At any one moment the relationships between neighbouring settlements

ranged from hostility to friendliness, depending on the nature of the most recent interactions, and varied across time as events unfolded. The reason for this is that human agency is always potentially lurking behind misfortune, sickness or death, and who is suspected or accused as a result of such an event will depend on past experiences. The dance festival is part of a mechanism that produces a shifting pattern of alliances, for although there is the obligation and necessity to invite friendly outsiders to a dance, after the event is over they may no longer be friends. The reason for this is inherent in the dance festival itself, as will be explained below.

In *Marriage among the Trio* (1969: 258) I noted that the Trio dance festival exhibits the classic tripartite structure of a rite of passage, although I pointed out that its nature more closely resembles that of sacrifice as described by Hubert and Mauss (1964). As mentioned above, a dance festival essentially involves the participation of people from other villages, and the first stage of the ritual is clearly concerned with the incorporation of visitors, bringing the outside inside so to speak. The outside–inside distinction, perhaps the most fundamental of Trio ordering principles, having been transcended, the middle stage or liminal period is marked by what Victor Turner (1969) would have called 'communitas' and which the Trio call *sasame*. It is a period of euphoria in which cosmological unification is achieved. In behavioural terms it often takes on an orgiastic character with not simply dancing but drunkenness and adultery. The final stage sees a return, together with hangovers and bad memories, to the distinctions and divisions of everyday life; with the departure of the guests, the outside is returned to where it belongs. The enmities that arise from the feast are often later compounded by sickness. Dance festivals, where people from a number of different settlements come together, provide the ideal opportunity for spreading any infectious disease there is in the region. Since sickness may be seen as the result of sorcery, any ill health following a dance festival may well be understood as resulting from the malevolence of a participant. The state of *sasame* which is engendered in the middle stage of the feast holds the seeds of its own destruction.

To take this further I want to go back to something I wrote in *Marriage among the Trio*, and about which I have not thought much since then. While discussing Trio dance festivals I noted that a key to part of what was going on depended on an understanding of the vernacular term, *sasame*. I continued:

When I asked an informant why the Trio no longer dance, he answered that previously the Trio had danced when they were *sasame*, but they do not dance now because it displeases God, and since the Trio are now always *sasame* there is no need to dance. In its simplest connotation this word means 'happy', but its deeper meaning implies a sense of inner contentment and the feeling of belonging not only to society but to the whole of nature and the universe. Thus when a group of people are *sasame* they are sharing these feelings, and in so doing are expressing a set of common values. It is to achieve this that the Trio dance, but *sasame* is not simply the reason for dancing – it is also the sensation which dancing engenders.

(Rivière 1969: 256)

Folk etymologies must always be treated with considerable caution but there may well be some accuracy in the one given to me for *sasame*. The *-me* is a common suffix with a complicated set of meanings, but for present purposes and in this context it can safely be translated as 'being'. Thus *sasame* means 'being *sasa*'. The Native explanation of this term is onomatopoeic, and this is not exceptional since onomatopoeia is common in the Trio language.[2] *Sasa* is said to be the sound made by the beads, shells, nuts, pieces of aluminium and other objects which are used to decorate the fringes of women's bead aprons shaking together while they are dancing (for an illustration of this, see Plate 2 in *Marriage among the Trio*). If this etymology is correct then it certainly ties the notion to dancing, at least so far as its collective expression is concerned. I originally had the impression that *sasame* was a purely collective sensation, that is to say that this sort of happiness could only be achieved with others. However, it is clear from its use in certain myths that individuals can feel *sasame* on their own, and even more obviously feel unhappy or *sasameta*. In fact, it is not clear whether *sasameta* exists as a collective sensation.

What, however, to make of the comment by the informant in the passage I quoted to the effect that the Trio in the early 1960s were not dancing because it displeased God and anyway the Trio were now in a permanent state of *sasame*? The first part of the statement is easily explained by the influence of missionary teaching that condemned social practices such as dancing, smoking and drinking which they saw as being at odds with their fundamentalist Christianity. The second reason needs a fuller explanation. The Trio hold the view that it would be nice if they all lived together and there is the idea that they once did so. This fits well with another idea – the high evaluation of a large network of close, harmonious relationships. Indeed I have argued (Rivière 1984: 87–94) that the possession of such a network is a form of wealth which is highlighted by its absence, most stereotypically in the form of the orphan, almost everywhere in Amazonia the poorest member of a community and the most likely to become a scapegoat. Thus a large settlement of close and harmonious relationships is an ideal, because to be a member of it is to share in the wealth it represents. In fact it is an unachievable ideal, for under normal circumstances there are clear limits to the size of a settlement. These limits are set by various factors which interplay among themselves and include the authority and competence of the leader, composition of the community, quality and quantity of the environmental resources, lack of tolerance for dissension, and ease of mobility. Indeed this last factor represents a crucial aspect of Trio politics because people literally vote with their feet. If you dislike the political ambience in a particular settlement, you can go and live elsewhere. In other words, Goldman's (1963: 155) comment about Cubeo housebuilding being the equivalent of an election applies equally well in Guiana; you cannot be a leader without followers. Thus the tensions that might arise as a result of the failure to share game because it is in short supply may result in a village fissioning unless a diplomatic and fluent leader can resolve the ill feelings engendered. But the ability of the leader to do this weakens in proportion to the size of the settlement. The larger it grows the more likely it is that disputes will break out or ill feeling be engendered, and the more difficult it will be to resolve them. This means that the population of a Trio village, given traditional institutions, is unable to maintain itself above a certain size, probably about fifty inhabitants. The second point is that Trio settlements are what I have called 'single-cell political units' (Rivière 1970) in which there is no room for political opposition which, for the Trio, is by definition external. Any growth of political opposition, that is to say internal factionalism, can only result in fissioning and the redefinition of the settlement as politically undivided (cf. Santos-Granero, this volume).

These features may be greatly modified or changed by the presence of extraneous factors, resulting in far larger settlements than can be maintained under indigenous conditions. The missionaries were just such a factor and they had induced the inhabitants from a number of villages to settle round the mission, forming a settlement many times larger than those that usually existed. That is to say that at the time the Trio were more or less living all together and togetherness is what creates the sense of *sasame*. This is what the Trio was saying when he said that they were now always *sasame* and did not, therefore, need to dance in order to create the feeling. It is likely that at the time this sense of togetherness was strengthened by an overt enthusiasm for the Christian message and it was not something that could be or was sustained.

The semantic range of the term *sasame* clearly overlaps with the usual sense of the English word 'conviviality' (cf. the Preface to this volume). It involves a temporary level of social activity that is more intense than that of everyday living. In fact the Trio have another word, *onken*, for the proper state of day-to-day communal and cooperative existence.[3] This word has the general meaning of 'quiet', 'calm', 'tranquil', and has the sense of a low level of noise. Indeed one cannot fail to be struck by just how quiet and soft-spoken the Trio are (contrast Alès and Passes, this volume). Early in my time with the Trio I was astounded by a conversation across the village square carried on by two men in little more than a whisper. Indeed, sitting beside one of the men it took me a little time to realise what he was doing and where and who his interlocutor was.[4] This quietness of speech is repeated in other activities; both cases were drawn to my attention by the differing behaviour of other neighbouring Amerindian peoples. Thus a Trio will move round the village virtually silently whereas a Waiyana strides about banging his heels on the hard dirt of the village square. When eating, a Trio will carefully pick small morsels of meat off a bone to put in the mouth, whereas an Akuriyo gnaws away at the bone. There is also the sense of harmoniousness to the word *onken*; it is the ideal state of relationships (cf. most other contributions to this volume).

Noise, on the other hand, is closely associated with anger. There are quite a large number of different words in Trio for denoting varying degrees of anger that range from the rather mild sense of being anxious or annoyed to rage.[5] There is also a rough correlation between an increasing level of noise – in other words from whisper to shout – and the intensity of anger. However, and this is rather similar to when the cusp is crossed in catastrophe theory, ultimate rage is when noise turns to silence, when speech and communication cease. Indeed, while calmness and quietness are good, complete silence and uncommunicativeness are not and are associated with sorcery. The man who keeps himself too much to himself and has little to say is regarded with suspicion. Interestingly enough, the rather loud Waiyana have a similar idea and are wary of what Trio quietness might conceal.

In their speeches it is very usual to hear village leaders exhorting the people to be *onken*, for this is the condition of everyday contentment rather than the more climactic state of ritual happiness that is *sasame*. This contrast between the everyday and feast days is signalled in *Marriage among the Trio* by the contrast between the chapters entitled 'Life's dull round' and 'Dancing and distrusting'. The Piro (Gow, this volume) recognise an almost identical distinction between 'having a good time, having a festival' and 'living well, living quietly'. There is the same 'aesthetic intensification' during rituals that contrasts markedly with the tranquil harmony that is the dominant value of everyday life. What does seem to be a difference between the Piro and the Trio is that for the latter, because of the high level of residential mobility, visitors from other villages are only temporarily those with whom one does not live well. Those who stay perforce become members of the community through the internal network of giving and sharing that defines the sense of community.

When *onken* prevails communal life is being conducted according to a set of conventions, ideals and expectations, among which we may note generosity and respect for, within certain bounds, idiosyncratic behaviour. There is no need to discuss at any length the importance of generosity as the whole of Amazonian ethnography is replete with reference to its fundamental part in social and political relationships. There is no Trio word that readily translates 'generosity' but there is a word for 'to give' (*ekarama*) which can be nominalised (*ekaramato*) to mean 'gift'. There is certainly no difficulty in hearing and seeing the importance of giving in Trio society, and the refusal to give is a serious breach of etiquette, just as the failure to be included in a distribution is a clear indication of marginality. The constant passage of goods, in particular food and drink, is not simply the lubrication of the social life of a community but the highly visible expression of community itself. If, accordingly, a person is left out of the distribution it could not be a clearer message that membership of the community is in doubt. It is possible to hark back at this point to the remarks already made about the size of Trio settlements, for it must be clear that the larger the settlement becomes the less likely is everyone to be included in distributions, especially when there are limited supplies. Thus the shortage of whatever resource is responded to not directly but through the failure to fulfil the conventional content of social relationships.

The high evaluation of respect for personal idiosyncrasies requires more attention. Rosengren (this volume) notes how the Matsigenka place much emphasis on the freedom of individuals to do and think as they please. The Trio are the same, and their language contains a suffix -*hkatë* which succinctly expresses this value. The suffix can be fixed to any noun or pronoun and it carries the connotation of giving its subject freedom of action. It may be translated colloquially as 'up to': thus *nërëhkatë* meaning 'up to him'. As well as humans, it can be applied to animals (*kaikuihkatë* – up to the dog) and things (*kanawahkatë* – up to the canoe). It is used as a response to a query or comment about some form of behaviour. Thus I once pointed out to a Trio I was with that a poorly moored canoe had broken away and was floating downriver; the response was *kanawahkatë* – 'it's up to the canoe' or 'it's the canoe's problem'. This could prove mildly exasperating and on a par with that well-known informant's response 'that is the way we always do it', but undoubtedly the most irritating occasion on which I heard it used as an explanation was when I returned one evening to the house in which I lived to find that a bunch of overripe bananas had been placed in the rafters above my hammock on to which they had dripped. When I remonstrated about this, the owner of the house shrugged and said 'it's up to the bananas'.

The freedom for individuals to do what they want is tempered by the need for self-constraint; idiosyncratic behaviour is tolerated on condition that it does not impinge on the freedom and welfare of others. It also frees the speaker from responsibility for the behaviour of another person or thing. However, this freedom to do what one wants must not be exaggerated and I am also suspicious about the claim that is often made that among Tropical Forest peoples no one can tell anyone else what to do. Certainly it is not true for the Trio, among whom adults give orders to children and may discipline them quite severely if they misbehave – furthermore, I have heard parents upbraided for allowing their children to misbehave. It is possible that this last was the result of missionary influence, although the recently reported power of village leaders to impose penalties such as whipping and imprisonment on wrongdoers may to some extent reflect the change in settlement pattern and the corresponding reduction in the ease of mobility (Carlin 1998: 37 n.32). In other words, in the past an individual would not have waited to be punished but gone to live elsewhere.[6]

Among the Trio, as in any other society, there are conventional expectations about the content of social relationships and the nature of social behaviour. The potentially most conflictive relationship among them is the affinal one, particularly, in this mainly uxorilocal society where brideservice is expected, that between parents-in-law and son-in-law. It is the one relationship which is hedged around with considerable formality; it is described as being *kutuma*. There is a lengthy discussion of the notion in *Marriage among the Trio* because it is the reason given by the Trio for their practice of affinal avoidance. In one sense, *kutuma* means 'pain' whether this results from physical injury or an illness such as a headache. Something that has the potential to cause pain is described in the same way. The word also acts as an intensifier.Thus it is possible to say *kutuma sasame*, which might be translated literally as 'painfully or terribly happy'.[7] There is also a verbal form which when used transitively has the meaning of 'persuade', 'force', 'talk someone into doing something' and 'insult', none of which is too far from pain or hurt in Trio thinking (Carlin, personal communication).

With reference to affinity it is said that you do not talk to your in-laws because it is *kutuma*, although it has to be added that not all affinal relationships are equally characterised by this quality. In a marriage between closely related individuals *kutuma* is not present, whereas it features most strongly when spouses are unrelated strangers to one another. In its most intense form it is very easy to observe. Thus, even when in close proximity, a man will ask his daughter to ask her husband to lend him his knife; the woman then asks the husband, who hands her the knife which she passes to her father. It is, however, clearly wrong to translate *kutuma* as a feature of affinity as 'pain'. Certainly when I asked where the pain was felt when one talked to one's in-laws the Trio found the idea most amusing. I assume, therefore, in the affinal context we are close to the notion of painful by which we might refer to some embarrassing incident and the sense of shame it gave rise to. Indeed, the embarrassment of two affinally related men when they have to communicate directly because no mediator is present is plain to see. Certainly *kutuma* has the effect of keeping people, in potentially difficult relationships, socially if not physically apart, and by stopping such people talking directly to one another it prevents opportunities for disagreement and dispute.

But if *kutuma* as an aspect of affinity carries the connotation of embarrassment or shame, there is another term that more directly translates those concepts. This is *püme*, and it is used in not dissimilar contexts from the English terms, but it is a feeling that the Trio seem to have difficult living with. The best ethnographic example I have of it is the case where an influential man in a mission village threatened to take his family and go to live elsewhere because he had been cuckolded by his wife. The fact that he did not was the result of pressure exerted by a missionary, worried that the mission village would fission, but I was assured that removal of himself, together with a great or smaller number of his followers, would have been the normal reaction for a man in such circumstances and the reason for his doing so would have been because he was *püke*, 'with shame'. In another case it was the behaviour of an adolescent son that produced the crisis; his father, so ashamed of what had happened, planned to go and live elsewhere for a while. A recent (1999) example was the result of a political dispute which resulted in some sixty people moving from Surinam to Brazil, and for which being *piime* was given as an explanation (Carlin, personal communication).

Any sense of shame seems powerful enough to make people feel ill at ease in their relationships and, as we have already noticed, the Trio have a relative low tolerance as far as this is concerned. The unwillingness to tolerate any psychic discomfort is well demonstrated by a story, possibly with a kernel of truth, that is widely known. It concerns a man who went hunting and killed a sloth near the village. He returned home, handed his kill to his elder sister, and told her that, since it was still early in the day, he was going to work in his field; he would return to eat later. When he got back he found that all the meat had gone. He was so ashamed at his kin's behaviour that he left the village, never to return.[8] Fully to understand this story one has to note that sloth meat is not highly regarded by the Trio; in fact it is one of those animals which the Trio are in two minds about whether they eat it at all. Second, for the Trio, the younger brother/elder sister relationship is one of the closest and most enduring. I think this story is so well known because even for the Trio it represents an extreme example of their shame at the failure of themselves or others to fulfil the social norms of behaviour whereby a community exists in harmony.

Nor is this story unique, for as with most Amerindian mythology, that of the Trio is full of asocial and antisocial behaviour of every kind that acts as a moral warning for flouting conventions (cf. Overing, this volume). For example, there are a number of Trio flood myths, which differ according to the degree to which the biblical story of Noah has been incorporated into them, but which are similar insofar as they all start from the position that people were collectively wicked in some way. For example, in one version people were married to their own sisters or mothers and were warned that they would perish because of such behaviour. Although not exclusively so, wicked individuals are almost all shamans who abuse their power, mystically killing and then mystically consuming even their closest kin. Thus, the Trio mythical world is full of wrongdoing and wickedness, in direct contrast to the ideal of the everyday good life as expressed and exhorted by the term *onken*.

If embarrassment or shame is an acceptable explanation for why people should wish to go and live elsewhere, and thus at an individual level accounts for the geographical mobility that is such a feature of Trio society, there is a further emotional state which provides an equal, if not stronger, reason. This is *ëmume*, of which the simple translation is 'sad', and seems more often than not to arise as a result of missing or being separated from someone. This feeling differs from *piime* insofar as it may attract people to somewhere else as well as inducing them to leave where they are. Probably the most common reason given by any individual or group of people for moving from one village to another is that they have kin at the other place, are missing them and want to go and see them. It is a perfectly acceptable and legitimate reason for moving and although I have no hard evidence for it, I suspect it is also used as an excuse to get away from some unease or tension without revealing the true reason – a sort of conventional white lie. Ëmume has something in common with the Cashinahua feeling of homesickness (Lagrou, this volume) although it is nothing like as intense, nor is there any association with a wandering spirit. On the other hand, the physical symptom of both ëmume and püme is thinness, also associated with weakness and ill health.

The most clear-cut and strongest expression of ëmume, when the word might be better translated as 'grief' than 'sadness', involves death and mourning. It is a widely reported ethnographic fact from the Guiana region that a village is abandoned on the death of an inhabitant, but in fact this normally only happens on the death of its leader or another senior resident or as a result of some unusual occurrence (there is a case of the Trio abandoning a village because a visiting Bush Negro spat in the fire). On the death of a child or spouse, it is more likely that just the closest kin will move away and the reason given for the move will be grief at the loss.

In a society where there is little scope openly to express emotions, especially those that might give relief to tensions and frustrations, it is quite acceptable to be openly ëmume. The problem is that, among the Trio as elsewhere, there is a rather thin line between acceptable grief and anger. I once asked why someone was sad to be told that he was angry, and in certain contexts, such as at the loss of a close kinsperson, one can see how the two emotions may well merge. Anger is an emotion widely associated with bereavement, and in a society such as the Trio where death is more often than not regarded as having an anthropomorphic agent there is clearly the strong likelihood of grief turning into anger and the desire for revenge on the sorcerer. Indeed anger, in its turn, is strongly allied in Trio thought with fierceness; to be fierce is to be ëire. This notion is in many ways the opposite to onken, and has equally important sociological correlates (cf. Rosengren, this volume; see also chapters by Alès, Belaunde, Kidd, Lagrou, Overing, Santos-Granero).

As mentioned, the Trio's ideal of the goodlife is all living permanently together, and they refer to a past village called Samuwaka in which they did just that.[9] One of the reasons they give today for no longer all living together can be summed up by the word ëire. It is because people are fierce or aggressive, and it applies equally well to physical as to mystical aggression. Hitting someone on the head with a club or cursing him equally demonstrate the quality of ëire. As I stated in the 1970 article I referred to earlier, the Trio say that they live well away from one another because they fear sorcery, an attribute of outsiders. Indeed it is because strangers and outsiders are ëire that people, that is to say close kin and co-residents, are fearful, narike. This may be described as a sort of generic fearfulness, or literally 'with fear', and a different grammatical construction is required when the cause of the fear can be specified as a particular person or thing. A generalised fear is the standard response to the unknown, which is always assumed to be 'fierce'.

In the event of death, illness and misfortune the suspicion of human agency is never far away and any such occurrence may involve accusations of sorcery. Not being fierce (*ëireta*) is one of the claims that a visitor will make in his arrival speech when reaching a village, and the less well acquainted he is with the inhabitants the more strenuously he will have to make such a claim (Rivière 1971). Indeed the suspicion of sorcery, or at least malevolence, always hangs around the outsider or the stranger. At one level the explanation for this view that the other is malevolent is part of a self-reinforcing set of ideas. If misfortune is an inevitable part of the human condition and it is given that misfortune is the result of human agency, then the occurrence of the first proves the existence of the second.

There is, however, more to this than that. It seems to me that the Trio have that dismal view of human nature whereby people are seen as incurably careless and wayward, if not actually wicked. It is this quality which accounts for the Trio's present condition, for it has destroyed what was once beneficial and valuable. The evidence for this from myths is overwhelming (cf. Koelewijn and Rivière 1987). There is a whole series of myths in which some object or creature was in the past much better than it is now and human failings resulted in the loss of this quality. A few examples will suffice. In the most widely known origin myth, that of Përëpërëwa, the best crops were lost to the Trio because, through fear, the hero failed to take them from his father-in-law, the Giant Alligator. In the myth of how the Trio first contacted the peccary, it is told how present-day peccary meat is not as good as it was in the past because a shaman raped the Master of the Peccary's sister. This theme applies equally to what are now inanimate objects although they were in the past animate. Thus arrows used to make themselves and shoot themselves, until one day a man failed to look after his arrow properly and from then on arrows had to be made and shot. A very similar story is told about carrier-baskets that used to carry themselves until mistreated by men, after which they had to be carried by people (Magaña 1987: 138). Fish poison was originally a little boy who caused the fish to die when he bathed, but when people found out about it they abused the ability and caused his death, since when people have had to go and find the liana, beat it and put it in the water. Finally, it was people's ill treatment of them that caused spirits who were once friendly and visible to become fierce and invisible. There is no Trio myth that explicitly deals with the relationships between people in the same way, although there is no lack of myths concerning aggressive acts between even the closest kin. However, there is undoubtedly a theme which portrays a world in which things were or could have been better: a golden age which was lost through human behaviour running from stupidity to viciousness. The primordial village of Samuwaka appears to have belonged to that lost world, for today the Trio no longer all live together but are separated because people are *ëire*. It might be noted that this idea of a past golden age in which things were better and easier but which was lost as a result of human failings is not restricted to the Trio. The myth, normally known as the Tree of Life or World Tree, has an almost identical theme and is widespread through Guiana. With some variation this myth records a marvellous tree which is the provider of all vegetable food. The people merely have to collect what falls from its branches in order to be fully pro-visioned. But they want more and cut the tree down, thus destroying the tree and, in some versions, bring about a flood that inundates the world.

At the individual level, I recorded an interesting life-story from Eoyari, a Trio leader of some renown. When I met him he was ageing and had retired from the more active aspects of leadership although he was still listened to. He told of his youth when, like many Trio young men, he travelled extensively in order to 'see'. He stopped doing this when, on returning to a village he had previously visited, the inhabitants were angry with him, accused him of sorcery and threatened him. After that, he said, he did not travel widely any more but stayed in his village and was 'fierce' to visitors. This suggests that youths are regarded as relatively harmless, but with increasing age, and presumably knowledge, the chance of becoming the target of accusations increases. At the same time as one becomes politically more influential and a village leader, the duty to protect your co-residents from external threat grows. The cross-questioning that takes place in the ceremonial dialogue between host and visitor about the latter's good intentions may be fierce. Once again strong talk is closely associated with increasing age and knowl-edge, and is both the cause and effect of political prestige. Thus it can be seen that the notion of fierceness is two-edged (cf. Kidd, this volume). There is the fierceness that maintains the distance between settlements and people and the fierceness that is for the protection of one's own settlement. The response to fierceness is fear which keeps you at a distance from other people and them from you.

The Trio occasionally come together to dance and be convivial, but much of the time they prefer to stay at home and be quiet amongst those they know best because people in other villages are fierce. When certain things happen they feel that they must move elsewhere because they are ashamed or sad. For all these situations the Trio have terms which express individual emotions or feelings and they behave in response to them. These responses are likely to be to a large extent conventional in the sense of fulfilling the social expectation of the correct behaviour associated with the given emotion, although it is also possible that someone will explain behaviour, motivated by other reasons, by the appropriate emotion. The point I wish to make in this chapter is the close correspondence between the conventional behaviour of indi-viduals in response to their feelings and the features of Trio social organ-isation. Let me draw the two levels together. The main features of Trio social organisation are small, ideally autonomous, self-sufficient, relatively ephemeral, dispersed settlements mainly composed of close kin but where co-residence carries similar weight and whose everyday internal relationships are ideally characterised by harmonious sharing. The outside is constituted by potentially fierce and dangerous people whose presence not only reinforces the coherence of the village but, for them, explains why they build their settlements at some distance from one another. From time to time this outside has to be allowed inside for a period of ritual euphoria which often ends disastrously. The sought-for tranquillity of the settlement is inevitably disrupted by antisocial behaviour or misfortune which gives rise to the feelings of shame or sadness to which the response is migration, observable at the sociological level by the high rate of population mobility. I hasten to add that I am not proposing any causal relationship, one way or the other, but simply reflecting on the fit between individual explanations of their behaviour in terms of responses to inner states and the observable features of the social organisation.

I wish to conclude this chapter by briefly placing its argument within a wider theoretical context. As mentioned elsewhere in this volume, Viveiros de Castro (1996: 188–90) has recognised three major analytical styles within recent studies of Amazonian societies, 'the political economy of control', 'the moral economy of intimacy' and 'the symbolic economy of alterity'. The first point I wish to make about these approaches is that I think it is wrong to assume that each of these 'economies' is characterised by a particular form of relationship. Thus I am not convinced that relationships within the moral economy of intimacy are necessarily concerned with love any more than I am that the relationships within a symbolic economy of alterity are necessarily predatory. Indeed, as I have pointed out before (Rivière 1993: 513), the Amuesha appear to operate a symbolic economy of love, and it is noticeable that Viveiros de Castro himself switched between 1993 and 1996 from referring to the symbolic economy of predation to that of alterity. Love and hate both have a place in the world, and they are both strong enough emotions to power a symbolic economy.

A second point is that while I would unhesitatingly accept that most of my work on the region falls within the political economy of control, does this current contribution belong within the moral economy of intimacy? The answer must be 'yes and no', for whereas the inner states with which it deals are the feelings of individuals for one another, part of the argument is that the conventional behaviours associated with these feelings appear to have consequences at, or are the consequence of, the sociopolitical level in terms of the size, composition and distribution of settlements (cf. Rosengren, Santos-Granero, this volume). In other words, the domestic and supra-domestic levels are not divorced from one another but are intrinsically related. Viveiros de Castro (1993) described the symbolic economy as encompassing other economies, and encompassment suggests to me linkage between levels rather than separation. One of the most obvious candidates for what

Viveiros de Castro has called a 'sociocosmological operator', is alterity itself, so intimately associated with affinity throughout Amazonia. It is an armature that links the different economies, but with different degrees of intensity. At the domestic level or in the moral economy, alterity is at zero for the consanguineous nature of the community is emphasised and otherness firmly suppressed. In the political economy of marital, ritual and material exchanges between communities, otherness plays an integral part, but its greatest degree of intensity is reached in symbolic interactions with an imagined cosmos of dead people and supernatural beings. The three levels form a coherent whole and the different analytical styles are merely a matter of perspective, of theoretical emphasis as Viveiros de Castro says (1996: 188). No one approach is exhaustive and to privilege one does not deprive another of the insights it might provide (cf. Gonçalves, Santos-Granero, this volume).

Notes

1 The importance of mobility is well illustrated by the case of the Gebusi of New Guinea (Knauft 1985). The expectation among these people is that everyone should always get along well together and they seem to lack any conventional or acceptable means by which to express mild dissent or displeasure. This results in a build-up of pressure until violence ensues and there is a very high homicide rate among them. What is interesting in the Gebusi case, and clearly differentiates it from that of the Trio, is that they are hemmed in by other people and their mobility is restricted.

2 This is an appropriate point to express my sincere thanks to Eithne Carlin, a linguist at Leiden University who has recently been working among the Trio, and has provided advice and help on several aspects of this paper. She noted that *sasame* is strictly speaking a sound-symbol as opposed to an ideophone; the latter cannot change its grammatical word-class or be inflected whereas the former can. For a discussion of the element *-me* and its various usages in the Trio language, see Carlin (forthcoming).

3 I would like to express my unease with the meaning that Illich has tried to give to the term 'conviviality', as discussed in the Preface to this book. Furthermore, it is unhelpful in the case of the Trio since *sasame* covers conviviality in the normal English sense of the word, whereas *onken* is what Illich wants the word to mean. It is noteworthy that Illich himself had doubts about its suitability, but against the advice of friends used it (1979: 12). For anthropologists the fate of Lévy-Bruhl's 'preliterate', despite the warnings of Durkheim, should be caution enough against using terms that might be readily misunderstood.

4 Carlin (1998: 22) has observed exactly the same phenomenon and notes a feature of the Trio language which helps make it possible. She writes:

> [T]he Trio . . . are extremely soft-spoken people, who can communicate over large distances with a barely audible whisper. . . . Furthermore, the Trio language lends itself to whispering because there is no voice opposition, that is, speakers can whisper without neutralizing a possible distinction between voiced and voiceless obstruents.

5 Once again I am grateful to Eithne Carlin for trying to sort out for me the various 'anger' terms in the Trio language when she was with them in 1999. One of the interesting features of many of the words is that is that their root is the word for liver, *ere*. This word also occurs in such terms as *erepa*, 'food', and *erepasa*, 'life'. I do not know enough about Trio ideas on anatomy to explain this further, but it seems very clear that for the Trio the liver is a seat of the emotions.

6 There is clearly more to it than just this, for in the past not only would such action not be accepted but there would have been no way in which the acts could have been carried out. It is difficult to believe that the leader is depending simply on his own physical force to administer punishment and it would seem to indicate that he must now possess some sort of recognised coercive authority to act in this way.

7 As with other words, it also possible to provide further intensification by lengthening vowel sounds; thus *k-u-u-tu-u-ma*.

8 It is worth noting that in another version of the myth the teller refers to the man being angry rather than ashamed. It is not difficult to appreciate the interchangeability of the words, and their emotions and affects.

9 I hesitate to regard this as purely myth. It is quite possible that it is a memory of the pre-Conquest period when very large native settlements existed, in particular on the Amazon and Atlantic littorals.

References

Carlin, E.B. (1998) 'Speech community formation: a sociolinguistic profile of the Trio of Suriname', *Nieuwe West-Indische Gids* 72(1–2): 4–42.

—— (forthcoming) 'WYSIWYG in Trio: the grammaticalized expression of truth and knowledge', in L. Rival and N. Whitehead (eds) *Beyond the Visible and the Material. The Amerindianization of Society in the Work of Peter Rivière*.

Goldman, I. (1963) *The Cubeo: Indians of the Northwest Amazon*, Illinois Studies in Anthropology 2, Urbana: University of Illinois Press.

Hubert, H. and Mauss, M. (1964 [1899]) *Sacrifice: Its Nature and Function*, London: Cohen & West.

Illich, I. (1979) *Tools for Conviviality*. Glasgow: Fontana/Collins.

Knauft, B.M. (1985) *Good Company and Violence. Sorcery and Social Action in a Lowland New Guinea Society*, Berkeley, Los Angeles and London: University of California Press.

Koelewijn, C. and Rivière, P.G. (1987) *The Oral Literature of the Trio Indians of Surubam*, Koninklijk Institut voor Taal-, Land- en Volkenkunde, Caribbean Series No 6, Dordrecht and Providence, RI: Foris Publications.

Magaña, E. (1987) *Contribuciones al estudio de la mitología y astronomía de los indios de las Guayanas*, Dordrecht and Providence, RI: Foris Publications.

Rivière, P.G. (1969) *Marriage among the Trio. A Principle of Social Organization*, Oxford: Clarendon Press.

—— (1970) 'Factions and exclusions in two South American village systems', in M. Douglas (ed.) *Witchcraft Confessions and Accusations*, London: Tavistock Press.

—— (1971) 'The political structure of the Trio Indians as manifested in a system of ceremonial dialogue', in T.O. Beidelman (ed.) *The Translation of Culture*, London: Tavistock Press.

—— (1984) *Individual and Society in Guiana. A Comparative Study of Amerindian Social Organization*, Cambridge: Cambridge University Press.

—— (1993) 'The Amerindianization of descent and affinity', *L'Homme* 126–8, 33: 507–16.

Turner, V. (1969) *The Ritual Process: Structure and Anti-Structure*, London: Routledge & Kegan Paul.

Viveiros de Castro, E. (1993) 'Alguns aspectos da afinidade no Dravidianato Amazônico, in E. Viveiros de Castro and M. Carneiro da Cunha (eds) *Amazônia. Etnologia e História Indígena*, São Paulo: Universidade de São Paulo.

—— (1996) 'Images of nature and society in Amazonian ethnology', *Annual Review of Anthropology* 25: 179–200.

Chapter 15

The Sisyphus Syndrome, or the struggle for conviviality in Native Amazonia

Fernando Santos-Granero

Ever since the pioneering works of such people as Nimuendajú (1939), Fejos (1943) and Oberg (1949) were published, Amazonianist anthropologists have produced an impressive body of ethnography that has contributed significantly to general anthropological theory. Along with this process, and as discussed in the Introduction to this volume, they have shaped – more or less consciously – an ethnographic imaginary based on two radically opposing conceptions of Native Amazonians. The first image depicts them as 'fierce' peoples who exalt the value of war, entertain a 'macho' ideal of virility and are engaged in permanent intra- and intertribal fighting. The second image portrays them as 'gentle' peoples who value peacefulness, have an 'intellectual' ideal of manhood and attempt to maintain harmonious relations at both the intra- and intertribal levels by practising reciprocal generosity.[1] This bipolar imaginary is based in part on empirical observation. In effect, there are Native Amazonian societies that are more violent, or more peaceful – depending on where we put the emphasis – than others. But it is also based on emic models, conscious Native perceptions and ideals about how social organisation and interaction work which in some cases have seeped into the ethnographers' interpretations, and in others have been deliberately adopted as the basis of their analyses.

No Amazonianist anthropologist would support the notion that Amerindians are quintessentially violent or quintessentially pacific. In recent years, however, there has been a tendency to raise to the level of anthropological theory the emic perceptions upon which these stereotypes have been constructed. Presented as antithetical ways of apprehending Native Amazonian sociality, these two approaches have been labelled as 'the moral economy of intimacy' and as 'the symbolic economy of alterity' (Viveiros de Castro 1996: 190). According to this view the first approach focuses on the local level and the domestic domain, placing emphasis on consanguinity, endogamy and the solidarity induced by moral sentiments, whereas the latter focuses on the interlocal level and the political domain, highlighting the importance of affinity, exchange and ontological predation (cf. Introduction (pp. 6, 24 n. 9), Gonçalves and Rivière, this volume).[2]

One of the main criticisms made of the morality approach – whose followers I have elsewhere labelled as 'doves' (Santos-Granero 1999) – is that it over-emphasises consanguinity, as well as the consubstantiality that results from commensality or the continuous sharing of food and beverages, as the basis of Amazonian sociality. Followers of the predation approach – whom I have labelled 'hawks' – assert that implicit in this view is the (erroneous) conception that consanguinity is 'natural' whereas affinity is a cultural construct. They contend instead that sociality and identity is about exchange rather than consubstantiality, and that 'potential or symbolic affinity is the key category of sociability in the lowlands' (Viveiros de Castro 1995: 14, my translation). 'Hawks' further assert that even though it is true that at the local level affinity is encompassed (in Dumont's sense) by consanguinity, at the interlocal level affinity encompasses consanguinity, becoming a socio-cosmological operator that allows reference to all kinds of relations between 'us' and 'them' (Viveiros de Castro 1993: 181; 1996: 190; Descola 1993). At this higher level, the notion of affinity finds expression in the metaphor of cannibalistic predation, which, 'hawks' contend, is shared universally by Native Amazonian peoples. In this view affinity is the natural relation, whereas consanguinity is a cultural artefact in need of explanation (Anne-Christine Taylor, Eduardo Viveiros de Castro, personal communications).

A second important criticism levelled at followers of the morality approach is that by downplaying or ignoring conflict they present an idealised view of Amerindian communal life (Taylor 1996: 206). Being one of the multiple forms of social exchange, conflict is a basic factor in shaping Amazonian sociality. According to 'hawks', the notion of harmonious conviviality – in one way or another present throughout Native Amazonia, as the chapters in this volume attest – is nothing else but 'wishful thinking', an ideal, an aspiration rarely corresponding to the on-the-ground reality of constant, ongoing strife.

In this chapter I shall contest this '*tout noir*' version of Amazonian sociality, without, I hope, falling into the other extreme and advocating the 'rosy' kind of version 'hawks' accuse us 'doves' of favouring. The only way to escape from this Manichaean trap, I contend, is by incorporating a temporal dimension into the analysis. Instead of examining sociality at junctures of peace and harmony, or at junctures of conflict and feuding, we should look at the social processes by which conviviality is constructed – and also destroyed. I will attempt this task by examining ethnographic data from the Yanesha of eastern Peru and comparing it with cycles of sociality in other Amazonian indigenous peoples.

The pillars of Yanesha conviviality

Yanesha notions of sociality are summarised in the myth of Sanrronesha', the murdered ones. As in Hobbes's *Leviathan* (1651), in this myth the Yanesha exalt the positive aspects of daily social interaction by opposing the present era to a brutal pre-social age characterised by the presence of territorially bound, endogamous and incestuous descent groups engaged in constant war with each other (Santos-Granero 1991: 36–48). Marked by isolationism, individualism, greediness, war, feuding and murder, the pre-social era is endowed by myth tellers with all the features that the Yanesha regard as antithetical to the 'good social life'. In contrast to other Native Amazonian peoples that glorify warfare as an honourable endeavour (Chagnon 1968; Maybury-Lewis 1974; Viveiros de Castro 1992; Basso 1995; Descola 1996), the Yanesha view war and killing with abhorrence.

Such aversion is expressed in this myth through the gruesome description of Sanrronesho – the land located in the uppermost level of the Yanesha cosmos – where the souls of the murdered ones (*sanerr*) live. A woman decides to travel with her children to Sanrronesho after enemies kill her husband. There, she sees her husband – his body wounded and covered with dry blood, his head crawling with maggots – singing and dancing with other murdered men and women to the sound of *coshamñats* music. Members of the group invite each other to drink a concoction made of fermented heart, liver and kidney. At dawn, after celebrating all night long, the murdered ones turn into vultures and other despised carrion birds, and ascend to the heavens of Sanrronesho. Clearly, for the Yanesha being killed in war does not constitute a noble death (see Alès, this volume). On the contrary, it leads to an afterlife of defilement and cannibalism. After death, however, the murdered ones seemed to have learnt something they did not know while alive: namely, how to interact harmoniously.

The priceless knowledge the woman obtains from her journey to the land of the murdered ones is precisely that social interaction need not be predatory: that the divisions, rivalries and hatreds that pit human beings against each other can be overcome. Realising that the key to a good social life lay in the *coshamñats* celebration, the woman and her children learn how to make the panpipes and drums, as well as how to brew manioc beer. They also learn the songs and dances of the murdered ones. After returning to the land of the living the woman organises a huge celebration, inviting all her neighbours, including those who killed her husband. She asks them to stop warring and tells them that they should establish friendly relations and become like a big family, for she has seen the ghastly fate that befalls those who are murdered. Thus it was that the Yanesha learnt what Overing (1996: 5) calls the 'skills for social living'. From then onwards, according to myth, they stopped killing each other, taking turns to organise *coshamñats* celebrations and to invite everybody to eat, drink, sing and dance in praise of the divinities.

The *coshamñats* celebration embodies the virtues the Yanesha consider to be the basis of conviviality and a good social life: namely, love (*morrenteñets*), friendliness (*amo'tsteñets*), trust (*yemteñets*) and generosity (*yomateñets*). *Morrenteñets* refers to the bilateral, symmetrical love existing between two individuals or parties related either vertically or horizontally. It contrasts with *muereñets*, the unilateral, asymmetrical love that those who occupy the superordinate position in a hierarchical relationship (divinities, leaders, or parents) feel toward those who occupy subordinate positions (humans, followers, or children). The Yanesha claim that whereas *muereñets* is the primordial, timeless love/compassion that moved the divinities to create the cosmos and its inhabitants, *morrenteñets* is a historical type of love that appeared when the Yanesha obtained the knowledge of the *coshamñats* celebration. It is this latter type of love that moved the mythical woman to invite the murderers of her husband to the first *coshamñats* celebration ever held in this mortal earth. And it is this type of love that is expected to guide social interaction whether among consanguines, affines or friends.

Friendliness is a personal disposition, indispensable to the establishment of harmonious social relationships with unrelated persons, or with someone with whom one has quarrelled and is not on speaking terms (*amo'tsteñets*). The verb root *am'ots*, indicating a harmonious or friendly relation between any two persons, is also present in the term *namo'tsesha'*, or 'the group of people with whom I have friendly relations'. This is an ego-centred term having varying degrees of inclusiveness according to context (cf. Gow, this volume). These range from one's nuclear family, to one's bilateral kindred, and even to one's distant collateral relatives and friends. It can even be extended to include all Yanesha, as if they were one 'big family'.

Like the term *amo'tsteñets*, the term *yemteñets* refers to 'friendly relationships'. However, in the latter, the emphasis is on the dimension of trust. The Yanesha consider trust and friendliness as basic ingredients of a harmonious social life. Trust is conducive to friendship; friendliness promotes trust. However, neither trust nor friendship could be sustained without *yomateñets*, that is, without generosity. This is especially true within local settlements, where everybody is expected to display generosity by sharing garden products, game, cooked food and beverages (Santos-Granero 1986: 122). And where all are expected to cooperate with their neighbours in burdensome or long-lasting tasks such as clearing gardens, building houses, or constructing community facilities (schools, health posts, airstrips, etc.). The Yanesha are expected to be generous not only towards their kin, affines, friends and acquaintances, but also towards strangers. So much so that I have never visited a Yanesha household without having its owners invite me to eat or drink, no matter how strange or suspicious I might have looked to them.

Love, friendliness, trust and generosity are the pillars of Yanesha conviviality. However, rather than ideal values that can or cannot be adhered to, these feelings and dispositions are regarded as social virtues that need to be constantly reinforced for them to turn into effective social practices. They are taught to everybody from early childhood (cf. Alès, Belaunde, Kidd, Lagrou, Londoño-Sulkin, this volume). Children are never punished physically. Instead they are encouraged through praise to be generous, loving,

friendly and trusting, and discouraged through scorn from antisocial behaviours. Acts of greed are similarly dealt with. Outbursts of wrath or anger
are repressed by making fun of the culprit. Quarrelsome children are ignored
and excluded from collective games.

Mockery, scorn and indifference are powerful mechanisms to instil social
virtues and encourage harmonious relations among children. In the case of
adults, these mechanisms may turn into gossip, contempt and, in extreme
cases, ostracism. The greedy, irascible or unfriendly are never openly
confronted. Instead, people express their disapproval by treating them with
indifference, ignoring them in public, not taking them seriously in community
forums, and excluding them from day-to-day networks of commensality.
They force the culprits either to behave as expected or to abandon the
collective.[3]

An even more powerful deterrent to antisocial behaviour is the fear of being
accused of witchcraft (cf. Rivière, this volume). Selfishness (*mopateñets*),
wrath (*atsrre'mueñets*), hatred (*e'moñe'teñets*) and belligerence (*chetannateñets*)
express a dangerous lack of self-control – dangerous because they trigger the
bewitching powers that every human being contains within him- or herself
(cf. Belaunde, Overing, this volume). Those individuals lacking social virtues
expose themselves to sorcery accusations, which in time can result in coun-
ter-sorcery, or even in their being assassinated.

To prevent conflicts and, more specifically, to discourage the escalation of
existing conflicts, the Yanesha have a second informal mechanism: namely
controlled sociability. People enjoy visiting each other, getting together in
informal celebrations, sharing food and beverages, and cooperating in
collective tasks. But they are also jealous of their privacy. It is not that they
prefer to live behind walls. There are few walls, if any, in Yanesha houses
and everybody can see what is going on within them. However, people get
tired of so much exposure, and of the sociability that this openness imposes
on them: too many visitors, constant demands on their generosity, increasing
requests for cooperation and so forth. In the old days, sociability was not as
burdensome, for households were dispersed. Distances between them may
not have been big – in some cases as little as one or two hundred metres – but
they were out of sight of each other. Nowadays, the government requires
that people live in nucleated settlements if they want to be recognised as
comunidades nativas, or Native communities, and to be granted land titles.

To lessen the burden that conviviality places on their lives under the new
circumstances, the Yanesha have developed a two-house strategy. Most
Yanesha have a house in the community's centre, which is generally located
along both sides of a landing strip or on a square or rectangular plaza that
doubles as a football field. In addition, they also have a second house near
their gardens, located fifteen minutes' to one hour's walking distance from
the village; these dwellings are generally smaller and less carefully built than
their village houses. Some individuals live permanently in the village and

move to their peripheral houses only when they have had enough of socialising, or when they want to escape from mounting tensions with a neighbour.
Others live in their peripheral houses from Monday to Friday, away from
the intense conviviality of the village centre, and move to the village only on
weekends, to attend church services, play football, and socialise. Having two
houses allows people to adjust the intensity of conviviality to their personal
needs and provides an escape from social interaction in situations of friction
or discord with other settlement members.

These informal mechanisms help keep in check antisocial attitudes and
defuse social tensions, but they are insufficient to avert internal conflicts
altogether. In such conflict situations, the opposing parties turn to the settlement leader, one of whose main functions is that of pacifier.[4] Yanesha leaders
are quite effective in appeasing contenders, and in suggesting just solutions
acceptable to those involved. A problem arises when the leader, or one of his
close relatives, is one of the parties in conflict. The conviviality and harmony
laboriously achieved by settlement members begin to crumble when informal
social pressure has proven insufficient to maintain social harmony, or when
withdrawal to peripheral houses has not lessened tensions, and the formal
conflict-solving mediation of leaders is unavailable. In the case of the settlements of Huacsho and Camantarmas this is precisely what happened, as the
following pages testify.

The case of Huacsho

Huacsho was founded along the Cacazu River in 1963 by a small group of
families native to the area. The Cacazu valley was still quite isolated then,
being at least one day's walking distance from the nearest road, but several
colonist families had already settled in the area. Huacsho's founding families
– four married sisters and their children, some of them married – were quite
aware that colonist pressure was likely to increase in the future. To counter
encroachment by colonists they built up a nucleated settlement and requested
land titles from the government. To avoid further colonist exploitation they
also asked the Summer Institute of Linguistics (SIL) to establish a bilingual
school in the community. It was around this school that the founding families
settled in 1963 (Smith 1977: 54). Under the leadership of Muenaresa, the
active son of one of the founding sisters, the population of the settlement
grew rapidly from then onwards. Ten years later, Huacsho's population had
increased to twenty-one nuclear families (ibid., p. 55).

In 1973 the settlement was made up of two extended kindreds, each represented by four living generations (ibid.). The core of the dominant kindred
consisted of the founding sisters and their offspring, ten biological and classificatory siblings. The second kindred had at its core an old man representing the senior generation, plus five of his children and six classificatory
siblings. These two kindreds were linked through nine marriage alliances

(ibid., p. 56). Members of the first kindred were considered to be founders and 'insiders' – they played a dominant role in settlement politics and affairs. In contrast, members of the second kindred, though more numerous, were considered to be newcomers and 'outsiders' – they had lesser powers of decision. Surprisingly, however, the two extended kindreds did not behave as rival political factions.

Thanks to the concerted efforts of its inhabitants, and to the skilful leadership of Muenaresa, Huacsho became a successful and prosperous community. Muenaresa had all the good characteristics of traditional settlement leaders. He belonged to the *cornaneshamray*, the group made up of descendants of the Yanesha priestly leaders of old and, until 1965, when he became an active member of the Evangelical church, he had two wives. Despite being illiterate, a trait shared by most traditional leaders of the time, Muenaresa was extremely competent in his dealings with state authorities. To secure titles for his community he even travelled to Lima, becoming the first person from the area to visit the capital. He was able to undertake this, as well as other trips, thanks to generous support from members of the community, who gave him the little cash they could save from wage labour. In 1971 Muenaresa's efforts bore fruit, and Huacsho was officially recognised as a Native reserve with legal title over 175 hectares of land (SINAMOS 1975: 67), becoming one of the first Yanesha settlements to enjoy these rights. Muenaresa's already great prestige was enhanced further.

Despite its isolation, by 1975 Huacsho benefited from all the services associated with modernity. It had a bilingual school run by a teacher trained by the SIL but paid by the government. It also had a small dispensary run by a member of the community. Finally, it had a small Evangelical church where a Native minister held services every Sunday. The school, the dispensary and the church were built through the cooperative work of all the members of the community. The same was true of the settlement's airstrip, which was finished in early 1976; even the school children participated in its construction. Finally, members of the community requested, and obtained, credit to establish a communal cattle-raising project and a communal store.

In brief, members of the Huacsho community had acted in a concerted fashion since the beginning, pooling their labour and resources on behalf of collective goals. Settlement leaders and church dignitaries directed collective work in the various communal projects. Work in large construction projects was alternated with the sharing of food and beverages, in some cases elaborated from the produce of communal gardens made with that purpose in mind. Commensality and cooperation enhanced the sense of conviviality, reinforcing communal solidarity.

Conviviality was so important in those years that on the basis of the observations he made in Huacsho between 1973–5, Smith (op. cit., pp. 64–9) waxed enthusiastically on the central role that reciprocal generosity (*yomateñets*) played in Yanesha lives, forming the basis for a harmonious social life. Reciprocity involved food, whether garden produce, game meat, fish or gathered wild products, but the notion that people should be generous extended even to their money (ibid., p. 66). Every household was expected to display, and actually did display, generous offerings of cooked food for visitors, whether consanguines, affines or strangers.

Unfortunately, things began to change in 1976, mostly as a result of political conflicts (Santos-Granero 1991: 184–7). Muenaresa had played an important part in the creation of the Amuesha Congress in 1969 (Estatutos 1980: 19).[5] Thanks both to his prestigious ancestry and personal charisma he was elected as *cornesha'* or chief representative of the Amuesha Congress in 1972.[6] Indeed, he was so popular that he continued in office in 1976, although he should have been replaced in 1974. During those years Muenaresa shared power with Shollac, the President of the Amuesha Congress, who was the teacher in charge of Huacsho's bilingual school. An outsider to the community, Shollac belonged to neither of the settlement's two main kindreds. He was elected in 1973 and re-elected in 1975 (Estatutos, op. cit., p. 19). By 1976, the relationship between Muenaresa and Shollac had soured as a result of an ambiguity. The Congress's statutes did not establish clearly whether the *cornesha'* had predominance over the president, or the other way around. Meanwhile, Shollac persuaded Ma'yarr, the community's representative to the Congress, and Chom, the elected settlement leader, to side with him.

Ma'yarr was a much younger classificatory brother of Muenaresa – the son of one of Muenaresa's mother's younger sisters. He was literate and had worked for a while for a government agency. As a government official, Ma'yarr had played an important part in some of Huacsho's collective ventures, mainly the cattle-raising project and the communal store. Chom, who was Muenaresa's classificatory son – the stepson of a classificatory brother – was not only *añcha'tareĩ*, or settlement leader, but also minister of the local Evangelical church. He and Shollac were also involved in the administration of the communal projects. Shollac, Ma'yarr and Chom accused Muenaresa of political incompetence, of using Congress funds for personal purposes and of attempting to perpetuate himself in power. Muenaresa accused them of abusing their power, selling communal cattle for their own benefit and embezzling the profits of the communal store.

What began as a struggle between Muenaresa and Shollac turned into a major conflict between brothers – a common theme in Yanesha political history and mythology (Santos-Granero 1991: 183). With the support of Shollac, Ma'yarr convoked a Congress meeting in which he demanded Muenaresa's resignation and proclaimed his candidacy to the office of *cornesha'*. Muenaresa countered by convoking another meeting in which he denounced Ma'yarr's political intrigues. Their struggle had bitter results.

In traditional terms, the brothers possessed equal prestige, for both were descended from Huacsho's founding families and belonged to the prestigious *cornaneshamray* group.[7] Moreover, they were married to a pair of sisters, who also were descended from a priestly leader. However, they differed profoundly in their political styles. Muenaresa's was more traditional, being based on charisma, diplomatic skills and the power of kin and affinal connections. Ma'yarr had a more modern style, based on literacy, knowledge of the outside world and the power of votes.[8]

During my first stint of fieldwork among the Yanesha in 1977, the conflict between the two brothers had not only split the Yanesha communities into two blocs – with the upriver settlements supporting Ma'yarr and the downriver settlements supporting Muenaresa – but had also divided Huacsho into two political factions that cut across the settlement's main kindreds. Rather than being confined to consanguines and affines, the confrontation between Muenaresa and Ma'yarr pitted consanguines against each other. Members of each faction exchanged accusations and counter-accusations on every public occasion. People stopped visiting each other; they would not exchange greetings when encountering one another by chance along a trail or at the riverside. The mothers of the two disputing leaders, who had always been very close, were forced by the circumstances to stop communicating. All collective activities were interrupted, and no family organised an *orreñtsopo* or drinking party. As the normal channels of communication, exchange and conviviality were interrupted, life within the community became unbearable. Between October 1976 and April 1977 four families abandoned Huacsho, among them that of Muenaresa's eldest son. Many families began moving away from the settlement's centre, to its periphery, so as to avoid meeting their opponents.

When the Amuesha Congress held its annual meeting in August 1977, both brothers had great expectations. Muenaresa hoped to be re-elected; Ma'yarr hoped to become the new *cornesha'*. Expressing their disapproval of antisocial sentiments, lack of self-control and open confrontation, the Yanesha supported neither. Instead, they elected a third candidate who was little known in most communities. All those involved got the message: the public condemned the conduct of the conflicting brothers. Disappointed with the results of the meeting, the main protagonists in the conflict – Muenaresa, Ma'yarr and Chom – abandoned Huacsho. A few years later, Shollac went back to his community of origin. By the end of 1977 nine out of the twenty-one families extant in 1973 had abandoned the community. Those who stayed moved to its periphery. In 1973, ten families lived permanently in the village centre (Smith, op. cit., p. 56); by 1983, when I did my second stint of fieldwork, only three families resided there. As an informant told me, 'the community was silent', by which he meant that it was dead.

Participants and spectators alike asserted to me that beneath the apparent reasons for the conflict (political competition, economic gain and personal dislikes) there was a more important cause, namely, envy. In fact, people did not blame either brother. Rather, they contended that someone who was envious of the community's prosperity, and of the brothers' prestige – and thus hated them – must have laid a curse upon them and the community; for no one in his right mind would fight with his own brother. The protagonists themselves agree with this explanation. Years after these events had taken place Ma'yarr said to me: 'I don't know what happened to me at the time. It was as if I was not myself. Someone must have wished me evil.' Briefly stated, envy, hatred, temporary madness and sorcery are the emotions, actions and states of mind the Yanesha associate with the emergence of social conflict and the end of conviviality.

The case of Camantarmas

Camantarmas, a settlement located in the middle stretches of the Palcazu River, was founded in 1948 by Poyaren, a Yanesha Adventist pastor, together with his Ashaninka brother-in-law (Santos-Granero 1991: 177–82). Their goal was to disseminate the Adventist faith, creating a safe haven in an isolated region for Yanesha and Ashaninka Adventists who wanted to escape from the pressures of colonisation upriver. In the ensuing years the settlement experienced several reversals as a result of various epidemics. By 1957, once its founders had died, Camantarmas was almost abandoned. Only three families remained: the widows of the founders, with their respective children, and Orrno, an old Yanesha man, and his wife and seven children. Linked by several marriage bonds, the three families formed the nucleus out of which a new community emerged, with Matar, one of Orrno's younger sons, as the new settlement and church leader.

Despite its isolation – the settlement was five days' walking distance from the nearest road – Camantarmas entered into a period of rapid demographic growth after 1957. Doubtless, the establishment of a private Adventist school, which acted as a magnet both for local people and for Adventists escaping from colonist encroachment upriver, was an important catalyst. Matar's firm leadership was also crucial. By 1964, the population of the settlement had increased to around sixty nuclear families, and school participation had grown to approximately 150 students.

Matar was an enterprising and charismatic figure. His prestige stemmed not only from the fact that he belonged to the *cornaneshamray* descent group, but was also fluent in Spanish, knew the 'ways of the Peruvians', had considerable oratorical abilities and was very pious. Under his religious guidance, the inhabitants of Camantarmas complied strictly with the norms of Seventh Day Adventism. Consumption of coca leaves, manioc beer, tobacco, alcohol and hallucinogens came to an end. Performing, singing and dancing sacred *coshañats* music was forbidden; the same was true of shamanic activities and polygyny. Fish, game or domestic animals that were tabooed were avoided.

Despite the prohibition on holding drinking parties and *coshamñats* festivities, settlement members carried on an intensive social life centred on church activities and the Sabbath celebrations. Adventist morality coincided to a large extent with traditional Yanesha morality; they both emphasised generosity and solidarity. The principle of *yomateñets*, or reciprocal generosity, continued to regulate social interactions, ensuring that the redistribution of foodstuffs within the community always took place. Church celebrations replaced *orreñtsopo*, or drinking parties normally held on the occasion of the full moon; psalms replaced the singing of *coshamñats* sacred songs. Internal solidarity was enhanced by collective projects and activities, one good example being the construction of a 300-metre-long airstrip that mainly served the aeroplanes of an Adventist agency.

No Adventist missionary lived in Camantarmas; the community depended for church matters on the neighbouring mission post of Nevati, located on the Pichis River. Missionaries from Nevati administered the school at Camantarmas, collecting the fees that paid for its privately hired teacher. The fees imposed a heavy burden on parents whose only means of income in this isolated region was working for wages in cattle ranches. When parents could not pay in cash they had to pay in agricultural produce. Members of the community readily acknowledged the importance of sending their children to school, but many parents began to complain that the fees were prohibitive.

Most of the protesting parents belonged to the founding families. Matar, the settlement and church leader, was particularly outspoken. In 1968 he asked the Summer Institute of Linguistics to establish a state bilingual school in Camantarmas. The most devout Adventist families opposed this move, fearing the Evangelicals would have an overriding influence over their children. Contor, the leader of this faction, was a young Adventist pastor who doubled as health attendant. He belonged to a large kindred whose members came from Yorenačo. Married to the daughter of one of Matar's sisters, Contor was thus treated by Matar as a classificatory son.

Ostensibly, the replacement of an Adventist private monolingual school by a state bilingual school was the issue triggering the dispute between the two factions. The real confrontation, however, pitted the 'old' against the 'new ways'. Contor referred to members of his classificatory father's faction as the 'old ones': elderly folks who were the earliest settlers in the community and remained attached to the old ways, such as chewing coca leaves, drinking manioc beer and singing the traditional sacred songs in praise of the old divinities. In short, Contor accused Matar and his supporters of being 'little civilised'. By contrast, Contor argued that he and his followers adhered to the new ways; they complied with Adventist norms and 'had greater knowledge and more ideas'. In my opinion, there was a grain of truth in his argument.

Until then a devoted Adventist pastor, by the late 1960s Matar had become disillusioned with the missionaries. He thus began a process of *rapprochement* with traditional beliefs and customs. Whereas neither he nor his followers ever renounced their Adventist faith, they were definitely less fervent than members of Contor's faction. To avoid deepening the division, and wanting to hold the community together, Matar insisted that the issue was not religious but economic. He argued that the Adventist school was too expensive; that it made little sense to pay high school fees when they could have a school-teacher for free. In private, however, Matar remarked that most ongoing settlement conflicts resulted from the overzealous attitudes of young militant ministers, whether Adventist or Evangelical, who had no respect for Yanesha traditions.

When the missionaries of Nevati appointed Contor as the new pastor of the church of Camantarmas the conflict deepened. Matar and some of his followers stopped attending church services altogether. From then onwards, and for almost a year, the settlement had two leaders, neither claiming the full support of its inhabitants. The conflict climaxed in 1969 when the government approved the establishment of a bilingual school in the community. Contor's faction opposed transforming the old mission school into a state school. Being in the minority, and not having enough political support to impede this, Contor persuaded his followers to split from Camantarmas and found a new village across the river, on the left bank of the Palcazu. Some fifteen families moved with him to the new settlement, which was named Shetomaso. The division followed along the lines of the settlement's two largest kindreds, with Matar's and Contor's respective extended kindreds forming the core of each faction. Once again, however, the struggle was between consanguines rather than affines.

Not surprisingly, and in consonance with the Yanesha's disapproval of extreme measures, a third group of about ten families not closely related to the core members of the opposing factions followed neither of the contending leaders. Instead, they founded a third, smaller, settlement further upriver. Thus what had once been one of the largest and most prosperous communities along the Palcazu River ended up being divided into three small settlements.

Cycles of sociality

The fates of Huacsho and Camantarmas are by no means unique. Community fission has been widely reported from Native Amazonia. Except for Rivière's (1984) perceptive analysis of the Guiana region, however, few attempts have been made to determine whether these various processes respond to a common theme. Yet even a quick glance at the literature reveals that they do, despite the very different regions and social settings from which they have been reported. Most authors attribute settlement fissioning to a variety of causal factors. In order to compare their information, I distinguish between the following analytical levels: (1) the general conditions that favour conflict and fission; (2) the specific causes that trigger settlement disputes, which can eventually lead to fractures; and (3) the causes that make settlement fissioning inevitable. In addition, I examine the social lines along which fissioning takes place.

All authors seem to agree – whether explicitly (Chagnon 1976: 14; Whitten 1976: 125; Dumont 1978: 32; Bamberger 1979: 142; Rivière 1984; 27; Brown 1984: 103; Kensinger 1995: 269), or implicitly (Maybury-Lewis 1974: 171; Overing Kaplan 1975: 50) – that settlement size is one of the general conditions favouring processes of fissioning. But they differ as to how this happens, and as to how large a village can grow before being affected by such processes. One group of scholars argues that the larger the settlement the greater the pressure and competition over key natural resources – be they game or good garden sites. In time these lead to social conflicts (Whitten, op. cit., p. 125; Dumont, op. cit., p. 75; Kensinger, op. cit., p. 269).

A second group maintains that the larger the settlement the more complex its social composition – a correlation proposed much earlier by Carneiro (1967) – and the more likely that sociopolitical conflicts will emerge. Advocates of this latter argument differ slightly as to why greater social complexity promotes discord. Some say it does so by diminishing the 'general amount of relatedness' (Chagnon, op. cit., p. 18). Others claim it does so by increasing the proportion of 'intrinsically fragile' affinal relations (Overing Kaplan, op. cit., p. 118; Rivière, op. cit., pp. 28, 74), or by multiplying the number of social groupings – patrilineages or men's societies – that have the potential to become political factions (Maybury-Lewis, op. cit., pp. 169–70; Bamberger, op. cit., p. 138).

Finally, a third group of scholars argues that large settlement size induces both: competition over resources and an increase in sociopolitical conflicts (Brown, op. cit., p. 103; Hames 1983: 423). On the issue of how large a village can grow before fissioning processes begin, opinions vary from 50–70 persons (Overing Kaplan, op. cit., p. 49; Arvelo-Jiménez 1977: 109; Dumont op. cit., p. 75; Rivière, op. cit., p. 73), to 70–100 persons (Whitten op. cit.: 125), and even to 100–200 persons (Maybury-Lewis, op. cit., p. 172; Chagnon, op. cit., p. 18).

Authors generally agree as to the specific causes that trigger internal community discord. Foremost amongst them is competition over women, whether arising from rivalry over prospective spouses (Chagnon, op. cit., p. 17; Arvelo-Jiménez, op. cit., p. 109; Hames, op. cit., p. 423; Alès 1990: 91), or from adulterous affairs (Maybury-Lewis, op. cit., p. 186; Dumont, op. cit., p. 32; Bamberger, op. cit., p. 133; Rivière, op. cit., p. 27; Brown, op. cit., p. 104; Kensinger, op. cit., p. 178). Other factors causing serious settlement disputes are sorcery accusations (Maybury-Lewis, op. cit., p. 185; Rivière, op. cit., p. 27; Brown, op. cit., p. 103), theft (Maybury-Lewis, op. cit., p. 27; Alès, op. cit., p. 91), competition for power between incumbent leaders and younger pretenders (Overing Kaplan,op. cit., p. 119; Kensinger, op. cit., p. 177) and disagreements over strategic political decisions (Bamberger, op. cit., p. 132; Brown, op. cit., pp. 104–5).

There is also general accord over the main cause of fissioning: communities split when disputes escalate and cannot be resolved in a peaceful way. Most authors agree that this incapacity stems from limitations inherent to Native Amazonian political systems. Some attribute this inability to the 'diffuse system of political authority', which frequently results in the coexistence of several competing settlement leaders (Bamberger, op. cit., p. 133). Others contend that it is a by-product of the 'tenuous' or 'weak' political authority characterising Amerindian leaders. Together with the impossibility of kinship ethics holding together large groups (Chagnon, op. cit., p. 17), and with the absence of formal mechanisms to settle disputes (Rivière, op. cit., pp. 27, 74; Brown, op. cit., p. 103), such weaknesses result in settlement splits. For other analysts, the inability to resolve conflicts peacefully results from the contra-dictory qualities demanded of settlement leaders: they must prove to be force-ful and aggressive in order to become leaders, yet they must demonstrate patience, self-control and diplomatic skills once they are in office (Maybury-Lewis, op. cit., p. 204).

Briefly then, most authors concur on the fact that settlement fissioning results from a sequence of events, beginning with population growth, followed by greater competition, increased conflict and finally, unresolved disputes.[9] However, the fault line along which settlements divide varies substantially throughout Amazonia. In most cases it follows affinal fissures. But whereas among the Akwẽ-Shavante it separates patrilineages belonging to different exogamic clans and related through marriage ties (Maybury-Lewis, op. cit., pp. 167–9), among the Piaroa it tends to divide sets of brothers-in-law (Over-ing Kaplan, op. cit., p. 112), and among the Panare it usually disjoins fathers-in-law from sons-in-law (Dumont, op. cit., p. 76). In other cases, fissioning takes place along consanguineal fractures. Thus, among the Ye'cuana it affects extended families belonging to the same kindred (Arvelo-Jiménez op. cit., p. 109); among the Wanano it divides patrilineal sibs (Cher-nela 1993: 50); whereas among the Cashinahua it affects extended families belonging to the same patrimoiety (Kensinger, op. cit., p. 177). In yet other cases, such as those of the Canelos Quichua and the Yanomamö, settlement schisms may separate both consanguines – whether belonging to a stem kin-dred segment or a group of patrilineally related men – and affines (Whitten, op. cit., pp. 125–6; Chagnon op. cit., pp. 17–18; Alès, op. cit., p. 91). Finally, among the Kayapó fissioning affects neither affines nor consanguines, but non-kin-based men's societies (Bamberger, op. cit., p.134). In brief, although settlement fissioning seems to be a pan-Amazonian phenomenon, there is no universal pattern determining how they divide (cf. Gonçalves, Rivière, Rosengren, this volume).

The end of conviviality

Yanesha settlement fissioning basically follows the same sequence. Both Huacsho and Camantarmas were large communities when they split. The former had more than 100 inhabitants, whereas the latter had an unusually high population of more than 300 persons. Size increased considerably the complexity of their social fabric. Huacsho grew from one set of married sisters to two large intermarrying bilateral kindreds; Camantarmas grew from two sets of siblings linked through multiple marriage ties to at least four large intermarrying bilateral kindreds. In one of these cases increased social complexity became expressed in escalating friction between 'insiders' – the founding families – and 'outsiders' – families that settled later on. However, in both settlements internal disputes took the form of a competition between 'traditional' settlement leaders and more 'modern' younger men eager to replace them.

Following Yanesha models of power building – based as they are on the retention of both married daughters and sons, but highly dependent on consanguineal rather than on affinal relations – this competition involved a pair of classificatory brothers (Huacsho) and a classificatory father and son (Camantarmas). In both instances, settlement leaders attempted to damp down conflicts as much as possible. However, in the absence of formal mechanisms to resolve disputes, and being themselves one of the parties in conflict, leaders were powerless to prevent confrontations from escalating. In time, what began as a competition over political power between two men ended up in a dramatic fissioning involving the entire community.

With reference to the Panare, Henley (1982: 127) has labelled these processes of growth and fission as the 'developmental cycle of settlements', arguing that they typically involve three ideal stages.[10] Other authors provide similar two- or three-stage models (Overing Kaplan, op. cit., p. 118; Arvelo-Jiménez 1992: 54) that, although referring to settlement composition, also help us to understand the development cycle of Amerindian conviviality. In effect, when a new settlement is created, its founders constitute not only a tightly knit unit – irrespective of whether at its core one finds consanguines or affines – but also a group of people bound by common interests. Founding groups may be searching for more bountiful hunting grounds. They may also be looking for a safe haven, to escape war with other groups or to avoid colonisation pressures. Alternatively, they may be pursuing a religious ideal or even engaged in a prophetic quest for a sacred land. Thus, the underlying solidarity that marks founding groups does not result only from commensality, mutuality and the ethics of kinship; it rests on a firm foundation of shared ideals and goals.

Commonly held Amerindian ideals usually articulate notions about the 'perfect community' (cf. Rivière, this volume), including the value of living in large settlements. Thus, for the Kayapó, a 'beautiful village' is a large village that can sustain an intense ceremonial life (Bamberger, op. cit., p. 142). For the Cashinahua, a 'real village' (*mae kuin*) is also one large enough to 'contain persons with the requisite knowledge for leading rituals, for curing illnesses and for dealing with the supernaturals' (Kensinger, op. cit., p. 132). The same is true of the Piro notion of 'beautiful' villages (Gow 1991: 70). Even among the Yanomamö, who would be happy living in tiny family groups, the ideal village is one large enough to have enough warriors to maintain enemies at bay (Chagnon op. cit., p. 17). In other Amerindian societies, leaders strive to form large local groups because size reflects favourably on their political power (Rivière, op. cit.).

Native Amazonian ideals about conviviality are not unattainable utopias. They find their fullest expression when settlements are growing, social relations are still close and intimate and commonly held ideals still very much alive. But the ideals about the beautiful village and the perfect conviviality carry the seeds of their own destruction. As we have seen, larger settlements often promote internal conflicts, with unresolved disputes eventually leading to village schisms. What authors often fail to explain satisfactorily, however, is why this should be so. In our own society we can quarrel with a neighbour or a colleague, even to the point of not being on speaking terms with her or him. But this does not usually prompt us to move out of our building, change our friends, look for another job or seek a new neighbourhood. We might simply stop interacting with those persons, or reduce contact to the necessary minimum. Another option is just to ignore them.

In a Native Amazonian community these options are not open to its members precisely because conviviality prior to the emergence of conflicts was extremely intense. We rarely have such close, intimate relations with our neighbours or our colleagues. A break in our relations simply adds a bit more distance to that already in existence. Among Amerindians such distancing is not possible (cf. Rosengren, this volume). In the initial stages of the developmental cycle of their settlements community members create even closer ties – using such mechanisms as commensality, cooperation and shared ideals – with persons with whom they already share close consanguineal and affinal ties. In the Yanesha case, as we have seen, conviviality also entails strong feelings of love, friendliness, trust and generosity. A rupture in such close relations generates intense emotions of anger, hatred, shame and guilt (cf. Alès, Gonçalves, Kidd, Rivière, this volume). These feelings impede people from continuing to live in close proximity.

Among the Kayapó, unresolved disputes end in formal duels between members of different men's societies. The vanquished abandon the settlement because, as Bamberger (op. cit., p. 139) asserts, 'they have too much shame to remain in the same village with those people with whom they have fought, and to whom they have lost'. The same is true among the Aguaruna and the Cashinahua: individuals or groups that lose face in a given confrontation or are chastised by the collective leave the community in anger or shame

(Brown, op. cit., p. 104; Kensinger, op. cit., p. 189). Among the Yanesha, settlement conflicts generate intense anger and hatred. They also invoke feelings of shame and guilt, for they fly in the face of the close ties that should bind consanguines together. The closer the pre-existing relationship, the more intense the shame and guiltiness. This explains to a large extent why, as a result of Huacsho's division, both rival classificatory brothers abandoned the community in shame.

I suggest that these strong disrupting emotions account for what Rivière (op. cit., pp. 74, 81) calls the 'lack of tolerance for disharmony' and 'low degree of tolerance for conflict' that distinguish Native Amazonian societies. Because Amerindian conviviality is so intense, its rupture generates equally intense but opposite emotions – negative feelings that prevent people from continuing to live together. Like Sisyphus, the Corinthian king condemned for eternity by Zeus to roll a stone to the top of a steep hill, only to see it always roll down again, Native Amazonians are engaged in constant pursuit of the ideal of perfect conviviality. It is a doomed struggle from the beginning, for conviviality begins to wear out as soon as it is achieved.[11]

Notes

1   I have adopted the terms 'gentle' and 'fierce' from the titles of two books: *The Gentle People* by Colin Henfrey (1964), and *Yanomamö. The Fierce People* by Napoleon Chagnon (1968). I suspect that the title of Chagnon's famous ethnography is a play upon words of Henfrey's lesser-known travelogue.

2   I have discussed in more detail elsewhere the main points of disagreement between advocates of these two approaches (Santos-Granero 1999).

3   Here I follow Overing's (1996: 7) distinction between 'collectivity' – a group 'expressed through social structural imperatives (roles, statuses and juridical rules)' – and 'the collective' – a group expressed through a 'specific cultural and social way of being'. Native Amazonian social groups use informal means of enforcing expected social behaviour, yet they lack the coercive mechanisms more characteristic of collectivities in the Western sense.

4   In the past, a settlement leader was generally the founder of the community and the head of the settlement's largest bilateral kindred. Nowadays, settlement leadership is shared between the formal leader (*amcha'taret*) elected by the communal assembly for a period of two years, and the informal leader, generally the man who founded the community – or one of his descendants – who is recognised by most members as the 'real' leader. In some cases, both types of leadership rest in the hands of one and the same man (see Rosengren 1987 for a similar situation among the Matsigenka).

5   The Amuesha Congress was created in 1969 in a meeting sponsored by Richard Chase Smith, then a Peace Corps volunteer, and the linguist–missionaries of the Summer Institute of Linguistics. It brought together the representatives of twenty Yanesha communities. The organisational structure of the Congress resembled that of 'federations', or organisations grouping trade unions belonging to the same branch of production. It had a president, a vice-president, a treasurer and several secretaries in charge of the different areas of activity (health, education, land titling, etc.).

6 The term *cornesha'* originally referred to the Yanesha traditional politico-religious leaders, the last of whom died in 1956. In its new usage it came to refer to an elected official of the Amuesha Congress who had the task of representing the Yanesha as a whole. Since the creation of this office at the 1972 annual Congress meeting, there have been tensions between the *Cornesha'* and the president of the Congress, for it was never clearly established who had precedence over whom.

7 The importance of priestly ancestry in Yanesha 'modern' politics is illustrated by the fact that four of the first five modern *Cornesha'* belonged to the *cornaneshamray* group. And the one who did not, claimed he did.

8 This in no way means that Muenaresa was ignorant of the 'ways of the Whites'; or that Ma'yarr was dismissive of 'traditional ways'. On the contrary, Muenaresa celebrated every year the anniversary of his first trip to Lima, to emphasise his knowledge of the national society, while Ma'yarr did not lose any opportunity of dressing up in traditional garb to underscore his adherence to Yanesha mores.

9 However, this is not the only process through which settlements split. As several authors have pointed out, settlements also dissolve or fission when their leaders die, or when key persons holding together different individuals or groups of people die (Overing Kaplan 1975: 119; Arvelo-Jiménez 1977: 112; Dumont 1978: 75, 82; Alès 1990: 91).

10 In the first stage, the group consists of a man, his wife or wives and his children. In the second stage it is composed of a senior man, his wife or wives, his married daughters and his unmarried children. Finally, in the last stage the group consists of a core of married brothers and sisters, or, seen from another point of view, of a core of men related to each other as brothers-in-law.

11 This was not always so, however. We know that in several areas of tropical South America during pre-Columbian times ranked chiefdoms gave rise to large settlements with populations of several thousand inhabitants. These polities may not have had fixed boundaries, and were certainly fluid in composition, but they nonetheless enjoyed a remarkable continuity over time (Arvelo-Jiménez and Biord 1994; Whitehead 1994). The mechanisms guaranteeing conviviality in such large settlements and preventing the processes of 'endless mitosis' (Bamberger 1979: 141), more characteristic of egalitarian native Amazonian societies, remain to be established.

References

Alès, C. (1990) 'Chroniques des temps ordinaires. Corésidence et fission Yanomami', *L'Homme* 113, 30(1): 73–101.

Arvelo-Jiménez, N. (1977) 'A study of the process of village formation in Ye'cuana society', in E.B. Basso (ed.) *Carib-Speaking Indians. Culture, Society and Language*, pp. 106–12, Anthropological Papers, 28, Tucson: University of Arizona Press.

—— (1992) *Relaciones Políticas en una Sociedad Tribal. Estudio de los Ye'cuana, Indígenas del Amazonas Venezolano*, Colección 500 Años, 51, Quito: Abya-Yala/Movimiento Laicos para América Latina.

Arvelo-Jiménez, N. and Biord, H. (1994) 'The impact of conquest on contemporary indigenous peoples of the Guiana Shield. The system of Orinoco regional interdependence', in A.C. Roosevelt (ed.) *Amazonian Indians from Prehistory to the Present: Anthropological Perspectives*, pp. 55–78, Tucson: University of Arizona Press.

Bamberger, J. (1979) 'Exit and voice in Central Brazil: the politics of flight in Kayapó society', in D. Maybury-Lewis (ed.) *Dialectical Societies. The Gê and Bororo of Central*

Brazil, pp. 130–46, Harvard Studies in Cultural Anthropology 1, Cambridge, Mass.: Harvard University Press.

Basso, E.B. (1995) *The Last Cannibals. A South American Oral History*, Austin: University of Texas Press.

Brown, M.F. (1984) *Una Paz Incierta. Historia y Cultura de las Comunidades Aguarunas frente al Impacto de la Carretera Marginal*, Lima: Centro Amazónico de Antropología y Aplicación Práctica.

Carneiro, R.L. (1967) 'On the relationship between size of population and complexity of social organization', *Southwestern Journal of Anthropology* 23: 234–43.

Chagnon, N. (1968) *Yanomamö. The Fierce People*, New York: Holt, Rinehart & Winston.

—— (1976) 'Fission in an Amazonian tribe. What determines the size of primitive social groups?', *The Sciences* 16(1): 14–18.

Chernela, J. (1993) *The Wanano Indians of the Brazilian Amazon. A Sense of Space*, Austin: University of Texas Press.

Descola, P. (1993) 'Les Affinités sélectives. Alliance, guerre et prédation dans l'ensemble Jivaro', *L'Homme* 126–8, 33: 171–89.

—— (1996) *The Spears of Twilight. Life and Death in the Amazon Jungle*, London: Harper-Collins.

Dumont, J.-P. (1978) *The Headman and I. Ambiguity and Ambivalence in the Fieldworking Experience*, Austin and London: University of Texas Press.

Estatutos (1980) *Estatutos: Congreso de Comunidades Nativas Amuesha*, Cacazú: Pocoll Eñotentsopo' Yaneshacop Moncnem.

Fejos, P. (1943) *Ethnography of the Yagua*, New York: Viking Fund.

Gow, P. (1991) *Of Mixed Blood. Kinship and History in Peruvian Amazonia*, Oxford: Clarendon Press.

Hames, R.B. (1983) 'The settlement pattern of a Yanomamö population bloc: a behavioral ecological interpretation', in R.B. Hames and W.T. Vickers (eds) *Adaptive Responses of Native Amazonians*, pp. 393–427, New York: Academic Press.

Henfrey, C. (1964) *The Gentle People: A Journey among the Indian Tribes of Guiana*, London: Hutchinson.

Henley, P. (1982) *The Panare. Tradition and Change on the Amazonian Frontier*, New Haven, Conn. and London: Yale University Press.

Kensinger, K.M. (1995) *How Real People Ought to Live. The Cashinahua of Eastern Peru*, Prospect Heights, Ill.: Waveland Press.

Maybury-Lewis, D. (1974) *Akwẽ-Shavante Society*, New York and London: Oxford University Press.

Nimuendajú, C. (1939) *The Apinayé*, Washington DC: The Catholic University of America Press.

Oberg, K. (1949) *The Terena and the Caduveo of Southern Mato Grosso, Brazil*, Washington DC: Smithsonian Institution.

Overing, J. (1996) 'Under the sky of the domesticated: in praise of the everyday', Inaugural Lecture for the Professorship and Chair of Social Anthropology, University of St Andrews, 4 December.

Overing Kaplan, J. (1975) *The Piaroa, a People of the Orinoco Basin. A Study in Kinship and Marriage*, Oxford: Clarendon Press.

Rivière, P. (1984) *Individual and Society in Guiana. A Comparative Study of Amerindian Social Organization*, Cambridge: Cambridge University Press.

Rosengren, D. (1987) *In the Eyes of the Beholder. Leadership and the Social Construction of Power and Dominance among the Matsigenka of the Peruvian Amazon*, Gothenburg: Göteborgs Etnografiska Museum.

Santos-Granero, F. (1986) 'The moral and social aspects of equality amongst the Amuesha of Central Peru', *Journal de la Société des Américanistes* 72: 107–31.

—— (1991) *The Power of Love. The Moral Use of Knowledge amongst the Amuesha of Central Peru*, London: The Athlone Press.

—— (1999) 'Turning fear into friendship: Amazonian sociality beyond kinship and affinity', unpublished manuscript.

SINAMOS (1975) *Comunidades Nativas de Selva Central. Diagnóstico Socio-Económico*, Lima: Sistema Nacional de Movilización Social.

Smith, R.C. (1977) 'Deliverance from chaos for a song. Preliminary discussion of Amuesha music', Ph.D dissertation, Cornell University.

Taylor, A.-C. (1996) 'The soul's body and its states: an Amazonian perspective on the nature of being human', *Journal of the Royal Anthropological Institute* 2: 201–15.

Viveiros de Castro, E. (1992) *From the Enemy's Point of View. Humanity and Divinity in an Amazonian Society*, Chicago and London: University of Chicago Press.

—— (1993) 'Alguns Aspectos da Afinidade no Dravidianato Amazônico', in E. Viveiros de Castro and M. Carneiro da Cunha (eds) *Amazônia: Etnologia e História Indígena*, pp. 149–210, São Paulo: Núcleo de História Indígena e do Indigenismo, Universidade de São Paulo.

—— (1995) 'Pensando o Parentesco Ameríndio', in E.Viveiros de Castro (ed.) *Antropologia do Parentesco. Estudos Ameríndios*, Rio de Janeiro: Editora UFRJ.

—— (1996) 'Images of nature and society in Amazonian ethnology', *Annual Review of Anthropology* 25: 179–200.

Whitehead, N.L. (1994) 'The ancient Amerindian polities of the Amazon, the Orinoco, and the Atlantic coast: a preliminary analysis of their passage from antiquity to extinction', in A.C. Roosevelt (ed.) *Amazonian Indians from Prehistory to the Present: Anthropological Perspectives*, pp. 33–53, Tucson: University of Arizona Press.

Whitten Jr., N.E. (1976) *Sacha Runa. Ethnicity and Adaptation of Ecuadorian Jungle Quichua*, Urbana: University of Illinois Press.

Index